MW00609786

MEL'S
M&Ms

(MYTHS AND MEMORIES)

MELVIN M. KIESCHNICK • CARLSBAD, CALIFORNIA • 8/1/2020

Mel's M & Ms

Copyright 2020 by Melvin M. Kieschnick

All Rights Reserved. Please do not reproduce this work in part or in whole without the written permission of the author.

Published by Piscataqua Press

32 Daniel St. Portsmouth NH 03801

Ppressbooks.com

ISBN: 978-1-950381-55-5

Printed in the United States of America

INTRODUCTION

"Mel, you should write your autobiography." This was often said to me after I had told a few stories of my life. I had no intention of doing that. However, I was open to writing about interesting incidents in my life and also some reflections on a variety of topics that got my attention. So, 12 years ago I began writing a personal blog. I recorded a series of memories and reflections. After all this time I decided to put them together in printed format. Here they are. I have printed them in the sequence in which I wrote them. Thus, they do not tell a chronological series of events. The sequence is random. Also, I did not do a lot of careful editing. They just are the way I originally posted them.

I am sharing a few copies with family and friends in the hope that you might enjoy them-and that they might stimulate you to recall special moments in your life.

Enjoy.

NOT AFRAID

As I reflect upon some episodes in my life I marvel at my lack of fear. At the age of 13 my parents sent me off to a religious ministerial training prep school, a boys-only boarding situation. I was really quite naïve, having grown up in the country surrounded by a close-knit family, relatives and friends who cared about me and watched over all of us youngsters who were considered part of a very large congregation-wide extended family. I knew nothing about guys "from the city" or kids whose parents were something other than farmers, ministers or country trades-people. But off I went unconcerned and unafraid. The school was small enough so one could play on all sports teams. The profs knew us and our parents and most of us came from equally depleted depression-era homes. I was unafraid and it worked great!

When I later worked in Hong Kong, I always felt perfectly at ease everywhere I went in that colony, even in the relatively off-limits section called Kowloon City. Once I went roaring through there when I probably should have been afraid. My assistant principal had guaranteed some loans and then was unable to repay them. He contacted me to come in my car to pick him up from a designated location. I should have been forewarned when he ducked low and crept into the back seat of my car. He had glanced back just long enough to see another car about a hundred yards behind us ready to come get him. I sped away. Flying up and down streets and alleys until we lost our pursuers in Kowloon City. I found a route to the rural New Territories where he asked me to just drop him off and drive away. I do not remember being afraid.

When I worked New York, I had the privilege of serving Lutheran schools in all parts of that metropolitan community. Sometimes this entailed night meetings in all sections of Manhattan, the Bronx and Brooklyn. I always went, carefully and confidently, assured that my colleagues were not asking me to do anything they themselves did not also do. I had nothing to fear. I remember especially one evening when I met with a group of parents in a Harlem apartment. They had invited me there in an attempt to help save their Lutheran school. During the conversation they told me of a community network they had established which kept an eye on each of the pupils on their way to and from school, assuring their safety. Then they told me that they had made a similar arrangement for me that night to get safely to my car and home. I had no need to be afraid

On another occasion I had reason enough to fear and I wonder why I do not recall that emotion. My two sons and I had gotten caught up in the Tiananmen Square massacre in 1989. We were trying to get out of Beijing. We had actually hired a very small van driven by a man determined to defy the authorities. We drove past barricades, which had been run over by tanks. We saw burning busses. We watched crowds ebb and flow as the military approached and backed off. We smelled the odor of burnt bodies, some hung from lampposts. Just as we thought we had gotten through the worst of it we suddenly heard the sound of guns from our right. Bullets could be heard flying near our small van. We proceeded forward and suddenly all was still. In retrospect it seems to me that I experienced it somehow more as an observer than as a participant. I do not recall being afraid. I do recall praying, so that is probably the more accurate remembrance.

I do not fear death. I sometimes feel uneasy about what could be a painful process preceding death. But I have no fear of death and the after-life. I figure that God and God's Grace have that pretty well handled.

ഇൽ

ONE SUNDAY'S MUSIC

It was a Sunday much like hundreds of others in my life. It was a Sunday full of music - all kinds of music and all manner of emotions stirred, recalled, expressed. Even at 7:15 when we got into our car the all-classical music station to which Jane's radio is perpetually set welcomed the days with arias, cantatas and fugues. When we sat down in our pews, our extraordinarily gifted Minister of Music, Stan, was already doing one of his incredible riffs on the opening hymn. During this season of the church year our congregation is focusing on Christ's light shining throughout the world so the various parts of the sung liturgy featured the words, the beats, the melodies labeled "Peruvian traditional" and "Creek Indian" and "from the Norwegian" and "Finnish folk song." Our 50-voice choir sang the plaintive song, "Open My Eyes." So, it was no surprise that when after the service the visiting couple sitting in front of Jane and me turned and said "We always come to this church when we are in San Diego on vacation. It is such a beautiful church and we love your music!"

I must admit that during this service I had let my mind's eye and my inner ear roam the world. I wanted to hear the millions of voices and

4

instruments from New Guinea to New Hampshire, from Brazilian Pentecostals to New York Episcopalians, from black soul to white chorales light a spark of the divine within us all; each plucking strings deep within us that start to vibrate when music fills the space around us. The feeling lingered into the afternoon when daughter Liz called from Connecticut. "I had to call," she said, "because I cried in church today as I thought of you." "You see" she said, "We sang 'God be with you till we meet again'. It brought up all those memories of when your family all sang that song at the end of our family reunions. And since Uncle Hal died a couple weeks ago, he was the first of the nine of your kids to go-and so when you sing that song again it will have an added dimension."

Then Liz's reverie turned angry, as she was very upset. Her teen-age son had just returned from a Church Youth retreat. It was an interdenominational event and the keynote speaker was a narrow fundamentalist. He instructed son Ryan and all others in attendance "When you get home today, before you go to bed, I want each of you to destroy your iPods. Smash them to smithereens! Explain to your parents that this is a tool of the devil who in the siren songs of today's music is luring you all into hell!"

But my Sunday was not yet over. It was easy for me to skip the Grammys. My musical tastes don't really run in the direction of Lil Wayne or Alison Krauss. My kids are making a valiant effort to help me catch up on all the movie classics I have missed in my earlier life and the day's feature was Casablanca. The first notes coming from Sam's piano in Rick's bar touched me in the same place as it touched Ingrid Bergman and the memories flowed. I was back in the late 40's early 50's and the woman who is now my wife and I held hands etc. to the tunes of Glen Miller, the Mills Brothers, Rudy Valle, Perry Como. All I need is the words "Some Enchanted Evening" and I am again walking my date back to the dorm and all is well in God's wonderful world.

Then the day, as they all do, came to its end. But my life had again been changed by the power of the music of an everyday Sunday.

෨ඏ

INAUGURATION: A VERY PERSONAL REFLECTION

Sent to my sons and daughters, January 20, 2009

Kids,

I have spent most of the last seven hours watching the inauguration events. It has been an emotional experience. Several times I was aware of tears flowing down my cheeks. Why?

First, of course, is the reality of a black president. I grew up racist - and didn't know it. As a very young lad I would go to Grandpa Kieschnick's farm. The black workers would come to Grandma and Grandpa's house for dinner at noon, usually only one or two of them. They always sat at a table on the porch while we ate at the dining room table. They had good food, but not what we had. We ate better!

One night I sat in the dark with them around a well. I was maybe 10. They told stories and stuff with sexual content. At one point one of them even said to me "You know what we're talkin about?" I don't remember how I answered but the truth is I didn't have a clue! Grandpa respected his black workers who were more or less freed slaves. They were free to come or go but they were also completely dependent. I always remember Grandpa's funeral. As the hearse passed through at least one of the many gates from Grandpa's home to the country road to get to the church - a black man stood at the gate, dressed in very best, holding the reins of his horse in one hand and his other hand over his heart. He was respectful. It was completely out of the question that he could possibly go into the church as part of a white congregation at the funeral.

Sometimes we would drive past Weir, to go to Grandma Doering's farm. We were on the back of Uncle Ben's old International truck. There was a black family that lived near the road on the way to the farm. When we would drive by that place the black children would come out and we would hurl comments (and I am sure racial slurs) at each other. I remember once the black mother came out. She helped lower trousers and lift skirts and the kids mooned us. We laughed uproariously. Concurrently Aunt Mattie was consistently helping those families. When they had no money and no food, they would come to the Henry Doering Mercantile Store in Walburg and Aunt Mattie "extended credit" to them: Of course, that money was never paid. It was possibly an effort to save some self-respect for all involved.

When I worked at Wukash Brothers Cafe as a high school student I had very special relationship with Joe the black dishwasher. We bet five cents every day on the total number of lunches we would serve. I did the dishes for him when he finally got a day off for Juneteenth, the day slaves were freed in Texas. Yet if ever a black person or group wanted to eat at the restaurant, they were not allowed to enter the front door. They needed to come to the alley and then sit on the back stoop of the cafe to eat what was provided.

I have a clear memory of sitting in high school class and Prof. George Beto making a reference to a black lawyer. George Winkler, my classmate somehow or other indicated that this was incomprehensible. Beto jumped on him. I remember very clearly my feeling "Oh. I understand what George is thinking; I have never heard of and cannot possibly imagine a black becoming a lawyer. I wonder if Beto is really telling the truth!"

Also, during high school during World War II, I went to church at St. Paul's Lutheran. A black soldier (1st Lt. US Army) walked into church and sat in the middle of the church. An usher came to him and asked him to leave, finally agreed to let him sit in the back row!

Several of us Texans took the train to Chicago for our first year in college. We changed trains in St. Louis. We got to a car, which had seats available. I turned and said to the guys "Hey, we can't sit here. This is for the colored!" The black conductor in a loud voice instructed, "That car is just fine for you damn Southerners!"

The stories go on as did my all too slow enlightenment and repentance. I pause to give thanks to a few of those black people who helped me out of my ignorance: Pete Pero, Julius Jenkens, Bill Griffin, Orlando Gober. So, when today we inaugurated a black person elected to the highest office of the land, I rejoiced so much that I wept!

The second profound moments came to me during the speech. But first, a bit of background. I, of course, have been most unhappy with the administration of the past eight years - considering these years to be among the worst in our country's history. Yet I am proud to be an American and value my USA passport beyond words. That feeling is never stronger than when I travel overseas. In the last few years, however, I have almost become defensive. Whether in China, Brazil, Finland, Palestine or Germany, I have had persons come up to me (some well-known to me, others strangers). In each case they approached me respectfully and hesitantly. Yet in every case they came to question how it could be that the USA has changed its image in the world. It has been seen as a bully, a user of torture, a naysayer to immigrants, a country so admired and now so disappointing. When Obama spoke of reaching out to all, of having ideals, which we stick to even in the face of threat, of conversation rather than mandates. My heart rejoiced.

The road ahead is incredibly tough. The reality of what the president can accomplish falls far short of the promises made during a campaign or even an inauguration speech. Yet it is a moment of hope, a time to put into place our best instincts, a time to cling to our highest ideals, a time to hope.

One final footnote: I watched finally the Obamas get out of their limo to enter the White House. I tried to remember if this was the entrance, I had used some 35 years ago when I had been invited to the White House for a meeting with the president. I thought, "Well, I guess if a Lutheran teacher's son and a Lutheran teacher himself can be a guest there, and a black man can be president there then God indeed is hearing my prayer "God bless America and the world! "

Dad

ഇൻ

MEDICAL CARE: HOSPITAL VISITS

Today I visited a former colleague in the hospital. He is a patient at the UCLA Ronald Reagan Hospital for Neurological Care. It was my first visit to that not yet one-year-old hospital. It is a large, impressive and beautiful facility. There was valet parking with a greatly reduced fee for persons with a handicapped sticker. The entire building is gleaming white, inside and out. The corridors are very wide and spotless. Floors look like shining marble. Walls have marvelous nature photographs, many of them of graceful white polar bears frolicking in the arctic snow.

Staff went way beyond the normal call of duty. One attendant followed me to make sure I was at the right door. When I buzzed the intensive care unit an assistant not only admitted me to that unit but also walked me to the patient. The windows of his single room offered a vista extending to the Pacific Ocean a few miles away. He was attached to the latest in equipment costing thousands of dollars. When the nurses came to aspirate him through his tracheal inserts, they were efficient, courteous, proficient.

Tom himself may or may not have ever been aware that I was there. He had fallen, and hit his head hard. At least a third of his skull had been removed to relieve the pressure and to drain off massive bleeding. On a previous day he had been responsive, today less so.

I held his hands and spoke as warmly and gently as possible. I assured him of love, hope, and God's presence. I had the feeling that he was in good hands, in every sense of those words.

As I left Tom, another visit some time ago came into and flooded my mind. It was at the Kowloon General Hospital in Hong Kong. The hospital was vastly overcrowded. In spite of the efforts of many and the care of lots of compassionate people the place was dirty, overcrowded, understaffed; with ancient equipment and no air conditioning in 90-degree heat. I had come to see a patient with a head injury. One of my students riding home on his bicycle from Concordia High School had a terrible collision with a truck hauling reinforcing iron bar. My student was lying uncovered, still in his school uniform, on the floor on top of a stretcher. He was alive but blood was oozing from his massive head wounds. No one was attending him. My status as a foreigner helped me reach an attendant. I pointed to my friend and pleaded for attention. "Oh, can't you see? He is dying. There is nothing we can do to save him." His parents had not yet arrived. So, I got down on the floor with him. I held his hands, spoke as warmly and gently as possible. As best I could in my limited Cantonese, I assured him of love, hope and God's promise. Two days later we buried him on a hillside overlooking mainland China.

Two very divergent streams of thought fill my consciousness as I drive home. The first is simply gratitude that I have so often been offered the opportunity to visit friends in the hospital. What a blessing it is to me to just be there to provide presence and to draw even from their weak bodies a sense of connectedness that endures.

The second is much more cerebral and much less hopeful. Which of those two hospital alternatives can we as a nation provide to those who need it? What are the possibilities and the limits? If I or one of my grandchildren will lie in a hospital needing medical and human care, where will it come from?

ഇൟ

TO PRIVILEGE BORN

I am "holding rope" at a Texas wedding. It's as near to heaven as a 10-year-old boy can get in the 1930's. We live out in the country and the reception for any wedding we attend is held at the farm home of the bride.

Farm houses are situated down a lane in a tree shaded area of the farm. When there's a wedding, small boys stretch a rope across the entrance lane, blocking the passage of the Model A and Model T Fords. Occupants of the cars will throw pennies, maybe even a nickel occasionally or at the very most a dime, to the boys holding the rope. Then the rope is lowered and the car proceeds to the farm house at the end of the lane.

To be a part of the gang (boys only, of course) holding the rope is a position of rare privilege. The "tips" collected are distributed among the boys holding the rope. So, it's just good business to not have too many boys involved. The closest relative to the bride is the general manager. He chooses his partners with care and is careful to limit the number of partners.

I am always chosen to be part of this special group. It has nothing to do with my ability to "hold rope" or my ability to get a nickel rather than a penny from a guest. I am selected on the basis of birthright. My father is Teacher Oscar Kieschnick! He's the principal/teacher of Zion Lutheran School. He's the organist for every wedding at Zion Lutheran Church. He has taught Grades 4 to 8 since 1920 and is the TEACHER for every bride and groom traveling from church to rural wedding reception. And I'm his oldest son. So, I get to hold rope. I may get as much as 16¢ to 18¢ per wedding, enough for three ice cream cones at the annual church-school picnic.

I really do consider myself born to privilege. My family gets invited out for Sunday dinner. My father sings and tells stories at wedding receptions. My father is secretary of the congregation. My father's opinion counts in community decisions. My mother's father is the founder of the town and local Lutheran Church. My uncles are the bankers, the store owners, the cotton gin operators.

Later when I am sent away to a boarding prep school to prepare for a teaching ministry in the church, I feel special. At weddings, there may be the custom of passing the bride's shoe around to the guests who place change into the shoe. The bride selects me as the recipient of this gift because I'm off studying to be a Worker in the Church and I'm the son of Teacher and Mrs. Oscar H. Kieschnick.

Years later my perspective may change. I may understand that my father was indeed respected, but often it was deemed that since he had respect, he really didn't need that much salary. Others will make the judgment that I was sent off to be a "church worker" because I wasn't competent or strong enough to be a farmer. Relatives may have viewed me as "poor relations." But none of that mattered when I was a kid. I was born to privilege. I still feel it.

A sense of worth, of specialness, of worthiness instilled in a child, builds a base that lasts a lifetime.

ՀՅՀ

HEAT OF THE DAY

I wriggle my bare feet trying to find the shade under the cotton plants. I am 10 years old picking cotton in a Texas field sweltering under the 100° heat. My fingers are still not callused or scarred and so they bleed as I pull the fluffy cotton from the pointed bolls.

An eight to 10-foot long cotton-picking sack is dragged behind by a strap slung over my shoulder. I pick cotton boll by boll, transfer a handful from my left hand into my right hand and stuff it into the bag. When the bag is full (or when the bag of the farmer in whose field we are picking is full) we carry the bags to the wagon. There they are weighed. The cotton is poured into the wagon. When the wagon is full, the cotton is taken to the gin. There the seeds and debris are separated from the lint and the cotton is baled for shipment to the spinning mills.

For me, weighing time is relief time. For just a few minutes there's respite from the back torturing that comes from stooping. There are a few minutes of dispensation for the knees on which one crawls down the rows of stalks plucking the low-lying bolls. And best of all there are water jugs bringing relief to scorched throats.

Worst of all is the voice of the man weighing the product of my labor. He'll say something like "40 pounds," a meager effort for my two hours of labor. Everybody knows my little brother can pick twice that amount in the same period of time. Still worse: my sister (a girl - of all things!) beats my amount picked every time.

I'll heed my father's call, "In the field by sun up." I'll give it my best shot till sunset with an hour off for lunch. If the crop is good and if I don't spend too much time day dreaming of becoming the next Mel Ott, or if I don't get too caught up in picking and throwing unopened hard cotton bolls at fellow pickers, and if it's a bit damp in the morning so that the lint weighs a little more, and if all those "ifs" come together just right I might pick a total of 180 pounds of cotton that day. At the rate of 25¢ per hundredweight I'll earn 40 cents for my day's labor.

Mr. Mertink the farmer-philosopher for whom I worked was also a bit of

11

a poet. He wrote into my autograph book the profound words:

"When you get old
And tired of your fate
Remember how hard the work
And the heat of 1938."

I am now old and I think of others who know about work: hard, boring, physical work. I see children at the rug weaving looms of Egypt with the finger-crippling repetition damaging them for life. I see coal miners in the USA and China descending into the depths of blackness and unclean air. I image again the women of India sitting in the sun with their bamboo-handled hammers crushing granite into small pieces for use as aggregate in concrete construction. I see the coolies still pulling barges up stream, and half-naked Bangladesh men pulling steel-laden carts down a humid street. Hard work, physical work that strains the muscles, numbs the mind and shortens life is still a constant in the lives of millions. So I remember Mr. Mertink's little ditty and I feel grateful that for me cotton picking is a thing of the past and that my heart can still feel a touch of shared humanity with those who work so hard for long hours under terrible conditions just to eke out a marginal life with little promise of rest and reward.

ೲ

PURGATORY AT THE KYBER PASS

I am sitting at an outdoor table of the Intercontinental Hotel in Peshawar, Pakistan. I look to the left and see the Khyber Pass. For some strange reason I remember and visualize Alexander the Great moving his armies through that pass on his way to "conquer the world." I remember the story (probably apocryphal) that he wept because he thought there were no more worlds to conquer. (Apparently, he was unaware of say, China and North America.)

I look a little to my right, past the massive refugee center I'd visited earlier in the day filled with Afghanis fleeing their home country then being controlled by Russia. I knew that many of these refugees were mujahideen being secretly armed to wrestle control back from the Russians. I did not know that they were going to replace communism with an Islamic State as repressive as any Stalinist dictatorship.

My mind is in deep reverie, my thoughts puddle jumping from ancient Persia, to Zoroastrianism, to my long held desire to visit Kabul, to refugees

12

all over the world, and how this boy from the little town of Walburg, Texas, who assumed that all of his life would be spent teaching in small Lutheran parochial schools in that state should find himself overlooking the Khyber Pass drinking beer with an Irish Catholic nun.

The "beer part" is almost as remarkable as the rest of the scenario. With Pakistan being a very strict Muslim country, the sale of alcoholic beverages is severely restricted. As a foreigner I have secured and paid for a license, which allows me to purchase a limited amount of alcohol, three units, to be exact. Sister Sheila and I opted for three quarts of beer since the price quoted us for the pint of gin that we really wanted was US $32.00.

Sister Sheila is a remarkable woman. She has left her native Ireland and devoted her life to teaching the poorest of the poor. Her classrooms are the shaded areas of trees. Her school equipment consists of four-inch high benches. Paper is too expensive so each student has a 10" x 12" chalkboard used over and over. Sister Sheila has put together a whole network of schools, has trained a corps of teachers using a model I had taught her. She gathers the mothers for lessons as well. We talk about all that. We move to reflecting upon the legitimacy of teaching Christianity to children form Muslim homes, about comparative religions, about denominations, about Lutherans and Catholics, about life after death and about purgatory.

"I haven't even thought about purgatory for 20 years" she says "and here I am with a Lutheran Texan drinking beer, recalling ancient caravans coming down the Khyber Pass and talking about purgatory!" We laughed. We agreed that teaching little children to read, giving food to the hungry, care to the sick, and human dignity to the forgotten of the world is much more important than trying to particularize any of the zones of hell.

೮೦೧೩

RESPECT FOR THE GROUND

I am attending a dinner party in my honor in the ultra-exclusive Boat Club at the harbor of Karachi, Pakistan. My host is a justice of the Pakistani Supreme Court. Others present at this all-male event include the Counsel Generals from the USA and various European countries. Especially noticeable is an impressive elderly gentleman whom I will call Mr. Faisel. I am told he is the person who negotiated the distribution of water rights from the Indus River. The agreement divided the water supply between archenemies India and Pakistan. The terms were so equitably spelled out that the agreement was still working decades after it was confirmed by the two antagonistic countries.

We are sitting around a circular cocktail table engaging in the usual cocktail hour small talk. About half of us are holding alcoholic beverages while the other half honors the Muslim prohibition against alcohol and drinks fruit juice.

Mr. Faisel gently interrupts our conversation. "Enough of this chit-chat," he interjects. Looking at me he says, "Tell me about this training you're leading here and what its philosophical bases are."

I explain, "I am teaching interpersonal communication, problem solving and conflict resolution skills. The underlying principle is 'respect' - respect for self, respect for others and in my value system: respect for a higher being."

He looks at me intently. "Quite good," he says, "but you're leaving out one very important component.

"Tell me, please."

"Respect for the ground," he replies.

"Respect for the ground?" I query.

"Yes, respect for the ground and for all those buried there. Respect for the ground which holds the remains of all those who've gone before us. All of our interpersonal relations, our situations in life and our values for the future are influenced by the generations who have preceded us and, in whose works, we now find our identity."

John Donne, the English poet, reminds us that "No man (sic) is an island." because we are connected to every other living human. Mr. Faisel expands the vision. All of humanity is connected not only to all the living but also to those who have lived before us, those now part of The Ground.

℘ℭ

RUTH: RECONCILIATION

More than 2,000 students were enrolled in kindergarten through high school at Concordia-Hong Kong when I served as principal. I did not know each student by name. My first encounter with Ruth, a 10th grade student, came in the emergency room of the Government Hospital. She was struggling for her life after slitting her wrists in a suicide attempt.

Slowly I got the story. She had just endured three full days of being locked up without water or food in a dark closet. Her father had put her there to teach her a lesson.

On the previous Sunday afternoon after a youth activity at our church she and another youth (male) from the group walked the street together and had tea together in a tea restaurant. This behavior by his 16-year-old daughter angered and frightened her father. He wanted to make sure she would not make a similar mistake again so he locked her in darkness!

In her despair Ruth decided death was better than life. She survived.

Thirty-five years later Ruth and I were leaving a Chinese restaurant in San Diego, California. She had given me her business card, which confirmed what I had previously been told. She was married, with children. She was an exceedingly successful businesswoman, managing a variety of companies, a millionaire many times over.

Yet there was something more impressive. As she (quite solicitously) held my arm to see her old principal safely to his car in a darkened parking lot, she very quietly said to me, "Principal Kieschnick, my father is still alive. We see each other often. We get along fine." Then we parted.

I rejoice with her in the power of reconciliation and restored relationships between a frightened father and a hurt daughter and between a Heavenly Parent and all children everywhere.

ഇഇരു

ERNA

Erna, four years older than I, is the eldest of the nine children in my family. She learned responsibility early. When mother gave birth to child number nine in the dining room of our country home, because it was the only room with a stove in it, Erna stayed home from high school. She not only assisted mother and baby, but also cared for other sibs who chose that same time to come down with some childhood disease. I don't remember which disease it was, since eventually all of us had them all: measles, mumps, pink eye, scarlatina, whatever.

Staying home for a while to serve as care giver did not seem to have a negative effect on her scholastic performance. She graduated #1 in her high school class, valedictorian.

She was awarded a college scholarship. She did not accept it. Instead she went to the big city of Austin to earn money as a clerical staff person for a financial institution. She had to earn the money so that her younger brother, that's I, could go to the church's preparatory school for service as a teaching minister in the church.

She helped pay my tuition and room and board. And since I was in the same city where she worked, we spent some time together. She taught me some much-needed social graces. "When with a girl you must walk on the street side of the city sidewalk." Or,"Leave at least a nickel tip."

On the day of my prep-school graduation I was stunned to receive a marvelous wristwatch as a gift from my family. I learned that Erna was financing it, $5.00 down, then $5.00 a month for six months.

Two months later I was at college, on the football team. Early in the season we returned to our locker room to discover there had been a theft. While we were on the practice field someone had gotten into the locker room stealing everyone's valuables. My watch was gone.

When I told Erna she sympathized with me. Then she assured me that she would continue to make the remaining three payments on the watch I was never to see again.

In the 60-some years since then Erna has continued to be there, faithfully and lovingly supporting her little brother.

ഇൻ

MAKING A DIFFERENCE

I am in Washington, D.C. addressing the House Committee on Education. I am suggesting that patterns of schooling and education of some foreign countries, specifically Hong Kong, might provide some valuable lessons for America. The Representatives and staff listen politely, ask some good questions, thank me for my insights and excuse me. As I now reflect, I am clear on one thing: My presentation did not make any difference.

I am again in Washington, this time at the White House. I am with three carefully selected Roman Catholic bishops and an influential rabbi. Finally, after months of using the right channels, getting the schedule organized to the minute and having our respective "talking points" finely tuned, we await our time with the President. Just before we are to be with him, an aide appears. "An international situation has just surfaced. The President will be unable to meet with you." I quickly stuff into my pockets a few White House embossed napkins as souvenirs to prove that I did in fact have an appointment with the

President of the United States. My appearance at the White House certainly never made a difference.

It's as tough an assignment as I've ever been given. A major denomination is in the midst of an ecclesiastical civil war. Finally, the decision is made to bring together spokespersons from all over the USA for the various factions. Put them together for three days, face to face, heart to heart, and try to resolve the issues. I am asked to facilitate the process. It looks to me like it worked. There were open conversations, new insights, and overtures for peace. I feel good about it. But then "the powers that were" decided not to opt for peace. The denomination fractured. I made no difference.

I am the facilitator for an international gathering of the members of a venerable and highly respected order of Catholic priests. The order has ministries worldwide, owns multi-million dollars' worth of property, and is awash with liquid assets. However, it does not have new members of the order. By its own canons all members must live in community; but there are not enough "religious" to form communities at all of their ministry sites. They want to reach consensus on which ministries to close, which to transfer to other entities, which to consolidate. They have three days to complete the process. I am to facilitate this. At the end of the three days there is no consensus. My efforts did not make any difference.

I am with a young couple who have just (for the second time in 24 months) gone through the stillbirth of an infant. I am there to listen, to puzzle, to grieve, to pray, to just hold them in my arms. I make a difference.

I meet a man who is retiring after years of successful service as a classroom teacher. He tells me, "Remember that night in the parking lot in Hutchington, Kansas? I had given up. I decided to quit teaching, maybe go dig ditches somewhere. You listened, you counseled, you encouraged. I tried again and the last years of my teaching were by far the most enjoyable and successful of my life." I have made a difference.

Making a difference. Sometimes it's not at some grand national or international level, but in a quiet, virtually unnoticed private encounter among just two or three that a difference is made.

೮೧೦೪

PEBBLE BEACH: BLISS

I am standing on the 18th hole of the Pebble Beach Golf Links. It's the most beautiful and awesome meeting of sea, shore and fairway greens in the world. The prevailing wind will accentuate my natural slice from left to right. I nail my drive. The ball sails over the bay, is blown to the right and lands in the middle of the fairway of this incredible par 5 finishing hole. My golf cart like Elijah's chariot carries me to my perfect lie. My ensuing three wood is straight and on line. My hopes soar. A seven or eight iron to the green. There's hope for a birdie. I swing. I have duck-hooked it. The ball is somewhere under an incoming Pacific Ocean wave. I take my penalty, try again and end up with a double bogey seven. I regret the inability to convert promise into reality, but I do not mourn for long. I have been to golfer's Mecca and it is paradise on earth.

When I grew up during the depression, the son of a rural parochial school teacher, golf was beyond even my wildest fantasy. Once, an uncle "from the city" had given me a golf ball. I treasured it and hit it, fungo-like with a baseball bat, into the cow pasture. I sought till I found it and hit it again. Then I couldn't find it and I assumed my golfing life was over.

But it wasn't. I've ended up playing more golf than I ever fantasized about and in venues where I have to pinch myself to be sure I was actually there: Hundreds of rounds at Hong Kong Golf Club, Fan Ling (no longer The Royal Hong Kong Golf Club). I've worked my way around many of the most wonderful courses imaginable: Kapalua on Maui, Hawaii, Westchester Country Club in New York, The Palm and the Magnolia in Disneyland, Cog Hill in Illinois, Torrey Pines in California, Banff in Canada.

There are unique elements of the golfing experience understood only by those who've been there, done that: the anticipation that goes with opening a new sleeve of balls on the first tee. The posturing, complaining, negotiating that precedes the first swing. The downward spiral of feeling as a ball just catches a trap, lands beyond the white out-of-bounds stakes, lips out of a cup. The almost orgasmic sensation of a six iron that hooks around a tree and lands on the green, the 30-foot putt that drops. There are always the post-round autopsies over a few cold beers. Although we all know that no one (no one!) really cares about the final score of another golfer, we all rehearse selected agonies and ecstasies.

Yet, it is not unique. Every being that is still really alive is stirred by the anticipation of achievement, is exhilarated by possibilities, disappointed in failure, and longs for the companionship of a shared experience. Golf is, as

18

they say, a four-letter word. For me that four letter word is LIFE.

ഓരു

WHAT WILL PEOPLE THINK! A LESSON TOO WELL LEARNED

My mother of blessed memory taught me many things, including lots of memorized material. Night after night she sat with me to ensure that I had done my "memory work" for the next day's religion class at the Lutheran elementary school. Thus, we memorized not only Luther's Small Catechism but also the hundreds of "proof texts" in Dr. Schwan's expanded version of that classic. Added to that were hymns, a few poems and many proverbs and sayings. Some of the proverbs were known to all in that German community. I still hear "Eigenlobt stinck" (Self-praise stinks.) any time I come close to telling someone of a personal accomplishment. Other sayings she made up for the occasion: "Wenn du hungrig bist, denn schmueck auch jelly brot gut." (If you are hungry, then plain old jelly bread tastes good.) This came when I complained that there were no freshly baked cookies available.

There is, however, one frequent reminder that, I fear, I may have over-learned and that is "What will people think!" That was really important to my mom. She often reminded me that I was the son of the principal of that small Lutheran school and people would be watching my actions. What would they think if I misbehaved! We often wore hand-me-down clothes, but they needed to be clean and ironed or else, "What would people think!" I learned to say, "Thank You" and "Please" and "I am sorry" because if I failed to do that, "What would people think!" I had to watch my manners, my mouth, my eating and spending habits. The threat was there, spoken and unspoken. Mess up in any of these areas and people would think poorly of me, of my family, of German people and certainly of Lutherans.

As stated above, this lesson served me well. It caused me on occasion to reflect before I acted or reacted. I believe it helped me develop a sense of empathy. It helped me to not bring shame to my heritage.

And it has also not always served me that well. At times I have kept my mouth shut when the situation really demanded that I speak the truth. Fear of people's reaction trumped my obligation to speak up. I have accepted invitations, taken on too many assignments, expected too much from my children, hidden some of my political or even religious views and values, etc.… all because I was afraid that if I exposed my true thoughts, feelings, values or desires, then I would be thought less of. In the process I have sometimes compromised my integrity.

So, dear Mother, I have written this blog even though there is a voice in the back of my head warning me, "What will people think!"

℘ℭ

ALWAYS THE UNEXPECTED

It was spring of 1950. About 100 of us were excitedly assembled in that large oval room on the ground floor of the Administration Building at Concordia Teachers College, River Forest, Illinois. We were there to receive our "Solemn Calls." In those days the church-wide Council of Presidents (Bishops Conference) had met with the appropriate college and seminary placement directors. They had assembled all the requests from congregations across the church for the assignment of officially approved "teaching ministers of religion." Those decisions had been made without further consultation with the candidates (that is what we were called). Each of us was assigned to a particular congregation or other church entity. The assumption was that each candidate would accept the assignment as made.

The suspense in the room was great. None of us knew where we would be assigned or what our specific duties would be. Previous to this we had, of course, met with our Placement Directors and discussed our gifts, our preferences and any unusual circumstances affecting our placement. For me there was really only one overriding question "To which Lutheran church and school in Texas would I be assigned?" The general consensus of the time was that Texans would be assigned to Texas congregations.

I dutifully waited until my name was called and the Placement Director announced "Melvin Kieschnick St. Paul Lutheran Church and School, Tracy, California." Within 72 hours I informed St. Paul's that I was their newly assigned principal/teacher/youth director and that I was prayerfully accepting their call.

The surprises kept coming. When once a month I found myself collecting newspapers from garages throughout Tracy (the paper was sold as a fundraiser for the school). I wondered if that was part of the "divine call" but I really needed to raise the money somehow to pay for curtains in the classroom so that I could effectively operate that brand-new filmstrip projector. I unexpectedly played basketball in the city league as part of a

20

team sponsored by a not very reputable pool hall and filled in as preacher when my pastor's alcohol problems kept him out of the pulpit. I learned that one really could complete a Master's thesis if one's spouse was willing to type after midnight.

The unexpected never stopped. When, without prior consultation, the Church's Foreign Mission Board extended me a call to Hong Kong I had to locate a map to find out where Hong Kong was. Once there, I learned to take in stride visits to the poorest of the poor among the refugees in hillside huts and to go from there to a formal party for the British Queen at the Governor's Mansion.

An unexpected cerebral aneurysm in my wife's brain brought me back to the States and to roles as divergent as leadership for a church-wide capital funds drive, to District School Superintendent, to national churchwide offices, to parents training around the world and to the privilege of serving Lutheran schools in the South Bronx, Long Island and other parts of the Metro New York area.

Even in retirement the surprises never stop and all of them flow from One who I believe has both a sense of humor and wonderful surprises!

හ⃝෬

AGING PARENTS: AGING SELF

My spell checker insists that "aging" is not a word. But it is a reality, regardless of how one may choose to spell it. My last two days have brought me again face to face with people who age. It began with a wonderful presentation here at La Costa Glen, the continuing care community to which Jane and I moved four months ago. Our Executive Director gave us a report of her first ever trip to China and her work there in helping to establish the first ever continuing care community in that country. She reminded us of something that we already know: China faces a tremendous challenge in assisting its citizens through the later years of their life. Because of the one child policy there will soon be less than three people under 60 to support each person over 60. If each family has only one child then that one child may have to support not only his parents but also four grandparents. The multi-generational family under one roof may have worked in a rural economy but not in the modern urbanized China. The state guarantees of old age pensions from state run enterprises have disappeared.Meanwhile the life expectancy grows. The Confucian mandate of filial piety is still embedded, especially in the minds of the elderly who still insist that being cared for outside the traditional family home is a sign of failed parenting. Thus, even the one large facility for the elderly recently opened is not fully occupied. One consequence is that general hospitals have an overload of patients who have no option but to remain hospitalized.

But one need not go to China. I had only to visit a former neighbor. The story is familiar. The single older male is no longer able to care for himself. He refuses to look at options other than staying in his home. (Even though he does not know how to cook, has never done laundry, and needs regular infusions of saline solutions for his severe Sjogren's disease). Meanwhile one of his children lives in another state and one (who is in ill health herself) tries to cope. It isn't working. When I offer alternatives (fortunately there are adequate financial resources) there is a complete refusal to even look at any other options.

As I was on my way to visit the above gentleman a neighbor stopped me. "I am in a bind, Mel," he tells me. "My daughter is divorced. She has a mentally retarded child. Her ex-husband just lost his job and so can't make his child support payments. So, I need to send money to my daughter and granddaughter, but here I am on fixed income and goodness knows what has happened to my IRA and other savings plan." He thought he had planned well for his years of aging and now he is beginning to wonder how it will all end.

As I reflect on my own aging, my kids sustain me in my own images of the future. When I recently said something about a decline in assets they responded "Dad you have assets, five big ones. They are your five kids." And when I stew over the future, Jane has the perfect three-point response 1. "God has always taken care of us in the past and God is not about to change." 2. "If we die young, we have enough resources to see us through." 3. "If we live a long life the market will have turned around and the assets will be there"

And that is good enough for me.

৩০৫৪

FIT FOR THE QUEEN

I get out of the taxi and move toward the Royal Guard to present our official invitation to this gala garden party celebration. It is Queen

Elizabeth's Official Birthday. The fete is in the Governor's Home on the Peak in Hong Kong, then a Royal Crown Colony.

The prescribed dress is "garden formal." That has presented a slight problem. By all proper English decorum that means ladies will wear appropriate hats. My wife, Jane, had left all her "garden hats" in the States years before. Missionary salaries precluded a visit to any local millinery shop (of which there were none in the Colony anyway) to secure proper head wear. However, in her usual excellent taste, ingenuity and skill, and drawing upon genes inherited from a grandmother who had run a millinery shop in the haute culture center of Decatur, Indiana at the turn of the century - and with the assistance of missionary wives of several religious denominations she is, in fact, properly attired with a gorgeous hat most suitable for a garden party in honor of the birthday of Queen Elizabeth II.

I have been led to understand that "appropriate dress" is subject to a variety of interpretations. In the case of Jane's hat and the Queen's Garden Party one rule of chic was paramount: she dare not look like a missionary wife!

I recall other instructions on fashion statements given me by my parents. When, during the Great Depression of the 1930's I questioned the stylishness of the knickers handed down to me by an older cousin, my mother had instructed me, "If the clothes is clean and well ironed, it will be just fine."

My father added his advice, "If your shoes are freshly polished, everyone will agree you are well dressed."

Incidentally, we had a great time at the Garden Party, and I, for one, thought I had the most smashingly attired partner of anyone there.

♥ঃ

SCARCITY

I am a child of the great American Depression. I blame that for my mental outlook that my New Age friends' term "coming out of scarcity." For me it means a growing feeling of never being sure that I have enough money, enough time, enough food, drink, clothes, golf balls, filing space - you name it.

The late 1920's and early 1930's were, in fact, times of great scarcity. My memory is that at mealtime we were restricted to one tiny piece of meat. When there was no meat, we ate boiled potatoes and pickled beets. When my dad returned from an out of town teachers conference and he brought back a candy bar it was cut into many pieces so that each of the nine of us children (or whatever the number was at that time) could get the appropriate fraction. During nine months of the year we went barefoot everywhere. We saved our shoes and pair of socks for Sunday wear. After our house "got electricity" my parents told me a million times to "turn out the light." Money and electricity were scarce. To get ready for whatever eventuality, my mother, one spring and summer, canned 800 quarts of vegetables!

The amazing thing is that we always had enough. I never went hungry, wore rags, lacked love, warmth, attention, toys, tablet paper or ink. Things weren't really all that scarce.

Why then do I still "come out of scarcity?" If I'm to do a one-hour workshop I prepare enough material for two hours so I won't run out of stuff to present. Why is my garage packed with paper, boxes, clothes, old golf clubs, scrap lumber, telephone wire, half-empty paint cans, cracked flower pots, baby beds, 8' x 12' sheets of plywood, an old Weber barbecue, tarpaulins, old light switches, etc. etc.? Why do I buy 10 pounds of meat for the six guests we're having for dinner, and pack six shirts for a three-day trip?" Why do I invite eight people for dinner just to make sure that six will show up?

I blame it all on my childhood depression-era scarcity. My idea of heaven is that finally there'll be enough of everything for everyone, including me.

ଽଔଔ

THROWING OUT THE FIRST PITCH

The phone rang in my office at The Lutheran Schools Association of Metropolitan New York. It was the New York Mets. They told me the Mets were playing the Los Angeles Dodgers at Shea Stadium. The date had also been set as Lutheran Schools Day at Shea. They asked if I'd be interested in throwing out the ceremonial first pitch.

Silly question. Of course. What time should I be there?

Then reality hit. I haven't thrown a baseball in years. Can I get it from the mound to home plate? What if I bounce it or throw it over the catcher's head? The answer is practice. So, I visit my grandson. I step off the distance from the mound to the plate. I use an official regulation National League baseball. I get it. I can do it.

On the appointed day I go to the assigned box in the stands between home and first base. The manager and Todd Hundley, the catcher, come to greet me. The big right field scoreboard announces in lights, "Throwing Out the First Pitch is Mel Kieschnick of the Lutheran Schools Association." I'm ready. I ask for the best route to get from the box seat to the mound.

I am told, "Oh no, just stay in the box and throw it to Hundley. He'll stand right here."

So, I made my great FIRST PITCH, all 10 feet of it, from a box seat. Hundley caught the ball, handed it back to me and wished me a nice day.

Sometimes the excitement of anticipation is greater than the thrill of reality.

At least the Mets beat the Dodgers that day.

೮೦೦ಽ

FINE DINING

I am enjoying the Epicurean delight of a marvelous dinner at Gaddi's in the Peninsula Hotel Hong Kong. This is dining at its glorious best. In the midst of the late 1990's economic downturn in Asia, the number of diners a Gaddi's tonight is limited. Our candle-lit table for seven in the prime spot of the restaurant is the center of meticulous service. The peach champagne cocktail is chilled to just the right temperature. The bisque is perfectly ladled over the artfully arranged pieces of lobster in the monogrammed tureens. The salad seems to have come directly from garden to table with only a stop for its presentation to be enhanced. Entrées, whether from the kitchen or flamed tableside, are even more delicious than their Pulitzer-worthy descriptions by the maître d'. The wine is aged and the vintage appropriate. The soufflé is so light and fluffy it fails to float only because it is held down by the texture of the perfectly melted chocolate.

The dining companions are articulate, interested in topics of substance, and gracious in manner.

I'm not responsible for picking up the outrageous tab. It is a fine dining experience and I relish it.

Fine dining is, however, by no means restricted to Michelin starred restaurants. A modest farmhouse with Formica topped dining table can be a gourmet's dream come true. The menu: french-fried, never been frozen

25

chicken, cream gravy on mashed potatoes, freshly picked garden beans with homemade bread just out of the oven and finished off with cobbler made from peaches picked that morning.

Or how can it get any better than a full Cantonese-style Chinese feast with shrimp on toast, roast suckling pig, sharks fin soup, salt baked chicken, etc. etc. until all 12 courses are served?

This list could go on for pages: the jaeger schnitzel and spaetzle in Switzerland, marvelous all vegetarian food in Bombay, outdoor just off the pit barbecue in Texas, grilled salmon beside a stream in Idaho. Name your favorites!

Fine dining: for a newborn it comes from the mother's breast; for the poor it's anything that puts bulk into the stomach; for the recovering patient it's anything that stays down. For the Christian it's a sip of wine and a wafer of Eucharistic bread.

While eating is a common need and/or pleasure it is also something that separates the human family: Vegetarians from those who eat meat. Those who love pork from those who find this unspiritual. Those who eat around supportive families and those who eat in silent groups or in lonely solitude. Those who eat until sated or those multitudes who wait in vain for any morsel of nourishment.

Fine dining. May we hasten the day when an entire human family enjoys the answer to their simple prayer: "Give us this day our daily bread."

ജ

SANDRA

It was my first year of teaching, probably as close to hell as one can get this side of eternity. Grades one to four, forty-five students in one classroom. They were ordinary growing kids. I was inexperienced and not very competent. Among the 45 were Sandra Swain and her sister. Sandra was articulate and exuberant and in no way lethargic.

One morning before school Mrs. Swain told me this story. She said, "Last night I'd had it with Sandra and I exclaimed, 'Sandra, Shut Up!'

"Mom, you shouldn't say Shut Up! Mr. Kieschnick says that's a sin."

"Now wait a minute, Sandra. I know Mr. Kieschnick and I know you kids. I'll bet that when things get out of hand in your classroom sometimes Mr. Kieschnick, too, does shout 'Kids, Shut Up'!" "Oh yes, he does," said

Sandra. "But God forgives Mr. Kieschnick!"

It's more than 50 years since Sandra made that declaration. I hope that even if she has forgotten all about how to add common fractions, she still believes that God forgives Mr. Kieschnick and all the Sandras too.

ഇൻൽ

SISTERS AND BROTHERS

I experience it all again now, decades after the event. My wife Jane's mind struggled to focus as she lay in the Chinese hospital in Hong Kong after weeks of splitting headaches and blackouts. Neither her doctors nor 1965 available technology offered an appropriate diagnosis.

The doctor at the foot of her bed was the personal physician of Madam Chiang Kai-shek. "Sounds like a cerebral aneurysm to me," he said. "Get her to America for arteriography and treatment immediately."

Within two hours buds of help and hope started blooming everywhere.

An un-named civil servant granted an exit visa on the spot. A hero in the battle against the Communist take-over in China telephoned. "You don't really know me, but I heard about your situation. You'll need plane tickets. I can get them. If there's a financial problem, let me know." A Jewish businessman phoned. "I have connections with the world's best neuro-surgeon at Mt. Sinai Hospital in New York. I'll ask him to take care of Jane. Don't worry about the money."

At our home things were frantic. How does one pack up five young children to accompany a barely conscious mother for a flight across the Pacific in three days' time? Neighbors and friends from several countries and religious faiths came to pray, pack and wipe away tears.

Our home was just two blocks away from refugee squatter huts built of scrap lumber, cardboard and tin. From one of them a little girl was dispatched. "Here's an orange for the sick lady and a bottle of beer for her husband."

We carried Jane up the plane's loading ramp. Our five young children followed. We paused for prayer as the jet lifted off.

The moment the "Fasten Seat Belt" sign was turned off a well-dressed woman approached the patient. "You need to recline further," she said. "I'm putting you in my first-class seat. I'll help here with the kids." She never even gave me her name.

Strong headwinds forced an unscheduled stop in Alaska. Finally came the descent into San Antonio where arrangements had been made for care. While Jane was being carried from the plane to a waiting ambulance a couple appeared. "We'll take the kids home with us for the night. Don't worry."

The neurosurgeon doubted the accuracy of the Chinese diagnosis and ordered arteriography. Watching the monitor, he exclaimed, "Well, I'll be! There it is! An aneurysm in the right carotid next to the brain."

Additional specialists were consulted. A silver clip around the bulge might not hold. Brain surgery seemed problematic. A conservative non-surgical drug-assisted approach was agreed upon. Now Jane is well.

The recovery period was long, but the line of people offering assistance was longer. From New Guinea to New York prayers were offered. A car was loaned. Meals were provided. Children's clothes were bought. Dolls were given. And Jane was healed.

Thirty-five years later the aneurysm lies mute, but Jane's voice is loud and clear as we affirm together the ancient Chinese saying, "Within the four seas all people are sisters and brothers." And there is one God who loves and looks over us all.

8003

DINNER'S READY! COME EAT!

Among the most memorable and most pleasant memories of my childhood are the warm and wonderful daily welcome words of my Mom, "Dinner's ready! Come eat!" Those words epitomize my Mom. Sometimes it must have been tough on her. I am one of nine kids. Enough said. She had to manage on a parochial school teacher's salary - throughout the depression, even in those months when the congregation could not pay Dad's salary. Then there were guests. I brought them by the baseball team from Concordia in Austin. Even if our whole crew showed up unannounced Mom would still manage those beautiful words, "Dinner's ready! Come Eat!" I remember when the church where Dad was the organist had a new pipe organ installed. We lived on church property so when the organ installer arrived there was never any question. For two solid weeks each evening the invitation went to him, "Dinner's ready! Come Eat!" We kidded that potatoes and gravy were so essential for dinner that in the rare event they were not there we did not need to say grace because without them the repast could hardly be considered a meal... and Mom always had a meal.

In her old age Mom still trekked on her heavy and slow-moving legs to the Handy Andy store down the street to lug home whatever it took to feed children, in-laws, grandchildren, drop-ins, one and all.

My Mother's words "Dinner's ready! Come eat!" hit me this past week when we had our family devotions focused on the words of the Lord's prayer: "Give us this day our daily bread." I recalled Jesus' proclamation that dinner is ready for all, and his heart longs for the day when all the children of the world will hear the words "Dinner's ready! Come Eat!" It must hurt the very heart of God when that invitation is not heard by millions.

My thoughts went further. In this Lenten season I recall the special supper Jesus instituted. I have the radical thought that He still invites "Dinner's ready! Come Eat!" and I believe that invitation goes out with even less restrictions than my Mother may have had. It is an invitation to all. Of course, I know well the rules that have been set up by us later day children. Rules about who can come to that meal. One must qualify by belief, by membership in the appropriate church, by making proper preparations, by being of a certain age - all that stuff.

I recall with shame the thoughts I had some years ago on a Sunday morning in Hong Kong. It was during the Viet Nam war. Some service people on R&R from Nam had gone to all the trouble to actually locate a church in Kowloon and to get there. As they sat there, I suddenly had the thought, "I hope we do not have Holy Communion today." In my officially authorized understanding of my church's teaching in that day I would first have to check their credentials. Were they rightly confirmed in the right church? Did they have the right answers to the doctrinal questions etc.? Only if they could pass those requirements dare we include them in the invitation, "Dinner's ready! Come Eat!" At that time, I was afraid that they might have to be excluded and so I was glad that the meal was not to be served at all!

I have changed since that day. Today I would be bold to say to them and to all who might want to dine, "Come eat! Dinner's ready!"

ଆଔଓ

GRACIOUS HOST

Jane and I are in Barcelona. It's wonderful visiting our son, his beautiful Spanish wife and our, of course, exceptional grandchildren. Spanish hospitality envelops us, especially through the efforts of Ana.

She's not family. She met our son and family only a few months ago. She exudes acceptance, hospitality, and graciousness.

She has taken us on a personal tour of the city. She loves the place, knows its history and gives details about its architecture. She exudes a love for and an admiration of the people of her city. She serves us a dinner with refinement. We sit together in the ornate Gaudi-inspired Music Hall and listen to a powerful performance of Haydn's "Creation." As we part, she presents me with a marvelous picture book on the exotic architecture of her city.

After Ana drops us off at our son's home, I ask him to tell me more about our marvelous host. He gives the usual data re marriage, children, and employment history. He concludes: Her father and mother, you know, were executed by the fascist dictator Francisco Franco who ruthlessly killed any opposition leaders, often dumping their bodies into mass graves. Ana's dad was the former mayor of Barcelona and it cost him his life.

How does a child survive the execution of her parents? How can bitterness be mitigated? What resources can strengthen the soul to enjoy beauty and reach out with tenderness and affirmation to strangers?

ഇരു

REFUGEES

I have, it seems, been confronted by images and experiences of refugees all my life. As a young child I heard the stories and saw the photos of "refugees" from sand storms, Okies seeking refuge in California. In my late teens, war refugees from Europe came to the USA labeled DP's, displaced persons. In my late 20's I worked in Hong Kong among the hundreds of thousands fleeing Mao's Liberation Army. In more recent decades I have read about, walked among, ministered to and been ministered to by refugees from every corner of the globe: Vietnamese boat people, Lutheran Liberians fleeing slaughter even in their own church sanctuary, Albanian refugees fleeing from Kosovo, surviving and then returning to drive these same Serbs into refugee camps.

A very small humanitarian group called "Survivors of Torture International" ministers near my home in San Diego. The director informs me that with only word-of-mouth publicity her office gets appeal after appeal for help from the more than 11,000 survivors of international torture just in our county. They've fled here from Iran, Iraq, China, San Salvador, Columbia, the Sudan, Sri Lanka, Chile, Afghanistan, Turkey - the list goes on and on.

It's disheartening, but not surprising. The first-born Cain fled as a refugee - east of Eden. Moses fled to Midian. David escaped to caves. Our Lord was a political refugee in a distant land before he was two years old. Many of our ancestors came to this country as refugees from political, economic and religious oppression. Among the saddest of all refugees are those even today being sold and bought into slavery.

How to respond to refugees is one of the major political and moral issues of the day. The U.S. government, for example, will admit a limited number of "political refugees" and how can it adequately discriminate between "political" and "non-political" refugees? The persecution of Christians may well be at its highest ever level. Do I, as a Christian, advocate special treatment for my Christian brother or sister, knowing that my brother in the Sudan is being persecuted into refugee status because he is an animist, not a Muslim?

Refugee and immigration issues are closely intertwined. Is the poor Mexican peasant sneaking into California across the Mojave Desert an economic refugee, an illegal alien, both of the above or neither? What is my personal, political, ethical response to this, my brother and his family?

Do I support the Dali Llama and his claim to be a religious refugee from Tibet? Should I urge my senator to supply and support the Kurds in Iraq in their opposition to Sadaam Hussein? How can I best respond to the Christian in India who writes to tell that she's a "refugee" fleeing for her life from her Hindu oppressor? Can I do anything about the 150,000 Hindu and Pandit refugees fleeing for their lives from the Muslims in Kashmir?

I ponder these ambiguities and moral dilemmas even as I sit comfortably and write memoirs in an idyllic Mexican resort overlooking the Pacific Ocean. I reflect upon the reality of our common humanity, our shared complicity in evil and the eternal destiny facing each one of us. I pray for compassion, wisdom and forgiveness and for the courage to continue to reflect, care, and act.

৪৩জ্ঞ

RELIEF GOODS

I get off the overnight ferry from Hong Kong to Macao. It's still early and I want to arrive at the Lutheran school there in time to observe our pre-8:00 a.m. breakfast feeding program. After riding in the pedicab for about 10 minutes I am aware that I am being tailed. It's neither the first nor the last time this happens to me on my monthly trip to (at the time) the oldest European colony in the Orient.

There could be any number of reasons I'm being followed. On a recent trip I sat in a refugee hut being shown a packet of heroin. The owner was pleading for me to help him get a visa to the USA or else, regretfully, he would need to support his wife and three small children through drug trafficking.

Or it could be related to the fate of a gentleman who was a regular attendee at our "Introduction to Christianity" down at our church. He seemed genuinely interested and appeared to be asking deeply spiritual questions. Then one night as he stepped out of our church after class, he was shot dead and left lying at the entrance.

Maybe there was even something suspicious about our free breakfast program. I knew that we were not strictly following the rules. All the care sacks had the USA government message clearly printed on them: "Not to be sold, bartered, traded or exchanged." In spite of all my rationalization I knew that technically we were in violation.

The USA-supplied baking flour was of high quality coming in 50-pound bags. Southern Chinese are not much into eating wheat products; their staple is rice. The homes of our care recipients didn't have ovens or baking pans. So, we'd made a deal. We would supply the local baker with relief flour. Each morning he'd provide freshly baked products for our school. The hungry school children enjoyed them. I could see them gain weight. The baker did not charge us for his efforts. We were not overly exact in our accounting for how many bags of flour came back to our school in the form of breakfast-sized buns for our now thriving children.

Feeding the hungry, distributing relief goods, offering a cup of cold water even in the name of Jesus is not a piece of cake. Malnourished refugees who've never drunk cows' milk swear it gives them diarrhea. A pig farmer on the edge of the refugee squatter area says his hogs love cows' milk. Why not convert some of that good USA milk into Chinese pork? Some would be shared with the families who qualified for the milk, which they refused to drink anyway because their system just wouldn't tolerate it.

Or a food distribution center for the poor is set up in a church owned property. Who wouldn't assume that people with some stake in that property might not get some advantage at distribution time? Joining that group (or religion) may bring tangible benefits. Relief goods distribution problems are as old as first century Biblical widows, 19th century rice Christians or 21st century Islamic students in Khartoum.

Relief goods to one African country may be a key factor in keeping a despot in power. Hospital supplies to the Sudan fuel the civil war because it keeps alive some of the injured who return to the battlefield.

Yet it's also clear that to ignore the hungry, the naked or the prisoner is to hear the judgment voice, "I was hungry and you gave me no foo."

So, I continue to support relief efforts, especially Lutheran World Relief which is considered to be about the best in the world. And if some of those clothes or a bit of flour or a shot of tetanus is distributed contrary to strict protocol I'm not going to worry about possible complicity with conspirators.

&)(&

CEMETERIES PART 1

Cemeteries have always been a part of my life. I grew up in rural Texas in a home with the somewhat unusual designation as a "teacherage." It is the counterpart to a "parsonage." My father was a teaching minister serving a Lutheran congregation and school, so we lived in the teacherage. The church properties were all in a row: the parochial school, the parsonage, the barns, the teacherage and the cemetery. The graves, the tombstones, the arched entry gateway were all just next-door. Whenever a member of that rural parish died my father went to the church and tolled the bell. Within hours the gravediggers were there. Soon the funeral home people came with their tent, folding chairs and artificial green grass. From infancy I had attended every funeral and when I was in grade school we sang at the funeral services. We marched by the casket, looked at the corpse and paid our last respects. Then the bell again tolled our walk to the cemetery. After the committal ceremony I would stay and watch the dirt and stones go back into the grave, covering the casket.

I might walk along the row of tombstones. I would always pause at the small marker noting my cousin Ben who died in infancy. Through the years the number of my relatives buried there grew: grandparents, uncles, aunts, dad and mom and then brothers-in-law. It is a good place to visit, to reflect, to cry, to smile, to anticipate.

The Christian Cemetery in Kowloon Hong Kong is very different. It goes up a very steep hill. There is no vegetation. Funerals there use no artificial grass to soften the realities. The first time I climbed that steep hill, following four Chinese laborers carrying the coffin suspended from bamboo poles across their shoulders, I was assisting Dorothy Gehring. We were laying her husband Ralph to rest. Ralph had visited Hong Kong while in the US Navy. After discharge and getting a business degree he wanted to return as the church's business manager. First, he served in Japan. Then he joined us in Hong Kong. He was great. His wife and two kids were wonderful friends.

For reasons to be talked about in a different blog I was the only Lutheran missionary to ever be admitted into membership into the Royal Hong Kong Golf Club. Guest passes for local friends were extremely difficult to obtain. But I managed to host Ralph. Even as we were returning home that day, he said he felt inordinately weak. Before long he was in the hospital. Very early the doctor made the surprising diagnosis. He had polio. Within 72 hours he had died. It was then that we learned that before he left Japan to move to Hong Kong, he and his family had gone to get polio shots. He was told that the supply at the time was very limited. Some children were waiting in line. "Oh, by all means, immunize them first" was his immediate response. His wife and children received the vaccine. He never got his. And now we were taking his body for a final rest in Kowloon Christian Cemetery - and ever since then it is for me a sacred place, a place to remember a gentle, giving colleague named Ralph.

Not long after Ralph's burial I was in a very different cemetery. It was lush in greenery with impeccably well-manicured landscape, spectacular vistas in all directions and 33,230 plain small white crosses. I was in the National Memorial Cemetery of the Pacific in the extinct volcano now called the Punch Bowl in Hawaii. I stood in silence for a very long time. All those under the sod at my feet had given their lives and, in that action, made my life choices possible. The day before my standing there at the Punch Bowl and after an absence from the USA for five full years I had proudly and gratefully presented my USA passport at USA Customs. I was again enjoying the privileges of a citizen in my own free country. Without the sacrifice of those now lying there it is most likely that I would not have been standing on the soil of the United States of America. And so, I bowed in gratitude and in petition that the cost of my freedom would never again have to be paid, as it had been by those among whose grassy beds I was now standing.

34

CEMETERIES PART 2: LEWIS

I still remember the first time I saw Lewis and his wife Anna (as I will call them in this blog). It was in the very simple storefront church at 232 Tai Po Rd., Kowloon Hong Kong. I estimated that the combined weight of the two of them was less than 200 pounds. They sat among a large group of White Russians who, like them, had just finally been released from six years of Mao Zedong- imposed house arrest in Beijing. Somehow or other they made it to Hong Kong and got across the border. Lewis and Anna were not White Russians; they were American citizens, Lutherans at that.

Of course, Jane and I took them home for Sunday dinner and helped them eventually find a very small cramped upper story tenement house apartment with no elevator. Not long afterward I received word that Lewis had been taken by ambulance to the hospital. The attendant there told me his situation was grave, accentuated by the fact that the stairway to his apartment had been too narrow for him to be carried down on stretcher and so his body had been severely traumatized before he got to the hospital room. Fellow missionary George Winkler joined me there. I remember George recalling that Lewis had spoken German as a child. So, George prayed the Lord's Prayer in German. Within minutes we closed Lewis's eyes in death.

We took Anna to our home. Jane invited Anna to sleep in the same bed with her that night.

Burial space in Hong Kong is severely limited. We arranged for a space in the Kowloon Christian Cemetery. Next, I had to find a coffin and make arrangements for embalming. I found the coffin-making shop. I still remember quite clearly standing on the sidewalk next to the narrow shop in which the coffins were being hewn. I really did not want a Chinese-style coffin and negotiated as best I could for a somewhat more Western-style wooden coffin. My memory is that I finally secured it for HK $200.00 (about US $35.00).

The memorial service was solemn. Then the four wiry-legged coffin bearers put their ropes around the coffin, suspended it from their bamboo poles across their shoulders and started up the very steep hillside toward the gravesite. Several hundred yards up the hill they stopped. They set the coffin down. They spoke to me in agitated tones. My Chinese language ability was quite limited at that time but I soon got the message, "This is more of a climb than we negotiated for. This coffin sits right here until our increased fee is paid." I paid it. Our small entourage, including frail Anna, proceeded up the hill.

Once we got to the gravesite (no fancy artificial grass or anything other than bare dirt there) I was awed by the care shown by the coffin bearers. Two of them got into the grave. The other two lowered the coffin. They went to great lengths to make sure the coffin was positioned just right. They wanted it on a slight incline with the head above the lower body, the entire orientation toward the ocean. They checked repeatedly with me to ensure that everything was just right. It was all done with reverence and respect for the deceased. Then they left the grave. We concluded the service with the traditional "Ashes to Ashes. Dust to Dust."

ഇൗരു

FLOWERS

I stepped away from the small Lutheran church in Klittzen, Germany where my ancestors worshiped more than 150 years ago. I walked down the narrow street. It was obvious. The poverty resulting from the years when this little village struggled for existence under the harsh rule of the Russians was everywhere evident. The houses were in need of repair. The little country store exuded scarcity. The vegetables looked tired. The little trinkets had lost their luster. Even the lone gray-haired woman who ran the place looked tired beyond her years. When I approached an elderly couple working in their yard, they glanced at me briefly. Then they turned away with an unspoken but obvious message "We don't want to talk."

Yet there was something else I could not miss: the flowers. Each home had its own little flower garden. Even in fall there were blossoms everywhere, flowers planted in rows, row by row each with its own species of flowers. I recognized them all, yet to my embarrassment could name virtually none of them.

Flowers. Flowers of the Wends. Flowers of my ancestors. They were never too poor; the season was never so dry that no flowers could be grown. The yearning for the beauty of flowers had to find expression.

I remembered my Grandmother Kieschnick. In the hot arid sands of Lee County, Texas she would raise some flowers, usually in pots arranged on foot-wide board planks along the side of her home. My mother had struggled to raise flowers but the greater need was to plant, tend, harvest and can vegetables by the hundreds of quarts to help us make it through the winter. My older sister Leona keeps the tradition alive. Row upon neat row in all their blooming splendor the marigolds, zinnias, daisies, chrysanthemums, always in bloom and always a few to cut and place on the table inside.

Flowers. They are as much in my Wendish Kieschnick genes as any DNA. Nothing can remove or replace those eternal markers of beauty and identity.

⁂⁃

LOW SEE

I am nervous. Of course, I'm nervous. I am a 30-year-old school principal presiding at my school's first monthly faculty meeting. There are 45 of us. I am the youngest. I am the only American there. My colleagues are all Chinese. Of course, they are Chinese. The school is in Hong Kong, our students are all Chinese, the medium of instruction is Chinese. My colleagues include venerable scholars who have risked their lives to escape Mao Zedong's communism. They know life and death, Confucian analects, Chinese school systems, exam systems, the names of centuries of dynasties, filial piety, and respect for the elderly. And I stand in front of them with the weakest of all credentials: I was appointed principal by the American missionary board, which controls the school.

So, I give it my best shot. Of course, I need an English-to-Chinese interpreter to get through the agenda. But at least, I think, I can greet them appropriately, respectfully, in Cantonese, their dialect. I had practiced my greeting and so I began, "Low See," etc. The rest of the meeting was eventually concluded to the credit of their patience and my interpreter's due diligence. At the close of the meeting one or two even complimented me on my effort to learn to speak their language.

Many years later after many lessons learned and many occasions for me to learn humility, that first faculty meeting comes up in a discussion with a Chinese colleague.

He startles me. "Remember that first faculty meeting where you wanted to respectfully greet your new Chinese colleagues?" You called them "Low See," but what you really meant was "Low See."

In the Cantonese dialect each syllable can be pronounced on any of 10 different pitches (tones). The meaning of the word changes depending upon the tone. When I said "Low See" I thought I was using the tones to respectfully address my colleagues as "Low See" meaning "honorable scholars." In fact, because of the tones I used I had begun my career as principal there by calling each member of my staff "Low See" i.e. "Old Rats."

ഇരു

PEGGY, MY TEACHER

Peggy, only 16, but is a college freshman. (The reason she's in college at 16 is due to a complicated set of circumstances related to enrollment in a Hong Kong British school at age four.) As I walk into the family room of our St. Louis home, I see her sitting on the floor. She is crying, tears streaming down her cheeks.

"Peggy, what's wrong?" I inquire.

"I'm crying because of what you said, Dad."

"What did I say that makes you cry?"

"You said that you had reached the peak of your career. That from now on you would have no opportunity to make a difference on this planet. That it seemed like life was more or less downhill from here."

I don't know if Peggy was quoting me accurately. I do know that she was exactly reflecting my belief about my future. I had just resigned my significant position at the top offices of a major Lutheran denomination. I was in conflict with what I saw as a fundamentalist take-over of the Church. I disagreed with new official documents on the role of women, prayer with other Christians, literal interpretation of Scriptures. I had accepted no other job but I knew that I could not serve with integrity in the position I had held. I had concluded that any other job I might ever take would not match the one from which I had just resigned.

Peggy spoke, "Dad, you have many gifts. There are lots of people and places that respect your integrity, experience and ability. I don't know where we'll go from here but this is not the end of your ministry. God is not done using you."

It was then that I burst into tears. We hugged and let our tears mingle.

Peggy was right.

IN THE 80'S

When I planned this blog entry a couple of days ago, I wanted to begin by rejoicing that I finally again shot a full round of golf - in the 80's. But that didn't happen. So, the theme has a more expanded focus. The topic is how I am doing now that my age is slowly creeping up through those numbers commonly referred to as "in the 80's." The bad news: The down side of being in the 80's is most readily apparent on the golf course and in the bedroom. In my youth I often hit my drives 250 yards (before all these new technologies). Now, even with the latest in equipment, I barely and rarely hit the ball 200 yards off the tee. In the bedroom the libido seems asleep and when awakened seems to fail to notify the rest of the body. I still walk the couple of miles to and from the grocery, but when I carry a gallon of milk home, I am glad that it is in plastic and not heavy glass. The woman cutting my hair no longer checks my age. She just automatically charges the senior rate (which I guess she should as total time elapsed for shampoo and cut never exceeds eleven minutes!)

Professionally there are other clues. When my congregation no longer asks me to preach or teach a special class during the pastor's absence I begin to wonder. "Is it because I am no longer able to preach a stimulating, helpful sermon? Is it because there is a fear that if this old man in his 80's gets into the pulpit the younger generation will automatically tune him out? And are my teaching methods not sufficiently enhanced with the latest media and newest theories of Biblical interpretation?"

The good news: Being in the 80's has its upside. I still get those phone calls from colleagues at, for example, The Center for Urban Education Ministries or Wheat Ridge Ministries or search teams for heads of schools like the Hong Kong International School. These good friends seem very genuine when asking for advice, or when expressing appreciation for experience and expertise. At a different level it is very affirming when a congregation council member invites, "Let's do lunch. I want to pick your brain."

I've now been doing crossword puzzles (even the New York Times) long enough to have caught on to some of the traditional clues and I can remember that old #4 in the New York Giants was Mel Ott.

It was especially heartwarming when in two recent confirmation classes at church I received the word that a couple of teen-agers had specifically requested me as their mentor.

There has never been a time when I did not feel the love and support of my wife and extended family, especially kids and grandkids. Yet as I am "in the 80s" this affection is prized ever more deeply. Grandkids living so far away are achingly missed and Skype connections are particularly valued.

In assessing my own spirituality in the 80's I find myself more and more drawn to the radical message of what Jesus called the Kingdom of God, with its reign of love, its outreach to those on the margins, its call for commitment to the poor, the aliens, the humble of heart. And it is good to have that extra time at the beginning of each day to parade in prayer before God's throne an ever-expanding line of people about whom I care.

In the 80's I live in a marvelous facility with my loving, 100% supportive and totally well and strong wife of more than 57 years. Wine and food still taste very good. There are minimal aches and pains. The stock market will eventually turn around. Two weeks ago, I sank three long putts in one round. Friends still email. Kids are planning to visit. God is good. It's good to be "in the 80's."

ഈരു

RISK-REWARD RATIO

I am violently jolted awake out of a sound sleep. I struggle to get my orientation. I find myself in the middle of an Illinois cornfield 100 feet from US Hwy. 66. I'm still in the general area of the back seat of a vehicle whose driver somehow failed to react to the sharp left turn sign. Part of the huge danger sign has been knocked off, the front end of the car has some new dents, but the vehicle is upright. The driver puts the car into reverse, backs onto the highway, changes into first gear and we head back down the road toward Mexico. It's another hitchhiking experience in the late 1940's.

Hitchhiking was a generally accepted mode of transportation for young men then. I started doing it when I was in high school, just short 40-mile trips between home and prep school. Then in college we hitched between Texas and Illinois. Later there were trips across the Midwest and once to New York. Most trips provided at least some small addition to hitchhiking lore. There was the driver who kept bragging that he was a top representative for

Lockheed Aircraft Corporation that paid for everything and anything he did: travel, food, accommodations, expensive women, and the "buttermilk" he sipped continuously from the brown bottle he kept between his feet. After he took careful aim and still just barely made it between the abutments on the sides of a bridge, I decided that the next crossroad was my destination.

There was the flashy young woman (I still remember her electric yellow blouse and shimmering green slacks) who stopped in response to my extended thumb. She opened the door, invited me to sit in the front seat, concurrently very visibly and deliberately moving the cocked Colt 45 from the passenger seat to her lap. She said she was just looking for a little conversation, nothing more. I talked.

There are other memories: three a.m. along Lake Erie outside Cleveland trying to get a small fire started to keep me from freezing. The two young women from Mena, Arkansas who sincerely invited me to their home for dinner and a good night's sleep. I chose to decline. The trucker who locked me into his trailer atop empty beer kegs and bottles and who kept his word to let me out at my destination.

Hitchhiking was a way of saving money. It provided adventure and, of course, just enough risk adding value to the experience. Since then, the hitchhiking risk-reward ratio has gotten out of balance (and interstates do not allow pedestrians).

Yet, this I know, a life without risk is flat and dull. Irrespective of age, one needs to keep taking risks in making friends, in investing money, in sharing one's beliefs, in dreaming dreams and in creating visions. The trick is to keep the risk-reward ratio in proper balance

ഇരുന്നു

THE WENDS

Part 1

I am a guest in the home of a well-known Swiss educator in the town of Brigg. He is showing me around his ancient village pointing out all the columns, arches and friezes which clearly point to the ancient Roman origins of his town.

Then he tells me there's a smaller village not far away with definitive Roman markings. The little community is called "Windish." My interest skyrockets. I consider my ethnic heritage to be Wendish. I am a Wend. My

Wendish ancestors emigrated to the Serbin, Texas area a century and a half ago leaving behind many of their Wendish relatives in southeastern Germany. Could this "Windish" be a connection?

So, my friend and I head for Windish. Outside this small town we stop to look at the remains of an ancient arena, like a small Roman coliseum. "Oh yes," my friend explains, "There was a Roman garrison here. One of the Caesars even paid a visit to this place. This arena was built for his entertainment. It seems the locals (Wends) were stubborn Christians and in this arena, they were put to the test, 'Give up your Christian faith or face the consequences.' We're not sure if the consequences meant fighting animals, gladiators or just fighting naked against armed Romans."

He went on, "A recent excavation here found some previously undiscovered human remains, probably from those first Christians. They were a stubborn lot!"

I listened in stunned silence, moved to reflection. I sensed that I was standing on personal holy ground. I let my mind wander through the centuries, priests baptizing infants, parents teaching children from generation to generation, from Windish in Switzerland to Germany to Texas to Zion Lutheran Church, Walburg, Texas, to my family and my Wendish father, Oscar Henry Kieschnick.

Part 2

I am the designated Protestant lecturer at a religious retreat in Berchtesgaden, Germany sponsored by the religious education department of the U.S. Armed Forces-Europe. My designated Roman Catholic colleague is Msgr. Al McBride. It is Sunday morning and we've led our respective worship services concurrently in two different locations. In my message I had urged my listeners to pass on their teaching from generation to generation. I told them the story of Windish, Switzerland and the Wends.

Shortly after the service Father McBride excitedly came to see me. "I've just heard from someone in your "congregation" that you told a Wendish story and that you're a Wend. Let me tell you something. My religious order of priests was founded back in the 11th century. The original documents declare that one of the goals of the order was 'to convert to the faith the strong-willed heathen nomadic ethnic group called the Wends.' You are the first Wend I've ever actually met."

Part 3

My cousin John is interested in genealogy, including the family histories of Wends. He has discovered a little noted book entitled "The Christianization of the Nomadic Tribes of Central Europe."

From it I learn that the flow of Christianity from Roman times to the 20th Century was not so uninterrupted as I had first surmised. Until at least the 9th century that geographical area now called Germany, Austria and Switzerland was occupied by a whole host of tribes, each independent, each with its own language and system of social organization. One of the toughest, most stubborn and least successful was the Wendish tribe. They fought a lot and they lost a lot. This merely intensified their resolve to keep their own identity, to resist being assimilated. They would keep their own language, customs and gods! Christianity was not their traditional religion nor was it something to be adopted easily. They were the last of the Slavonic tribes to become Christian.

As I read of the Wends' determination to keep their own ways, including their ways of worship, I found one piece of myself rooting for them to resist. A part of my gut was almost hoping they would not convert to Christianity. Two sets of questions: 1. Which kind of Wendish blood still flows in my veins? Am I stubborn and slow of heart to believe all that the prophets have written or am I a person with strongly held religious convictions, convictions worthy of praise? 2. Why was a piece of my awareness hoping my ancestors would resist the evangelization efforts of early missionaries? What implications are there in this for me as I act on what I perceive as a mandate to "Go make disciples of all nations, baptizing them in the name of the Father, Son and Holy Spirit?"

೮೦೧೩

MOTHER'S DAY 2009: MENTAL IMAGES

Another image of Lina Doering Kieschnick, my mother. Image after image floats into my consciousness, hundreds and thousands of them. I select just a few, each one a pointer to others, possibly more important or profound.

Mother at Work

Some may say she didn't have a choice. The wife of a Christian Education Minister in a rural Texas parish, the mother of nine (count them:

nine!) with a miscarriage or two in between, she worked at providing daily bread. I still see her standing at the kitchen stove, at first only a wood-burning one, then kerosene, gas and finally electric. I see her sitting on the floor of the porch doing the prep work for canning peaches, pears, plums, berries, beans, peas, corn, pickles, beets, jams. jellies, relishes. (One summer she "put up" 800 quart-jars of them!) Baking was constant. We ate only home-made bread and pie from fruits in season, also biscuits, cornbread, jellyrolls, strudel, and the mandatory angel food cakes (using a dozen fresh eggs) for every birthday. She fed the chickens, helped butcher the pigs, milked the cows and then separated the milk, made the butter and lowered it in a bucket into the well so the cooler temperatures there would help preserve it.

Mother Responding to Crises

She was there as each one of us ran the usual gamut of childhood diseases: measles, mumps, intestinal worms, whooping cough, chicken pox, appendicitis (before penicillin), broken bones and broken hearts. One strong image is seeing her incredible strength, stamina and determination as she lugged two metal buckets each filled with five gallons of water and with wet burlap bags over her shoulders. A Texas late summer grass fire had erupted near our house. She led the way running full speed for over a hundred yards to the edge of the fire and kept the flames from spreading.

Mother at My Side

She was always there. She fought with unceasing resolve not to have a "favorite child" and yet each one of us considered ourselves her favorite. I was only 13 years old when she bundled me up and sent me off to the small dormitory prep school where future Lutheran ministers were trained. Years later she stood with me in her beautiful new blue dress quietly pleased that the first of her children was graduating from college. Later I saw her standing outside the train waving good-bye to my wife Jane, our son David and me as we were on our way to that great yet strange place called Hong Kong. In those days the church rules were that no one who went to "the foreign mission field" was allowed to return home for a visit until after one had served five years abroad. She may have wept for her little grandson but her heart was proud that her son and his wife had been seen fit to be called to this important ministry

Mother in the Spot Light

This she could never imagine. In her eyes she was too unworthy to ever be in any kind of spotlight. And she certainly wasn't going to put herself there. "Eigen-lobt stinks" (Self-praise stinks) was a mantra, so she kept a very low profile when her husband or one of her kids received an honor, but her deep gratitude could not be hidden. When she was named Texas Lutheran Woman of the Year, she was almost embarrassed and assumed that someone had made a mistake.

Mother at Prayer

Prayer was as natural (and often as quiet) as breathing. We prayed all the time, before and after meals, at bedtime, before dashing off for school, after a safe trip. Yet it was never a show. It was just quietly there. "Evening devotions" were absolutely routinized: a scripture reading and commentary, a written prayer, The Lord's Prayer in unison and the blessing. Dad was always in charge. The leader for the readings and prayer might vary (it was never Mom) but the blessing was Dad's prerogative. On the day of Dad's funeral most of our vast family crew gathered in Mom's home. We ate, drank, celebrated, cried and remembered. Finally, it was time. Mother said, "It's time for bed. Let's have devotions." As we went through the ritual my mind wandered: "Who will say the blessing? Should Erna do it? She's the eldest. Should I do it? I am the eldest son. Would she prefer one of the official pastors in the group to do it?" Then the moment came. There was not one second of hesitation. Mother's voice was instantaneous, loud, clear, completely at ease and in charge. "The Lord bless us and keep us. The Lord make His face to shine upon us and be gracious to us. The Lord lift up His countenance upon us and give us peace. Amen."

The mantle had passed. Mom wore it with dignity and grace.

෫෨ඥ

CITIES

I love New York! My heart races just thinking of getting off the train in Grand Central Station. I am swept up by the crowds that carry me up the stairs into the massive, yet beautiful terminal and into the throbbing streets outside. I sidestep the frenetic cab catchers to walk toward Fifth Ave. It's fun to watch the eyes of the Nigerian street hawkers. The pupils of their eyes try to focus on many places at once to concurrently see the potential customer, the ally who signals the coming of the cops and the open case holding the fake Rolodexes. It's a big game, more or less enjoyed by all.

The ethnic mix of the city energizes me. When visiting Lutheran schools, I am lifted up by the beautiful accent of a Jamaican principal in the Bronx. I share workshop memories with the cadre of women teachers from the Philippines. I marvel at the classroom discipline of a Brooklyn school presided over by staff from Belize. I visit with a principal in Queens who was born in Pekin, Illinois. His school includes recent arrivals from Beijing, China. I drop in at the oldest Lutheran school in America. It's in Manhattan. Once again, a shift is occurring among the ethnic mix of the community. The waves come and go; German to Chinese to African-American to Puerto Rican to Colombian to who knows what next. In Queens Lutheran School I can hear 21 different native languages in one student body. On Parents Nights interpreters from Korea, China, Honduras, Yugoslavia and Russia facilitate parent-teacher communication. Just a few miles away it seems simpler; it is overwhelmingly Asian. Only Korean, Chinese and Vietnamese interpreters are necessary.

Within the poly saturated ethnic mix, unsaturated communities thrive. I'm meeting in an apartment in Harlem with a community group of long-time residents. I'm the only white person within miles it seems. This tightly knit group speaks of their care for the students. They tell how neighborhood shopkeepers, hawkers, housewives and police officers all keep their eyes out, ensuring that the school kids make it home or to public transportation. They care deeply about their community and the institutions that enrich it.

The feel is very different in the section of Brooklyn dominated by close-knit immigrants from Guyana. To move from there to another school celebration in another part of Brooklyn (Bay Ridge) is like hopscotching into Italy where the sense of ethnic solidarity is celebrated with entirely different sets of rituals.

The city! It's full of hope and aspirations, from the newly certified MBA down on Wall Street putting together an IPO, to the recently-arrived San Salvadoran hawking peeled oranges on the streets of Washington Heights.

Pick a Topic. Food: Four Seasons to street hawkers; Housing: The Trump Tower of midtown Manhattan to the street hot-air vent sleepers on the Lower East Side to the tenements of Brownsville or the burnt-out shells of the lower Bronx; Entertainment: Les Misérables to hookers, to cock fights; Salvation: St. Patrick's Cathedral to St. Peter's Jazz vespers, to Pentecostal glossolalia to Jamaican voodoo.

I love the city.

I am not alone. The biggest movement of people in the history of the world is underway: a worldwide migration to the city. Millions upon millions are moving from the countryside into Shanghai, Mexico City, Khartoum, Sao Paulo and into city after city, each with a population in excess of five million. For the first time in the history of our planet most of the people will never have experienced a season of planting and harvesting, never have seen a sunrise over an open horizon, never have walked a country lane, never have gone to bed without making sure all the doors are locked.

How will the new urbanization affect families and values and the world's great religions? How will the Christian church transfer its pastoral images, parables and liturgies from the countryside to the curbside?

It's a great time to be alive and to be part of the challenge of living out a theology as big as the city.

ଛୠ

DOWN THE RIVER

Twelve-year-old son Tim and I are having a FATHER-SON BONDING EXPERIENCE! Together with two other fathers and sons we are on an overnight river adventure, each pair of us in separate canoes, floating down the idyllic Michigan river called the Au Sable. It is both wonderful and terrible. I am creating a disaster.

There are some complications. I'm afraid of any flowing water more than six inches deep. Neither Tim nor I have ever paddled a canoe before. Within five minutes our fellow campers are so far down the stream we can't even see them. I don't even know from which end of the canoe the control is supposed to come. The stream is swift. We ram the shore on the right. We move away, across the stream, and ram the shore on the left. Tim at the back of the canoe, Dad in the middle, we end up going down the stream backward. We change positions and barely miss a fly fisherman in waders who, I'm grateful to say, was not able to exchange his fishing rod for another type of rod. Our cargo gets wet. We sweat. Blisters develop. We continue to careen from shore to shore.

Finally, we spot our fellow travelers. They've set up the tent, have a fire going and believe it or not are enjoying before dinner drinks. Tim and I have traversed four times as much distance as they to reach the same destination.

We (or at least I) are complete failures. It is wonderful. Tim and I are learners together. We fail together. We reach our destination (if not our goal) together. We laugh. We celebrate.

Now Tim is an experienced hiker, camper, boater. He has hiked high in the Cascades, rafted down the Rio Grande, explored Death Valley. I just write memoirs and reflections and recall two of the most wonderful days of my life, canoeing down the Au Sable with my son.

℘℃

FAREWELL

I am in the hospital in San Antonio visiting my ill father for the last time before my wife and I return to our home in California and for the last time before he returned home to the arms of God who first gave him life. My siblings who saw him daily had told me that the cancer seemed to be "in its final stages." Yet I was shocked at his gaunt appearance. It was hard to see my father so weak. He had always been for me the very epitome of strength: of body, spirit, faith, and integrity.

While his body was weak, his mind was sharp. So, we spoke of love, of family, of the church, of God, of hope. In the last minutes before our final visit we recalled together the many years during which our family had what we called "evening devotions." They were simple: a reading from the Bible, Martin Luther's Evening Prayer, the Lord's Prayer and the singing of an ancient hymn titled "Abide with Me." We agreed to repeat the ritual there in his hospital room. However, instead of just singing the first stanza of the hymn we sang the last stanza also. Dad's voice was not only audible. It was strong. He sang not the melody line, but the strong tenor part. My wife Jane sang alto and together we ended our time together:

"Hold thou, thy cross before my closing eyes;

Shine through the gloom and point me to the skies;

Heaven's morning breaks and earth's vain shadows flee;

In life (long pause), In death (another long pause)

Oh Lord, abide with me."

It was my farewell and my intimation of when we'll again say to each other, "Good Morning."

℘℃

48

PRAISE DENIED/PRAISE JUNKIE

My recent thinking about praise began simply enough. A colleague wrote a book and sent me a copy. On the title page he wrote a few words of affirmation (maybe even praise) of me. It felt good to read that. Yet as I took my morning walk the thought came up, "Mel, have you become a 'praise junkie?" I knew where that thought came from.

For years I was a colleague of Dr. Thomas Gordon, the author of "Parent Effectiveness Training" and other best sellers. He and I disagreed about the role of praise in parent-child communication. Tom was very leery of parental praise for children. He was afraid the praise might be empty or just be flattery. He feared that a child's self-esteem might become too dependent upon the evaluation of others. He coined the phrase "praise junkie," a person who regularly needs a fix of praise to maintain self-worth and positive self-image.

I was concerned about children who were not affirmed, not praised or whose positive actions would receive no comment from significant others in their life. I argued that praise was actually necessary, provided it was honest and given without hope of personal gain or favor, I argued that praise is most helpful when three conditions are met: 1. A person acts in a way that is commendable. 2. The person receiving the praise feels that the cause for praise is merited. 3. The praise comes from a person who is significant to the one receiving the praise and there is no hope on the part of the praise giver to get anything in return for the praise given.

I further recalled a conversation I had with our son John when he was in junior high. I do not recall what he did that pleased me. I do recall saying, "John, you are a good boy." I meant it. Yet John's reply to me was "Dad, I do not like it when you call me a good boy." So, we explored that a bit. Part of it was that John heard me making a judgment on him as a person. If I reserved the right to call him "good" I would also have the right to label him "bad." Further: in the culture of junior high being called "a good boy" may, in fact be not at all what a young person is looking for. So, I decided I needed to express words about his actions that pleased me rather than making a general statement of judgment of his total character.

My mind then went to my wife Jane. The fact is throughout much of my career I was often in the public eye as a speaker, teacher, leader. In those contexts (especially in formal introductions) people would say nice things about me and about my accomplishments. Of course, that felt good. Yet often sitting right next to me was Jane. Often her presence was completely ignored, even as it was in the cocktail hour conversations before dinner at these events.

Jane has a strong self-concept, yet I often wished she could get a bit more praise. Then I wondered if this were more a statement about me than about her.

Of course, the matter of bestowing praise or speaking words of praise varies from culture to culture. In Chinese culture there is often lavish praise that we Westerners might consider flattery. Yet for them it is simply a form of politeness. It is said that in certain Nordic cultures one must win the Nobel Prize to ever merit a "not too bad, son."

Finally, there is the entire matter of being evaluated by others, always a two-edged sword. When I would receive 49 positive evaluations and one negative, why did I seem to focus on that one negative? Had I, in fact, become a "praise junkie?"

Conclusion: I choose to run the risk. I will continue to speak words of praise as long as they are honest and heartfelt, with no hope for personal gain. There are so many put-downs and so much negativism in the world that a bit of positive affirmation (and yes, even praise) just might help make someone's day.

ഇരു

GRADUATIONS

My own and many others. First, mine. Graduation from 8th grade at Zion Lutheran School, Walburg, Texas was a big deal. We dressed up in freshly starched and ironed shirt, tie and coat. We graduates sat on the outdoor stage under the trees between the school and the area where the kids who rode horseback to school tethered their rides. The motto "Climb Though the Path Be Rugged" was emblazoned on the wall behind. The class salutatorian welcomed all. The guest preacher preached the appropriate words. The diplomas (duly rolled and ribbon enclosed) were distributed. Then the valedictorian (that would be I) gave the closing address, carefully following the rules: thank the parents, the congregation, the school board, and the teachers. Assure your classmates of everlasting friendship and say it LOUD so that all can hear because there was, of course, no speaker system. Lemonade, cookies and angel food cake climaxed the celebration.

Four year later there was very little focus on my or anyone else's high school graduation. It was May 10, 1945 just two days after V-E Day (Victory in Europe) had been declared. To my own surprise I still remember the graduation address/sermon was based on John the Baptist's words "He (Jesus) must increase, but I must decrease!" The class was all male, all preparing for rostered church ministry. I remember my Aunt Elizabeth being there and I especially remember her telling me that what made her proud was that I had been recognized for my high marks in religion classes. A teen-aged female friend who came on her own all the way from Thorndale (35 gas-rationed miles away) was not someone whose presence I could really acknowledge and I do not even recall speaking with her. A few of us guys celebrated afterwards by going to the amusement park and enjoying the baseball-pitching machine. I look back frankly in great surprise that I do not even recall trying to buy an underage beer in that beer-saturated culture.

I remember nothing of my college graduation ceremony. Of course, I was extremely proud to have my mom and dad there (dad had graduated from the same school exactly 30 years earlier). I wish I had been more sensitive to the financial sacrifices they made to come from Texas to Illinois to be there. But the big excitement of the day was that a couple hours before the ceremony I had slipped a package into Jane's hand. It was our engagement ring. (Incidentally, it was made possible financially when the one head of cattle I owned sold at auction for $100.00) So graduation activities quickly fell much lower in matters to which my head or heart was attuned.

Years (and many other graduations later) I was the pleased parent as each of our five kids received diplomas, in each case with high honors from bachelors through Ph D's. Tim's (forever the middle child) was in the midst of other compelling events. The news of my father's death arrived just as he was lining up for the procession into the beautiful Valparaiso Chapel. (He and Jane got the message and had decided to tell me only after the ceremony.) The next day we rushed to my dad's funeral and then later, back to Valpo where daughter Peggy was getting married. Never did attend son John's graduation from high school, college or graduate school. He is really not into such things and attended none of them.

In the many years since my own I have attended countless graduations. I figure I have been the speaker for at least a hundred elementary and high school graduations. It has been a challenge and a joy to speak at five university/college graduations and always a humbling experience to receive honors and awards at others. All are merely pointers to the blessings of an education, a reminder of the challenge to use what has been taught and to be an instrument so that an increasing number of people around the world might receive the benefit of developing their gifts through education for the cause of service and world peace.

GRANDPARENTS

Someone has told me that grandparents are like golf scores. Nobody ELSE cares about them. Yet as I took my walk today, I reflected upon my status as an absent grandfather and upon my own grandfathers and grandmothers. Images of Grandpa Kieschnck quickly flooded my mind. He seemed ancient as he toiled in the very hot mid-summer's day sun down on "the bottom" of his Lee County Texas farm. He trudged very slowly alongside the mule drawn wagon. He was "pulling corn" which means he took the ears from the stalks and threw them into the slowly moving wagon. I was about seven years old, walking beside him and I was scared. I was scared that it was too hot, Grandpa was too old, the work was too hard. I feared he would to die right there in front of me. I imaged myself running to tell Grandma.

He survived that, of course. The next morning, he was ready to go again, but not before "morning prayers." He took out that old well-worn devotion book, read very slowly yet loudly, the appropriate section (in German naturally) and then prayed in that long slow firm voice the prayer he prayed each morning. He took his usual noontime nap on the old leather sofa until the day he went to sleep for the last time.

I remember the wake. The open coffin in his living room. Then the funeral procession to the country church. Along the way we needed to go through several fence gates to get to the county road. As we went through each gate there stood one of his black hired hands. Each stood solemnly next to a black horse. Left hand holding the reins. Right hand holding his hat over his heart. Bidding farewell to the "old man" on whom the whole family depended for livelihood.

My memory of Grandma K focuses on the humble yet proud woman wearing a gold tiara. It was her 50th wedding anniversary and she was queen for that one day. I admired her with a smug feeling for I had just made it through an extremely difficult yet important assignment. It had been my role as one of the grandchildren to recite from memory (in German, yet) some kind of a poetic ode to Grandmother, and I had made it. Grandma eyed me; wanting to make sure that I did not feel too proud of my accomplishment because one must always be wary of the sin of pride. Her smile acknowledged that I had done okay and inwardly my heart sang!

A whole different Grandma K is recalled in her encounter with the chicken thief. Grandmother had noticed that the size of her chicken flock seemed to be diminishing. So, she kept her eyes and ears open. In the middle of the night she heard a slight commotion in the hen house. She strode outside. Sure enough, there sat the thief cowering in a corner. He recovered quickly enough to ask "Which is the best way to Giddings?" (the town 10 miles away). Grandmother's response (in German, of course) was the equivalent of "You S.O.B., you know the way to Giddings as well as I do. Just never let me catch you in my hen house again." With that the disappearance of chickens was over.

My Grandfather Doering died before I was born. One of my most heart-warming and stomach-warming images is that of coming home for second grade and finding Grandma Doering in our kitchen. She was sitting, peeling apples for the very special apple pie she baked. For some strange reason my mind jumps immediately to the time I found her there calmly peeling away and then telling me that an hour earlier a 22-caliber bullet had flown through the window and by her head. She surmised a hunter in the area was not careful enough, but the pie would still be warm for supper. And now I am a grandparent eight times over. But my kids are strewn across the world. As I write they are in California, Connecticut, Ireland, The Czech Republic and Hong Kong. I wonder what will have replaced blogs 75 years from now and if they will have any memories of their Grandfather Mel.

&ԹՇ

REFLECTIONS ON THE 20TH ANNIVERSARY OF THE TIANAMENN SQUARE MASSACRE

Hope

I'm standing next to the sculptured Goddess of Democracy in Tiananmen Square, June 3, 1989. Together, she and I fix our eyes intently across Chang An Avenue onto the portrait of Mao Zedong guarding the Forbidden City. Never before (or since) have I been in the midst of such exhilaration, such sense of community, such hope.

As our son John had told me over the phone from Beijing University a week earlier, "Dad, you must come. There's hope that for the first time in the history of China, there may be a bloodless revolution!"

Students by the thousands had marched in orderly columns to the Square. Workers by the millions were joining the surge toward freedom. One middle-aged man with whom I spoke had brought his crippled aged mother in a wheelbarrow to the Square. "She never dreamed that she'd be present for the birth of freedom in her country. Her grandchildren will have opportunities now undreamed of!"

English speaking Chinese students surround me. They joyfully speak of America and China forgetting their decades long enmity. "Democracy is coming to China and our two countries will be united in freedom."

Days earlier the sheer mass of humanity had prevented a military convoy from reaching the Square. The Peoples' Army wouldn't dare fire upon their own people. Even the old guard around Deng Xiaoping would finally make the concessions to at least receive the written petition from student leaders. Conversations would begin. Political and economic freedom would begin to seep under the doors of the old imperial palace, now the Communist seat of power. One student even quoted to me, "Mine eyes have seen the glory of the coming of the Lord!"

Despair was dissipating. Doors to political, economic and intellectual freedom were opening. Hope welled up. It was intoxicatingly energizing.

ഇറ

HOPE SHATTERED – DREAMS DESTROYED

I am surrounded by weeping students in the quad of Beijing University. It's the evening of June 5th, 1989. Mournful funeral music sweeps from speakers across the campus. The banner in front of the campus gates, in black characters on white cloth laments, "Tiananmen bathed in blood. The whole world weeps."

By now the world knew what those milling about us had experienced in the hours before. The People's Army did fire on students. Tanks rumbled through the streets and the square. Bodies were bullet ridden and crushed. Soldiers were captured, strung up from light posts and burned while the crowd cheered. Buses were parked together to form barricades. One side or the other torched them. Sporadic skirmishes and resulting deaths would continue for another day. But the outcome was immutable. The student led foray for freedom had failed. The Party won.

Now cadres of students come into the weeping cauldron, returning from the morgue with news of whose bodies they found and who was still unaccounted for.

My two sons and I are the only Americans in the crowd and so the target for unrealistic pleas. "Can't you contact President Bush? Can't the US military intervene? Will the free world just stand by and let hope be crushed?" It was a cry not only for themselves, but also for their fallen colleagues and their now under suspicion parents. It was the unrealistic plea for some kind of rekindling of the flame of hope which had been definitively quenched.

We weep with our new student friends. We wince as they show us wounds in their bodies. We remember with mixed feelings the female student friend of John who was safe in the country-side. The day before, her mother had come and physically carried her out of the square where she had been on a hunger strike. We know we cannot reach our family back home but are confident we will get there. Other student friends will not make it home. Without a doubt many others will make their homes in prisons. It seemed almost secondary to think of two years of John's work reflected in Chinese to English translations now stored "somewhere" on campus. Yet in the magnitude of the suffering, death, and shattered hopes those concerns seem minor. Many have died. More will. It's a long, long road to freedom for too many.

೮ා౦ෂ

TELEPHONES

My telephone number is 760-702-6361. It may seem strange to some for me to just put it out there like that. But there is a story, of course.

I have only recently learned that currently my phone number is not listed in any kind of public directory. When we moved to this retirement community last year, the number we got is the number assigned to this room (and not to the name of the room occupant). The only public listing is the name of this community. This has resulted in some problems. Out of town relatives who were in the area and wanted to call and stop by could not find us listed anywhere. Several international callers have been unable to find my number anywhere and, in the process, a very important contact was never made. A blog reader who wanted to call knew there were Kieschnicks serving as ministers in the Lutheran Church, found an official directory and reached my sister-in-law who provided my number

When I was growing up in rural Texas there was no telephone listing for my family, simply because we did not have phone service. Then came the old party line. When there was one long and two short rings, we knew it was for us.

In the 1950's in Hong Kong we were told that only through the payment of significant under the table bribes could one secure a telephone without a year or more wait. However, we just applied for ourselves and for our school and within a week the phones were installed. During my years with The Lutheran Schools Association of Metropolitan New York we did not yet have emails, but plenty of phone calls. I still remember when I had been out of my office for two days and returned to my very full answering machine with 51 calls waiting to be returned. (Now my email aficionados say, "I had 100 emails yesterday." The response: "Lucky you, I had 150 by 10:30 a.m.!")

Last week I met my next-door neighbor returning to his unit muttering. I asked, "What's up?" "Oh, I forgot my (expletive deleted) cell phone! Would you believe that I am going just a few blocks to the dog park with my dog? I have my GPS to get me there but I don't dare go without my cell phone!" Then he mused, "What will it be like a hundred years from now? I bet all this stuff will be embedded in our bodies. I just bet that cell phones, iphones, iPods, direction finders, blood pressure, radar units, etc. etc. will all be right in my cells! But for now, I've got to find my cell phone!"

෨෨

HUNGER

This morning, once again, I saw a picture of a hungry child. I have decided that never in my life have I really experienced hunger. Of course, I have been hungry and have eaten as though I were famished and would never eat again; yet I was just hungry, not in a condition of hunger.

I grew up during the Great Depression. Dad was a teaching minister in a Lutheran church and we didn't always get his meager monthly salary. Money may have been scarce, but food was not. Even in the bleakest months my mom would have me crawl under the house to retrieve some of our homegrown potatoes that we stored there. She would open a quart or two of canned red beets. That red juice/water made a great covering for the potatoes. We had butchered hogs and saved the bones from which almost all the meat had been cut to make sausages. The leftover bones we called "knochen fleish." Mother boiled these. We added a bit of mustard, combined that with the boiled potatoes and beets and a glass of fresh milk. Soon we certainly did not have to deal with hunger!

When I came home from school hungry. If all that was available was a slice of bread with a bit of jelly on it, I soon learned that if I complained to Mother her stock reply would come echoing back, "Wenn du hungrig bhist, dennn scheckt auch jelly brut gut." If you are hungry then jelly bread tastes good!

Another hunger lesson taught me by my father was a Biblical quote: "If any would not work, neither should he eat." The message was clear. If you expect to eat, do your chores. Yet dad was always equally quick to say, "Now remember, too, that some people want to work but are unable to do so. They are in danger of hunger. Those we must help feed."

My first encounter with persons who were suffering from hunger came in Hong Kong in the mid-1950s. To this day there is an encounter burned into my consciousness. We had been there less than a month. I had taught a late-night class and was walking back to our tenement flat along the northern end of Nathan Road. I walked by a middle-aged man. In his arms he held, pieta-like, his starving young son who may have been 10. His stomach was not extended but absolutely flat. There was no flesh or fat on any of his skeleton. His eyes were those staring orbs always seen in the face of those starving. The father looked at me with pleading eyes, not saying a word. I did not know a word of Chinese. I paused just long enough to pull out of my pocket and place into the hands of the father a one Hong Kong dollar bill. The father's eyes looked back at me with a full-bodied look of gratitude as he thanked me. I went on my way home and yet I remember the whole incident as though it were last night. A father on the street holding his son dying of hunger, completely dependent upon some stranger walking by and dropping in one dollar (17 cents in US money!).

Since then I have seen a few of the approximately one billion hungry people in the world and am still haunted by some of those extended stomachs, vacant eyes, pleading parents in India and Africa. Some of the four percent of American citizens who are hungry confront me even in affluent San Diego County

It is easy for me to become so overwhelmed by the enormity and complexity of this challenge that I am tempted to try to just push the whole issue out of my mind. But that doesn't always work. So, in my very small way I try to help the hungry at the San Diego TACO homeless feeding program, at Bread for the World which deals with hunger in the USA and Lutheran World Relief which takes a global perspective. Mine is just a drop into an empty food plate but I do put in the drop.

Much more to say, but I need to run. It's time for lunch. Food.

ℰꙅℭ

KILLERS

I am in my office in downtown St. Louis. It's noon on a Saturday. It's the one time of the week when there are no scheduled meetings, no co-workers seeking appointments, no telephone calls. The telephone rings. Beyond my wildest expectations (it had never happened before) my Mother is calling from Texas.

"Melvin, I have bad news," she said with a firmness of voice held steady by sheer force of will. "Your sister Miriam has been shot in the head. I'm afraid the whole back of her head is gone. There was a bank robbery at the Walburg State Bank. She lay face down on the floor just as the robber ordered. But as he left, he still fired the gun at her. And, oh yes, your Uncle Reinhold has also been shot. We're quite sure he'll survive. But we are not so sure about Miriam. I know you'll join us in prayer."

My thoughts turn to Mimi, one of my six sisters. Intelligent, vivacious, Director of Nurses at a hospital - shot - critically - dying. Of course, I pray, fervently.

What about the robber? I assume it's a male. I assume he thought this small bank in a small Texas town was an easy Saturday morning target. I assume he was frightened or on drugs. He had the money. Why did he have to shoot to kill?

Soon further details emerge via phone and radio: The robber had fired again. This time he instantly killed the Texas state trooper who had stopped his fleeing vehicle.

Further developments: miraculously Miriam survives. The robber is apprehended. Giving thanks for the miracle my mind turns to the murderer. He has already admitted guilt. What should be his fate? Texas, of course, has the death penalty. The murderer killed a peace officer, for crying out loud! My sister is alive, but she'll always have a black hole in that part of the brain where the bullet blasted away her optic nerve.

Yet, even as I mourn for the trooper, his widow and young daughter left behind, even as I struggle with my anger at the brute who attempted to murder my sister, I cannot force myself to wish for him the death penalty.

58

In this apparent bleeding-heart liberal response, I am out of step with the very Texas culture in which I was raised and in which so many of my values were shaped. Texas is where the death penalty is more common than in any other state. Texas, in fact, accounts for one third of all public executions in the USA. Texas is where six convicted killers were recently executed in the span of only two weeks. Texas is where I was taught in church catechism class, "All they that take the sword shall perish by the sword."

But my heart won't buy it. I can't get myself to believe that killing to punish killing, or killing to prevent killing, or killing to teach people not to kill is rational, nor has it ever proved to be a detriment to further killing.

So, in my sometimes lonely meditations I thank God for saving Mimi from the would-be killer. I pray that I will not be a party to another killing even in the name of justice or for the purpose of teaching someone a lesson.

℘℃℞

RACISM

I grew up racist. I still haven't overcome it.

In my childhood years in rural Central Texas racism was as pervasive and unquestioned as the air I breathed. There were certain a priori, never questioned assumptions. Blacks and whites don't attend the same church or school. They drink from separate water fountains, eat in different restaurants, ride in different sections of public transportation. Blacks are less intelligent. They suffer from the curse of Ham. Their cute children are called "pickannies." They are tenants, never real estate owners.

I have no memory of my assumptions ever being challenged. In eight years of parochial schooling and daily religious instruction, I don't recall ever being presented with an alternative perspective. Of course, we all shared our fallen humanity. Christ is the Savior of the world. We are to love everyone, but love for blacks was a love expressed within a segregated context with more than a hint of condescension.

In the all-male, all-white dormitory prep school that I attended for my high school years, most of my prejudices and presumptions about race were reinforced, with a few assaults upon my blindness.

It was during World War II. A black army officer and his wife came to worship in the church we attended. They were quickly escorted out of the church by the thoroughly prepared white ushers.

59

Some twinge of conscience within me was stirred. This was not right.

One day in class the teacher made a reference to a black lawyer. I was silently incredulous. How could a black person be a lawyer? The teacher must have noticed a similar look on the face of a classmate. He berated my classmate for his unwarranted racist assumptions. I had avoided the face-to-face chastisement of my teacher, but my consciousness was raised.

World War II was raging. I was exempt from the military draft with a 4D classification because I was studying to become a minister of the church. However, I had a certain amount of uneasiness about this arrangement, especially as I noticed that the young black men of my community all seemed to be classified 1A, were drafted (albeit into a segregated military), sent overseas and too often returned home in body bags. My conscience was awakened.

During succeeding years, I slowly, entirely too slowly, saw the error and sinfulness of my attitude and actions. Usually my teachers were black persons. I read their writings: *The Autobiography of Malcom X, The Algiers Motel Incident, Black Like Me, Black Rage,* etc. etc. I attended lectures and conferences. Slowly I was led out of my ignorance by people like the Rev. William Griffin and Dr. Pete Pero. I was driven to deep reflection after I listened to black activist Fred Hampton speak of how the police would find a reason to kill him. Within weeks, he was shot dead by the white police while on his bed in his Chicago apartment.

Theologians like Paul Schultze, James Cone, and civil rights leaders like Dr. Martin Luther King, Jr. inched me along. Personal contacts with blacks around dinner tables, shared bedrooms, long walks, harsh confrontations, animated conversations with persons like Orlando Gober all helped move me down the stony path my soul desperately needed to tread and so did my children.

Now in the later year of my life I am grateful for the progress made. Yet I must confess I still have a need for purging pieces of my consciousness. When I hear of certain criminal behaviors my first instinct is still to image a black person. When I hear of a significant literary or research publication my initial, seemingly unconscious belief is that a white person (white male, actually) must be the author.

So, my struggle goes on and I say with the Apostle, "Not as though I were already perfect, but I follow after..." (Phil. 3:12)

TRYING TO TEACH A PIG TO FLY

In the late 1940's the national Lutheran body of which I was a member had an unshakable conviction (which had nothing to do with theology). It believed that every person whom it certified as a recognized rostered member of the teaching ministry could be taught to play a keyboard instrument, if not a pipe organ, at least a piano.

I was brought into that system when I entered the ministerial preparatory school at the age of 13. I was assigned a piano teacher. Mr. Bentrup was his name. He showed me how to curve my wrists over the keyboard. He assigned music with no sharps or flats. He reserved for me specific practice pianos at designated practice times. He encouraged me. He threatened me. He praised me. Once he even slapped my hand. Finally, he gave up. He thought the solution was to get me a different teacher, a woman.

Ms. Schneider was wonderful. She seemed especially young and attractive as one of only two female teachers on an otherwise all-male faculty for the all-boys prep school. She was wonderful to me, supportive, kind, affirming, appropriately confrontive and patient. And when, after three years I graduated from that prep school she was at the ceremonies thanking God, I am sure, that she no longer had me as a student.

Post-prep school meant university in the Midwest. The doctrine was still believed, "All certified teaching ministers will be able to play a keyboard." The elderly piano teacher assigned me had been at it for some 40 years. After a few months of disastrous piano lessons, she came up with the brilliant solution. She recommended that I try to qualify for pipe organ lessons. For weeks she had me do one simple piano piece in preparation for the placement test. I actually got through it. But at the placement test I was asked to sight-read a piano number. It could have been written in Sanskrit instead of music notes and it wouldn't have made any difference. The results of the placement tests were announced: Promoted and qualified for pipe organ instruction: Melvin Kieschnick.

I'll spare the details. I was assigned to an outstanding organist whose compositions are still being played in church services all over the world. We came to an accommodation. The student who had her lesson just before mine would get 50 minutes instruction instead of 30 and so there were only 10 minutes left for me. I learned how to turn on the organ, clumsily move my feet across the foot pedals, and push the stops to get a trumpet effect - and all of this in only three academic years. It was conveniently agreed that no grade on instrumental music would ever appear on my transcript and I was graduated and certified for the teaching ministry of the Lutheran church.

I really do love music. I married a woman who was outstanding on the pipe organ and still plays marvelously on the piano but as for me, the closest I've come to being an accompanist was a surprise tribute from a wonderful Christian couple. They donated a marvelous grand piano to our congregation. The inscription says simply, "Donated by an anonymous couple in recognition of the ministries of Mel and Jane Kieschnick." And that's as close to a keyboard as anyone will ever permit me to go.

ഇരു

HOSPITALITY TO STRANGERS

I find it interesting (and have been greatly blessed) by the commandment central to all the great faiths of the world, "to show hospitality to strangers." But last week I found myself railing against inhospitality. Jane and I had just taken a young student from China to her first trip to the university at which she had been accepted for study. We arrived at the appointed time and place only to find no one there. After finally solving that problem we discovered that when her classmates arrived at the airport their promised university escort who was to have met them there arrived about an hour late, had inadequate space for their luggage and had no apparent understanding of what it felt like to be stranded in a new country and get only recorded telephone messages when pleading for help. As an educator I railed, "Why can't universities ever learn the art of hospitality!" I have too often had assignments on university campuses only to find that no one knew where my materials for the workshop were stored, or where I was to stay or who could find me a key to my assigned guest suite that more than once had no bedding in place. Then a couple days ago all of that despair was disproved from being universally true of institutions of higher learning. I went to a board meeting for the Van Lunen Fellows program at Calvin College in Grand Rapids, Michigan. A driver was waiting for me at the airport. My beautiful room in the Prince Center was waiting, complete with welcome basket and a full agenda of activities was on the desk. Ah! Hospitality!

On further reflection I got in touch with the reality that my life has been one succession after another or people showing me hospitality. Even though I was part of a large family of nine children the people of my home congregation in rural Texas always opened their home to our entire family for

62

Sunday dinners, wedding receptions, birthday parties and golden wedding observances. Once when I was hitchhiking from Illinois to Texas a couple of young women from Mena, Arkansas picked me up late in the day. In genuine purity of heart, they expressed concern that I would be thumbing a ride in the dark. They offered to have me come to their home for dinner and a night's sleep. When I was in an automobile accident in Oklahoma, a complete stranger took a couple sibs and me in for medical care and got away before I even got his full name and address. Later on, in that same trip (now continued by train) a stranger was concerned, when it appeared I had no money, (He was right.) and offered to buy us dinner in the train diner. When my family was home on leave from missionary service in Hong Kong families in 17 states took us in and housed, fed and welcomed us.

Hospitality around the world has consistently enveloped me. Once I was overtaken by a local gentleman in Peshawar, Pakistan. He followed me down the street and asked me anxiously about a pakul (cap) I had just bought. He wanted to know where I had gotten it and what I had paid for it. Slowly he made it clear to me that he wanted to make sure that I had not been overcharged. He even told me that hospitality was essential to his belief system. Another gentleman in Brazil discovered late one night that one of my travel companions was having a birthday the next day. At 10 o'clock that night he found a bakery that would have a nicely decorated birthday cake waiting for me in the morning. In Calcutta a total stranger learned of my interest in the arts of India and found a member of the India National Dance Troop who came to me and showed me around. In Cairo I was nearly in trouble because I had been accidentally seated at a hotel table exclusively reserved for a very wealthy sheik. When the sheik's personal aide (an Egyptian Coptic Christian) discovered me at his boss's table he worked through his fear and I ended up sharing a delightful meal with the sheik!

The Bible says that by showing hospitality people have been found to be "entertaining angels unaware." In my case I have found myself as the one being entertained by angels unaware!

ℰℭ

CHURCH PICNIC SOFTBALL

Last Sunday my church once again sponsored Sunday Church Picnic in the Park. It was wonderful. Lots of hamburgers, hot dogs, potato salads, homemade cakes and cookies. The fellowship was great. Persons of all ages milled around together enjoying a gorgeous day.

After the meal there was the usual: putting contest, hula hoops, water balloon toss. The works. Then came the announcement, "Time for the softball game. Get your glove, bat and balls and let's head for the ball field."

It was at that point that I hesitated. Should I join in? I remembered our last church picnic softball game, now some 10 years ago. Of course, I was younger than, only 71 and anxious to get into the game. First came the matter of choosing teams. One chooser was a middle-aged softballer, the other an eager teen-ager. By turn they made their selection. Almost all had been selected when it hit me. "Hey, I haven't been picked." This was a pretty new experience for me. I used to be always among the first ones picked. I felt a tinge of rejection.

Finally, all had been chosen, all except me, that is. Then to add injury to insult the middle-aged guy said to the kid, "Why don't you just take Mel?" The reply, "No, that's okay. You take him." So I joined my team in the field. Naturally I was assigned short right field.

When it came my turn at bat, I was ready. I rejoiced as I belted a single through the infield. I admit it was not a screamer, but I was safely on base. The next batter hit a slow roller. I was not about to be doubled off at second. I took off with every ounce of energy my legs could generate. About half-way between first and second it happened. I felt my hamstring snap. I fell to the ground. I was assisted off the field. I watched the rest of the game in silence trying not to show any pain. It was the first time in all of my life that I declared a church picnic a disaster.

That was why I hesitated last Sunday about joining in the game. I made the right decision. I wished my fellow congregants well. I went home and watched the Padres lose on television.

ℰᏜᏟℛ

ENERGY

It is the bottom of the tenth in the 1986 World Series. The slow grounder off the bat of Mookie Wilson has just gone through the legs of Red Sox first baseman Bill Buckner and we win! Mets win! Mets win! We don't want to leave the stadium. We are all friends. We are all exultant. It doesn't get any better than this. ENERGY!

I am walking as fast as I can, being jostled pushed, propelled out of the mouth of the tunnel from the subway. I am being carried on the motion of the crowd of thousands right into the heart of Tiananmen Square in Beijing China. It is June 4 1989. Everyone is hopeful, ecstatic, that reform is coming to Communist China. People talk to me in Mandarin whether I understand them or not. Music blares. Flags fly. Arms hug. Youths exult. Elderly contemplate. I am part of a sea, the crest of a wave, moving in concert with a sea of humanity toward the shore of freedom. ENERGY!

The city swoops me up into her arms and carries me from midtown to downtown. It's the Centennial Celebration of the Statue of Liberty and we are all celebrating it in the pulsating heart of Manhattan. People are everywhere. They are eating, singing, break-dancing. There is reggae and salsa and military marches. Kids wear Statue of Liberty head decorations. Adults wave America flags. Even dogs are attired in red, white and blue. The people sweep me along all the way across from Manhattan to Brooklyn on the Brooklyn Bridge. Later in the darkness, sirens howl, spectacular fireworks explode, laser beams soot up into the sky. There is massive motion and no violence. There is brotherhood and sisterhood among people of every color, multiple dress styles, uncountable different languages. All are celebrating and I am part of it. This is the celebration of the open arms of America, land that I love! ENERGY

Hang on, little Peggy. Let's hold hands tightly so we don't get separated. We are once again a part of that happy company of crowd-loving Chinese going down the ramp of the Star Ferry to cross from Kowloon to Hong Kong Island. The signs warn, "Watch out for pick-pockets" so we are careful, but not so careful as to detract from the pure exhilaration of being a part of the crowd, a connected piece of humanity, a couple of cells in the body of all God's people.

Crowds can do this to me! They give me SYNERGY! ENERGY!

ഇൽ

PRAYING

It was on a quiet hill called Tao Fung Shan (the mountain of the wind of the way). Behind me Hong Kong swarmed with tens of thousands of desperately poor street-dwelling refugees. In front of me lay Mao's China where as many as 3 million were starving because of his misguided Great

Leap Forward. Around me were the young restless teenagers facing a most uncertain future. We sat under a naked white cross inscribed with only two black Chinese characters pronounced, "sing leo" meaning "It is finished." I prayed for the terrible past to be finished, the unsettling present to be handled, and that the future to be open. The voiced 'Ah-moon' of us all, the end of the prayer, came from deep within and floated heavenward in doubt, faith and hope.

The auditorium in Disneyland was still tense. Among the 2,000 there, some were anxious. Some rejoiced. Others feared. Some threatened. Some cursed. It was the end of an exceedingly stormy session of a large churchwide convention. All day in the name of God, people had fought like the devil. I had been asked to lead the closing prayer at the end of the day. So, I began, "Dear God, those of your children called the Lutheran Church-Missouri Synod have kept you very busy today..."

The other passengers were already off the plane at the Lincoln, Nebraska airport. Only my seatmate whom I had met an hour earlier and I remained. She was not sure she had the courage to get off the plane to face her father. She planned to inform him, a Lutheran pastor, that she had filed for divorce. She feared her father would be angry, disown her, damn her to hell; or maybe ... understand, forgive, support. While the flight attendant waited, I held her folded hands in mine and we prayed.

Only two of us stood before the simple altar in the chapel at Maxwell Air Force Base where I was conducting a weeklong workshop for military chaplains. The Jewish chaplain and I were the only ones in the room. He had invited me to come with him as he prayed. Yesterday I had been in the much larger Catholic chapel where the Catholic chaplains had violated official policy and had invited me (a non-Catholic) to share with them the sacred elements of the holy mass. And just two days previous some twenty of us had held hands surrounding the altar of the Protestant Chapel where together we prayed saying, "Our Father in heaven."

The eyes of all wait upon you, Oh Lord.

ॐ

A TIME TO SPEAK

It was mid-December, 1949. I had joined a significant number of my college colleagues in the on-campus women's dorm lounge. In fact, the place was packed. We were jammed into every square foot of sofas, chairs, floor space. The place was aglow, not only from the warmth of the fireplace, but also from the ad hoc harmony of Christmas carols. It was our pre-holiday all-school Christmas party and everything felt just right. The snow was glistening. Home for Christmas was just days away. Engagement rings were anticipated by some and homemade Christmas cookies, candies, eggnog by many others.

We had moved through "Jingle Bells" to "Let It Snow" to "O Little Town of Bethlehem." Then it was my turn to speak. I was the president of the student body and so was invited to give the devotion/homily/speech, whatever one wants to call it.

So, I spoke on "Let us go to Bethlehem." We were going home and that was great. We were going to be among those who loved us and that was wonderful. I suggested that all of this was part of going to Bethlehem, to the crèche, to the place where we meet anew the infant Jesus, to the place where angels assure us that this is where acceptance, hope and love abound.

The speech worked. Since all in that room were preparing for public ministry with the Lutheran church, most were touched at a deep spiritual level of the meaning of their life.

It was a great time to speak. Since then I have spoken to a hundred (maybe more than a thousand) different audiences in settings as varied as convention centers in New York City to the tiny chapel of the Baptistery of Lydia in Greece. Every once in a while, it all worked.

The crowded low-ceilinged meeting room was in a Colorado Springs hotel. It was the 6190's and Lutheran schools shared in the upheaval. Young and old were questioning institutions, even schooling itself. I spoke to some 300 teachers in the schools of the "4-corners" area. My theme was "The Church That Meets in Your Classroom." I reminded those teachers that their classroom met all the criteria of church: the Gospel was shared, faith united the community, and the demons of ignorance, racism, and sexism were being exorcised. Miracles like learning to read and write were happening every day. And each teacher was the minister in that classroom that God used to make it all possible. The addressed worked. It was a time to speak.

Every once in a while, the magic occurred. Speaker and audience reacted in unison. Thoughts were stimulated. Emotions were evoked. Hope and promise seemed real.

Of course, sometimes it just didn't work. (See next blog entry: "A Time to Keep Silent). Sometimes it was just another speech. But when it all came together it reassured me that even in the age of multi-media there are still occasions when the best communication occurs because "it is the time to speak."

઼ଔ

A TIME TO KEEP SILENT

We are in a staff meeting checking calendars. Mine lists lots of speaking engagements. My colleague comments, "Mel will speak on any subject, anywhere." I still don't quite know what Don meant by that remark. I took it as much more of a put-down than as a vote of confidence.

In later years I realized that I should have taken it as a warning. Sometimes I have made speeches when I really should have chosen silence.

A rather fundamentalist congregation was sponsoring a weeklong revival. I was asked to speak on "The Battleground for the Gospel." I knew what they wanted: Warnings against secular humanism in public schools, the shame of removing posters of the Ten Commandments in southern courtrooms, The threat of radical feminism, free condom or drug needles distribution. I chose another route.

I suggested that the real "Battleground for the Gospel" lay deep within the heart of each one of us. Our struggles between knowing the good, but not doing it. The continuing wish to earn God's favor in place of freely accepting grace. The constant seeing of the speck in my neighbor's eye, ignoring the beam in my own.

As I spoke, the usual "Amens" were very sparse. "Tell us brother" was not to be heard. At the end of the day I decided that I should have suggested a different speaker while I remained silent.

The event was a national conference of construction workers and spouses. It was in a very fancy Hollywood hotel. I was scheduled to speak at a 3:30 p.m. sectional on effective parenting. Attendees there were hoping to forget their children for a few days. Vendor hospitality suites next door were stocking their bars. My audience had one goal: get out of here. Let the good times roll. Effective parenting: well, I'll think about that when I get home. I should have chosen silence.

Not just a lecture, but a whole course. I was asked to teach General Psychology to a class in a seminary. Two problems: I was to teach it in Cantonese (even after six years in Hong Kong, teaching a psychology course in Chinese was not to be recommended.) The second problem: the only psychology texts available in Chinese were translations from Russian behaviorists, hardly the best grounding for future Lutheran pastors. The students (at least outwardly) were marvelously patient. I was terrible. I should have remained silent.

There is one whole class of speaking opportunities that has no equal. Give a lecture, conduct a workshop or lead a seminar. Do it for a faculty that is required to attend. Speak at the close of the school day on a Friday afternoon in any (especially urban) school in America. Forget about it. Stay silent.

The ancient writer had it so right, "There is a time to speak and a time to remain silent." Why is that silent part so hard to put into practice?

ഇൗരു

PHARAOHS WHO KNEW NOT JOSEPH

The Bible tells us that at some point Egypt got a "new Pharaoh who did not know Joseph." He forgot the history of how Joseph had saved the Egyptians from starvation. So…

This forgetful Pharaoh made the Jews his slaves and, in the end, he lost them all and even lost his own son. All because he failed to remember Joseph.

The story is repeated straight up to this morning. It is called "loss of institutional memory." Others call it forgetting one's roots. Still others find it demeaning to admit that they stand on another's shoulders. Some talk blithely about that was then, this is now and it is time to move on - now!

I just returned from my annual family reunion. My niece and her family orchestrated it wonderfully. She was determined to be a female Pharaoh who remembered Joseph and Joseph's queen and so our parents were recalled in gratitude and appreciation.

On the other hand, I have seen schools and congregations currently led by Pharaohs who do not remember anyone named Joseph. There is no acknowledgment of those who have gone before. That is why (even before I was in my 80's) I believed in celebrating the anniversaries of institutions. The early Josephs and their female counterparts not only deserve to be remembered but also, they are forgotten at the peril of the current power wielders.

Citizens can all too easily enjoy the freedoms, life style and opportunities of the present while all too off-handedly dismissing those who whose efforts, sacrifice and even life blood makes it possible for them to have the blessings currently enjoyed. Of course, I read Kibrahn's "The Prophet" and agree with him that "life goes not backward nor tarries with yesterday." However, I cringe at the all too true joke that the most commonly passed resolution at the annual meeting of the congregation in which I grew up was the one that ended with "therefore be it resolved that we stick with the old!" Of course, we move on. But we also remember Joseph and if he is around, we consult with him and his sisters, we stand on those shoulders and then see new vistas and dream new dreams and even celebrate new paradigms.

Now I must run and have a long talk with an elderly friend named Joseph!

ℰℭ

MORE THAN A SEX SYMBOL

I regret that I recall neither her name nor the name of her son. But I do know that the boy was a student in the first grade and that I was his teacher. The boy's tuition was being paid by an elderly woman from our church who was the landlady for the woman and her son.

I remember what the mother looked like. She was stunning. Tall, slim, well-endowed, long, flowing hair. She was a Southern California carhop, a waitress at a drive-in. She came to the cars to take and deliver food and drink orders. Her scanty halter-top uniform, I'm sure, helped her generate generous tips.

It may have been because she was not home in the evening to assist her son with homework or it may have been something else. For whatever reason, he was not doing well and it was time for a parent-teacher conference.

We met in the principal's office and discussed the issue. I soon learned how much she loved her son and was saddened by his slow progress. She really wanted the best for him. She wanted to be a good mother. We discussed a variety of options. I assured her that her efforts would bear fruit.

As we came to the end of the interview, she thanked me. Then tears suddenly began to roll down her cheeks. She looked across the desk at me and said, "Thank you. You must know that no man in my whole life has ever talked to me in this way."

It was probably an exaggeration, but I got the message. no human wants to be deemed merely an object, or symbol. We all yearn to be accepted as being more than a title, just someone's spouse, someone who's rich or poor, or any other symbol. "See the me who's a real person" is the plea of us all.

ഇൻ

RETIREMENT

Sometimes I think I ended up as head of Lutheran Education for a major Lutheran denomination as a result of a fluke. For a very brief period (before it was ruled to be illegal age discrimination) the Church had a rule that heads of major departments had mandatory retirement at 65. My predecessor, Dr. Arthur Miller, got caught by that rule and entered forced retirement, the only officer ever required to do that.

One of the saddest moments of my stint as his successor was when he came to see me not long after I assumed office. He told me that he had taken a new job. He was going to be a door-to-door salesman peddling encyclopedias.

I saw (and still see) this as a tragedy. Art was a man of great passion for Christian education. He himself earned a Ph.D. when few professional church workers made that choice. What he lacked in personal charm or charisma he made up with meticulous attention to detail, astute management of budget, surprising skill at getting larger fiscal appropriations for his department and great ability at hiring and supporting very competent staff. And for that he ended up knocking on doors, selling books on credit.

Out of that came a personal resolve. I would retire at 65 by my own choice, not by bureaucratic rules. I would manage my finances so that we would not feel impoverished. In retirement I would pursue interests congruent with my skills and values.

That is how I planned to retire. That is how I have done it now - many times.

ഇൻ

THE BENEFITS OF GIN AND TONIC

The Building Committee of the Lutheran Church of Hong Kong for which I served as chair made a mistake. We hired a construction contractor to do the site formation for Saviour Lutheran Church and School on Tai Po Road. He was a fraud on many counts. I did not know that when we had the first of many "unfortunate incidents." He was blasting away a rock hillside to create the level building plot. He had erected a huge bamboo screen to contain the blasted rock. Then one day he used entirely too much explosives. One of the rocks flew over the screen. It landed on and shattered the front windshield of the Rolls Royce parked there. The owner: the Chief Justice of the Hong Kong Supreme Court.

By the next morning I had the official notice from Crown Lands. "All site formation at said site is herewith terminated until further notice."

I knew that I did not have a strong case when I went in to make my appeal for another chance. For over a month all work on that site was suspended.

Through the kindness of the Director of Kodak International, a wonderful Lutheran layman from the USA, I had been accepted into associate membership in the exclusive Royal Hong Kong Golf Club and I regularly made use of that privilege.

Since only British citizens had the right to full membership, we associate members did not always interact with those with higher status. But one day after a round of golf one of "them" invited me to join him on the veranda. I offered to buy the first round. We made our introductions. When he learned of my work with Lutheran schools, he asked me if I had any connection with that new building planned for the Tai Po Road site next to the new court building. I confessed that I did indeed have some responsibility. He informed me that he was the person responsible for all blasting permits in Hong Kong. His next sentence was unequivocal "Well, blasting at that school site will continue on exactly the same day hell freezes over!" I hastily ordered another round of gin and tonics that I offered as apology for his having to deal with a very upset judge.

And so, we commiserated: my problems with greedy contractors, my deep desire to get that school built and open for the poor children of the community and his having to respond to people living or working near construction sites and all their unreasonable objections and complaints. One more round of gin and tonics and we might be able to endure!

Exactly 10 days later I received the registered letter on official crown stationery. "The blasting permit for the site on Tai Po Road is herewith immediately reissued."

BARS

I was six years old. Prohibition had just ended. I walked into that small Texas town saloon with eyes wide open, my nose sniffing the new smells, my ears hearing the debate as to whether this 15-cent bottle of bought beer was really better than home brew. I eyed the muddy boots, the Oshkosh overalls, the sweated Stetsons. The barkeeper behind the simple bar wore a white half-apron drooping from his waist. The dominoes clicked. The language became guarded as we entered because my father who brought me there was the principal of the local parochial school and had taught them all. Even in that saloon I knew he was probably the most respected man in the community. He bought a beer for himself. Then he slid over a nickel for a big bottle of red strawberry soda pop for me. I had been introduced to the world of bars, saloons, pubs, lounges.

My Uncle Otto was in town, staying in a big fancy hotel in the downtown loop of Chicago. He had invited me, a college freshman in suburban River Forest to come see him. When I arrived, he invited me to join him in the bar. He said he would buy me a beer. "Buy me a beer - but I'm not of legal age," I thought. But he took me in. We sat in a booth. He ordered two beers. But I'll never forget it. What surprised me was not that the waiter never questioned my age, but that he asked for $2.00. "That's a dollar a bottle!" my mind screamed. I had never in my life heard of a beer costing more than a quarter. It was one of the memorable beers of my life.

I either was 21 years of age or at least appeared to be. I sat in a dark midwestern neighborhood tavern, in a high wood-paneled booth. I was there with my new girlfriend Jane. I ordered her a bourbon and 7-Up. We looked into each other's eyes. We held hands. We sipped our drinks. We swam in our love.

I had tipped the maître d' generously and he had come through. Immediately he led us to a choice table. We were at the Windows of the World cocktail lounge at the top of Tower II of the World Trade Center in New York. The table was right next to the window. The view of New York on this beautiful day stretched magnificently below us. I ordered a bottle of good wine. It was great to be in New York. Wonderful to be with a wife and a sister I loved. Perfect to be in the best seat at the best bar in New York. All was well with the world.

Nevermore!

9/11 TO 9/11/09

The date is September 11, 2001. It's 9:30 p.m. And I have just left a dinner at the American Club in Hong Kong. I was the honored guest of the alumni association of Concordia Lutheran School, Kowloon. It has been a wonderful evening of memories, laughter and hope. A car and driver had been sent to pick me up and return me to my hotel. The driver is obviously agitated, paying very close attention to the car radio. My Cantonese is surely not what it used to be, so I don't catch all of what he and the radio are announcing. But I do get the message than an airplane has hit a building in New York. I do understand enough Cantonese to know that the driver keeps repeating, "This is terrible, terrible!"

I rush to my hotel room. Worldwide CNN is there live to air the tragedy. Like millions all over the world, I watch in horror as the second plane hits, the twin towers collapse. Throughout the night I watch in sadness, horror and anger. In light of the indescribably terrible consequences so many experienced, because of this tragedy, my messed-up plans, cancelled flights and delayed trip home, of course, amount to nothing. Further, in view of all the sadness so many endured because of this tragedy, my own memories of the world trade center amount to nothing.

Yet for each one of us, our memories are personal. And mine of the World Trade Center are all wonderful. I loved the bar at the top at the Windows of the World restaurant. It was a "must stop visit" with any relatives and friends who came to see us in New York. There was the private club on that same floor at which Jane and I (and a host of private donors) arranged for an appreciation luncheon for all Lutheran school principals of the metro New York area. For all those urban principals this was their first experience in the marvelous exclusive setting. It was on the 98th floor of the other tower where I had conducted workshops for the staff of an international bank. It was in the basement where we always found parking to explore so much of what those towers offered.

Now all that made up the physical components of that center has been pulverized, melted, or carted to a dump on Staten Island. As I write this, more than eight years since that fateful day, the whole world continues to weep, to cope and dares to hope.

BRIEF ENCOUNTER: ROCKS

It was one of the best parties I've ever attended. Beautiful site, incredible food, aged wine, stimulating, supportive friends. Allan gave the party for Brenda, his wife who turned 60. The focus of course was on Brenda. So, I was surprised when Brenda and her friend Nancy came to Jane and me with little gifts. They were in appreciation of our roles in leading a just-completed tour to Luther Land in Germany.

One of the gifts was a small rock, nothing more than a pebble. It was picked up at the Wartburg Castle in Germany, the site where Luther was held safe from those who sought to kill him. We had explored that castle, stood where Luther stood, peered in the cubicle that was his home for nine long months. This little rock spoke to our friends saying, "Take me to Mel and Jane." They did. It is indeed a precious stone.

Stones have not always seemed so precious to me. When as a young child I dug in the dirt, pesky stones prevented me from digging very deep. When I picked cotton and the knees on which I crawled down the rows landed on a stone it really hurt. Years later I fought a nasty legal action against a corrupt construction company which only took stone from a church/school site instead of leveling the site for construction of the building.

I spent more than two years on a church fund-raising effort built upon a Biblical theme of an Old Testament stone set up as an icon for remembering the greatness and goodness of God.

And now this little stone takes on surprising meaning for me. Like Luther, I struggle. Like Luther, I get upset with the institutional church. Like Luther, I feel like hurling things at evil forces. More importantly, like Luther, I find something outside myself to rest upon, to hope upon, to rely upon: a Rock of Ages

ಏರ

IT STILL HURTS

Scene at a Conference.

He was principal of the oldest Lutheran parochial school in America, St. Matthews, Manhattan, New York City. What he was speaking of was his need to fire a teacher. There were plenty of reasons for the dismissal. The teacher was failing. The kids were not being well served. He had tried to help, but to no avail. So, he fired the teacher. It hurt both him and the one let go. It was not the first time he had fired someone. Yet we all knew he meant it with all his heart when he said, "I'm glad that it still hurts. It hurts to end another person's employment."

It stirred up memories of the times it has been necessary for me to terminate a colleague's employment. It's never easy and never more difficult than in my early years in Hong Kong. It was really difficult to find a job in those days. It was often especially difficult for some teachers for they were frequently without documents to prove their educational background. They had fled for their lives with only the clothes on their backs. They didn't always have the remotest chance of carrying their official diplomas and the schools from which they had graduated were now closed by the Communists. The school records were all burned.

However, we had gotten Mr. Wong certified to teach. He was overwhelmed with joy and appreciation. Now he could get off the street. He could feed himself. After a few months he was able to buy a suit to replace the one from the charity bin. However, I soon discovered that he was (in King James language) not apt to teach. There was no classroom discipline. The only method he used was lecture. I observed him often and made suggestions. I had my academic dean try to assist him. It was decided that we would not renew his contract. This would have tragic consequences. In the Chinese idiom, "His rice bowl would be broken." He would have a very hard time getting another job. His loss of face was overwhelming.

I will never forget the day I had to give him the bad news. It was the right thing to do yet it hurt me to do it. It still hurts. I'm glad it still hurts.

૭૦૯૨

EDITH

I hardly knew her, but 25 years later I can still picture her. She was the only English woman in my class of 45 Pakistani parents I was teaching in Karachi. I see her now, sitting on my right, two rows from the back. She seemed to hang onto every word. She engaged in the role-plays with intensity. The topics of active listening and honest self-disclosure seemed to especially grab her attention.

On about the third day she spoke with me briefly during a break and asked if we could arrange for a longer interview. Of course. We set that up. When we met, she spoke of the importance of being listened to and of the deep pain of not having anyone with whom one can be totally open.

Slowly she poured out her story. She was one of two wives of a Pakistani gentleman. This was perfectly legal. The other wife was Pakistani. Her husband was kind to her and not like other husbands she knew who beat their wives. He provided for her and even gave her an adequate allowance to purchase personal items. Yet, she said, she was missing something. She knew that she was "number two" in the relationship. She knew that she was never fully accepted into his family. She knew some of her husband's friends asked him about her and asked some painfully intimate questions about the relationship. She said she could endure all of this.

But what was most difficult for her was that there was no one, absolutely no one with whom she could share her experiences, her thoughts, her feelings., her longings. Nor was there anyone who would just listen without judgment, moralizing, advising, or even blaming. So, we talked for a long time and she felt free to release what had been building up in her for more than two decades.

She came to see me again after the last session. She said to me, "There is one place I can express myself. I write poetry. And I collect the poetry of others who share my feelings. I have actually compiled them into a little book of which I have only a very small number. I would like to give you a copy of that book if you would accept it."

In my retirement I have disposed of almost all of the thousands of books I have owned in my lifetime. The one given to me by Edith I hang on to.

ഇന്ദ

SO CLOSE

I am in Harrod's Casino, Reno, Nevada on January 28,1952.

My wife Jane and I have traveled there from our home in Tracy, California, some four hours away. We are dirt poor, combined income of some $2,000 a year. But we'd spent some Christmas gift money for gasoline and planned to drive to Reno and back on the same day because we don't have the $6.00 required for an overnight stay in a motel. We do have, however, one dollar each for the slots. We feed the nickel machines.

The slots smile on us. By the time we feel we need to head home we have parlayed our $2.00 into $5.00. We take a breather, have a discussion, and make a decision.

We'll take two dollars of our gain (two neat rolls of nickels) and secure them in the glove compartment of our car. Then we'll take our $3.00 worth of winnings and hit the slots again. If we can just win $2.00 more, we'll have enough for a motel room. We'll spend the night in Reno and head home the next day, just like the high rollers.

Twenty minutes later Jane and I are pulling out of our parking slot, heading back over Donner Pass on the way home for a very late dinner.

Fifty-nine years later I still feel the rush. So close! I'm not alone. From Las Vegas to Atlantic City to Mississippi River boats to Indian reservation casinos to state-run lotteries, every day there are millions who feel the rush. "Just maybe..."

§O©R

GOLFING PARTNER

When we lived in Hong Kong during the 1950-and 60's we did not have many vacation options. US law prohibited travel to the China mainland. Financial limitations precluded travel abroad. So once in a great while I would take a day off by playing golf and then spending the night at the Royal Hong Kong Golf Club.

I was there alone on one occasion when the starter asked me if I wanted a partner for the afternoon round. Of course, I did. The guy was good. I noticed immediately that he had a very good swing and played at very near par. He was not very talkative and I had learned that British protocol precluded me from prying. He did tell me that he was a Scotsman that he had just come from India and was on his way to the USA.

After the golf round we agreed to share a drink and dinner. He ordered "whiskey." In Hong Kong, of course, that meant Scotch served neat. I ordered bourbon. He asked, "What is that?" I explained. He stuck up his nose at the thought, especially when I asked for it over the rocks. However, when I also asked for a Seven-Up mixer, he told me that was almost more than his stomach could handle but in a good-natured way we had our drinks and dinner.

Then he asked me if I would be around the next day and if I would care to play with him. He said that he was playing with the Captain of the Club.

I was surprised at his good connection but felt pleased to accept the offer. I asked him if he knew the Club Captain.

"Not really," he said. "But you see he is playing with me because I am on my way to the USA to represent my country in an international competition. It is called The Eisenhower Cup.

ഇൗ

PREJUDICE AND PRIDE

The year is 1961. I'm on a "missionary-on-furlough" lecture tour in the Deep South. My primary target: black Lutheran churches in Mississippi and Alabama.

Even though I grew up immersed in the racism and prejudice of central Texas, I am struck again by the racial arrogance of the whites: color-segregated schools, restaurants, water fountains, motels, churches. When my black driver picks me up from the airport in Birmingham to take me to a black church, he asks me to sit in the back seat. I refuse, "You're my brother, not my chauffeur!"

I get in the front seat next to him. At the first stop light the white in the car in the lane on our right glares at us and cuts us off. We narrowly avoid colliding with his vehicle.

In Montgomery the white taxi driver almost refuses to take me to a black church. He's both afraid and very skeptical of my intentions. He's suspicious of outside agitators who go to black churches.

I grieve at the facilities and resources in our black Lutheran schools. I can hardly believe the diet at the Lutheran college dining room. I bask in reverent awe as I sit together on her front-porch swing listening to a black saint, Rosa Young. She tells me about her unflagging ministry through black schools and churches.

After Dr. Martin Luther King Jr., the Civil Rights Act, Brown vs. the Board of Education, elimination of the poll tax, no more water fountains, busses or restaurants designated "For Colored Only," surely the 1960's or at worst the 70's would see the end of segregation and racial prejudice in the USA.

It's a Sunday evening, 1999. We are sitting in liberal California, enjoying a dazzling sunset over the multi-hued Pacific, enjoying a glass of crisp California chardonnay.

Our guest, a teacher in a nearby public high school speaks. He tells us of a story nowhere reported in the local press. One of his students, Roxanne, has committed suicide. She, the only black in her class, was hounded to death by racial slurs spoken to her, written in her books, scrawled on the blackboard. She was shunned, spit at, known only as that damned n_____. It went on for three months. Our guest had tried to be a friend and counselor. He sought assistance. The community claimed he must be a communist. A promising young woman is dead.

I hang my head in shame for my own failures at not more intentionally confronting racism. I feel anger at any system, which still claims some sort of superiority by virtue of a white skin. Once more I examine my own heart. I image the face of a Creator God with tears streaming from h\His eyes, watching us humans still failing to see that we are all of one blood, all of us sisters and brothers.

ℰᏩ

FEARS

I have finally gotten around to reading Mitch Albom's "Tuesdays With Morrie," subtitled "an old man, a young man, and life's greatest lessons." One of the topics they discuss and upon which I have been reflecting is FEAR and my experiences around fear.

I have no recollection of the common childhood fears of dark places, ghosts, or things that go bump in the night. With one exception: I must have been - oh, maybe in the third grade. It was after dark. I was all alone in the dining room doing my homework. Dad was in his "study" and I guess Mom was putting my sisters and younger brother to bed. Suddenly I was sure I heard a noise in the dark room just off the kitchen. I perked up my ears and looked. Sure enough, a shadow was moving across that dark neighboring room. I quickly ran across the hall to Dad's room alerting him," There is a prowler in our back room." He ran out his door and through the yard to the back. He rushed into the room. I heard a loud shriek! He had caught the intruder, only to discover that it was Mom looking for an item she wanted to retrieve. Then we laughed, but for a few minutes I had been afraid.

A second incident about that same time in my life left more lasting effects. I had somehow or other secured a broad-rimmed black hat. I thought I looked great in it and proudly wore it to school the morning after I had received it. As I neared the school a group of men from the congregation were on the water tower working on a leak. They noticed me. I could hear them laugh. Then one said in German "Na, hut, was hast du denn in zinn? Wo willst du mitt den jungen hin!" (Rough translation: "Now hat, what is in your head? Where are you taking that little lad?") I knew it was a put-down. I was being laughed at. And I felt it in the core of my being. It produced a fear of people making fun of me, a fear of what would people think of me. That ingrained fear resides in me still and I have not yet overcome it. (See previous blog entitled "What Will People Think.")

I have been afraid when I feared loved ones would die. Daughter Elizabeth at less-than-a-year lay in intensive care on Christmas Eve and the doctor had warned us that she might not be with us on Christmas Day. On a later occasion, wife Jane was in a coma from a cerebral aneurysm and our emergency flight from Asia to the USA encountered headwinds forcing a stopover in Alaska. Three times I have been in intensive care units wondering if persons who had attempted suicide would die. My guess is that these fears were not so much the fears of death, but of the consequences of death on me and my family or close friends. Now those are fears worth contemplating.

Fear, of course, is often a natural and God-given response, which helps us protect ourselves. So I am glad that sometimes I am still able to be afraid.

ೂಬ

ARABS

Arabs. I thought I knew about Arabs. They lived in the desert. They owned camels. They were the descendants of Ishmael. They were Muslims. I was pretty sure about all this until I went to Beirut in 1968.

My objective was to meet with American missionaries there to discuss education opportunities. They were hospitable: a lunch of 30 small dishes of Lebanese delicacies. They were helpful: a tour and contacts at the American University of Lebanon. Then they threw me a curve. For the rest of my trip they assigned me to a local guide; an Arab in a business suit; an Arab who was a university graduate, lived in an apartment and drove a car; an Arab who was a devout Christian; an Arab who was very gentle with his arrogant and ignorant guest.

He taught me about the cedars of Lebanon and the many different ethnic, cultural and religious groups who have walked under those majestic trees. He took me to Tyre and Sidon, recalling for me the history of Phoenicians. He took me to where Jesus walked. He showed me the remaining Crusader Forts built by Christians who had come to annihilate non-believing Arab Muslims who were called infidels. He showed me the massive military build-up by Israel which he correctly predicted would be used to invade his country.

He spoke with no bitterness or animosity. There was no condescension toward my American inspired pro-Israeli bias. He just shared his experiences, his fears, his hopes, his faith.

Now 50 years later I need to remember him as post 9/11 images and rhetoric would ask me to forget or ignore what I experienced in those few days and what I learned from my Arab brother. Arabs, like all ethnic groups, come with a variety of values, beliefs, aspirations. Some of these points of view I despise – others I share.

೮೦೦೮

BRAVADO

Earl was a dominating presence. Well over six feet tall with broad shoulders, taut muscles and aggressive tenacity he controlled the lanes of the basketball court. He and I were both in our early twenties with lots of stamina. Our team was sponsored by D & W Billiards Parlor from the wrong side of the tracks in Tracy, California. We took on all comers from the local city league or neighboring small towns and even from Stockton, the county seat.

I don't quite remember how I got to be asked to play with that particular team. After all, I was the supposedly pious principal of the small Lutheran elementary school and my teammates were not likely to often find themselves in my or any other church.

Earl stood out and sounded out. His oaths were articulate. Highly descriptive threats intimidated many. His after-game relaxation fit right in. Beer was guzzled. Tales of female conquests were recalled. When we drove to some urban sites for games in certain parts of town Earl enjoyed calling the street-walking prostitutes by name and telling of their particular skills.

After playing for the Tracy D & W Billiards team for three years I ended my career with them by missing an easy lay-up that would have won the game. A few months later (unconnected with my missed lay-up) I accepted a call to serve in another church and school 500 miles away. A few years after that I was even further away, in Hong Kong, serving as a missionary.

I was stunned the day a letter arrived from Tracy, California, from Earl. In it he recalled our time together. He informed me that his business was doing well. He told me that he was a changed man. Christ had entered his life. He had cleaned up his act. He was happily married, the father of two and determined to raise them up properly. He wrote that he thought I might like to know that. So, he went to no small pains to get my mailing address. He just wanted to wish me blessings and express the hope that Hong Kong still provided an opportunity for me to shoot a few baskets.

ଽୠଔ

FIVE FAR APART THOUGHTS

Usually I try to focus on only one thought or experience per blog posting. I have just had a very interesting five days that brought up five different reflections. So here goes.

1. Really Big Bucks.

I attended a Board meeting of the Van Lunen Fellows Program. We provide executive management skills for administrators of faith-based schools. We get our fiscal resources from the Van Lunen Foundation. When Mr. Van Lunen died about four years ago, he left behind a Trust, a group of four Trustees, some money and the simple instructions, "Do something good with this money." The surprise: the money he was speaking of came to approximately $100 million. What "good" does someone do when suddenly having available $100 million?

2. *What's a University for?*

I also attended a conference of university professors. The focus was on teaching practices at the university level. The keynoter challenged us with the proposition that the sole function of a university professor is for the experience to teach the students to think. Is that correct? Does the university professor want the students only to think or does s/he have in mind a particular way in which they should think? Does the professor care about what conclusions the students reach from their thinking? Does it make any difference if the university is secular or church related?

3. *Vices and Virtues.*

One of the outstanding lectures was on teaching students to reflect upon the seven vices and their counterpart seven virtues. The vices, defined as habits or character traits, are envy, vainglory, sloth, avarice, gluttony and lust. The virtues, defined as excellences of character, habit or disposition, are faith, hope, love, wisdom, justice, courage and temperance. So, what vice do I still have embedded in my character? What virtue do I feel I possess and which am I still seeking? (Note: I decided to try to help myself answer that question by teaching an eight-session course on the topic at my church.)

4. *The Limits of Humor.*

On the plane I read Garrison Keillor's newest book, "Pilgrims." I decided that I did not like it. I thought that the author had lost any sense of sympathy for his characters and was just enjoying poking fun at their sincere eccentricities. Am I fair? Does a writer need to have sympathy for the characters in his or her novel or does s/he just describe them and hopefully produce a few understanding chuckles?

5. *Nobody Knows Me.*

To balance Garrison Keillor a bit I was reading the diary of the great Danish philosopher/theologian Soren Kierkegaard. While still a young man he wrote this: "How awful it would be on Judgment Day when all souls return to life again … then to stand completely alone, alone and unknown to all." Does this have anything to do with my decision to write a blog?

಄಄

DEATH

Death is a natural part of the human experience. From my earliest memory I was taught to not fear death. It was always assumed that children were present for the funeral and burial rituals. In the rural part of Texas in which I grew up we went to the home of persons who had died and often "viewed the body" laid out in a casket in the parlor of the home where the deceased had lived.

During grade school years all of us students in the Lutheran school attended all funeral services in the church situated next to the school. At the close of the service we would all walk by and look into the coffin. My father tolled the church bell as the coffin was moved from the church to the nearby cemetery. The church-owned "teacherage' in which we lived adjoined the cemetery. Death was not a stranger.

But dying was. It was not until years later that I was physically present when a person died. By then I was in Hong Kong. A student from the school of which I was principal was involved in a traffic accident. I was called to the emergency room. In those days medical services in Hong Kong simply could not cope with all the challenges of a refugee-swollen population. I found the student unattended, lying on a stretcher on the floor, bleeding profusely. I grabbed a medical staff person and pleaded for assistance. I was told, "Can't you see? He's been fatally injured. There's nothing we can do for him. He will soon be dead." I knelt next to him, held his hand, prayed, and felt him die.

There were other death experiences. The aged Lutheran gentleman from America was finally released from house arrest in China by Mao Zedong and allowed into Hong Kong. He was frail, weak, unable to stay alive. So, I stood by the side of his hospital bed. Since he spoke German, we prayed the Lord's Prayer in German - and then he died - with his aged wife virtually the only one who knew him.

I immediately took the grieving widow to our house where she sobbed inconsolably and went to sleep only when my wife took her into bed with her.

Then I went to the casket-making street in Hong Kong, negotiated a casket, found a grave site and hired four coolies to carry the coffin up a hill to an open grave. Halfway up the hill the bearers set the coffin down. They refused to carry it further up the hill until I paid them an extra stipend. Then we laid Mr. Henkel in the grave, conducted the interment liturgy and made our way slowly back down the hill.

Since then I have been present for peaceful deaths, the quiet death of a still-born and the lingering death of those ill with cancer.

So, I see death as one step in the God-given journey of each human. Because of the death and resurrection of Christ, I think I am moving to my own death completely unafraid.

ಐ ಗಿ

HERB

Tomorrow the "mortal remains" of Herb Brokering will be laid to rest. But this I know: neither he nor his "remains" will ever be completely at rest. Herb will continue to inspire, evoke a shake of the head, create a smile and stir a tug at my heart.

Herb was dubbed the "Leonardo DaVinci of the Prairies." So, when we see him identified as pastor, professor, or staff associate of Wheat Ridge Ministries, we know that those titles don't get close to describing him. When we recall him as poet, hymn writer, author, lyricist, "master of free association" or creative provocateur then we come closer.

Many others are writing official obituaries and well-deserved paeans of praise. For me it all becomes personal.

The first time I met him he had all of us writing poetry. When I told him that my teen-aged daughter was a better poet than I, he encouraged me, but also insisted that I take to my daughter a poem he had written along with his encouragement for her to continue to write poetry.

Once when he was at my church with our very creative musician Stan Beard and they were doing a presentation together, Herb looked at Stan and said to him, "Play something orange!" Stan did and the two of them were off where previously only angels had made music and musings.

When we were in India together (running hours and hours behind schedule because Herb kept finding more immediate signs of God), he left behind those of us looking for traditional souvenirs. He went to the open-air clothes market. There he bought baby socks. He took them to the States and gave them to infants as a sign that all the babies of the world share a need for warm toes and hopes for a wonderful life.

When he and I were to have a planning session at a hotel 30 miles from Chicago he excused himself. The front desk had called and said someone whom he had never met before was looking for him. The young man had alcohol and other drug problems. Someone, somewhere in Chicago, had told him to find Herb. He did, came to the hotel and Herb lifted the man's vision – and then most likely never heard from him again.

Just weeks before he died, he telephoned me. We have a mutual friend about whom Herb was concerned. Herb said, "Mel, call him. He needs some advice and encouragement from you. So just call him and talk to him."

So I muse with Herb as he writes "Cat Psalms" or "Dog Psalms," or "Earth and All Stars" or "Thine the Amen" and I hope that with his unmatched vision to see what others cannot see, Herb is smiling and telling me to get ready for just one more surprise.

୫୦୦୫

SICK CHILD

It's Christmas Eve, 1961. At midnight I sit next to my 10-month-old daughter, Betty. She's in a hospital bed in the intensive care unit of Lutheran Hospital Ft. Wayne, Indiana. She is fighting for her life, threatened by pneumonia and a serious staph infection. In spite of oxygen tents, respirators and I don't know what other catheters, plug-ins and tubes, she can hardly breathe. It breaks my heart to see and hear her struggle for every breath. Worst of all is when she tries to cough, tries to get mucus out of her overburdened lungs. With each cough she grows weaker. The nurse had told me that if Betty survived until midnight then she would probably live. So, I have prayed. I have meditated on another Child at Christmas midnight. I have tried to trust the goodness of God. I cannot stop my tears as another forced cough shakes her little body.

Is there any more agonizing experience for a parent than seeing one's child hurt or sick or dying? Is there any greater challenge to one's perception of how things ought to be than to see or to fear that one's child will precede one in death?

It was not time for Betty to die. She not only survived, but has thrived. Even today as a mother and a clinical psychologist she has a special bond and care for little ones.

And her father has never again experienced Christmas Eve without thanking God for the gift of the Child and of His child, Betty/Lyzse/Elizabeth.

CHRISTMAS CARDS AND LETTERS

I love getting them. And though I write a blog I actually prefer getting these Christmas messages the old-fashioned snail mail way rather than electronically (and I will be pleased to get any reply you might choose to send via whatever medium.)

For more than 30 years the first one has come from the now long retired Senior Pastor of St. Peter Lutheran Church in Manhattan, New York, Dr. John Damm. He always includes a well-thought-out homily, an Advent theme.

This is followed by the assortment with which we are all familiar. They run the full gamut: highly artistic versions of ancient classic paintings, silly ditties with cartoon figures, messages allegedly written by pets. Some feel like the same sermon said in the same way year after year. At least three or four will feature the family biographies of budding Nobel Prize winners, the next Babe Ruth, Michael Jordan, Mother Teresa or Abraham Lincoln. I read them all with always a touch of disappointment when there is no personal note and even the signature is pre-printed.

Each one is guaranteed a second reading. Jane and I save each of those greetings where we can get at them every day. Then each morning we pull one out, re-read the message and say a short prayer for the sender. Since we get about 300 of these a year it works out great and by the following Christmas our Christmas Letter box is empty.

Of course, we send out our Christmas letter too. My wife Jane is the organized one in this marriage so we can find many of the letters of the 58 years of our married life. In re-reading them I find no literary masterpieces or eye-watering narrative. Yet these Christmas messages (both those sent and those received) are precious. They provide glimpses into the joy, trauma and everyday routines that make up our lives. And because they are in relation to a very special religious observance, they point not only to things transient but also to the friendships, love, values and hope that transcend not only the Christmas season but our very lives.

So, keep those cards and letters coming.

HORROR STORY: HOME

Breakfast at our home in Hong Kong in the early sixties was probably like breakfast in many homes; kids and adults gotta eat, everyone needs to be properly dressed for work and school with lunches packed and milk glasses drained. And it's time for morning prayers. In the midst of all this I suddenly heard a scream from nine-month-old son Tim. He had gotten away from the table and was on the floor. He had discovered the basket of washed and dried clothes waiting to be put away. Inside the basket he had found a wire coat hanger. In the process of playing with it he had managed to get the hanger hook lodged between his eyeball and his eye socket. Amidst his screams he was frantically swinging the hanger back and forth. I picked him up and slowly withdrew the hanger.

Then it was off to the emergency room, always a nightmare. When we arrived, we saw what we always saw at street clinics: a line of persons waiting that stretched to the end of the block. Never one wanting to claim any special treatment I held Tim in my arms and went to the end of the line.

However, in only a matter of minutes a staff person was there and invited us to the head of the line. My desire to see my son treated speedily overcame my reluctance to accept special treatment because of my "foreign status."

The doctor examined the eye. He noted a gouge in the eyeball, but said that it was not too deep. He applied some antibiotic ointment, assured us that he saw to it that it got to the bottom of the gouge and sent us home

Tim's eye healed well. But there are still moments when in my mind's eye I see that hanger being shaken, attached to Tim's eye socket. And the horror returns.

ೞ

HORROR STORY: LUTHERAN SCHOOL FINANCES

For centuries Lutheran schools around the world have been blessed by the outstanding commitment, skills, and sacrifices of their administrators. Each year their task becomes more complicated. Today's Lutheran school administrators and especially also the preschool administrators need to manage not only academic excellence and Christian distinctiveness but also public relations, buildings, heightened parental expectations, ever changing regulations, public health issues - and finances. And when it comes to finances some meet the challenge exceedingly well. Other cannot cope and end up with horror stories.

The Lutheran preschool director from New Jersey was in tears as she spoke with me on the phone. She had consistently withheld all FICA taxes (Social security, income tax etc.) from her staff. However, she had never sent in those funds to the appropriate government agencies. She had needed the funds just to keep her much loved school functioning. The day of reckoning came when she heard from the IRS. First, she cleared out her own personal bank account in an effort to keep her school alive. That was not enough. She knew she had to report the situation to her Church officers, when they would find out, she was sure she would be fired. She reported, was fired and the school was closed.

The national offices of the Lutheran Church asked me to pay a visit to the Lutheran school in St. Thomas in the Virgin Islands. Something down there didn't seem to be going well. I was happy to investigate. After all this school is one of the oldest Lutheran schools in the Western Hemisphere. I was pleased with what I found: good teaching-learning. The top citizens of that island were sending their children to this school. The principal was new. Finally, I asked him if there were any significant problems. He hastened to explain. "You see," he said, "I have been withholding FICA payments but have not sent them in to the USA Government to which we are accountable for them. Now I have received word from them of our delinquency. I don't even have the money for the base amount, much less for the deferred interest penalties." I asked him if his school board had a plan to deal with this. He replied, "Oh, no. I haven't told them yet. There is a meeting with them tonight and I was hoping you would tell them this story and give us directions for solving this problem." At the end of the term the school closed.

But the saddest of these horror stories took place in New York. The school was large and excellent. Teachers, pupils and families were all cared for. Learning was taking place. Self-esteem was being built. So, I was startled to get a telephone call shortly after midnight. One of their best teachers (a single mother) was calling. She was calling from her hospital bed and she was devastated by two terrible pieces of news she had just receive. First, she had been diagnosed with a fatal disease with a very short life expectancy. Secondly, the hospital finance department had called to tell her that her medical insurance was not in effect because the school had not submitted the monthly premiums. As she was trying to cope with this, another thought flashed into her mind. "I wonder if the school has sent in the pension and retirement fees they had deducted from my monthly salary." These were critical for the survival of her daughter. She said she knew it was after midnight but she wondered if I could do anything about it at once and come to the hospital to give her some hope.

To my (and her) dismay we learned that, in fact, the school had sent in neither health premiums nor retirement deductions for over a year!

I grieved deeply at her memorial service only a short time later.

A bit of good news in the midst of it. I contacted our wonderfully caring and competent attorney, Howard Capel, and he got right on the case. Together with his associate they got the Internal Revenue Service to drop all interest and penalty charges and arranged for time payment of the balance. And the Lutheran Church at the national level came through in a very compassionate way to assist with the medical bill and survivor benefits.

The lesson has been relearned; when finances are not handled appropriately the results create incredible horror stories.

80CR

PAT ROBERTSON AND OTHER RELIGIOUS FIGURES

Well, Pat Robertson has done it again. He asserted that the terrible hurricane which hit Haiti is the result of a pact the Haitians made with the devil long ago and that deal made long ago to sell their souls in return for freedom from the French has now come back to strike them with unimaginable devastation.

This kind of logic and religious belief is not new for Mr. Robertson. He has, of course claimed that Florida hurricanes of 2004-2005 were because Disney had Gay Day at its parks. Katrina was brought down by God in anger over the sins of Bourbon Street. Even 9-11 was essentially self-inflicted and sent by an angry God.

Naturally, I do not lay these disasters at the feet of a vengeful God. Rather the God whom I worship sees people hurting and suffering and weeps and calls us to reach out in compassion and sacrificial care.

Yet there is more. I think this is a time for leading spokespersons of the Christian faith - and especially those with an evangelical leaning - to publicly and insistently speak out. They should say, "Pat Robertson does not reflect Biblical (and especially Christian) thinking or dogma. He is wrong." Authentic Christianity points to a God with a special heart for those who hurt, and who mourns in sympathy with all who suffer loss and pain.

While I ask the Christian leaders to do this in connection with Robertson, I make a similar appeal to leaders in the Muslim world in their response to Umar Farouk Abdulmutallab. I would hope that every time an Islamic terrorist claims to take or attempts to take innocent life in the name of God and hope for eternal blessing, that leaders in that world should proclaim loud and clear, "This is not what we believe. This is not the Islam which we preach."

Let us all, if we must speak in the name of God, speak of a God who calls us all to strive for peace, prosperity and a reverence for life.

ℰ⃝ℛ

BOYHOOD DREAMS

I recall only two overarching boyhood dreams. The first (probably more fantasy than dream) was to be a professional baseball player, especially one in the image of New York Giant Mel Ott. Didn't we even share the same given name? During the baseball season I would hurry home from school, dig into the sports page of the newspaper and look at the stats for Mel Ott. Someday only the last name would be changed. That dream, of course, died young.

My second dream was to be Lutheran parochial school teacher just like my dad. That was a wonderful calling. Dad was one of the most respected persons in our entire rural community. He was a TEACHER. People asked for his opinion. He wore a white shirt, tie, coat and freshly polished black shoes to school - every day. When boys who had graduated from Zion Lutheran School went off to serve in World War II, the one person they made sure to write letters to was my father. Since he was also the church's organist and choir director, he played a major role at every wedding, funeral, baptism, anniversary. He even directed the brass band on a special bandstand at the annual school picnic. Lutheran schoolteacher, that was my dream. I never even considered any other option.

Thus, I was shocked once (and only once) when my mother startled me (I must have been about 6 years old) when she looked at me with loving eyes and asked, "Melvin, are you sure you want to be a Lutheran school teacher? Surely there must be some better option!" I now know that she asked this question out of a specific reality. It was during the Depression and the congregation had been unable to pay Dad his salary. We had even become dependent upon her more affluent brothers and sisters for clothes and extra food. Also, there had been some conflict in the congregation and some unkind things had been said about my dad. Mother spoke to me out of genuine mother's love. I explained to Mother that I had only one dream and was hanging on to that. She never again suggested an alternative and loved and supported me throughout my career and even told me she was proud to be my mother.

As I now look back to that dream of some eight decades ago, I affirm that it was a good dream and the reality of my career far exceeded my wildest dreams.

ℰᏉᏉ

MALE AND FEMALE

I recall with gratitude and appreciation the 100 or so principals who were my colleagues when served, first in Tracy and then in Glendale, California in the early 1950's. We met together often. They served me as mentors and models. They impressed me by not only serving as principals, but at the same time being full-time classroom teachers and more often than not also being their congregation's organist and choir director. One other factor stands out: All 100 of them were male.

In the mid 1950's I accepted a position as a major leader for setting up a Lutheran school system in Hong Kong (which today enrolls some 25,000 students). My memory is that when the World Mission Board considered candidates for that position, they looked at no female possibilities.

I recall with admiration and appreciation the Lutheran school principals who were my colleagues in Michigan when I served them as their District Superintendent in the late 1960's and early 1970's. They served from the heart of Detroit to the village of Bach. There were over 100 of them in those days. I visited in the homes of as many as possible. This, too, I recall, 109 were male; one was female.

In the later 1980's my duties took me to the Center for Urban Education Ministries in New York. It didn't take long to notice that more and more principals of urban Lutheran schools were female. We convened a significant number of them and asked them to share their stories. They told us that often they had been selected only when no male would accept the position. The more we listened the more we learned another obvious point. These women were committed, capable, professional models for all.

Today when I read the websites, blogs and other literature I am struck by the fact that one of the most challenging positions within the entire Lutheran Church is the position of Early Childhood Center Director. These leaders deal with incredibly complex issues ranging from extremely complicated tuition and fees schedules, to complicated salary schedules, to concerns ranging from peanut butter to recording devices hidden in the kids' back packs. Another reality hits me. Almost all of these competent servant leaders are female.

In reflection I am saddened again with the realization of how any society or segment of society deprives itself when it chooses to not utilize the gifts of all members of the society, male and female.

ℰℭ

LAHORE, PAKISTAN: PAIN, PLEASURE AND PRAYER

The headline screams: "43 Killed in Pakistan Blasts." The story gives the details. Suicide bombers hit a military section and the crowded market known as the R. A. Bazaar in Lahore, Pakistan. I read the details of another wave of violence carried out by Islamic extremists. Even though I am removed by time and distance from the place and the events, I hurt inside.

Twenty years ago, I was in that Lahore bazaar and in recalling it my mind floods with pleasant memories. I had done a series of workshops in Karachi with school, business and religious leaders from around the country. As I neared the end of my stay my host offered to fly me to Lahore. A class member said her uncle lived there and would be my host. And what a gracious host he was. He welcomed me to his home. Dinner was set before us and his wife who cooked it, hurried back into the kitchen for it was deemed inappropriate for this woman to be in our presence while we ate. As I got better acquainted, I told my host that I enjoyed the meal. And I asked for permission to personally tell his wife that. He agreed and said it was okay for me to have a conversation with her - with him as interpreter.

The next day was tour day. My host showed me the marvelous centuries-old beautiful sites of Lahore. He took me to the famous Shalimar Gardens. While there he explained that it was the hour of prayer so he took out his prayer mat, knelt on the grass and prayed.

Later he offered to take me shopping for some take-home souvenirs. To

94

my surprise he invited his wife to join us. She watched me but said nothing as I bought a small brass vase to take home. Then she disappeared. A little later she returned with an identical vase. "These would make a nice pair," she said. "I think your wife would enjoy these side by side."

When I left the next day, she came to say good-bye. Her husband translated for her. She asked him to thank me: I was the only non-Pakistani male with whom she had ever spoken. Together they gave me a peacock feather as a symbol of a brief but beautiful friendship.

And now I read of that beautiful city being blown up in the name of God. My prayers go to a God of all creation, whom I know desires peace upon earth.

ဆူဃ

CHRISTMAS MEMORIES: CHILDHOOD

My memories of Christmas in my childhood are all positive. This is amazing. I grew up during the Great Depression and my family had very limited financial resources. I am one of nine children and so there must often have been illnesses over the holidays. Early on I believed in Santa Claus and when I learned that was not true, some disappointment must have accompanied that. But all of those negatives have been erased.

The anticipation of Christmas still stirs my heart. On December 10 we were allowed to "hang stockings." And we did. They were those long ugly woolen grey things we hated to wear. But always on December 10 (my birthday) there would be something in that stocking; maybe an orange or a pencil. It was great discovering them.

We had a German song we sang counting off the days. The literal translation of the title is "Tomorrow Something Will Happen." The key line (which rhymed in German) was "Once more must we awake; then it will be Christmas Day." We changed the words to, for example, "10 more days must we awake" and we counted down the days. We loved singing that song.

About two weeks before Christmas I had to leave my precious (and usually rusted and in poor state of repair) little tricycle out overnight. During the night the birds would come and whisk away my trike. It was taken to Santa who happened to be my Uncle Walter who ran a blacksmith shop that doubled as Santa's workroom where trikes got repaired and repainted, always in red! It always reappeared under the Christmas tree.

I attended a Lutheran parochial school and we were responsible for the Christmas Eve Church Service. It was far from the Disney-like productions one finds today in many churches. It was utterly simple and maybe simplistic. No costumes, magi gifts or manger scenes. The teacher would ask a question, e.g. "Which high feast are we celebrating in these days?" The answers were all assigned ahead of time. And the previously designated student would be called up to give the answer "The high festival of the birth of the Christ Child." And thus, the Christmas Eve catechism went on for about 75 questions and answers. In between, some of the students would march to the front of the church and recite a little poem. This was followed by the entire classroom singing a traditional Christmas carol. (Throughout my eight years of elementary school this program was always conducted in German.)

It was tough to keep our focus on our assignments. Distractions were everywhere. We were wearing our new Christmas clothes, carefully sewn by our mother. To our left stood a massive cedar Christmas tree. In the early years an usher was positioned nearby with a wet rag on the end of a stick to douse any flames that might erupt dangerously from all the wax candles which lit the entire tree. And our eyes could simply not be diverted from glancing at what was piled under the tree. Under that big tree were arranged piles of plain brown grocery bags, one for each child! The bags held dreamed-for treasures: a fresh orange; several walnuts, some loose peppermint-like Christmas candies, and chewing gum. If it was a bit better year there might be a full package of Wrigley's Juicy Fruit gum in each bag; in leaner years there was only one stick. We pondered for days as to just when we would chew that rare gum.

The Christmas Eve Service was always early enough to allow families to go home, open their gifts, enjoy them, and return for early worship services on Christmas Day. At my home everything was according to ritual. For days we had not been allowed into my dad's study where Santa would decorate the tree and bring gifts. When it was time to enter, we lined up outside the door, eventually all nine of us kids, always by age, from the youngest to the eldest. The tree was full of fake icicles, homemade decorations and lights. The gifts were opened in reverse birth order and for at least three consecutive years Santa brought me my incomparable trike all decked out in new paint.

Christmas Eve celebration continued at my Grandmother's house. I have no memory of any gifts being involved. I do remember the food: fresh pork sausage and ham, homemade candy and cookies everywhere, freshly made eggnog with gallons of whipping cream in enormous punch bowls (duly spiked with bourbon). To the side was a smaller bowl without the alcohol for some delicate women and little children - and to the best of my memory no one ever monitored who drank from which bowl.

Then came a Christmas tradition apparently unique to Texas, the fireworks. We shot firecrackers, and rockets, roman candles and sparklers. Once a group of cousins of mine got very brave. They "borrowed" a couple of massive anvils from local blacksmith shops, filled a cavity in one of them with powder extracted from other fireworks, placed a fuse appropriately, positioned one anvil on top of the other, lit the fuse and produced the loudest Christmas Eve blast ever acknowledged in all of Williamson County, Texas.

Finally, home to bed so we could get up very shortly to head for Christmas Day Worship services and the special dinner to follow!

ଯଠଔ

HOLY THURSDAY: COMMUNING WITH THE SAINTS

Communing PLACES

This Holy Thursday marks exactly 70 years since I had my first holy communion. It was around the simple wooden altar of Zion Lutheran Church, Walburg Texas. In the years that followed I repeated the experience thousands of times at hundreds of other holy places. From cathedrals in New York and Helsinki to store front chapels in Hong Kong. From quiet secluded sanctuaries to the floors of bustling hotel meeting rooms. From among the olive trees of the Garden of Gethsemane to a rustic chapel at Yosemite National Park. From places of somber meditation to arenas filled with the jubilant sound of a thousand hymn singers. From places with names like Zion, St. Paul, Good Shepherd, and St. Thomas to Calvary. Always the PLACE in that moment was holy ground.

Communing PEOPLE

I recall those 12 nervous teenagers with whom I first communed and wonder where they now are, here or in heaven. I recall the multitudes of others who shared with me those precious elements: my sainted parents, my children now scattered around the world, the black saints who welcomed me as the only white in the assembly, those with whom we now share full communion in denominations with names like Methodist, Presbyterian, United Church of Christ, Moravian. I recall people next to me at the rail who exuded the scent of exquisite and expensive perfume and those who came in their sweat-filled work clothes. I recall an ancient Chinese grandmother and the tense bodies of GI's on R&R from Viet Nam. Always with those PEOPLE we heard the words "For You."

Communing PRESENCE

Today I recall that in every place, with whatever people, there was always bread and wine. There were always words. But there was more. There was the PRESENCE. Yes, it was the PRESENCE of mystery, of prayer, confession, reflection and resolve. But beyond it all was a greater Presence. For in with and under the forms of bread and wine was the very REAL PRESENCE of the One who said "This is My body; This is My blood."

ℰⱮℛ

I AM GLAD THE TEARS STILL FLOW

For the second Sunday evening in succession I felt the tears roll down my cheeks. I was surprised to find myself so emotionally affected by a television program. Both times I had been watching "60 Minutes." The first time the copious tears rolled was as I watched the images of children injured in Iraq and the efforts of one American woman to get them new legs, to correct terrible facial scars, to bring healing to body and soul. Those kids, damaged and repaired, touched me at the heart of who I am.

The second set of visuals was entirely different. They were of older men and women, some with scraggly dirty beards; others with clean clothes and eyes that betrayed bewilderment and disorientation, aloneness. These persons, too, had been in Iraq and in Afghanistan. They were adults, veterans from the US military. The other thing they all had in common: they were homeless, living on the streets of America. I became deeply aware that I, as a citizen, had asked them to go to war for me and now I, as a citizen was playing a role in the homelessness, despair, inadequate physical and mental health resources. And I wept.

ℰⱮℛ

Like millions of other kids on this day, today I remember my father. Of course, my memories are biased. They should be as I hope every kid has a positive bias in recalling their father. I certainly hope my kids bring a very positive prejudice (free even from justly deserved negative judgments) to this special day. So here go a few of my very fond and strong memories of my DAD.

Faith

My father was a man of deep religious faith. He believed in grace. I recall that at Dad's funeral the pastor said that he had a problem preaching on the text which my father had requested. My father had selected a text that referred to himself as "a chief sinner." The pastor said that no one who knew my father would ever have used that designation - but for Dad it was a take-off to point to grace, boundless love and unconditional acceptance. My father's faith in God, in family, in kids, in the possibility of a preferred future, continues to ground and inspire me. He even had faith that someday his beloved Chicago Cubs would actually win a World Series!

Trust

My dad trusted me. I recall that when I was still quite young, I lied to him. Even in that undeserving situation he trusted me and took me at my word. Toward the end of his life I came to tell him that I had made a major decision regarding my future and I wondered how he would react. He said "Mel, I raised you in a way that I could trust your judgment. I have always trusted your judgment 'Do what seemeth right to thee.'"

Worker

Dad worked hard, probably too hard. When I was young, he taught grades four to eight, was the principal of a two-room Lutheran school. He concurrently served as the congregation's choir director, organist, youth director, brass band director, custodian, and congregation secretary, all the while raising nine children, and sufficient pigs, chickens, cows and vegetables to provide food. During the hot Texas summer, he took himself and his kids into the fields to pick cotton, always with the injunction "In the field by sun-up!"

Story Teller

Dad told stories at home - especially when we kid pleaded with him to tell the stories of his childhood when wolves howled at night, horses suddenly stampeded, grandmother encountered chicken thieves, and his dad's black farm hands shared their own dreams of greatness. In school he told the stories of the Bible in such a way that recalling them sustains me to this day. At the Texas rural weddings (after he played the organ for the ceremony) there would come a time after much beer and barbeque when Teacher Kieschnick was asked to tell his fantasy stories about the bride and groom. Then he closed the entertainment with the appropriate version of how fortunate the bride or groom was to marry either a very large or a very petite spouse, always changing the words to fit the situation.

Teacher

For his entire career my Dad was often just called TEACHER Kieschnick. And that was certainly the most appropriate title. He taught all those years at the elementary school level. He taught the values of faith and trust and humor and integrity, but I also marvel at how much academic stuff he taught. In that little two-room school I, for one, learned proper grammar and to this day know how to diagram sentences and determine if a verb is transitive or intransitive. He taught us how to multiply and divide fractions, the names of the capitals of all the states, the three branches of government, and regularly checked to make sure we knew the names of all the secretaries on the US president's cabinet.

Lover

Each of us nine kids is convinced that we were Dad's favorite child. Later this love was extended to in-laws and grandkids. One night there must have been near 20 of us in his small house. We were sleeping all over the place with our blankets and pallets on the floor from wall to wall. I woke up during the night to see Dad just walking by that mass of sleeping family and his heart was aglow. He loved us all and thought we were all great. He often spoke of and constantly demonstrated his great love for his wife, our mom. One of the saddest moments I remember of my dad was when in his old age once late at night he confessed to me that his one regret in life was that he never made enough money to give Mom all that he would have liked. Of course, Mom would join us and especially me in saying "Dad, you gave us riches way beyond your wildest imagination!"

SOUNDS, SILENCE, COMMUNITY

Sounds

There are so many sounds I just love to hear. The doctor's voice, "Mother and baby are both fine." The grandkids in the room next door just having fun together. The key opening the front door as my teen-ager returns from her date. The Hallelujah Chorus. The roar of the crowd at a home game with my team scoring the winning run. The plop at the bottom of the cup after a long putt. The intimate whisper that says, "I love you." The very personal sounds of satisfying sex with one's spouse. The train whistle in the dark distance. The hustle and bustle of people, cars, buses, policemen, hawkers of central Hong Kong or downtown Manhattan. Soft and gentle or raucous and lively, I love sounds.

Sounds

There are so many sounds I hate to hear. A parent yelling putdowns to her child. Heavy rock metal music. Your flight has been delayed. The stock market is down 500 points. A religious zealot telling me that "if you just…" The answering machine telling me I have 21 messages. "Unfortunately, the test results came out…" The talk show host who just won't shut up. The alarm clock after what seems like just minutes since I fell asleep.

Silence

There is a silence I love. I walk in silence under the majestic redwoods of Muir Woods. The TV is off, no one speaks, no cars are within earshot. The rare quiet of the sanctuary before the prelude. The moment after the loud couple at the restaurant table next to ours has just signed their credit card slip and left. Parent-teacher conferences are over for the day and I sit at my desk alone. I stand alone at sunset over my parents' grave in the Texas country church graveyard. I lie awake at 2:00 a.m. and just reflect and all is okay.

Silence

There is a silence I don't like. I wait for the phone to ring with good news, but there is no ring. I make a presentation to a class, ask for reaction

101

and no one speaks. I ponder a tragedy, I ask, "WHY?" and can hear no response from anywhere. I do something well and await some affirmation but no words reach my ears. I seek for just the right words to say to someone in pain but come up only with silence.

Community

I reflect upon SOUND and SILENCE as I read about David Brooks' new book, "The Social Animal." From it I learn an essential truth: in all my sounds and silences there is a part of me that is seeking a "connection, a closing of the loneliness loop, an urge to merge a community." In all my sounds, in all my silences, I am never completely alone. I am connected with nature, with others, with the eternal.

So, when I find myself crying because a fellow human being is hurt, or sick, or disfigured or homeless or lost, my heart aches a lot. In the midst of the flowing tears I hear a tiny voice whispering, "I am glad the tears still flow"; for if those tears ever stop then I have stopped being fully human.

ဆဣ

THREE STRONG WOMEN

I have been blessed to be in a family line that has included many very strong women. Lately I have reflected upon just three of them.

Aunt Elizabeth became a widow responsible for two young children when she was just in her thirties. She managed it all by raising chickens and marketing them and the eggs they produced. In her old age she lived alone. One night a young man (possibly on drugs) appeared in her room. He was armed. He demanded she go get him money. She refused to budge. Instead she started a conversation. She reminded him that somewhere he must have a mother who loved him and who would be disappointed to see him robbing an old defenseless widow. She kept the conversation going as the would-be robber became more reflective, decided not to pursue the robbery and was about to leave. At that point Aunt Elizabeth said, "No, wait. Sit down. We are going to have a prayer." And so, she prayed for the young man, his mother and his future. She was never intruded upon again.

My mother had to be physically strong. She bore nine children. One summer she "put-up" 800 quarts of vegetables and fruits to feed us through the winter. She washed our clothes without a hot-water heater, wrung the clothes dry by hand and hung them up on wash lines. Then she starched and ironed basketsful of them. She nursed us all through red-eye, measles, mumps, whooping cough, scarlatina, poison ivy, broken bones and broken hearts.

One image stands out for me. Somehow or other the very large pasture surrounding our house, barn and sheds caught fire in the midst of a dry Texas summer. The parched grass and broom weeds were blazing and heading toward our home. Dad was not at home. Mother marshaled us. She got out five cans holding five gallons each and some old burlap bags. I can still see my mom lugging two enormous cans each holding five gallons of water. She ran to the edge of the fire some 100 yards away, wet down the burlap bags and beat down the flames at the edge of the on-coming conflagration. Then she ran back, refilled those cans and again she lugged them to the fire, instructing us to join her. She repeated this until the fire was extinguished. I still see her, not only struggling with those heavy containers, but after the fire breathing very heavily, completely exhausted, sweating, black with ash and sighing after saving our home from disaster.

My sister Mimi had already proven herself by rising to be first the head nurse and then the widely acclaimed administrator of a community hospital. Then one average Saturday morning she walked into the small Walburg State Bank to make a simple transaction. In the midst of this, two angry men walked in, armed and aggressive. They ordered Mimi to lie face down prone on the floor. She did. They ordered the teller to turn over the cash. He complied and still they fired at him with the bullet grazing his head. One of the robbers stood over Mimi straddling her body. Then just before exiting he fired and blew off the back of her head. Ambulances arrived; emergency care was provided. Contrary to every prognosis and due to Providence, old ammunition, and the strength and determination of one very strong woman, Mimi recovered enough to advance in her profession and receive statewide acknowledgment of her skills and leadership. Then recently she had a "medical incident." The attending physician who had not really studied her medical history said to her "Hmm, this activity seems to be the result of some severe trauma to your brain. Do you have any memory of something like that happening?" She remembers, of course, but it has not kept her from being one more of those strong women who continue to be for me, much-valued models and inspiration.

OBJECT OF CHARITY

Throughout my life I have been the blessed object of charity, well beyond my deserving or anyone's imagination. It begins with the early memory of me as a five-year-old kid at our church/school picnic. My uncle gave me a quarter. That amount was huge, enough for five ice cream cones or a hamburger, a cone, a candy bar, a strawberry soda pop and then another cone.

When I was in high school preparing to teach in the church, I received a most unusual gift. A bride from my home church had gone through the ritual of that time to pass around the bride's shoe and the guests would put in coins as a special gift for her. She decided not to keep it but to send it to me to help with my tuition.

When I was in college, I did not have the money even for a bus ticket from Concordia Chicago to Texas at Christmas time. So, on December 23rd I was busy as a bartender at a Christmas party at the Oak Park Club. When I got to my dorm after midnight there was a check from another uncle for $100, a full term's tuition at that time!

My first assignment after college graduation was as principal of St. Paul's Lutheran in Tracy, California. At Christmas the parents of my students gave me the cash to spend Christmas with my fiancée teaching in Michigan. When we returned a year later as a new couple, the pantry shower held for us caused our kitchen to overflow with goodies. This was followed by chicken for the fryer, tomatoes to can and an occasional six-pack to enjoy.

The gifts kept coming. One night at my next parish in Glendale, California we went to a dinner at the end of which a big television was rolled into the room. It was our first TV ever.

From there we went to Hong Kong where colleagues and parents of students, in spite of their poverty, were most generous with gifts of many kinds, including, for example, two freshly laid eggs a grateful mother sent from her meager little operation in gratitude for the education her children were receiving. Just before we boarded a flight to the USA to get medical care for my wife, who was suffering from a cerebral aneurysm, my 12-year-old son came running into the house. "Dad, the woman at that little shack of a store at the end of our street heard that Mom was sick. Here, she sent an orange for Mom and a bottle of beer for you!"

When a long recuperation period for my wife was demanded, the generosity we experienced more than matched our anxieties. The faculty wives of Concordia Chicago baby-sat a couple of times a week. Mabel Warnke who had visited us in Hong Kong provided a refrigerator and meals twice a week. When the editor of the church's periodical realized I did not have an overcoat he literally took his off his back and placed it on my shoulders.

It goes on to great lengths which overwhelms me (and might bore the reader): "The green fees are on me." Gift cards like "dinner for two at the steak house. "I'll host a meal at Gaddi's in the Peninsula." "Just take those hearing aids. I have been looking for someone who could use them."

Next month Jane and I take off for three weeks in China, all First Class and all paid for by friends, old and new! Probably most amazing of all is that when I get all these undeserved gifts the donors have never made me feel like an "object of charity." I have never felt like an object, but always like a person who reflects in gratitude, wonder and praise to the Giver and the givers of all these good and perfect gifts.

ଌୠଔ

CHINA/HONG KONG 2011 VISIT PART 2: HOSPITALITY

Almost all of the world's great religions call upon their followers to "practice hospitality." I have tried to follow that important injunction. However, on the trip from which Jane I just returned the tables were turned: We were the objects of others' hospitality, and at a level beyond my wildest imagination. I am still reeling in overwhelm.

It all started simply enough. One Sunday morning after I taught a class at my church, I announced that I would be gone for a few weeks as I was headed to China. A gentleman by name of Leon came up to me and asked if I needed assistance with air travel. I explained that that was not required, as the organization for which I was doing this trip had already purchased my round-trip ticket. However, in response to some impulse that I am not sure I know from whence it came I added, "But if my wife and I make it through 60 years of marriage next year and our health permits, we would like to celebrate with a visit China, and if you could help us out with a few frequent flyer miles so that we could move from the back of plane to the Economy Plus that would surely be appreciated."

This almost casual remark yielded a marvelous gift. Leon and Sarah booked us First Class to Beijing with return from Hong Kong. On top of that they provided accommodations at the top JW Marriott's in each of those cities. And more: they got us our visas, facilitated access to the Executive Lounges, and picked up all meal costs in Beijing.

When we arrived at our hotel in Beijing, Leon casually announced that Jane and I were there to celebrate our 60th. Immediately the check-in person slipped next door, spoke with the manger and returned with the announcement: "To help you celebrate, we are upgrading you to a corner suite with an extra sitting room, two baths and office space." We had barely arrived in that glorious space when the manager and a butler arrived with a magnum of champagne, two flutes and an assortment of sweets beautifully arranged on a bed of rose petals. And (believe it or not) this process was repeated some 10 days later when we checked into the Marriott in Hong Kong.

Of course, it didn't stop there. There was a Peking Duck Dinner at the premier Peking duck restaurant in Beijing (complete with a certificate showing the registered numbers of the two ducks we had eaten certifying that they were indeed of the genuine highest quality available anywhere in the country). When our host took us for dinner in the home of the top ophthalmologist of China, we tagged along as guests. We were greeted with a beautiful personal gift of a tea set, served a 20-dish meal, and fêted not only with Qingdao beer but also with a very good Moa Tai.

All of our travel and accommodations within China were given us by a marvelous friend, Laurie Li Xiao Hung and her husband Wang Qing. I first met Laurie when she was my country guide on the first of four tours I led in China. Our relationship went beyond the professional. When she visited the States, I was blessed to baptize her into the Christian faith.

Laurie is a very smart and effective businesswoman. When she was about two years of age she literally lived in a pigsty when her father as an intellectual was sent to the countryside by Mao Zedong for "re-education" during the Cultural Revolution. Now 50 years later she has utilized her amazing organizing, marketing, and service skills so that she now owns two apartments and two offices. One of those apartments she made available just for Jane and me for our stay in Xian. This was not just a place to sleep: She equipped it with a well-stocked bar, new silk bed coverings, specially arranged computer and phone access, and (get this) she moved a piano into the apartment and had it specially tuned so that Jane could play the piano while we were visiting. Of course, she hosted us everywhere we went. We couldn't even pay for a cup of tea.

It keeps going: Because Laurie is in the travel business, she arranged for one of the very top tour guides in all of China to give us a personalized tour of the Tierra Cotta Warriors with reserved VIP parking space included. When we went to visit the Shaan Xi Provincial Museum, Ping, our guide, was really such an expert that I commented upon it. Lauri's reply, "Of course, she is the best. You must know that when Bill Gates and Warren Buffet were in China, she was appointed their official guide!"

Laurie and her husband Qing (whose government official boss had loaned us the car for our visit) took us everywhere, served us in special restaurants (including the one where our menu was a succession of eight different kinds of specially prepared mushrooms), entertained us at a Tang Dynasty Cultural show and helped us meet a university professor who had taught our son years ago when he studied in China.

It was Laurie who gave us the tickets to Guilin and who paid for Peter, our guide, who took us down the Li River. It was Laurie who had her colleague in that city host us for a gorgeous dinner and sent us on our way with gifts. (See my upcoming blog entry on Religion in China, for Laurie took us to a very special worship service with her family.)

In spite of my protests that I wanted to be the host, the Parent Effectiveness Training licensee in Shenzhen feted us at the plush Seaside Sheraton Hotel, which at lunch featured a gorgeously decorated 60th wedding anniversary cake, all documented by the official photographer whom she employed to record our little celebration. The host by the name of Coco hired a private car to ease our exit from China and entry into Hong Kong where this amazing hospitality just kept going. Private transportation everywhere on a Mercedes driven by former student Kim Lin Chu who hosted us with meals at places like the Peninsula and Repulse Bay hotels. This happened after another couple of former students met us virtually upon our arrival at our hotel to give us a relaxing massage, provide us with a generous wad of "walking around" money, gave us a cell phone and an assortment of other gifts. Other alumni and friends just kept feting us: at their home, at The American Club, the Yau Yat Chuen Club etc. It all came to a grand finale when some 150 alumni threw a massive 60th wedding anniversary celebration formal dinner with much multi-media, humongous wedding cake, free-flowing wine, gifts, excellent emcee, thanksgiving prayers, dedicatory books, the naming of Kieschnick Garden etc., etc.

Then first-class travel home and now the memories to last beyond a lifetime.

CHINA/HONG KONG 2011 VISIT PART 3: THE CHURCH IN CHINA

I make no claims on being an expert on the Christian church in China today. I simply reflect upon my personal experience in the churches my wife Jane and I visited there last month. The first Sunday we visited the Beijing Chongwenmen Church. Like all registered churches in China today it does not claim any denominational affiliation, as denominationalism has been declared illegal in China. However, the brochure of the Chiongwenmen Church speaks of it being established in 1870 under the auspices of the American Methodist Church. Today it is a registered "Three-Self Church." As such it has three important characteristics. One, it must be self-governed, that is, not accountable to any foreign hierarchy or Board like the Vatican or an American Mission Board. Secondly, it must be self-propagating. Foreign evangelists are not permitted and the evangelistic preaching must all be done by Chinese. Thirdly, it must be self-financing. Restrictions for the operating funds of local churches in China are severely enforced.

The service we attended was one of five that the congregation held that day. Four were conducted in Mandarin and one in Korean. The church was packed - at least a thousand worshipers. I noted the great diversity. While women were in the majority there were certainly many males present. The age grouping was fairly representative of the general population. The dress was "middle class informal." Two female pastors served the congregation. The beautifully robed women's choir sang beautifully. The hymns and readings were posted on the overhead screens and the audiovisuals were all done very professionally.

As foreign visitors, we were seated in the section equipped with headphones and we could select English as the translated (interpreted) language. We were only four Americans among the many visitors who were introduced and the attractive young woman who sat next to me introduced herself (in English) as coming from Russia.

The liturgy was traditional, with the readings the same as those read by thousands of other Christian churches around the world. Aside: This is one reason I like the traditional designated readings. I can be in a Christian church anywhere in the world on any given Sunday and know that the people of Calvary Lutheran Church, Solana Beach, California will be listening to exactly the same reading on that Sunday. Note: no offering was received, but offering receptacles were at the door as one left.

The second Sunday we went to church in a smaller city some 60 miles west of Xian. We attended there because our Chinese host, Laurie Li, has a mother and brother who are members of that congregation. It is quite unusual for any foreigners to be in that church and very rare (if ever) for a foreigner to address the congregation. I was very clear that I did not intend to "preach the sermon." The elders did get permission from their duly-appointed Government Liaison Officer for me to bring greetings, to lead a prayer, and to speak the benediction. This church, too, had about 1,000 in attendance that day. The church was packed. The women and men's choir were beautifully robed and did an outstanding dramatic presentation of readings and song. Even with several thousand members this church does not have a pastor, as there simply are not enough pastors ordained to serve all the parishes. So, this church, Immanuel by name, was led by three elders, one of whom is part-time at the seminary and hopes to be ordained and then serve as pastor of this church.

This church, too, had, of course been closed during the Mao years. The churches were all converted to warehouses, factories, even arsenals. But now they are being restored (sometimes even with Government assistance).

Just three asides: 1. When the pastor introduced us, he mentioned that we were celebrating our 60th wedding anniversary. The congregation applauded vigorously. During communion tens of members stopped by our pew and used their cell phone cameras to have their pictures taken with us. But most surprising was that after telling about our wedding the elder announced the Psalm reading for the day. And it turned out to be exactly the verses (Psalm 34:1-4) that the pastor had used as the homily text when we were married all those years ago in Ft. Wayne, Indiana. 2. After the service Jane and I and Laurie's family were hosted to a very simple, yet profoundly moving luncheon in a little room in the back of the church. It was just salted peanuts, a green vegetable, some bean curd and a lovely steamed fish, but in that setting and out of that poverty (the lead elder's monthly salary is $80) I was moved almost to tears. 3. Our host's brother is a member of that church. For years he was a silent member as he was a Communist Party member and dared not be exposed as a Christian. However, the climate has changed, he is "out" as a Christian and even sings in the choir where all can see him.

Fact: There are probably over 100 million Christians in China today. They come from all classes of society and are of all ages. They meet in registered state-approved churches and in non-official house churches. Sometimes they are persecuted, jailed and even killed. But generally, the church is seeing a renaissance which is affecting all levels of society and the individual stories could fill volumes

ഇ൦രൂ

CHINA/HONG KONG 2011 VISIT PART 4: ONE CHILD POLICY

The trip to China from which I recently returned was trip number seven since 1989. On each trip virtually every one of my Chinese hosts has chosen to talk about China's one child policy. This is very understandable because almost everyone in China is affected by it. First put into action in 1978, it limits family size to one child for all couples except those in selected rural areas, minority groups and parents whose first children are a set of twins.

The results are dramatic. It is estimated that half a billion births have been prevented. In the past, births of female fetuses were often avoided through abortion. It is now illegal for any person to reveal to a pregnant mother the gender of a fetus as shown on a sonogram). Births of daughters were often unreported so that the couple would wait for the second child (hopefully a male) and that birth would be recorded as "first child." All of this has resulted in a situation where there are approximately 117 young males for every 100 females. Another result from this endeavor is that India has, or soon will, exceed China as the world's most populous country. Another obvious outcome is that the number of younger people in the workplace who support the elderly is now dramatically reduced.

Family dynamics are, of course, significantly influenced. People have no aunts, uncles or cousins. Two sets of grandparents have only one grandchild among the four of them. Parents wonder if their one child will be able to support them in the traditional way of caring for them. There are even for-profit endeavors to provide Senior Citizen retirement communities that can be a source of profit for those who operate them. And, to date, there are virtually no state-mandated regulations for such endeavors.

Enforcement of the one child policy has also become more difficult. Three years ago, I still heard female elementary teachers saying that if they already had one child (a daughter) they sometimes were forced to take a pregnancy test to ensure that if they were pregnant, they would be required to get an abortion. In my last two trips I was told that this practice has now been stopped. In the past, all persons had severe limitations as to where they could live. This was all government-assigned. Now, there is much greater freedom of choice and people buy their own apartments. In the past, families with more than one child were on a lower admissions priority for hospital care than families with only one child. That, too, is not something I heard about as still being practiced.

A significant impact has been on parenting styles. While this may be true in all cultures, it is my belief that the "authoritarian' or "permissive" reality is doubly true in China. Each parent will have only one child. Each grandparent will have only one grandchild. One response is that some really want that child to be an absolutely outstanding perfect child in every way and so the elders are very strict, very authoritarian, often quite punishing of unacceptable behavior. On the other extreme, are those parents and grandparents who say, "You are our only child (grandchild). You are the empress/emperor in our family. Whatever toy, or clothing, or gadget, or second McDonalds you want. It is yours!" To suggest to parents that there is an alternative to these two options is a very hard sell, is counter culture and is why the introduction of Parent Effectiveness Training in China is moving ahead very, very slowly.

A recent change I have noticed: I had several people, especially women, say they would be just as happy or even happier to have a girl child than a male child. One taxi driver father with whom we chatted even said that he wished that one of his two children were a girl so that he would get at least one dowry!

As indicated above, there is a growing concern as to how the younger generation will be able to support the much larger older generation. Just last month I was told that in March there was a significant change in policy. Under the new policy, if both husband and wife are themselves single children, then they are allowed to have two children. The other thing that I experienced, especially in Shanghai and the more affluent urban areas is that couples are choosing to have more than one child because they now have incomes to overcome the state-imposed penalties (poorer housing or higher taxes et sim). They have the resources for a second child so they choose to have them. Concurrently (especially in places like Shenzhen), young couples are choosing to live together without formal marriages and those couples are either not having any children at all or are significantly delaying the birth of their first child. Lastly, the divorce rate in urban areas is rising dramatically (50% now in some areas) so those couples, too, are choosing to not have even that one child.

Three things are certain: 1. China central government will continue to adopt and attempt to enforce a countrywide "population growth policy." 2.

Enforcement will vary greatly from province to province. 3. Children of both genders will be conceived, born and grow up in a very complex interconnected world that last week experienced the birth of its seven-billionth living resident.

ℰᴑℭℛ

TOUGH AND TENDER

My colleague Marlene gets it. For years she was principal of a large urban school, Queens Lutheran in New York. She served so well that she was named a National Distinguished Elementary School Principal and honored for that at the White House. She knew how to be tough.

One day as the kids were being released at the end of the school day, she heard that the older kids were being confronted outside the school by a drug dealer. It took her about one New York minute to get to him. "You get out of here – now! And don't ever return!" But the dealer was not so easily rebuffed! "Lady, this is a public street. Now you let me alone or I will break your leg!" Marlene got into his face and replied "You can break not only my legs, but every bone in my body and you will not get to my kids! Now get your ass out of here before I call my friend Bob at the police precinct office just down the street." The dope pusher left and was not seen again around Queen's Lutheran School. Marlene's toughness paid off.

Some years later when Marlene was at her desk in Manhattan as Executive Director of The Lutheran Schools Association of New York tears were streaming down her face and she had to avert her eyes. She was looking right down Columbus Avenue all the way to where she looked in unbelief and horror as the Twin Towers crumbled on 9-11. It was then that her tenderness took over.

Marlene with great assistance from John Scibilia and others at Lutheran Disaster Response moved in to help the victims and their families. Marlene's special concern was for kids in Lutheran schools of New York. At least 60 of them, preschoolers through high school had lost a parent or grandparent in that disaster. Marlene was at the funerals; she was there to comfort children. She was there to hug teachers. She was there to cradle in her arms those who had lost loved ones. She was there to embrace the little ones who came running to put their arms around her legs whenever they heard an airplane

112

come in for a landing. She was tender. Her tenderness moved her to action. Funds were raised so that the tuition of those kids who had lost parents or grandparents were guaranteed Lutheran school tuition up to the time of their graduation. To this day her tears flow when she goes to the Twin Towers Memorial Fountain and lets her fingers scroll over the names of those who had kids in Lutheran schools.

Tough and tender. That's the paradigm for what it takes to be a successful urban school principal or teacher. I see it especially in the Lutheran schools of New York and Milwaukee. Those teachers and principals are tough. They hold their kids and their parents accountable. No excuses for homework not finished. No excuses for not showing up at assigned parent-teacher conferences. No excuses for using street language on the school campus. Those teachers and principals are tough.

And they are tender. They love those kids, hug them when they are afraid, pray with them when they feel hopeless, tutor them when they have academic problems and pat them on the back when they succeed.

That's the way Marlene does it and that is the way kids who attend Lutheran urban schools still experience it. That is how I hope to live: Tough and tender!

ဆာ

RITUALS

I was surprised to feel the tears streaming down my cheeks. That seldom, if ever, happens when I am watching television. But it happened last Monday while I was observing the inauguration of the USA president. My tears were not related to the politics of the day. Rather they flowed because of my emotions being caught up in the ritual. I was moved by the singing of the ancient American classics like "America, The Beautiful" and "The Battle Hymn of the Republic." My eyes joined the poet as he verbally toured us from the redwood forests to the lobster traps of Maine. The waving of handkerchiefs by the thousands. The peaceful passing of the torch. Yes, the ritual stirred up patriotic feelings aroused by Zion Lutheran School picnics in Walburg, Texas to hot dogs at the American Consulate in Hong Kong. All it took was the ritual to lead to remembrance, pride and petitions.

That's what rites and rituals do. And that is why each of us must play our part in preserving them. Keep those family rituals alive. Recreate those birthday party rituals with birthday cake loaded with candles, and home-make chicken salad sandwiches and ice cream. Some are silly like singing a crazy version of the O' Tannenbaum Story told with a new twist each Christmas Eve. Others are formal like the prayers and blessings of late-night family devotions.

Lovers of all ages need to keep the rituals alive, the times and way we kiss, the gifts we exchange, the looks we sneak, the special touches.

Those of us who are spiritual know that all faiths have rituals around births and deaths and new beginnings. In my church the Holy Eucharist and Baptism are absolutely essential.

And so, too, our country is well served by all those wonderful rites around inauguration. Regardless of our political persuasion we reflect as the oath of office is taken, as the National Anthem is sung, as the pledges are made, the prayers spoken, the military parades…

Rituals connect us to the past, ground us in the present and propel us into the future.

છાબ

LAZY SATURDAY

I'm having a lazy Saturday. Got up late, ate a leisurely breakfast, took my walk, watched golf, replied to emails. Nothing scheduled for this evening. This is a new experience in my life and I am enjoying it.

Saturdays were big when I was a young kid. My father was a teaching minister in a rural Lutheran church and school. We lived in the "teacherage" - aka "parsonage." There were a couple acres of land that went with that. So, there were gardens to weed, what seemed like acres of grass to be mown with the hand mower, corn to be husked for the chickens and cows, and manure to be piled up.

While I was doing this my dad was "up at church." He cleaned the church, posted the hymn numbers, practiced the pipe organ and prepared the Bible Class he taught every Sunday for decades.

I felt like I had a role in helping Dad in his ministry. My job was to polish shoes, especially his. They were always patent leather black. They had to be able to give off a reflection from the buffed shine. I loved getting them ready for him.

In my high school days, I attended Concordia Academy, a boys-only ministry prep school. We had classes until noon on Saturday. During football season we ran directly from class to the University of Texas football stadium. For 25 cents each we could sit in the end zone and cheer on the Longhorns. In my four years there twice I had a date. They were nice - and led to nothing exciting.

Saturdays at college were wonderful. Sports and dates, especially the three years with Jane, who is now my wife. If I had set enough pins in the bowling alley to have a bit of cash, we would take the El to the Chicago loop and see a movie. Always (except for one 1:30 a.m. permit per semester) required to have her checked in to her women's dorm by 11:00 with the house mother waiting to make sure our good-night embrace did not last too long or ever dare to end in a kiss witnessed by another person.

Then came 50 years of teaching, administering, raising kids, traveling the world. Saturdays were always full.

But now I have passed my 85th birthday and I am keeping my vow (most of the time) to be retired. Today I am doing that. I wonder if it will be true for me that on this Saturday, I will be ready for bed at around 9:00 p.m.

☜☞

AUSTIN, TEXAS: PERSONAL MEMORIES

In 1941-45, Austin Texas was my home. It was about 35 miles from my rural Texas home one mile from Walburg. Walburg still welcomes all visitors with its town sign that announces: "Walburg: Home of 88 friendly people and one old Grouch." I went to Austin after finishing eighth grade and enrolled at Concordia Academy of Texas, a boys only dormitory school for persons preparing for the pastoral or teaching ministries of the Lutheran Church.

That Concordia campus was home. We ate, slept, played sports and endured lower classman hazing. We were not allowed off campus except for Saturday afternoon and to go to church (twice each Sunday). Our dorms had two to a room. Times were tough and our meals were spare. Cereal, the same boxed stuff every morning for breakfast and cheese and baloney for the evening meal at 5:00. Chapel services every morning and every night. At 10:00 p.m. the dean came to each room to check and make sure we had pulled down our Murphy beds from the closet and were in bed. It was a close-knit community with lots of good and some not so good or ethical stuff going on in the lives of the forty to fifty of us young boys studying there in a very cloistered, girl-free environment.

To go down town to Congress Avenue was a treat. We went for five cents each way on the city bus. The state capitol was always an attraction. There was a place for wonderful chocolate shakes (which at 15 cents each we could afford a few times a year). We would not venture below Sixth Street, as that was the hub of really bad stuff we weren't supposed to even know about.

Austin was where my eldest sister Erna worked. She had given up a college scholarship to work and send home the money so that I, her younger brother, could "study for the holy ministry." She helped me get a job at Wukash Brothers Café where I slowly advanced from a potato peeler and dish washer to waiter and where I could earn twenty cents an hour plus tips. In the three years I worked there never once did a customer leave a tip as high as one dollar.

Austin was and is the home of the University of Texas, Memorial Stadium and Saturday football. I never missed a home game. We ran there after classes on Saturday, scrounged up the twenty-five cents needed for a seat and cheered them on. At one point we discovered that the Coliseum was left open after the games so on Sunday a bunch of us went there, found a group of equally eager and foolish black teen-agers and played each other in tackle football on that hallowed field, all without helmets or any other protection. The septum in my nose is still not straight.

Now I need to get back to Austin with its 850,000 people doing electronics and computers and its wonderful music and bands. But until that happens, I will let my very selective memory recall to me four glorious years of adolescent discovery, growth and dreams.

ഔൽ

CHICAGO LATE 1940'S

Making my first visit to Chicago in late August 1945 was a big deal. The train-ride from Texas to there was my first ever experience with rail travel. World War II had ended only a couple weeks earlier. I knew the city would be immense to this 17-year-old boy from Walburg, Texas. My father who had made the same first-ever train trip some thirty years earlier had given me very detailed instructions on how to use the El to get me to Concordia Teachers College in suburban River Forest. But I was met at the Union Station and my first El ride didn't come until weeks later.

Yet the El rides help define Chicago for me. As we went by crowded tenements it was a new world for this rural kid. Encountering people of many different ethnic groups and black people at all economic levels was ever eye-opening.

Visiting the Loop was (and still is) always special. Perry Como at the State Theater, New productions (at very low student ticket prices) at The Goodman theater, the Lakefront, Buckingham Fountain, Outer Drive, Michigan Avenue, the stockyards, the South Side, Maxwell Street (where I reinforced my biased ethnic stereotyping.) Just imaging these still stirs my heart.

And in the middle of the heart is Jane Addams Hull House: a community settlement for "young girls." We visited that as a class assignment. But what attracted me was not Jane Addams but another Jane who wore a unique pair or earmuffs. I introduced myself and told her I liked those earmuffs. Now sixty-five years later the earmuffs are long gone but Jane and I still share those memories and five kids and eight grandkids.

It was in the Chicago area that Jane and I got certified to be Lutheran teaching ministers. In that role we have traveled the globe and lived all over, yet without Chicago's Hull House it might never have happened. Together we still visit Chicago and I still love that city. Pick any ethnic food and you know some of the best will be in Chicago. If you need to keep hope alive after decades of evidence to the contrary, visit Wrigley Field. Want to see good art, look at Picasso at the Art Museum or other ancients and moderns at lots of other places. Look at the exotic sea creatures and enjoy the cafeteria at Shedd Aquarium close to Soldiers Field. Listen to good Bach music at worship at St. Luke's Lutheran. I can stop by (as close as security allows) at the Obama Chicago mansion and recall visiting my son when he lived in that very home as a street worker for alienated youth, or go just a little farther south (but lock your car better than I did as it cost me my new expensive camera) and visit the University of.

I think O'Hare wasn't even there in my college days. All subsequent school-time trips were via the thumb of a hitchhiker until I got my own car. So, whether it was or is by train, plane or thumb I am always ready to head there.

Chicago - it's my kind of town.

ഇരു

HONG KONG 1956

Welcome

Jane and our four-year-old David stared out the window of the descending TWA Constellation. We skirted (it seemed like by just a few feet) the hills around Kai Tak Airport. When we walked down the ramp into the sweltering September heat, the first thing I noticed was that we had actually landed and taxied across a public street that had barriers put up to allow for our landing. Then came the typical Chinese welcome. Some Chinese teachers from a Lutheran school, a group of Lutheran missionaries and even the President (Bishop) of the Lutheran Church-Missouri Synod were all there to welcome us. We were immediately herded into small cars and taxis and were off to Winter Gardens where a 12-Chinese meal awaited us. We were welcomed. And that was typical of all. Fellow workers who were overwhelmed with challenges could hardly wait for a few new hands. Our Chinese colleagues were welcoming beyond any reasonable expectations. They endured our terrible attempts at Cantonese. They laughed with us and not at us as we negotiated chopsticks. They graciously held us back when we forgot that cars traveled on the left side of the street. They understood when we were slow to bow or when we did not immediately have a name card to exchange when we were introduced.

Assaulted

While the welcome was warm, the entire experience felt like an assault. Chairman Mao had won in China. Refugees by the tens of thousands were fleeing into British Hong Kong. In 1945 it had a population of 500,000. Ten years later there were two million (and now there are seven million). People everywhere, on the streets, under staircases, on the roofs, in the parks, in every stairwell. With babies in their arms and on their backs, mothers grabbed at us as we entered the restaurant and eagerly clutched at the bags of leftover food from the meal when we departed. Two weeks after arriving I was walking down the road in the midst of a riled-up mass. Unrecognized by me, I was walking in the middle of a riot. Bullets entered the wall of the classroom I had just vacated. On the street the wife of the Swiss Consul General was tragically killed while riding in her car, just below where I had been teaching. A man ran at me with what I thought was a half-drunk bottle of Chinese wine. Minutes later I learned it was a bottle of explosives. We stayed cooped up in our little apartment and waited until things calmed down under the excellent response by the British and local police.

Challenged

I can still list a few of the many challenges: finding an affordable apartment, keeping Davey occupied in that tiny upper-floor apartment we shared temporarily with two women not used to having a kid around, figuring out when to take a bus or a ferry or a rickshaw or a tram, or a taxi, or to just walk. Learning to never, never drink un-boiled water. Even my faith in a just God had to face the reality that I had just walked by a 12-year-old who I am pretty sure was dead of starvation before the next day's sun rose.

Inspiration

Yet it was all-inspiring. My colleagues, both American and Chinese were determined to make it work. Everyone wanted schooling and that is what I was there to help provide. Faith had been discovered and was rewarded with the sight of belief, trust and moving forward confident of the future.

Within a very short time I learned to love Hong Kong. I still do. I am encouraged by my Chinese friends, I am energized by the resourcefulness of the Hong Kong people, I am enthralled with the beautiful lights and architecture, I am blessed by four children born to Jane and me in Hong Kong. I still salivate at the thought of the good food and remember the contrast of the city pavement and housing blocks with the greens of the Royal Hong Kong Gold Club. I loved Hong in the late 1950's. Now I go back at every opportunity and there are several more Hong Kong blog entries in me just waiting to get written.

శ్రీఆ

ANN ARBOR, MICHIGAN

The late 1960's and early 70's was a great time to live in Ann Arbor, Michigan. It was a typical university city full of the then current unrest. Students were in protest. Young men went without shaving and young women without bras. I went with my teen-aged son, David, to my first (and only rock concert) where marijuana smoke filled the air.

I was Superintendent of the 117 Lutheran elementary and high schools in the state. Our office became "occupied" by a group of black activists who insisted they would not leave until they were paid several million dollars in "reparations' for past injustices. We dialogued with them, served them coffee and assured them no money was forthcoming but that we would stay with them as long as they stayed. My memory is that well before 10:00 p.m. they had decided to "call it a day." They left and they never returned.

But for all of us it was time to reassess our ministry to and with our black brothers and sisters. Dr. Pete Pero who was serving in Detroit and his black allies taught me a lot. There were 17 Lutheran schools within the city limits of Detroit, some of them with all-black enrollments. Those teachers, students and parents were patient with me, accepted me and broadened my horizons.

My memories of the principals across the state are very positive. While the schools of Detroit may have had very diverse student bodies the schools in places like Bach or Frankenmuth were still all-white and often all-Lutheran. Interestingly one of the things I remember of those days forty years ago is that the state highway department did an incredible job of keeping all highways open during snowstorms and I do not recall ever having to cancel a school visit because of weather!

It was a great time to be politically active, especially in the interest of school choice. I helped form the Michigan Association of Non-Public Schools, sat on a special Education Committee of the state Senate, was invited to meet with President Nixon, and served as Vice-president of the now defunct Citizens for Educational Freedom. One of the great joys of all this was that I had two associates, Don Kell and Roland Boehnke and the three of us together with our aide, Elinor Donohue, were always challenging and supporting each other into new ways of thinking and acting.

We lived in Ann Arbor for only four years but that was enough time to learn to know its excellent restaurants and friendly bars where Lutheran principals (all except one were male!) could gather, drink a few beers together and sing songs to our hearts content. The University of Michigan football stadium was the site of some great football fetes and the frozen feet of a whole den of boy scouts whom I took there. The memory of that university may have played a role years later when our daughter Elizabeth returned there to earn her Ph.D.

Ann Arbor - a good place of fond memories and intellectual growth.

ஓௐ

BEIRUT, LEBANON

My memories of my time in Beirut, Lebanon are all positive and strong with an undertow of emotions calling me to return. The year was 1968 and I was on my way to chair a conference on Lutheran Education around the world. The Conference was to be held in Hong Kong and on my way there I visited educational institutions in Europe and Asia, with Beirut being a highlight.

One of the things that made it so memorable was my guide. He was an Arab who was native, had converted to Christianity and was very insightful into the history and the special dynamic of that centuries-old domain called Lebanon.

He gave me a wonderful tour of the city of Beirut: the harbor overlooking the tranquil Mediterranean is breath taking. The drive through the countryside down to the historic Tyre and Sidon plunges one into Biblical history. The well preserved as well as the abandoned fortresses of the Crusades pointed to a darker time of humanity's inability to live peacefully among people of different faiths. Unfortunately, we did not have enough time to visit the majestic Cedars of Lebanon.

My host explained some of the unique features of life in Lebanon. Then, as now, representation in the governments is on a rationed basis. Seats and offices are divided up in the same proportion as the faiths represented, presently Christianity, Islam and Judaism. When I was there Christianity actually was entitled to a small majority of positions. Now Islam is dominant, just about equally divided between Sunni and Shiite.

After returning from Tyre and Sidon we spent several hours on the beautiful campus of the American University. Originally established by Christian missionaries it continues to be a seat of higher learning for people of all faiths. The tree-lined campus is home to many professors from America and some of them graciously hosted me for stimulating conversations.

The highlight of the visit came when it was time to eat. We sat in a gorgeous restaurant at the very edge of the sea. We were eating the meal long-ordained as the official repast of the country: mezze. There must be a minimum of thirty dishes. They just kept arriving. There were items that looked like tapas from Spain and anti-pasta from Italy, multicolored dishes of vegetables, fruit, meat, tea leaves, sea creatures and plants. Delicious, every one of them and all washed down by arak, the anise flavored liquor of the region.

Tragically, the history of Beirut and Lebanon has seen painful and dark days since I was last there. The worst disaster for U.S. Marines since World War II was when 285 were killed in an attack by a suicide bomber which resulted in President Reagan ordering all U.S troops out of Lebanon in 1983. Recently the militant Islamic group Hezbollah has established a strong presence. And now Lebanon is caught up in the Syrian revolution and coping with sectarian violence and an avalanche of refugees.

My heart goes out to the people of Beirut. Even as I reflect upon their current struggles, I have wonderful memories of a warm people who love their country and are models of hospitality that I would do well to emulate.

ഇൽ

SELMA, ALABAMA

My first visit to Selma AL was in 1962 - three years before that city gained everlasting fame as the site of the Bloody Sunday racial confrontation at the Edmund Pettus Bridge, one of the sparks that ignited the entire civil rights movement in America. I was there to visit Concordia College, an institution of the Lutheran Church-Missouri Synod. The Board for Lutheran Higher Education knew that I was putting together a school system in Hong Kong and they wondered what lessons that experience might bring to the development of black schools in the south of the USA.

Concordia Selma had been established already in 1922. While it was called "college," my memory is that it served only students in grades eight to twelve with a few in the first two years of college.

I spent the day visiting classes, meeting with students and eating lunch and dinner together in the dormitory dining room. At the end of the day I was in overwhelm. I was deeply disturbed and saddened at the very low academic level of the students - in spite of the extraordinary commitments of their teachers. Then I was very upset by the amount and quality of the food. I knew that the students in "my" schools in Hong Kong had much higher academic achievement - and even though they were poor refugees, their daily meals were so much better than my new friends at this school.

As mentioned above, this was not due to a lack of commitment of the teachers - nor even of the desire to learn of the students. It is just that the elementary school education was of such inferior quality that good high school/college work was exceedingly difficult.

I walked through the town. Even then I noted that well over half of the population was poor and black. Now the percentage of the Selma population that is black has reached 80%.

The president of the college was Walter Ellwanger, a most remarkable man. He was deeply committed to racial equality; his family had helped found the Lutheran Human Relations Association, the first formal group in the Lutheran church advocating for our black brothers and sisters. Dr. Ellwanger and his wife spent almost twenty years at this school and he did it all: taught, managed the dorms, raised the money, maintained discipline and even directed the choir. I will never forget that choir practice. Even though this was an all-black school the songs all seemed to be English translations from old German tunes and chorales. The choir was good, but somehow or other their mood just wasn't right. And then at 9:30 pm Dr. Ellwanger announced, "And now, as always, we will close with the Negro National Anthem." And with that the choir plunged into "Lift Every Voice and Sing." The music got louder, the harmony deeper, the spirit moving, and the emotion transforming. I hear it and feel it to this day

I also remember my experience after that late choir practice. I went to the home of the president, a distinguished old southern mini-mansion. I was assigned an upstairs bedroom. There I finished reading the novel, which had been engrossing me: "To Kill A Mocking Bird."

The next day I met with the legendary Rosa Young who must have been in her eighties. Here was a woman with an unmatched devotion to black children in the south. She knew that the public schools were not available to many of them. The quality of their black schools was a shame. She started a group of 18 or more church-related black schools in Lutheran congregations and there, using all black teachers, she provided basic literacy for kids for whom this was otherwise unavailable.

Side note: I visited one such school outside Mobile. I noticed that some children did not even have their own desk - and were sitting on the floor using a church pew for the writing surface. Fifty years later a distinguished educator Dr. Vernon Gandt delivered a talk at a national convention of educators. After his lecture we spoke. I learned that he was one of those students who used that church pew as his desk - and went on from there to a distinguished career after earning his doctorate.

Today Concordia in Selma is a fully accredited university of excellent reputation and even awarding doctorates in education.

Now and in the last decades many of the products of that Concordia in Selma have provided lay and professional leadership for the church and they are one of the reasons that that branch of the Lutheran church has more blacks among its membership and leadership that any other Lutheran group. Persistence, education and overcoming adversity continue to reap rich rewards!

NEW YORK

NEW YORK! I love New York. Actually, I love all five boroughs of that wonderful city, but my favorite is The City, Manhattan, The Big Apple. From the first time I visited in the late 1940's through the eight years I lived just up the railway in Eastchester (while I served as head of the Lutheran Schools Association of New York) I jump at every opportunity to get my New York fix!

I love the people; and, of course, one is enmeshed in them the minute one steps onto almost any Manhattan street, but it seems to be at its most frenzied pace around Times Square. What a thrill it is to be caught up in the swell of people from all corners of the earth, speaking every conceivable dialect, all wearing all styles of dress, all sharing one common characteristic: they are in a hurry, each person with their own agenda and a fierce determination to meet that agenda.

It was always a special treat when I got to Times Square with my long-time friend Howie Capell and he chose to drive his car. We would pull into Times Square. He'd spot a cop, get out of the car and wave to the cop with a "Hi." Immediately the officer would be at our side, direct us to the nearest parking space (most likely marked No Parking) and wave us into the spot. If none of those were available the cop would personally walk alongside our car to the nearest public garage. He would signal the attendant and order, "Take care of my friend." The valet would park our car at the entrance and there was never a fee. (These cops all know of how well Howie represented their fallen colleagues in the lawsuits following 9/11.)

Another way to experience Times Square and Manhattan streets, the Empire State Building and Rockefeller Center, etc. etc. was with my nearly ninety-year old mother who was determined to "do New York." She was in her wheelchair. Every time we got to a curb or an elevator or a rest room, which she needed to use, someone was at her side asking how they could help and then doing it squared! My mother declared, "New York is the friendliest city in the world and I am from Texas where we know about hospitality."

I, of course, love to eat. In New York the picks were literally beyond imagination: Chinese food in Chinatown, Little Italy, street vendors with their pretzels, hot dogs, etc. very expensive famous eateries, delicatessens and bars ranging from the one with a view at the top of the Marriott to the neighborhood pubs around Union Square.

Entertainment on And Off the Street 24/7: Theaters, Carnegie Hall, The Met at Lincoln Center, and The Blue Note for Jazz. Every conceivable Museum beckons. Madison Square Gardens awaits, but you have to slip across the border into the Bronx to get to Yankee Stadium

Naturally I find the churches to be important to me, I never miss a chance to drop into St. Patrick's on Fifth Avenue for a few moments of silence. St. Peter's Lutheran sits inside the Citicorp Building and the reredos behind its altar is a massive window framing the city it is called to serve. If one is around on Christmas Eve the thing to do is go to St. Luke's Lutheran in the theater district. Just before midnight singers come from many of the shows, concerts, clubs in the areas (professionals all) and gather to sing in incredible harmonies the ancient Christmas carols.

I try to end my New York visit with the most meaningful worship of all. I go the site of the new World Trade Center. I stand silently for a long time at the Memorial Fountain. I let my fingers trace the names of the 9/11 victims; I image especially those who were numbered among the sixty who left behind a child or grandchild enrolled in a Lutheran School. I remember and I pray that the Lord of all cities would stop especially all killing done in God's name and send flocks of special angels to the big cities of the world, beginning with the Big Apple.

ℰℭ

SAN ANTONIO, TEXAS

I love San Antonio and always jump at any excuse to go there. I love its diversity. While the population is predominately Hispanic the city bursts with the energies of a variety of people. The military bases, like Lackland, Ft. Sam Houston and Randolph Air Force Base, constantly bring in persons not only from across the USA but from our allies abroad. While there are massive areas of low-income and not a few very poor people, the city has its share of the wealthy, many living in beautiful estates. Together they reflect the military, the health industry, the higher education world, all within an ever-prevailing aura of the Old West with plenty of cowboy boots and large Stetson hats abounding.

One of the words that always pops up when I reflect upon my time in San Antonio is sweat. Yes, that stuff that flowed out of my body during the summers of my college years. I worked in construction at the very lowest

125

level. In weather, which was consistently over 100 degrees, I was the one (back before sophisticated Bobcats) digging foundation trenches with pick and shovel. My hands were seared with the iron of the foundation steel. My back blistered as I laid the roofing panels. The good news: I was in the best shape of anyone who reported for fall football practice in September after surviving an unforgettable orgy of fresh tamales and Lone Star beer when we finally had the topping out celebration of the building at which I was working.

I also did my share of philosophical and mental sweating. After a couple of years of teachers college, I took off a year to teach in a two-room Lutheran school. I had forty-two in grades one to four. I hope by this time they have forgiven my inadequacies and plain old mistakes. Believe me I tried!

The mental stress was at its highest twenty years later when the ambulance met us at the airport upon our arrival from Hong Kong. My wife, Jane, was in a virtual coma and it was at San Antonio's Baptist Hospital that she was properly diagnosed and treated for a brain aneurysm. Family and friends provided unbelievable support to me and our children.

Of course, San Antonio is a city of romance. The historic Alamo hastens the blood flow of any true Texan. The San Antonio River and the River Walk stir up romantic feelings in even the most jaded. And for me San Antonio is the place where my now-wife of some sixty-two years was first introduced to my mom, dad and family.

San Antonio evokes a feeling of sadness and absence. It was in San Antonio that I saw my mother slowly lose her formerly unquenchable energy. And it was at a bedside in San Antonio that Jane and I joined my father in a harmonious rendering of "Abide with Me" shortly before he left us to be forever with our Lord.

I wish I could conclude this little reflection by just sitting at a comfortable table on the River Walk savoring a margarita and some chips but that will have to await my very earliest convenience

෨ൠ

MACAU

Macau in the 50's and early 60's. That little note specifying the 50's is critical. The current Macau bears virtually no resemblance to the old. Today's Macau is the biggest gambling Mecca in the world. Its volume way exceeds

Las Vegas. It has enough neon to shine half-way up to Guangdong. That is nothing like the Macau that I visited probably 100 times fifty years ago, but have not set foot in now for some twenty years.

Macau was a Portuguese colony. It was only thirty miles from Hong Kong where I lived. But it was tricky to get there. We were not allowed to go through China. Borderlines in the South China Sea were carefully monitored and if the ferry I rode to get to Macau would stray it could become an international incident.

There was much to love about Macau. The view from the balcony of the Bella Vista Hotel was fabulous. The African chicken served at the Macau Posada was unrivaled. The hotel room in which I stayed did not have a bathroom or toilet, but the beer at the bar was always cold.

The ancient façade of the St. Paul Cathedral had survived a fire and a typhoon. The battered cross on top of it still stood and became the focus of a wonderful hymn written by the then governor of Hong Kong. The hymn: "In the Cross of Christ I Glory, Towering O'er the Wrecks of Time."

I went to Macau because there were people there with lots of needs: spiritual, physical, psychological and educational, people in need of hope. The Lutheran Church did (and does) a good job there.

The first Sunday I was there I was told that children had to bring last Sunday's leaflet with them to be admitted to class this Sunday. There was no space for new students. I am not so naïve as to not know that one of the factors causing this very large attendance was that a limited amount of relief food and clothing was made available at the church.

We wanted property to build a Lutheran Center and eventually received a title from the Government for a wonderful plot of land. However, when we finally got a decent translation of the deed which we had signed, we learned that in fact, the holder of the deed was listed as 'Chinese merchant Titus Lee," the same person who was our evangelist there. It was explained that no government official (fearing censure from the Catholic Bishop) would ever sign a deed, which showed a Lutheran Church as a property owner so the "merchant" phrase was used. We were assured that later the property could be transferred to the church. That never happened. (See addendum below.)

Many refugees from Mao were desperate and wanted to get to Hong Kong. I recall one gentleman who lived with his family in a most primitive hut with no water, light, or furniture. He pleaded with me to help him get a visa. Then he told me, "I am desperate." With that he pulled out a packet, which I immediately recognized as street heroin. "If I don't get my family to Hong Kong soon, we will all be existing on this," he told me. Maybe that had

127

something to do with the fact that I noticed that on some of my subsequent trips I was always followed. As soon as I boarded my rented pedicab at the ferry station I noticed that I was being followed. This happened throughout two subsequent visits. Then it stopped. I don't know that there was a connection but I do know that all of this coincided with the murder of a gentleman on our church steps as he was leaving Christian instruction one night.

Some of the immigrants, through sheer force of Chinese determination and effort managed to survive in Macau, and find jobs besides, making fireworks in their homes. But most wanted to get to Hong Kong. One of the families that I was able to assist in getting there was a great blessing to many. One of the sons became head of Lutheran Social Services of Hong Kong, a massive center of assistance to thousands. His sister is now a famous Hong Kong surgeon.

Macau is now, of course, famous for its gambling and extravagant hotels. But I am grateful for the people whom I was able to meet, who found their chances for a much better life than at the crap tables.

Addendum: Years after I left Hong Kong, I received a call from a Lutheran Church official in America. He informed me that the Macau church building, school and the land on which they had been situated had been sold. It appeared that the person who had been named as owner of the building as indicated above, had sold the property, taken the money and disappeared in America. Fortunately, church officials did eventually go to Macau, deal with the new buyer and were able to secure for the church a repayment to the church in what I believe was a total of US $1 million.

ౠ

PESHAWAR, ISLAMABAD, RAWALPINDI, ABBOTTABAD, PAKISTAN

Prior to visiting these Pakistan cities in the mid 1980's I doubt if I had even heard of them. Now each of them is firmly etched in my memory. In 1983 (and again in 1984) I spent time in Pakistan teaching Parent and Teacher Effectiveness Training. It was a great and extremely rewarding experience. My classes included Christians, Muslims, Buddhists, Zoroastrians and persons of no faith. At least one was one of multiple wives. One who attended all of my workshops later publicly immolated himself in

128

protest of the government. To a person they treated me with respect and extended hospitality beyond my wildest imagination. On my second trip I was invited to the area near the Khyber Pass bordering Afghanistan.

But first I stopped in Islamabad and even then, was amazed at the build-up of troops all around that city extending into the area right next to Abbottabad of later Bin Laden fame. My host was one of the greatest living saints I ever met, Sister Sheila from Ireland. It was she who startled me when I knocked on her hotel room in Rawalpindi and stepped in. "STOP!" she shouted. I recoiled. Then she was immediately in my arms with words of apologies. "You see, Mel," she said, "If I, as a woman, was noticed inviting a single man into my hotel room I could be killed for it." After my apology she recanted, "What the h.., Mel. Come in. It's worth the risk."

She took me to the Bishops' residence. He kindly lent us his driver and beat-up old Ford to take us over the camel-crowded passes to Peshawar. There I was to present certificates to a class of teachers to whom she had taught the model I first taught her. But then a problem arose. This was a big event and the head of the Education Department was to distribute the certificates, but was unable to attend. He asked if his wife could make the presentation for him and deliver a short address. The problem was that she, as a woman, was not permitted to speak to an audience that was not all women. I agreed to step out of the room until she was finished. But Sister Shelia did some negotiating and I was permitted to attend.

After the presentation I was taken to a bazaar where some beautiful embroidery was bought for me. Then I bought a type of turban/hat from a street vendor. I had gone about a block when a gentleman ran up to me from behind. I finally figured out that he wanted to know how much I paid. When he found out the price he explained (as I finally got it through an interpreter) that he just wanted to make sure that as a foreigner I had not been taken advantage of for that would be anti-Islam; but since I had been charged a fair price I was sent on my way.

My way took me to the Pakistan-Afghanistan border. Once again, I viewed the tragedy of hundreds of thousands of refugees fleeing from the Afghanistan-Russian fighting, like millions of others through the ages. Now again, especially on the Syria-Jordan border, people are fleeing for their lives. They live in hot, dirty, dusty, little tents, scrounging for food and water, trying to keep hope alive.

On this pleasant California evening I sit and reflect on my brothers and sisters in places with names like Peshawar, Islamabad. Rawalpindi and Abbottabad and I feel like my life is so different and so blessed. At the same time, regardless of the name of the place in which we live we all yearn for the same things: someone who loves us, people who respect us regardless of our gender, religion or nationality, and a place where we can lie down and sleep in peace.

ဆကၡ

NEW ORLEANS

I love New Orleans. One big reason I love New Orleans is because I love food and New Orleans is loaded with good food. I can begin the day with some great beignets in the French Quarter. For lunch I can stop at almost any street corner and take my pick from among po-boys, jambalaya, gumbo, crawfish etouffee, or just plain red beans and rice. Dinner offers anything my pocketbook can afford including two of my favorite restaurants, Brennens and Broussards.

Music and New Orleans are all part of one wonderful orchestra. Jazz was born there. The Blues still fill the streets. Sunday black churches have music that lifts the soul. For my funeral I would be very happy to have my body accompanied by a traditional street funeral band. And if my Memorial Service was on a Sunday it would be great to have all the mourners go the Quarter for a Gospel Brunch.

But good memories of New Orleans go deeper than food and music. For many years my late brother, Harold, lived in New Orleans. Harold always inspired me (and he lives in me today) with his commitment to hard work, his unflinching care for the black Lutheran schools of the South and especially for those who taught in them. And on top of that, at the end of every one of his long days he knew that his specially designed refrigerator was stocked with some good cold tap beer for him and any who cared to joined him

Honesty requires that I also share the things that really bother me about New Orleans. It has one of the highest poverty rates of any city in America. Racism is still rampant and blacks are still denied entrance to restaurants, homes on favorite streets and equal opportunity in the work place or in the courtroom.

While I have gone to some very enriching conferences and conventions in New Orleans, my mind also often goes to one New Orleans gathering that for me was a disaster. A major Christian Church body adopted a formal

130

resolution that stated that anyone who refused to teach that the world was created in exactly six days of 24 hours each was to "be considered a heretic and not be tolerated within the Church of God."

But I will try to forget about that this weekend when I head to New Orleans to join some 100 members of my eight siblings and our families. We will remember Mom and Dad, honor the memory of brother Harold and enjoy the food, the music, the Gospel and the family. And it will be good!

ℰℭ

CHILDHOOD MEMORIES PART 1: FOOD

I grew up poor. However, I never ever went hungry. There was always plenty of good food, most of it homegrown, home-canned, and home-cooked. If I ever complained to my mother about the food (which was usually if there were no cookies because we couldn't afford the sugar) Mother always replied "Venn du hungrich bist, den schmeck auch jelly-brut gut." (If you are hungry then also jelly bread tastes good.) And jelly on top of home baked bread was always available.

I have no memory of ever eating a meal (or even a hamburger) in a restaurant until I was in high school. We always had plenty of vegetables, almost all of which we grew ourselves in our large garden. Almost every meal featured potatoes. Potatoes were so common that we had a joke that if there were no potatoes on the table at a meal other than breakfast one was not required to say grace because without potatoes there could not be a real meal.

Our meat came from hogs, cattle, chicken, turkeys, an occasional sheep, goat or rabbit, which we raised ourselves. Our fried chicken was always fresh as Mother would catch a fryer or two, cut its head off with a hatchet, batter it in flour and fry it in lard. Friends by the name of Schwausch would come to assist with butchering the hogs. The hog's throats were cut, bled, immersed in scalding water and the hair scaled off. Then the cuts were made, the intestines and stomach cleaned and stuffed with sausage. The ham and sausages were smoked in our own smoke house. One of my jobs was to keep plenty of tree bark smoking so the flavor would really penetrate the meat. Most of the meat was cut off the bones to make sausage, but even those bones were salvaged, cooked and served with mustard on top and mashed potatoes with beet juice over them as the side dishes.

Fish were a rare treat. My father and Uncle Otto would catch over a hundred small perch, which we deep-fried. (Always outside over a corncob-fueled fire.) Once in a while an itinerant fisherman would stop by and at very low cost sell us a couple trout or more likely a big string of catfish. If my memory is correct, the first time I saw shrimp was when I was about twenty years of age.

Vegetables were in abundance. The earliest crops each spring were those we did not can, like radishes, onions and lettuce followed by mustard greens, spinach, turnips, sweet potatoes and carrots. Eaten fresh, or canned by the multitudes, were string beans (the plants growing up the slender bamboo poles alongside them), peas, corn, cucumbers, tomatoes, okra, kohlrabi and beets.

Of course, there was plenty of fruit (either from our own trees or from neighbors and relatives). I still see my mother sitting on our back porch, peeling away enough for literally hundreds of fruit jars to be filled with peaches, cherries, pears, blackberries, apricots, figs, and pickles.

There was always plenty of fresh milk, butter, homemade bread and gravy. Desserts were for special occasions like Sunday or birthdays. I have not a single memory of wine ever being at the table, but Dad did enjoy home-brewed beer, especially during prohibition. At Christmas time Dad (much to Mother's disapproval) would buy a quart of Four Roses bourbon and we would have Christmas eggnog with all the fresh homemade whipped cream the cup could possibly hold. I do not remember ever having even one bottle of soda or cola in my home until I was in college.

Of course, this was all long before television, cell phones (we did not even have a line phone) or computers. There were no after-school baseball games, dance lessons, or baby-sitting jobs. So it is that my memories of food enjoyed while growing up are all warm and fuzzy. They are filled with images of our large family gathered around the table (I am one of nine kids) saying the table prayer (often in German), then passing around those wonderful dishes of fresh nutritious food, enjoying every bite and trying our best to keep our mouths shut while we energetically chewed.

80CQ

CHILDHOOD MEMORIES PART 2: WORK

My parents taught me the value of work. Early on they taught me the Bible verse: "If any would not work, neither should he eat!" In summer we lived by Dad's mantra "In the field by sunup!" And they practiced what they preached. Dad was principal of the school, taught grades four through eight, and was church organist and choir director. He taught a Sunday morning Bible class and was the adult counselor for the youth group named the Walther League. He also cleaned the church and saw to it that hymn numbers were posted for Sunday worship. Before and/or after school he raised nine kids. Beyond his family and the local congregation, he served for many years as Chair of the Texas District Teachers Conference and organized the annual statewide conference.

Mom, of course, washed diapers continually, served three hot meals a day, did hundreds of loads of laundry (always carrying the hot water in buckets to the washing machine). She used the hand-turned clothes wringer before hanging the laundry on the drying line, taking them down when dry. Dad always wore ironed shirts; the girls wore homemade dresses sewn by Mom (often made from the material of flour sacks et sim). She cared for the sick, always saw to it that "the beds were made," canned up to 800 quarts of home fruits and vegetables in one year. And still made time to hear our daily recitation of Bible verses and catechism lessons.

Within that context my work was pretty simple. Of course, I milked the cows, gathered the eggs, and watered the hogs. We shucked an awful lot of corn, sometime made less tiresome when my sibs and I would have contests to see who could get 100 ears shucked first.

My memory is that I was forever pushing a lawnmower. Mom's idea of the expanse of our lawn (our house abutted a major pasture) kept expanding. By the fifth grade I was busy mowing for my relatives. Uncle Walter wanted to be helpful. He was a very clever blacksmith so he rigged up an electric motor on top of the lawn mower blades. Big problem: Before I had cut even a tenth of his lawn I had run over the electric cord. I hastily repaired it with "black tape" only to run over and cut the extension cord at another place. My cousin Olga had what seemed to me to be an acre of front lawn, and try as I might I never cut the mowing path as straight as she liked and so had to recut the lawn in 100-degree heat.

It was obvious early on that this boy would never make it on the farm and this just got proven again when I was sent to pick cotton. My younger brother Harold and my elder sister Leona both out-picked me, and remember that we were paid by the pound-picked, 35 cents for a hundred pounds. On a really good day if I picked from sun up to sundown, I might hit that 100 pounds and earn my 35 cents. My sibs could double that!

My most enjoyable little job may have been digging for worms that

Uncle Otto used for bait when he went to the lake for perch. He would slip us a full nickel when we had a good pint-sized can full of wriggly worms waiting for him. What I remember most vividly is not the nickel but a near disaster. We moved a small water tank to get to the moist ground underneath. It was full of wriggly worms. I hoisted the heavy grubbing axe above my head to really get into the earth. Just then brother Harold spotted a worm in the middle of my target. He ran to grab it. Angels descended from above and averted the swing of my digging axe that would have shattered his skull. We got the worms and shared the nickel.

৪০৫৪

CHILDHOOD MEMORIES PART 3: ZION LUTHERAN SCHOOL

My first eight years of schooling were at the two-room parochial school named Zion Lutheran School of Walburg. As its name indicates, it was a parish school. As such it had three distinct aims: to teach the Christian Lutheran faith to the children who had been baptized as infants in Zion congregation, to help preserve the best of the Lutheran German heritage and thirdly, to prepare its students for productive citizenship in the USA. And in my judgment, it achieved all three goals in an outstanding way.

Teaching the faith was primary and the methods were traditional. Tell the Bible stories, ask the questions of the Catechism and get the correct centuries-old answers, and memorize the "proof texts," the hymns, prayer and Martin Luther's Small Catechism. Up until my graduation in 1941 these were all learned and taught in German!

We were taught to read the old-fashioned way, pure phonics. I can still see the wall charts. I remember the primer "I am the gingerbread man; I am. I am." We had no library and no access to a public one. When I was in the seventh grade, we (rejoice greatly) received a set of thirty-eight condensed versions of children's classic books. My only regret: I had read them all in the first two weeks after they arrived. But then we got a set of World Book Encyclopedia. As diligently as I read, I never finished that!

Writing was just penmanship - no essays, books reports or creative writing. Spelling was a separate class. But grammar was paramount. We diagramed sentences and I can still put it all down: subject, predicate, object, adjective, adverbs, subjunctive clauses, the whole bit.

History was as much Texas history as US history. At one point I tried to

134

memorize the names of all fifty-two counties in Texas and their county seats - but, of course, that was all secondary to the Alamo and the San Jacinto Monument!

I don't remember any science course. Yet my father, Principal Kieschnick, wanted his students to have new learnings. I am sure that neither I nor any of my classmates had ever been to a zoo or an aquarium. Once he contracted with a gentleman who brought a mature elephant to our school. As the elephant walked around our playground, we felt its trunk - and a few students even rode it. Another time a large preserved full-sized whale was brought to the school. We felt its skin and marveled at how whalebones could be shaped into useful objects.

We had two classrooms (Grades 1-3 and 4-8) taught by Teachers Bleke and Kieschnick. Outside of my piano/organ and one high school teacher of Spanish, I had not one single female teacher from Grade 1 through grad school!

We drank water drawn from the school well and dispensed in little tin cups for each student. Lunch came in sacks - except for mine, as I lived close enough to school to always go home for lunch. No school busses and in the early years some classmates rode to school on their horses or in buggies drawn by horses. There was a place for the horses to rest and be fed, just next to the outdoors hole-in-the-ground toilet for boys. In winter the boys got coals from an outside bin and kept the pot-bellied stove stoked.

We had plenty of fun. Recess time was generous. We chose up sides and played softball. At other times we "shot marbles" played "Red Rover" and "Andy Over." Christmas was time for wonderful Christmas programs in church on Christmas Eve where we each received a brown paper bag with goodies - the one time in the year when I had a stick of gum and an orange just for myself, and some red and white Christmas candy! End of the year school picnics were time for the oompah band, softball games, ice cream cones, and a "program" with candidates for public office in the 1930's assuring us they were against "child labor laws" which allegedly might prohibit parents from sending their own children into the fields to pick cotton!

My memories now are all positive. For its time, the school was perfect for me. Today is a new day and I am glad my grandchildren have so much more than I had. And I look with dismay at the many in our country and in our world, who would be so blessed to have the simple lessons and eternal values, which were taught me at Zion Lutheran School in Walburg, Texas.

CHILDHOOD MEMORIES PART 4: FUN AND GAMES

I had lots of fun and played many games as a child. It always amazes me that the games we played as children seem to be the same games that other kids my age played all around the country at the same time. We had no interaction with each other, often came from different ethnic backgrounds, certainly had no access to modern social media and yet we played many of the same games.

Like so many others in the late 1920's or early 30's, I played "Hide and Seek," "I Spy," "Draw a Magic Circle," "Sheep Pour Down" (where did that title come from?), "Kick the Can" and "Red Rover." I played very few, if any, board games. Of course, being a Texan I played lots of straight dominoes, and early on learned to play "Shoot the Moon" and "Texas 42." "Old Maid" seems to have always been around. I sat by my father (often sleeping on the floor next to him at wedding receptions and other celebrations) when he played the card game "Scot," but I never learned it.

Softball was omnipresent as long as there were at least two of us. In school we always chose up sides, played at every recess and even competed against two near-by public schools (Walburg and Thrall), but not against the neighboring Catholic school. When the older kids in the church youth group (Walther League) played against other church groups I got to be "pig tail" which means I backed up the catchers as we had no backstop behind the catcher.

The holiday seasons, wedding receptions and birthday parties were much anticipated. At Easter we went out to the pasture and found the most beautiful wild flowers (especially Texas bluebonnets if they were already blooming) and decorated fancy Easter egg nests. On Easter morning these would be filled with chocolate Easter eggs and a few single-color painted hard-boiled eggs. We looked forward to weddings. The receptions were always in the country home of the bride. There was usually a lane that ran through a gated fence. At the entry little boys were allowed to "hold rope." We stretched a rope across the lane and "demanded" a contribution from the arriving cars before we would lower the rope and let the car in. After all the guests had arrived the pennies and nickels (very, very rarely was there as much as a quarter) would be distributed. Of course, the fewer boys (NEVER a girl) that participated the better the per-boy yield. I was lucky. My father was always the wedding organist and was the local church school principal so I was usually permitted to be one of the rope bearers. Another good thing about those weddings was the wonderful Texas barbeque that was absolutely essential to the celebration. Then around midnight the chivaree players arrived. They banged on the plowshares, the kettledrums, the shovels and whatever else was around to make a din. Then they were served beer (homemade during Prohibition) with my dad singing a special humorous song for the bride, and then ending with a "midnight lunch."

Rare, but very special were the times when Dad would finally give in to our perpetual pestering and tell us stories of "von alten" - old-times. Over and over we heard the yarns of the time he and his sister were afraid to complete their walk home from school because a pack of wolves got between them and home. Or the story of the afternoon riding of the calves and his friend who got pitched off the calf right into the cow dung; or the story of his grandmother who sat in her chicken coop in the dark all night with flashlight in one hand and a rifle in the other and confronted the "you bastard" who had been coming to steal her chickens!

So, there was no television, no social media, no movies (for us), but I would not trade my childhood fun and games for any of the wonderful gadgets, theme parks or organized Little Leagues providing entertainment for my grandchildren today.

೫೦೦೩

CHILDHOOD MEMORIES PART 5: HEALTH

Mother's bed had been moved into the dining room, as that was the only room with a stove to provide heat in the central Texas December cold. Dr. Wiedemeyer was there as always with his black bag and was assisted by my Aunt Mattie Kurio. I weighed in at a healthy 10 pounds. After eleven days I was taken out of the house to the church for my baptism.

My health continued to be excellent. Of course, during the first 10 years of my life I (together with all my sibs) had all the usual childhood diseases. I know that I had measles, mumps, whooping cough red eye, scarlatina and chicken pox.

Living "out in the country" and always going barefoot I stepped on myriads of pieces of glass, pins, nails, splinters and bristles. We'd dig them all out with assistance from sisters or Mother if necessary. If we couldn't get them out, we applied a generous dab of some very black gooey salve that allegedly has "drawing power." Whenever we had a deep scratch or an itch that wouldn't go away, or the beginning of something like athlete's foot we applied a generous dose of kerosene and that usually took care of it.

I had an unnamed aunt who always supplied us with a drink that was supposed to be very good at preventing nasty colds or cure them if they had arrived. It came in a 20-ounce bottle and was called "Alpenkrauter). She used it generously and it sustained her health until she was well into her 90's. It was only then that I looked at the label and discovered that its alcohol proof was something like 90%!

Bees, wasps, ants and spider bites were simply facts of life. Mercurochrome seemed to fix most of that and if things got really bad, we went to iodine. Yet we were always told to be careful lest we get infected and we end up with "lock jaw."

There were other homemade "wonder drugs." For chest colds there was a mustard plaster. For sore throat a big slice of fatty bacon wrapped around the neck brought instant relief. Any pain in the abdomen area required a whiskey rub. This was much preferred to detested castor oil. If a cough simply would not stop Dad would have to spring not only for a rare fresh lemon but also use some of our carefully limited whiskey. This was mixed with just a tiny bit of sugar and warm water. I don't remember it ever failing!

But there was one major health issue which very nearly proved fatal. Somewhere between the ages of 5 and 7, I developed a terrible stomachache, which could not be helped by any of the home remedies. Finally, Dr. Wiedemeyer was called in. He said "You have got to get this boy to the hospital." So, Uncle Reinhold and Dad got into the Model A Ford and took me to King's Daughter's Hospital in Temple, Texas, more than an hour away where Dr. Harland (a nephew of Mom) would take care of me. Ether put me under. It was a ruptured appendix. Peritonitis was all over my insides. Of course, there were no antibiotics. Three tubes were inserted to drain off the pus. I was on the critical list. Obviously, I survived. And I marvel at the tidbits of memories I carry with me some 75 years later. I remember the embarrassment of not being able to deliver a urine sample unless I was standing. I remember a wonderful plump nurse named Miss French. She told me I was beautiful and that she would wait until I was grown so that she could marry me (and I half believed her!). I remember Uncle Frank giving me a store-bought little 12-inch sailing boat. And I do remember the anxiety on the faces of my Mom and Dad and the relief and prayers of gratitude when I was returned home. And Mother always insisted that the one side effect of my appendectomy was that it slowed down my running. She claimed I was very swift before and just barely normal after the surgery.

⁎

CHILDHOOD MEMORIES PART 6: FAITH DEVELOPMENT

Seven days after my birth my parents rustled me off to Zion Lutheran Church, Walburg, Texas where I was baptized into the Christian church. My mother duly noted in my Baby Book that I "behaved well" when Pr. John Sieck performed the ritual and, that I was dressed in the same white and pink dress in which my sister Leona had been baptized just two years earlier.

My parents took seriously their responsibility of nurturing the faith development of me as an infant and young child. I was immediately immersed in the daily rituals of morning and evening prayers, table grace, Bible reading and hymns. Every morning and evening we had the ritual of Dad reading a section from the Bible, a reflection upon that text, a prepared prayer, and the pronouncement of the Aaronitic blessing.

My life was always in the context of the local congregation at which my Father served as school principal, organist, choir director, youth minister, etc. etc. Every Sunday found us at church where I was well monitored by Mother. In those days we "went to church" a lot. Every Sunday, midweek Lenten services for six weeks, church festivals that did not fall on a Sunday such as Christmas, the Holy Week Events, Ascension and Reformation Day. Mixed in were funerals, weddings, anniversaries, mission festivals and concerts. It was pretty much total immersion. If my memory is correct this was all fine with me and I enjoyed the rituals, was proud to get dressed up but very much resented having to wear shoes as that interfered with my nearly year-round seven days a week of going barefooted.

At age six I enrolled at the two-room Zion Lutheran School. Of course, we started the day with religion class. It was classic Lutheran indoctrination with heavy focus on doctrine and dogma, always quoting Luther and Scripture (often even in that sequence). There were four basic elements to this instruction: 1) Bible Stories (we all remember the blue covered book with the title "100 Bible Stories"); 2) Martin Luther's catechism and Dr. Schwan's Explanation of the same; 3. Memory work. We memorized hundreds of Bible verses and Martin Luther's Small Catechism; 4. Hymn

139

singing. We sang every day usually in German and often in three-part harmony.

I recall that instruction with appreciation. I learned the fundamentals of the Christian faith. I was taught very clearly that God is a God of Grace and that God is for me, not against me. I learned the virtues and rewards of leading a pious life. I learned that in God's eyes I was special and that God had a dream that I would lead a productive, ethical life, sharing my faith, values and gifts with the world.

In retrospect I also see some things in my religious training that I now reject. The Bible was presented as needing to be interpreted very literally. I was taught that only my branch of the Lutheran Church had "the Word of God in all its truth and purity." I learned little about anyone not of my very specific faith and denominational tradition. It was a very narrow view of the work of God and my role in the larger parts of God's scheme for all of creation. I also was not introduced to some of the worship practices which I now wish I had developed, specifically meditation, contemplation or silence.

When I reflect deeply on my early religious training I must do so with very deep feelings of gratitude and appreciation. The seeds that were sewn went deep. I trust that they continue to bear fruit that endures into eternity.

ഇരൻ

CHILDHOOD MEMORIES PART 7: POVERTY

I grew up poor. I hasten to add that I was certainly not alone. Also, I am deeply aware that there were and are millions who had/have much less than I. I recently checked on-line and found detailed records of the 1940 US Government census. That record showed my father's income for the previous year listed as $720.00 (although I seem to have the memory that while that was indeed the promised salary the local church he was serving was, in fact, unable to pay his total salary for that year).

I certainly never went hungry, but I remember things that I longed for. I wondered what it would be like to eat a complete candy bar. When Father went to Teachers Conference, he would bring back a few candy bars (Baby Ruth, Butterfingers, or Milky Way). Mother would get out the kitchen knife and carefully cut the bar into seven pieces and distribute them to my six siblings and me. Occasionally our neighborhood grocery store would display a box of seedless green grapes on the counter. My mouth salivated at the sight, but I could never possibly purchase any. Mother would, on occasion, make a banana pudding and I would stare at the banana and wonder what it would be like to have the luxury of eating a whole banana, all by myself. When at Christmastime the bag of goodies we got from our church was given us on Christmas Eve I spent a lot of time trying to decide as to when I wanted to chew that lone stick of gum that was enclosed. But I also knew that when dinner time came there would be meat and potatoes on the table and plenty of fresh milk

Mother insisted that we dress neatly and cleanly. She sewed many of the clothes, especially for my sisters, and pants often had many patches. But they were clean and the white dress shirt my father wore as he taught each day was always starched and ironed. To this day I remember the really good-looking suit that was purchased for my confirmation ritual at church and that the suit cost $7.00 and was paid off over an agreed upon time period.

I went to one movie in the first 14 years of my life. Uncle Otto, who wanted me to see Shirley Temple, provided that. One of my most proud grade school projects was that somehow or other I collected enough Post Toasties box tops to send them in for a brand new 12-inch softball. I remember the day it arrived in the mail and how it was passed around at school and we learned to know what a new softball felt like. I never owned a storybook but my cousin Ben loaned me those small fat little Dick Tracy books. The 1927 Model A Ford we drove lasted us until Uncle Fred helped us get a new Chevy in 1946.

One of the lessons my parents insisted upon was that we were not to ask for "government relief" and I regret to say that we looked down disdainfully on those who were working in government-sponsored relief programs like the WPA even though that government project provided us with our first in-the-ground cesspool outdoor privy.

Those early years of very limited money served me well. I learned to appreciate what I had, to enjoy the reality that the best things in life are free, that God always took care of me and that I was and am very richly blessed.

☙❧

CHILDHOOD MEMORIES PART 8: REGRETS

I was blessed to have a wonderful childhood. There was food and clothing, wonderful parents, good modeling, strong spiritual direction. My memories are overwhelmingly positive. When I asked myself, "What do I regret about my childhood?" I found the list to be very small. Here are just two little items on my lists of regrets.

I never learned to swim. Mother made a note in my baby book: "He always enjoyed his baths till he was eight months old when we took him into the Gulf of Mexico at Galveston. From then on until he was over a year, he never liked his bath." I learned to enjoy my bath but never flowing or deep water. Of course, there was very little deep water in Central Texas. I certainly never had access to a swimming pool. I do recall that when I was quite young, Teacher Meier of our Lutheran parochial school went swimming in the San Gabriel River, got caught in some quicksand and drowned! I decided to not get into any water deeper than about six inches. But then came high school. A group of us boys headed for Barton Springs in Austin. They all jumped in. I could not be chicken so I jumped in too, actually swam a way and then panicked. I made it back to shore completely traumatized. I tried to hide my embarrassment. And I never learned to swim. I regret that and it led me to resolve that when my kids grew up in Hong Kong they would learn to swim. If I should ever find myself in deep water today (of whatever kind) I hope my kids will be there to rescue me.

I also never learned to dance. It was the teaching of my local congregation that "dancing is a sin." It would have been cause of significant scandal if any of the Kieschnick family was ever seen on a dance floor! Later, even though my beliefs about dancing changed, I never learned. Jane, my wife has a wonderful sense of rhythm and she knew how to dance. I was clumsy, self-conscious and not fun anywhere near a dance floor. Now I really regret that. I would love even now at 85 to join my friends here at La Costa Glen (and elsewhere) and enjoy a waltz, etc. but instead I just sit and watch and dream; but I do know that if I tried to learn now it would be a disaster all the way around. So, I write about my regret and move on.

ℰᏅᏣ

LEGACY

What legacy will I leave when I die? No, I am not morbidly contemplating my last days. However, just this last week I had several little nudges that stirred me in the direction of contemplating my legacy

The first was a radio interview regarding our recently sacked San Diego mayor. He admitted to grossly inappropriate (even illegal) behavior in sexually harassing women of all ages. When asked about the specifics of his guilty plea, the attorney being interviewed stated, "I think what the ex-mayor is sort of calculating is his legacy and very specifically: what will be in the first two lines of his obituary when it is published in the media upon his death." Interesting. What will be in the first few lines of one's obituary? Will it be very dependent upon whoever happens to write that obituary or will there be general agreement, "Yes, this is Mel's legacy."

I happened to mention this to my daughter Liz who has a private family therapy practice. She told me that she had just seen several clients who had significant challenges in mother-daughter relationships. She told me that she had asked the mothers to consider: "Many years from now when your daughters will be recalling your life, what is it that you hope they will remember about you?" That is another legacy question.

I have now been retired for 20 years. Tomorrow I go to an international education symposium on Lutheran education. There I will listen to the latest in the "Kieschnick Lecture Series," an endowed endeavor set up by my friends at the time of my retirement. Most of the people at that lecture will never have heard of Mel Kieschnick and I surely get that! The person delivering the lecture is much younger than I and we have spent little time together. But I have read his speech and it is good stuff. It is about his dreams and visions for international Lutheran schools.

That is good. And as I listen, I will be reflecting upon my dreams and my nightmares, my successes and my failures, my satisfactions and my regrets. I will be driven again to my vision of a God who is loving and forgiving. And I trust God's verdict as to what my legacy shall be.

᠅

LUTHERAN INTERNATIONAL/URBAN SYMPOSIUM – REFLECTING, REJOICING AND REGRETTING

I have just returned from a symposium to which I looked forward with much anticipation. My colleague, Marlene Lund, from the Center for Urban Education Ministries had helped pull together a symposium of some sixty Lutheran educators from around the world. Her hope was that, by combining leaders from international schools with those of urban Lutheran schools in the USA new learnings might emerge and new relationships might be formed. A

143

part of that goal was well achieved, some of it not very well. Here is a sample of a few of my Reflections, Rejoicings and Regrets

I rejoiced to look at the cities/countries from which these Lutheran school leaders came: Hong Kong, Hanoi, New York, Australia, China, Ghana, Frankenmuth, and Papua New Guinea. It continues to thrill me to image kids from each of these places having the opportunity to learn and grow and to have faith born and sustained in every one of those places. I regretted seeing no one from any South American or European country there.

I appreciated looking at titles of the participants: Executive Director of International Education, Science Teacher, Head of School, Evangelist, Board Member, Treasurer, Elementary Teacher. Of course, many of them could also have identified themselves as "parents." It takes all kinds of expertise to make schools places of growth. I regretted seeing no title or position related to a denomination head or regional offices, such as at a church-wide, synod or district. It again pointed to the quickening demise of denominational leadership in the USA.

I thought about the contrast between the small, very financially poor Lutheran school struggling in, for example, Ghana, and the relative wealth of international schools in places like Hong Kong and Shanghai. Yet as I spoke with heads of those schools of whatever country or size, they all spoke of the on-going challenge of responding to parents' concern, or lack thereof.

It was wonderful to see the representation from Lutheran colleges and universities and their departments of international studies. (I reflected upon the fact that way back in 1968 I was asked to start up the first one of such in the LCMS but decided my educational career was headed in another direction.) I wondered what insights we would have learned had there been someone there from the largest Lutheran University in the world – in Brazil. It has 32,000 students on campus out of a total of some 140,000 in their extended network.

I enjoyed looking at names like Gyamfi Kwadwo, Betty Lingenfelter, Philip Ohene-Abrefa, Moyo Tawango and Tarirai Doreen. I regretted seeing no names of obvious Hispanic heritage. The highlight for me was the keynote address by Martin Schmidt. His theme was "Grace and Vocation." He challenged all Lutheran schools to be places where students and staff experience grace, a God who cares about and loves all creation, and vocation and the calling for each one of us to be of service and ministry in and to the world. He gave marvelous examples of how teachers at all levels can lead their students into this wonderful direction. I left this symposium just as more than 3,000 teachers in Lutheran schools from all over were gathering for a three-day convocation. I bowed my head in respect for them and in prayer that each of their students might indeed discover and live out Grace and Vocation.

୧୦୬୫

SURVIVORS OF TORTURE

I spent most of yesterday in jail. It was in the US Detention Center near the Mexican border. Thank God I was not a detainee. I was there, however, on behalf of a particular class of detainees, survivors of torture in other countries who are seeking asylum in the USA. There are at least 2,000 a year. Probably as many as 50,000 refugees in America were tortured prior to their arrival in the USA. They arrive having escaped torture in their home country, but not yet having all the papers to legally stay in the USA. Unfortunately, they are placed in the same prison with all others who are held for illegal entry or are waiting to be sent back to their country of origin.

I went there because I am on the Board of Directors of a local organization called Survivors of Torture, International. Our mission is to identify legitimate asylum seekers who were tortured in their home country, had to flee for their lives and are seeking a new life in America.

I am getting to know these brothers and sisters personally. Just this week: a woman from a Middle Eastern country. Her teen-aged son foolishly wrote a less than friendly note about his country's leader in one of his computer tweets. He was identified, told that he was "dead." He made it home. Fortunately, his mother had the resources to buy a ticket for her son and herself to the USA (leaving behind her husband and other children). Of course, when she landed in the USA, she did not have a visa. She was sent to a prison detention center - she to one, her 14-year-old son to another!

Another survivor: Her family was pro–USA, but the real offence her father committed was to send his daughter to school. The Taliban stopped her on her way home from school, told her to drop out. She went back to school. She was stopped again. The persons who stopped her found she had an English as a second language textbook with her. They came to the house, took away her father and killed him. She is a Survivor seeking asylum in the USA.

There are stories like this every day. Survivors of Torture, Inc. (started with the assistance of a Wheat Ridge Ministries grant some 10 years ago)

145

assists these brothers and sisters get legal status, helps them find doctors who assist with their physical and psychological trauma. Sad disclosure: I have yet to meet an adult female asylum seeker who was NOT raped!

My efforts are feeble in the light of the need. I raise funds for the organization. I met with and wrote the warden at the detention center expressing my thanks to him for protecting me from people who want to hurt America but also asking him to treat humanely those who are here because they believe the invitation on the Statue of Liberty, "Give me your tired, your homeless, your tempest-tossed, those yearning to be free." And I am working for Congress to pass legislation separating asylum seekers from suspected criminals like the gentleman of whom I heard yesterday. He was in Afghanistan assisting a USA helicopter force. He was threatened. He fled. When he got here, he was handcuffed, incarcerated, treated like a violent criminal. Tough calls: but I want to be sure that I am on the side of those who are truly Survivors of Torture.

കായ

AGING UPDATE

This I know: Nobody else really cares about my aging. This I also know: anyone who reads this blog is in the same process as I. So, here are a few of my personal reflections and I really would be pleased to hear how you are doing.

First the good news: My body is okay. As long as I do my exercises and drink my two glasses of red wine a day, things go pretty well. I have not been able to get my doctor to actually officially prescribe those two glasses of red wine a day so Medicare does not reimburse me for my now-Three-Buck Chuck. My golf drives get shorter and shorter. The other day I had to use a five iron to reach a green only 130 yards away and I can't blame age for my lousy putting. Fortunately, there are some things that my brain still handles okay. I recently was able to give a brief three-point speech without having to consult my manuscript.

With age my concepts of God and my vision of reality keep getting expanded more and more.

Yet aging is obvious, especially when I sit down at this darn computer. I screw up all the time, get frustrated every time I try to use this machine that I cannot get along without and that drives me to distraction when I use it and it

146

doesn't stop me from writing run-on sentences.

I keep forgetting numbers. Can't even remember a house number that I had memorized when I had left my home. I left behind (so far not retrieved) my annual calendar that had not only my appointments but also my phone contacts, prescriptions, and computer passwords!

My lack of alertness bothers me especially after someone honks at me when I made a right turn on red in front of him or her. (I KNOW THIS COULD GET SERIOUS!)

I notice now that occasionally people show deference to me because to them I obviously appear as an "old man." I also notice that others now seek my opinion or consultation much less frequently and when I give my suggestions they seem to be ignored more often.

So I wake up each morning especially grateful that my wife Jane is patient with me, that she is the one who insisted that we move to this retirement community, that we can still afford the monthly payments (even after working for the church virtually my whole life), that I have a family which supports me even though we just cancelled the planned visit of all six of my sisters, two sisters-in-law and one brother because within 48 hours one had unexpected cancer surgery and another had to accompany a spouse to the hospital for urgent blood vessel work.

So that's the word for today. I will put it in my calendar that next November I will again give an update provided I remember and/or don't lose my calendar…and am still among the living.

❧

HOLY LAND TOUR PART 1

Why lead a tour to the Holy Land? "No more tours!" I said it and I meant it. My participation in leading four trips to China was memorable, educational and inspirational. But now I was 80 years old and it was time to quit.

"One more tour - to the Holy Land!" I announced. Why? The aging process affords the opportunity to reflect upon missed (or yet available) new experiences. As Jane and I together once again read through the four Gospels, I thought, "I'd like to walk where Jesus walked. I'd like to sit in places where Jesus taught. Maybe I should go there - with a group."

There was a second motive. I wanted to go to Bethlehem. In my work for

147

Wheat Ridge Ministries I learned more and more about the situation in Bethlehem. I listened to and watched Arab kids (Christians and Muslims) studying together in our Lutheran School there. These kids drew me to Bethlehem.

Of course, there were concerns. Do I still have the physical and mental stamina to be a group leader? Is it safe? I felt a very heavy responsibility for the security, especially also because all in my tour group were key members of my congregation, Calvary Lutheran Church. I dare not irresponsibly lead them into harm's way. Support from Jane is always essential. Of course, I had no way of knowing that two weeks before our departure she would have full hip replacement. Typically, Jane kept her reservations about my trip to herself and supported my dream. Our kids, as is also typical of them, were supportive with Peg coming from New Hampshire and Lyzse from Connecticut, and contact via computer Skype conversations from my son in Taiwan.

Then there were marvelous co-hosts: Bill and Marian Duncan. Bill handled the finances and paper work and Marian the interpersonal stuff.

Once again absolute unconditional support came from the tour members. As anticipated, they were responsive and wonderful. In spite of significant difference of opinions regarding the Middle East political issues and the US role in them, the members remained more than civil. They could not have been more cooperative, loving and understanding.

And so, we went. We traveled safely. We ate (or just looked at) the food provided. We found a land that instead of floating with milk and honey flowed with wine (and cola for Al!).

I've said that in a way the trip was more informational than inspirational – as commercialism and conflicting church claims at many of the holy sites tended to remove the aura of holiness. Yet I gained not only new information, but also moments of deep inspiration. In the following sections I share special moments of inspiration and moments for which that adjective does not apply.

The Garden of Gethsemane was a highlight, a place of deep reflection and spiritual awakening. As we drove across the Brook Kidron my anticipation heightened. The chapel in the Garden was quietly affecting my mood. Then we entered the Garden. I looked for and found the oldest of the olive trees, gnarled, ancient, sturdy, still bearing fruit. Some, I believe, have been there since the days our Lord went to pray among them.

We found a quiet spot where all who chose could sit. We sang, "Go to dark Gethsemane, ye who feel the tempter's power. Your Redeemer's conflict see. Watch with Him one bitter hour. Turn not from His griefs away. Learn of

Jesus Christ to pray."

Judy read reverently and movingly the account of the agony and prayer of our Lord under those old olive trees, and of the sleepy eyes of the disciples that just kept being closed in sleep.

For us gathered there the climax came in the Holy Communion. We had previously been in Cana where Jesus turned water into wine. I had secured wine from Cana. The previous day we had been in Bethlehem. There I had secured individual communion cups, chalice shaped, made of olive wood. The bread was a full loaf baked in Jerusalem. As Christ invited, we did this to remember Him and to unite us. Calvary!

Addendum:

We lingered in the Garden. We had our group picture taken there. We went to the edge of the Garden. We looked over the burial tombs of centuries of Jewish brothers and sisters. We looked across the Brook Kidron to the upper room, to the home of Caiaphas the high priest.

And I recalled Jesus sitting there. Sitting there and weeping over Jerusalem. He wept, He said, because Jerusalem had not been able to secure the peace God intended for that place.

Now 2,000 years later I felt Jesus sitting next to me. Again, He weeps. Not yet has peace come to Jerusalem or to many other places on this earth.

෧෬

HOLY LAND TOUR PART 2

Sea of Galilee Tour

We had come down from the mountain where Jesus preached, "The Sermon." We had visited the home of Peter's mother-in-law and the synagogue next to it. Now we were on the shore of the Sea of Galilee. It was the place where Jesus appeared to the disciples after his resurrection. It was the place where Jesus restored his apostolic call to a Peter who had thrice denied him. I liked the metal sculpture depicting Jesus restoring Peter. It felt right to look at the large stone formation running from the church to the shore of Galilee.

I made a decision. I would walk to the seashore. I would take off my shoes and socks and stand in the shallows. Then I would hear the voice of Jesus,

"Melvin, do you love me?"

"Yes, Lord, you know I love you."

"Then feed my sheep.

"Melvin, do you love me?"

"Yes, Lord, you know I love you."

"Then feed my lambs."

"Melvin, do you love me?"

"Yes, Lord, I love you."

"Then feed my sheep."

My mind went back 58 years and 10 days. That was the date the bishop's representative at St. Paul's Lutheran Church, Tracy, California, commissioned me to serve as an officially rostered teaching minister in the Lutheran church. The text was the one above, the call to Peter. And what a ministry it has been! (But that's a topic for a different set of reflections.)

Cana 2008

It was startling! As we got off the bus to walk to the place remembered as the site of the first miracle of Jesus, I nearly walked into a huge banner hanging next to the street. I don't remember the exact words, but the impact was there. It was something like, "Remember there is only one God, Allah, and his prophet is Mohammed."

I refocused as we all entered a room reportedly the site of Jesus' first miracle. We saw an excellent sample of a clay water pot capable, according to the King James version of the Bible, of holding 30 firkins of water. The first miracle!

Then we went to the chapel that Anes, our Guide, had reserved for our Sunday worship service. (A major accomplishment, as couples reserve this chapel for their wedding at all hours of the day, with reservations required months in advance.) We had just come from Nazareth so we began our service with Julie doing her usual amazing and stirring introduction to the Annunciation as sung in Holden evening Vespers. "An angel sent by God, to a town called Nazareth, to a woman whose name was Mary…" and we responded with Mary's Magnificat.

I very intentionally asked 92-year-old Gerry Hendrickson to read the lesson for the day, the account of the first miracle. I wanted Gerry to read this because he was the first president of Calvary Lutheran Church. Just like Jesus began his ministry of miracles, Gerry has led and been faithful at Calvary, a congregation alive and active because of God's continuing miracles.

We prayed very purposely at this wedding site where Jesus was present. First, I asked each of us to recall one marriage for which we especially thanked God (our own, our parents, some friends…). Each in their own way thanked God. I thanked God for Jane and our marriage of more than 57 years.

Then I asked each of us to pray for a marriage that is facing special challenges and threats. I had promised one particular Calvary couple that I would do this and I was pleased to keep this promise.

Our third prayer was for God to find a partner for someone currently unmarried but having a desire for marriage. I imagine some prayed for themselves or for a friend. I prayed for the one member of my family who is not married but would like to be. I continue to ask God to hear that prayer.

I closed with the thought, "God still changes water into wine." There are times in our life when we run out of wine. All we have left is simple H_2O. We turn that over to God and the first miracle is repeated: God once again changes the water into wine

෭ඥ

HOLY LAND TOUR PART 3

Christmas Lutheran Church

It had been very difficult to convince our tour company, NAWAS, Travel to include Bethlehem on our tour. There were issues: security, no four-star hotel in Bethlehem, the Nawas family is Lebanese and Lebanon/Israel relations are strained. Yet, I insisted we go to Bethlehem or we don't do this tour. Bethlehem was included.

My work with Wheat Ridge Ministries called upon me to assist in supporting Lutheran work in Bethlehem. Wheat Ridge funded the Wellness Center there. Wheat Ridge friends helped build the school. Wheat Ridge helped establish a Parish Nurse program and sponsored short mission trips for doctors, audiologists and nurses who donate their time for brief periods of time there.

So, we visited. We listened to Pastor Miter who tries to keep hope alive in a place where hope is a rare commodity. And we worshipped on Sunday at Christmas Lutheran Church.

We had agreed (or, more accurately, I had decided) to have our group sing a special number during the service. I decided it should be Stan's version of The Lord's Prayer. We rehearsed it (especially on the bus). I loved it and so did others. However, others with better musical ears than mine came to me and said, "Mel, this is not working. Listening to our botched-up harmony does not make it easy to feel like a prayer. We must go to Plan B." Plan B was to sing "Alleluia." Great song. I didn't think it fit. I felt it kind of went on without an ending. I made an executive decision. We will sing that old Lutheran favorite "Beautiful Savior." Problem: We didn't have the music for that with us. Through Barbara I e-mailed Jane to fax it to us. And we got just the right arrangement when we visited Bethlehem ministries on Saturday: 33 copies clearly copied.

Sunday morning found us at church 30 minutes ahead of time (a minor miracle for folks from Calvary) but in time with that specific request from Pr. Mitre. As we entered the beautiful chapel with its exquisite stained-glass windows we were met by a large group of white people, certainly not the Arab members of the congregation. It turned out to be a big brass band from Germany. They had come to support the Lutheran ministry in Bethlehem, had a benefit concert, taught children in the Lutheran school there how to play some band instruments, and donated instruments. A gentle, tall Lutheran pastor led them. Now we needed to negotiate how their playing and our singing would work together to enrich the worship. Surprisingly, my German was better than the director's English. "Beautiful Savior" is well known in Germany by its German name, "Schoenster Herr Jesu." The band director thought we wanted her to accompany our group. Not a good idea. When I mentioned our hymn choice to Pr. Mitre he said, "Wonderful. This is a favorite hymn of my congregation. Why don't you folks sing the first three verses and the congregation and the organ will join in on verse 4." We did that. It was stirring: "Beautiful Savior, Lord of the Nations."

I was also glad that we had dropped singing "The Lord's Prayer "when Pr. Mitre said, "We do the same thing every Sunday. When we pray 'The Lord's Prayer' during the service I ask each person to pray it in the language of their choice." It was powerful, Arabic, German, Swedish, Norwegian, and English. (I chose Cantonese.) God sorted it all out.

Another decision had to be made. Pr. Mitre had asked for someone from our group to read the Epistle lesson for the day. Of course, many wanted to do that. Several volunteered. I chose to offend them all and made the decision that I would read the lesson. And what a lesson it was to hear God's call for justice, peace and consideration for the poor. Once again, the right word of God for exactly that time and place.

Two disappointments: The sermon was, of course, in Arabic. Pr. Mitre chose to not give a brief summary in English. I learned later that Pr. Mitre struggles on Sunday in finding a balance between being the pastor for the members of his flock, and also paying adequate attention to the needs of guests.

The second disappointment: The church was built by German Lutherans more than 100 years ago. The stained-glass windows all depict the life and ministry of Jesus in and near Bethlehem. Stunningly beautiful! My disappointment: The Bible verse accompanying each window was there in German. I wish it had been in an Arab language. To compensate, upon the 100th anniversary of the church, the congregation had the words of the Gloria in Excelsis done in beautiful Arabic script around the dome.

The conversations after the service were an important part of the experience. Once again, the tour members were wonderful as all of us met the Arab members, some ELCA youth volunteers from America and guests from Norway and Germany. My conversation with one of the members was sobering. He explained the great difficulty he has getting around the "security walls" to land, that has been in his family for generations. He said to me, "I must get there. I must continue to plant olive trees there. If I fail to go, if I fail to plant, my family's ancestral lands will immediately be 'appropriated.' So, I go. I plant with my bare hands. I have planted 400 olive trees."

"Mitre, how do you feel about the future?" "Not hopeful," he said. "I see almost no signs of us moving toward a peaceful solution." "Yet," he said, "we must keep hope alive." As Martin Luther said, "Even if I knew I would die tomorrow, today I must still plant an olive tree." (Luther, of course, had said, "Plant my apple tree" but in Bethlehem the apple tree became an olive tree.) I heard that and tried to keep my teardrops from becoming too obvious.

ℰᏡℭℛ

HOLY LAND TOUR PART 4

The Sea of Galilee
Now this was a surprise. We are all together in the boat. The Sea of Galilee is calm. We are about to leave the seashore at Tiberius. The boat crew hoists a flag: Old Glory. The recorded music blares out "The Star-Spangled banner." What can you say? I stood at attention, full of pride - and hopeful of peace.

But the highlight came when we stopped in the middle of the Sea of Galilee. Ruth (as always - decked out in just the right attire) opened the Bible

153

and with deep reverence and just the right intonation read the account of Jesus walking on the water and of Peter's not completely successful effort to do the same.

My mind was flooded with reflections. Suppose it was I whom Jesus invited to take that walk. I decided Peter was a better man than I.

Outside Bethlehem: Angels We Have Heard on High

It was hard, very hard to really feel the presence of Christ or to recreate his walk along the Via de la Rosa - midst the shops, the noise and the solemn cross-bearing pilgrims. It got really tough to feel reverent at the Tomb of the Holy Sepulcher as warring denominations argue over who controls what portion of the floor, or door, or even tomb - while ornate brass lanterns give the whole scene an almost bazaar atmosphere.

But when we walked out of that cave on the hills of Bethlehem, when we sang, "Gloria in Excelsis," I got it. I could see that angel and then the heavenly host. I could feel the rustle of angel wings. I could hear the announcement, I could get the impulse and say the words, "Come, let us go to Bethlehem to see this thing which the Lord has made known to us." I was ready to go with haste - to the manger.

The Wailing Wall, The Holocaust, The Holocaust Children's Museum

I combine these three for they all speak to me of a profound spiritual mystery: The Silence of God.

The Wailing Wall is a magnet. It draws to it Jewish people of all subgroups from the ultra-orthodox to the secular. It speaks of past glory, of great mourning for the temple, that was destroyed, deep anger because of the Islamic Dome of the Rock now sitting above, of great hope for the restoration of hope for the ancient chosen people of God.

Access to the Wailing Wall, especially also for non-Jews, is not guaranteed. Some recent travelers had told me they had not been allowed to approach it. Issues regarding where non-Jews, or inappropriately dressed people, or women kept surfacing.

So, I was grateful when I knew we were going, men and women, just as long as men's heads were covered and we stepped away from the wall before turning our backs to it.

For obvious reason,s security and access were carefully controlled. I fully understood why we went through the metal detectors, etc. The men and the women went to different sections, although we were in sight of each other.

I had expected more people, even though the entire area was crowded by an eclectic mass of people: Hassidic Jews and pilgrims from all over the world, Sri Lanka, Poland, Rwanda, Canada, Thailand, Russia and USA. About 20 feet from the wall scholars sat   with their texts. Nearer the wall many bar mitzvahs were being celebrated by ecstatic young men with their fathers and male friends while mother and females "cheered them on" from beyond the barrier, which separated men from women.

I wrote my simple prayer, approached the wall, placed my hands and head in reverent attention and placed my prayer between the cracks. I added a few more petitions, just reflected a few moments and then stepped back.

On one level it was only a ritual. On another level it was much more.

I am glad we had time on our last day (and paid the extra $15.00 fee) to go to the Holocaust Museum. Nothing really new there. We all know the tragic history so well. But the presentation was so exquisitely well done, just the right tone, the architecture moving us along from the early stirrings of German patriotism to extreme nationalism, super-race belief, blind followers of clever politicians. Then came the prejudices, the faultfinding, the exclusion of "the other" and on to (as we all know and as it was so movingly narrated by survivors) the pogroms, the Star of David, the trip to the concentration camps, to the ovens.

Who can possibly have this experience without deep moments of reflection, repentance, and resolution! And the realization that instead of "Never Again" we humans repeat the tragedy again and again: Mao Zedong, Cambodia, Rwanda, Darfur, Myanmar.

The Holocaust Children's Museum overwhelms with its stark simplicity. Almost total darkness. Just illuminated with candles, one for each child victim. And a reading of the names and ages of the killed children, solemnly and slowly read - one, by one, by one...

In it all I experience the Silence of God. Where is God when the temple is destroyed and mad men throw children into ovens? My heart screams, "My God, my God, why has Thou forsaken us?" It is in these often-deep periods of reflection that I find God; and God is not absent, but just beside me, and then I notice that God too is weeping. God's tears mingle with mine and with many others. God made the decision way before time began to give to human beings, freedom of the will. They were not to be automatons programmed to do only good. God gave us choice. So often we have chosen very, very poorly - and God weeps.

And sends a Redeemer to forgive, to point to better possibilities, to kindle more pious plans, to relight the candle of hope in the darkness - and finally, the darkness does not overcome it.

HOLY LAND TOUR PART 5

In Jerusalem we moved slowly out of the place where Jesus faced his trial before Caiaphas, the high priest. Then we walked down into the dungeon where Jesus may have been held before being taken for his trial before Pontius Pilate.

I wandered into the nice adjoining gift shop run under the auspices of a group of catholic nuns.

Nancy Rinehart had a question, "Mel, we are thinking of buying a stole for Pr. Lubs. It could come from the group - about $3.00 from each of us." I immediately focused on the red festival stole with the beautiful Jerusalem cross-embroidered in it. Nancy stood holding that and I went on my way.

During the following days I wondered when Nancy was going to ask each tour member for his or her three bucks. I thought about bringing it up, decided that maybe Nancy decided not to buy the stole after all. Besides, I've learned long ago that if Nancy has a need she'll take care of it without any assistance from me.

Then came the meal at the Bethlehem Hotel when Al, on behalf of the group, presented me with that beautiful red stole with a gorgeous embroidered Jerusalem Cross.

I was/am deeply moved. This group had been great. The trip had been amazing. In the midst of it, my mind occasionally thought about my future. I have resigned from Wheat Ridge Ministries. I have terminated my service with the Center for Urban Education Ministries. My role at Calvary has steadily diminished. I'm ready to move to a retirement community. What does all this say about my ministry?

I saw the stole as an affirmation of the past - and as a symbol of continued opportunity and call to be a minister to whomever God calls me.

Slight ecclesiastical hitch. My official ministry category in the ELCA has been a challenge for some. Without going into all the details - it has to do with what's the appropriate ministerial status for me. Since I was originally commissioned in The Lutheran Church-Missouri Synod as a minister of the Gospel for the educational ministries of the church - and the ELCA does not have this category, what is the appropriate stole for me? Most would say it's the red diaconal stole, worn over one shoulder, connected by a gold chain at the waist. But that was not the stole presented to me.

And so, Step II happened. The bus driver, guide and group all readily agreed to return to the shop in Old Jerusalem. Gary went with me to the shop. The manager could not have been more helpful. She traded stoles and I now have the appropriate stole, from a very special place, given to me by a very special group of people. I cherish it deeply.

෬ට෬

HOLY LAND TOUR PART 6: MEMORY FLASHES

Highlights

There were the moments when the stimuli of particular places produced an immediate reaction. Sometimes the reaction was fleeting. It came. It was there. It went. Yet, as I sit here now, they once again invade my consciousness. Some samples:

a. Walking down those layers of civilization at Megiddo, each one thriving, fighting, dying, and now silent as an archeological dig.

b. Masada, vacation and security of Herod, then place of resistance and death each and every day of Jewish defenders. What if I had been among them? What if I had been the leader? Would I have made the same decision? Is there any circumstance under which I could kill my family to save it from greater torture?

c. The gardens of the Bahai shrine. How beautiful nature can be, all tended and nurtured and laid out with only one goal: to be beautiful. It stirred my memory of a book written three decades ago by a famous Biblical scholar, Jaroslav Pelikan, in which he challenged me to answer the question: What is finally the true, the good and the beautiful?

d. The Mount of the Beatitudes with Edie's moving reading of those beatitudes. Blessed are the meek, the peacemakers... and the quiet prayer, Lord let me claim those blessings.

e. The Quran, the Dead Sea Scrolls, the Museum of the Books. Centuries of written fragments miraculously confirm and then testify to the amazing accuracy of the Biblical texts over all these years. Can this all just be chance? What an amazing example of the providence of God.

f. Sitting near the Garden Tomb, listening to our evangelical guide, and then seeing The Place of the Skull. Maybe this is Golgotha.

g. I had never heard the theory of Jesus being kept in a "dungeon" after

157

his Maundy Thursday arrest, his trial before Caiaphas - and awaiting the morning trial before Pontius Pilate. The site makes a pretty compelling case. Could it be? Yes, yet I doubt.

h. Just wondering. The security at Tel Aviv as we left was tight. The questions I was asked were "No Nonsense" e.g. "Did anyone join this group who had not been a member of your church as long as the rest? Why is she not with you now? Do you know where she is at this moment? Aha, so someone gave you a gift (a small oil lamp given to me by the shop owner in Bethlehem)." And after all of this, and a thorough bag inspection, yet we were not asked to remove our shoes.

i. Just wondering: Did the Golden Tulip Hotel in Tiberius change its alcohol policy after we left, namely, free beer, wine and Israel-produced liquor (all included in the price of the room)?

Lowlights

I've listed some highlights, some highly inspirational moments. Naturally there were a few matters that did not make it to the top ten list.

a. The Blue Bay Hotel in Netanya and our first night check-in. We did not get off to a good start with accommodations. It was close to 7:00 p.m. when we arrived. We were told our rooms would be ready. They weren't. We were told to go have dinner and then our rooms would be ready. We did. The rooms still weren't ready. Finally, everyone had their keys, but no bellmen to take luggage to the assigned rooms. I hadn't even gotten to our room before my roommate Ken came with the news, "Mel, did you know that we are sharing the same bed?" When I protested to the manager she was surprised at my displeasure. She said, "Sir, I gave you a nice room with a nice view!" When my protests continued, she said, "Well, okay. I'll send up a roll-away cot for you." My protests continued. Eventually she assigned Ken and me a room way beyond the swimming pool which I had great difficulty finding in the dark - and to which a bellman did not want to accompany me.

Of course, by this time I learned that virtually every twosome of unrelated persons all had rooms with one double bed - and we never did get satisfaction.

The answer was the same, "You folks arrived on the Sabbath. Jewish people can't drive until after sunset. They don't check out until after sunset. You are unreasonable to expect rooms to be ready and all bed arrangements right. You should know better than to arrive on the Sabbath."

I didn't sleep all night, even called at 1:30 a.m. to complain about a malfunctioning air conditioning system. The same person who thought she had given us good rooms answered the phone. She was consistent. "Well, we certainly can't do anything about that at 1:30 in the morning. You must have messed with the controls!"

The breakfast was wonderful. The next hotel had rooms ready for us but we didn't really care because free beer, wine and Israel-produced gin was just waiting for us, as was the $7.00-a-bottle tonic. But we didn't complain.

The wine and beer even flowed from the spigot into water glass-sized glasses. The Calvary group (including me) could handle that!

b. The food. I eat what is set before me. When I travel to a foreign country, I don't expect American menus. The meals by and large worked great for me. Yes, I had to turn my eyes away from most of the breakfast items at the Bethlehem Hotel. I regret that Bob and Judie got some salmonella and were really sick for a few days after their return. I learned that Ken has an amazing appetite and capacity for herring. In Jerusalem Olga Nawas brought me a dish filled with sweets. I said to her, "Wow! Thanks! I'll have a hard time finishing all this before we leave Israel." She responded, "I brought it for your wife!"

c. Floating in the Dead Sea. Being afraid of water from my earliest years I am a very poor swimmer and an even worse floater. I imagined it would be great to calmly lie on my back and float serenely on the Dead Sea. Wrong! It was a slimy, dirty, slippery mess. I didn't have the courage and the patience of Suzanne to get beyond the waves near the shore. She had a great float. Ken and I hung on just to make it and were happy to get showered and back on the bus. So, I never floated - in the Dead Sea - or anywhere else.

d. Biggest disappointment - and yet. I was not surprised and yet was somewhat saddened by the commercialization of all the sacred sites, from the Annunciation to the Ascension. The hubbub around the Holy Sepulcher was especially disturbing, making it almost impossible to be reverently respectful.

And yet, suppose no one ever came to the sites. Suppose nobody ever visited Nazareth, Bethlehem, or the Mt. of Olives! Suppose the story of the life of Christ was a forgotten one. Suppose no one cared. That would be the bigger tragedy.

℘℘

PLAIN BROWN ENVELOPE

It is now 64 years since I opened the first important plain brown envelope addressed to me. I sat with some 100 others about to graduate as seniors from Concordia University, Chicago. We were assembled to receive our "assignments." In that day church leaders decided where we would serve in our roles as Christian educators. Oh, we had been asked about where we might want to serve, but the decision was for others to make. When we entered that room, we had no idea as to where we might be called. I sort of assumed it would be a church school in Texas because it was a strong tradition that Texans were assigned to teach in Lutheran schools of Texas.

I walked to the front of the room where Dr. Albert Maurer handed me my brown envelope. I rushed to my seat, tore open the envelope and saw the assignment: "Teacher and Principal; St. Paul Lutheran School, Tracy, California." And within three months I was in the classroom of St. Paul's, Tracy.

It was actually a good assignment. The school was at the forefront of dramatic changes within the Lutheran school system. I had known only the traditional parochial school that served only children of the sponsoring congregation. There was no tuition, all costs covered by the congregation. While that was my experience, Tracy introduced me to a body of students of many or no faith. Congregational financial support was minimal; school costs were raised through tuition and major fund-raising efforts. I had to learn fast. Many helped teach me. They were patient, affirming, and supportive. It is an experience I recall with pleasure and gratitude.

The second plain brown envelope arrived via second-class mail on a Saturday morning in 1956. I hardly noticed the envelope and didn't open it for a few hours. I was too busy installing the antenna for our very first television set that had been given to us the night before.

When I looked at the return address on the envelope there was no big surprise. I received lots of mass mailings from The Lutheran Church-Missouri Synod Board for World Missions. But when I read the enclosed letter I was shocked to the core of my being. I was being asked to be Co-Coordinator of Education for a Lutheran School System I was to establish in Hong Kong. I had never expressed an interest in "foreign" mission work. At that time, I had no idea of where Hong Kong was even located.

A few months later my wife Jane, son Dave, and I were in Hong Kong where we spent 10 marvelous years. They were years of challenge and growth; years of mistakes and forgiveness; years which played a role in establishing a Hong Kong Lutheran School System which now enrolls some 25,000 students in 10 secondary schools, 6 primary schools and 12 kindergartens; all way beyond the dreams enclosed in that plain brown envelope.

Today I realized that in a way the plain brown envelope was more than paper. It was a challenge, a call and a commitment. I too, am just a plain brown envelope which God used to accomplish a great purpose. One final reflection: On this Easter weekend I await one more destination for the plain brown envelope: the final call, and the best which is yet to come.

ഏരു

BIRTH

I entered this world from my mother's womb on a cold night in the "teacherage" (a home for parochial a school teacher) outside of Walburg Texas on December 10, 1927. Dr. Wiedemeyer was there with his black bag and my Aunt Mattie Kurio was there to assist. The delivery took place in the dining room of the house. That is because it was cold and that was the only room in the house that had a heater, a venerable wood-burning stove that had served for decades.

I was the first-born son and third child of Oscar and Lena Kieschnick. Oscar was known throughout the community as Teacher Kieschnick as he served as teacher for Grades 4 through 8 and principal of Zion Lutheran School. Ancestry was not much talked about in my early years and what I know about my family heritage is limited. I know that my grandfather John Kieschnick was born in Malschwitz, Germany and came to American in 1854. He settled on a farm in New Ulm near Brenham, Texas. It was there that my father (one of 10 children) was born in 1899. My grandmother Marie Friedrich was born in Kleinbautzen, Germany in 1868 and came to America in 1882. John and Marie settled in Lee County, worked very hard as successful farmers and had seven children.

My maternal grandfather, Henry Doering, was born in Walburg, Hesse, Germany in 1855. He came to the United States in 1880 and settled in Berry Creek in central Texas. He suffered a severe sun-stroke, gave up farming, opened the general store, post office and bank and is recognized as the founder of Walburg, Texas.

My maternal grandmother is Lena Braun who was born in Fayette

County, Texas. She and Henry were married in 1882. My mother Lena was born in Walburg, one of eleven children

My father was born in 1899 and my mother in 1902. They were married in Walburg in 1923.

As was the custom I was baptized soon at the age of eight days at Zion Lutheran Church by Pastor John Sieck, with an aunt, an uncle, a cousin and a Lutheran schoolteacher as sponsors. The notes my Mother recorded in my "baby book" are sparse but contain the note that I first said "papa, mama" when at 10 months I heard my father deliver a sermon at church. One other note explains why I never really learned to swim and to this day am somewhat afraid of water. Mom wrote, "He always enjoyed his baths till he was eight months old. Then we took him to the Gulf of Mexico at Galveston. From then on he never liked his bath - or running water."

ဆဝ

ANCESTRY

I have never been into family genealogy. While there are, of course, family records I recall only a few isolated stories handed down from generations past and present.

There is the story of my maternal great-grandfather. He left Germany for Texas in 1847 with his wife and two daughters, one of them a newborn. While making the long journey across the oceans his wife died. When he arrived in Texas with his six-year-old and an infant, the German Consul General "adopted" and raised his infant. He remarried and one of those children was my Grandmother, Lena Doering.

Grandma Doering was a strong woman who raised 11 children, with her husband dying when the youngest was only nine years old. The death of her husband came within one year of two big fires; one destroyed their barn and the other their large beautiful family home.

My grandmother on my father's side has a slightly different Texas legend. She lived "way out in the country" in Lee County and noticed that her chicken flock seemed to be diminishing faster than she figured it should. She decided that there might well be a nighttime raider of her chicken house. So that evening instead of going to bed she armed herself with a big flashlight and a hunting rifle.

Sure enough in the middle of the night the would-be thief arrived. She even recognized him as probably being one of the poor recently-freed-from-slavery farm hands who lived on their place. She confronted him, shone the light directly into his face. Quick to respond, the intruder stammered, "Oh, I am lost. Can you direct me to the nearest road to Giddings (a town nearby)?" She kept the light on his face and shouted "You (expletive deleted)! You know the way to Giddings as well as I do. Now get out of here and never return or I will use something stronger than this old flashlight on you!" Her chickens stopped disappearing.

I loved to visit my Grandmother Kieschnick even though I knew I was expected to spend some time hoeing and weeding her very large garden that had a lot of many-thistle berry bushes. It was worth it because we would always leave with large bags of beans, radishes, peas, carrots, and onions. And at mealtime there was always a freshly baked berry pie.

She seemed to always be at that wood-burning cook stove. I especially remember how she served dinner (always at noon.) Grandpa and us would all sit at the dining rooms table (or once in a while at the kitchen table) and we would be served first. Then she would take food out to the porch where she served "the hired help"- who were always black. They sat at their own table and ate their own food – which while good, was not quite up to what we were eating. Yes, it was racism, paternalistic racism, but clearly blatant racism.

I never met my maternal grandfather Doering. As he died eleven years before I was born. He was born in Walburg, Germany, lived through the deaths of four younger sisters who died at the ages of two, three, eleven and 18. He came to America and settled in central Texas.

Soon after arriving he suffered a serious sunstroke and gave up farming. He quickly utilized his considerable entrepreneurial skills and, in succession, opened the Henry Doering Mercantile, the Walburg Post Office and the Walburg Bank. He apparently passed on his business skills to all his children who were successful in the grocery, banking, hotel, insurance, cotton ginning and farming businesses.

He was known as an intelligent, humble, devout Christian citizen. When he opened the post office the US Postal Service suggested the settlement be called "Doering" in his honor. He declined and opted instead for Walburg, the name of the town in Germany from which he had immigrated. He was an active, generously contributing and founding member of Zion Lutheran Church and School of Walburg.

My mother was only 14 when her father died, but in her life, she exemplified his virtues of hard work, humility and Christian service; yet I remember very little of her even speaking to me of him.

I knew Grandpa John Kieschnick much better. He was born in 1864 near Brenham, Texas. His heritage was Wendish (Sorbian), a distinct ethnic group with its own language, tragic history of persecution, poverty, losers at war, that dates back to the first century of the Christian era. He married Grandmother in 1886 and they were blessed with seven children who survived infancy. My father was child number five.

I have three strong images of Grandfather Kieschnick. One is from a period shortly before his death in 1941 when I was 13. My sister Leona and I were visiting, allegedly to help bring in the crop. Grandpa and we were in the sweltering bottomland of his farm. Two mules pulled the wagon while Grandpa walked along side limping all the way from the lasting effect of a broken leg suffered previously when mules ran wild and he was dragged from his wagon and severely fractured his leg. In the 100° temperature Grandpa limped, sweated profusely and resolutely picked ear after ear of corn and pitched them into the wagon. I looked at him with deep concern, greatly afraid that he was about to fatally succumb to it all right before my young eyes. But he made it back to the farmhouse and instructed me to unhitch the mules and take them down to the water tank (pond) so they could get their thirst quenched.

My second image of Grandpa Kieschnick is of him leading family devotions, a ritual which was for him absolutely essential every single day. I doubt if he ever got beyond 6th grade in school, but he read the German devotional material and prayers with such solemnity, quiet eloquence and conviction that I still hear his voice today.

My third memory relates to his funeral. After his death his embalmed body was returned to the parlor of his farmhouse. There, church members, neighbors and friends all came to pay their respects. Then there was a brief pastor-led ritual after which his coffin was placed in the hearse for the trip to St. John Lutheran Church in Lincoln for the formal funeral.

To get from the Kieschnick farm home to the main road required going through several gates. At each of the four gates there stood one of his hired black laborers. Each one stood next to a sleek black horse and each black man held his hat solemnly across his chest, honoring the man for whom they all worked.

Grandpa combined his deep devotion to God and church with hard work and wise investments. Beginning with very little he departed having fulfilled his vision of being able to provide via inheritance a separate farm for each of his children.

Early on I learned a skill that serves me to this day. Our whole family was often invited to people's homes for birthdays, holidays, weddings, etc. The women and men were, of course, separated. After dinner the women conversed. The men played cards, especially a game called "Scott." As the evening progressed and I got more and more sleepy, I learned to find the bedroom where all hats and coats of guests were laid. I shoved them aside, made myself a bit of space and slept peacefully. And to this day I can fall asleep in my chair, on a plane, during dull lectures or while watching Jeopardy or the San Diego Padres.

ഔൽ

PRESCHOOL

Some people, including son David, have an incredible ability to recall events of their early life, even prior to the age of six years. I have very few memories of my life prior to Grade 1.

Of course, I didn't go to preschool. That was unthinkable in those days and I doubt if there was even a single kindergarten in the Lutheran School system then even though it had some 2,000 elementary schools.

I do remember our family growing. Seems like a new baby came every two years. I was born in December 1927 the third child with two older sisters, Erna, born in 1924 and Leona in 1926. Doris arrived in February 1930, Mimi in March 1932, Harold in 1934 and Ethel in 1935. Mom must have had a couple of miscarriages for John and Darline were not born until 1942 and 1943. I have no memory of awaiting a new birth. The word "pregnancy" was never mentioned in mixed company.

Whenever it was time for the arrival of another sibling, I was taken to Aunt Mattie Kurio's to spend the night. (I wonder how old I was before I caught on that there would be a new sibling by the time I went back home.)

Each of us were loved and provided for by our parents. Mom just kept on breast-feeding, cooking, sewing, canning, cleaning and caring for the sick ones. Every night we had family prayers complete with Bible readings and a hymn.

Every Sunday (and I do mean *every* Sunday) found us all in church for which, to my constant dread, I was obligated to wear shoes. The rest of the time for ten months of every year we were all barefooted.

Mentioning church helps me recall two embarrassments. It was the custom at Zion Lutheran Church for young children to sit together up front in

165

pews arranged at right angles to the rest of the congregation. One Sunday I acted inappropriately. Mom left the two little ones sitting with her, marched to the front of the sanctuary and gathered me under her left arm to get me out of church – fast. Unfortunately, one of my legs dangled somewhat freely and as she carried me out that foot hit the wainscot wall on the side of the church. So, the rat-a-tat-tat of my shoe against the wall followed us all the way out of church. By this time Mom was so upset that she waited no longer and gave me my well-deserved spanking just outside the church door. The sound of her slaps and my screams filled the sanctuary.

My dad, who was school principal and church organist, also served as church janitor and his duties included posting the hymn numbers on the hymn number boards on either side of the front altar. Once when I was about four, I asked him the names of some of the hymns. I immediately recognized one (in German, of course, because all of our services then were in German). The next Sunday I proudly announced to a friend, "I can read the hymns! I opened the hymnal to the appropriate number and began acting as though I was reading; but my faking was exposed because I was looking at hymn 356 but was "reading" the words of hymn 282. My somewhat older friend, who could read, called my bluff!

One of my special preschool thrills was when I was asked to be ring bearer at a wedding. I would get some new clothes and lots of attention. Sometimes I carried the ring lightly, stitched to a pillow. Once it was inside a big white blossom. I remember being asked to kiss the little flower girl but I steadfastly refused to do so.

ɛɔCʁ

ELEMENTARY SCHOOL JOYS

My elementary education was in the wonderful two-room Zion Lutheran School in Walburg, Texas. Maybe it's because one remembers pleasant times and blots out the bad, but my recollections are all happy and joyful.

I eagerly anticipated school. My teacher "Teacher Bleeke" was a family friend. My dad was principal. My two elder sisters and some 10 cousins were schoolmates. All the other pupils were from the same Lutheran Church-German community. I had strong self-esteem. I was eager to learn.

We lived almost next to the school in a "teacherage." This is like a "parsonage" except it was for teachers. It took just five minutes to get to school in the morning. I had "dinner" at home every day at noon.

Recess was always a highlight. Softball was the recess activity of choice. We always chose teams and the competition was friendly but fierce. Morning and afternoon recess times were often extended and the lunch hour was always an hour. By the time I was in the 5th Grade we played softball games against public neighboring schools but we were not allowed to play the Catholic school team only four miles away. We were German Lutherans. They were Czech Catholics and in those days we stayed apart.

It was also while I was at Zion that we got the first ever set of swings for the school. When we weren't playing softball, we rode the swings or played marbles (playing "for keeps" was forbidden and all "won" marbles needed to be returned at the end of the day). Other games included Andy Over, Red Rover, and a little basketball. Strange as it now seems for one growing up in Texas, I do not recall us playing football though every Saturday had me listening to the Texas Longhorn games on the radio.

The school building and classrooms were simple. The toilets were plain old "outhouses." When it was cold the older boys stoked the stove in the center of the classroom with coal from the coal shed. We boys also took turns pulling up fresh water from the well and putting it into central outdoor containers. We were supposed to bring our own drinking cups but most of us forgot them so we all shared a common cup.

There was no school bus. Those who lived within three miles walked. Some rode horses or came in horse drawn "buggies." Others were brought by car, usually a Ford Model A or Model T.

A major fun day was the school picnic held near the end of the school term. It began the night before when "the men" spent the night making barbeque on the immense outdoor pit. The 400 pounds of wonderful meat, which was slowly barbequed for 12 or more hours, was sold for the dinner. There was a concession stand and my memory is that I received an incredibly large amount of money to spend, 25 cents. That was enough for five ice cream cones or one bottle of pop, one package of gum, one candy bar, one ice cream cone and one lemonade. It took a week to plan my budget!

At the picnic the church brass band (which my father directed) played from their specially designed bandstand. In election years political candidates were invited to shake hands and make short speeches. I always remember the one question all adults asked of the candidates, "What is your position on child labor laws?" The rumor was that Congress was about to pass strict "Child Labor Laws," one component of which would forbid farmer parents from having their children pick cotton or even milk cows twice a day.

Everyone at the picnic was anti-Child Labor laws.

Of course, school was more than fun and games - and I'll get to that in my next blog entry - but the point here is "I loved school – every day!"

ಬ೧ಚ

THE FIRST OF THE FOUR "R"s: READING AND RITING

Everybody learned to read at Zion Lutheran School. There was really only one method of teaching reading and that was phonics. We used the same Bobbs-Merrill Primer millions of others did after its first printing in 1929. We both read and memorized the immortal first pages about The Gingerbread Boy. "I am the gingerbread boy, I am, I am. I can run from you, I can, I can." From that primer we went directly to the phonics charts. "can, man, pan" and "fast, last, past." It worked.

Unfortunately, there was no library at school or at home. It was the time of The Great Depression and nobody had money for books. I never owned a "child's book." I had no public library card. When I was in about the 6th grade the school suddenly received a treasure: a collection of some 60 books of the classics. Each story was condensed to about 30 pages. I devoured them all, finishing them within two weeks.

In addition to reading English we learned to read German, using the German alphabet and style. We began with a book called, "Die Feeble," then "Erste Lesebuch" and after that "Zweite Lesebuch." This was taught from Grade 1 through Grade 8.

As I reflect upon my reading instruction I wonder where and how I developed my lifelong love of reading. Maybe it was the deprivation in the early years or maybe it was my father who was my Grades 4-8 teacher and who would read to us with a great animation. Something stirred up within me a passion for reading that remains very strong to this day.

"Riting (writing), the second R had two points of stress: correct grammar and good penmanship. Proper grammar was drilled into us. By the 6th grade we spent hour after hour diagramming sentences. In retrospect I am very grateful for this experience. We learned all about subject, predicate, object, prepositional phrases, major and sub-ordinate classes, and the parts of speech – carefully noting transitive and intransitive verbs etc. etc. I loved it. I still remember in the 8th grade being challenged to diagram one of the longest sentences Martin Luther ever wrote (at least it came out as only one sentence in English). Imagine diagramming this sentence. "I believe that Jesus Christ, true God, begotten of the Father from eternity, and also true man, born of the Virgin Mary, is my Lord, who has redeemed me, a lost and condemned person, purchased and won me from all sin, from death and from the power of the devil; not with gold or silver, but with His holy precious blood and with His innocent suffering and death, that I may be His own and live under Him in His kingdom and serve Him in everlasting righteousness, innocence and blessedness, just as He is risen from the dead, lives and reigns to all eternity." Just imagine your teacher saying to you, "Melvin, I want you to diagram that one sentence – do it on the blackboard."

Handwriting was taught as a separate subject and given a specific grade on each report card. And I never made an "A" in that subject. I remember my teacher using something called "The Palmer Method" that was supposed to involve one's entire arm and not just one's fingers. I failed miserably.

Regretfully my elementary schooling did not stress actually writing reports, essays or anything creative. When I now see what my grandchildren are doing in elementary school writing assignments, I am regretful at my never receiving that kind of inspiration. Yet I am grateful that at least my grammar is usually correct.

But I must end this blog entry on a positive note. Certainly, the grounding of my faith in Zion Lutheran School has given me the faith, strength, courage and hope to live a wonderful life following the One who said, "I am the Way, the Truth and the Life."

ഌരു

PRIMARY SCHOOL PART 1: THE FOURTH "R" RELIGION

In this series of blog entries on my elementary school I have called the fourth "R" to be religion. I am sure that the founders of my elementary school, namely Zion Lutheran School, Walburg, Texas would insist that R for Religion should be the first R. The primary purpose of the school included teaching the Christian faith to the children of congregation members (and only to them). Usually a separately listed goal was "to prepare children for the ritual of confirmation." This was such an important aspect of congregational life that I recall a discussion as to whether parents who chose to not send their children to Zion should actually be excommunicated from the church as they were deemed to be neglecting the best resource for

169

learning to grow as Christians.

So, obviously, religion was the critical component of our curriculum. We had a formal class on religion every school day, each class lasting from 30 minutes to an hour. At the heart of our lesson was learning Bible stories (also called Bible History). We learned the narratives well. The teacher told the story. We were questioned about the story. We students told the stories to the class or we asked the class questions on the story – or we volunteered to stand in front and have our fellow students ask us questions about the story. We had large colored pictures of the Biblical events posted on the wall. They all came from Concordia Publishing House and I think were the only pictures in our classrooms. We had the stories in printed form also (in both English and German). I learned those stories and loved them and to this day am grateful for the experience.

The second aspect of our religious instruction was learning Dr. Martin Luther's Catechism and an extended version of this with appropriate questions, answers and Biblical references. I memorized the catechism first in German, then in English (and much later in Cantonese). My recollection is that the primary teaching method was "question and answer" and my grades 4-8 teacher was an absolute master at that.

The third aspect of our formal religion classes was music. We learned to sing hymns. By the time I was in the sixth grade we were singing them in three-part harmony. One strong memory: When I was in about the fifth grade a schoolmate burned to death. She had gotten up before her parents arose, decided she would surprise them by preparing fried bacon and eggs for breakfast. Unfortunately, the kerosene stove exploded costing her her life. We sang at her funeral, "I am Jesus Little Lamb." We sang it in German and my entire being recalls the moment.

When we reached the 7th grade, we were excused for the first hour of the day to go to "confirmation class" taught by the pastor. My reflection: "Total disaster!"

It is now some 73 years since I was taught that fourth R and for much of it, I am forever grateful. I learned, among many other things at least, an important life lessons 1) God is for me, not against me. God forgives me, accepts me, loves me. 2) The Christian life is a life of grateful responses, daring fullness, filled with service to neighbors around the world. 3) The power of prayer: God hears and responds. 4) Eternity is a mystery, but wonderful. 5) My teacher continues to be a model of what it means to be a Christian.

There were also some significant weaknesses and failures in my elementary school religious training. Probably the most serious is what I call "religious arrogance." We were taught the official teaching of the Lutheran Church-Missouri Synod - that it was the only body of Christians who believed and taught "the Word of God in all its truth and purity." We had it like a clear glass of water. Others had part of it, but their glasses of water were filled with lots of dirt. We were never to worship or pray with or even play softball against other Christians, like Roman Catholics, Baptists, Episcopalians or even Lutherans who were not Missouri Synod. If a graduate of our school married a spouse of another Lutheran denomination and that spouse joined our congregation, we called him/her an "adult convert."

A second failing in my religious upbringing related to the above was the importance of the "proof-text" manner of teaching. We were taught a certain piece of doctrine which was stated as truth and then there was a small verse from Scripture to prove this teaching. I now know that it is probably true that one can find a particular "proof text" in Scripture for anything. Sometimes this proof-texting was taken out of context and the true teaching was distorted.

The third failure was in the area of skills and practices for personal reflection. I went to Lutheran schools and college for 16 years and not once was I asked to "just observe a few moments of silence." Not once was I taught how to meditate. Not once was I given any real guidance on what it means to "be still and know that I am God."

ℰᏁ

PRIMARY SCHOOL PART 2: PHYSICAL HEALTH

My memory is that I was a healthy strong boy. Of course, I together with my siblings and friends had all the usual childhood illnesses, none of which was considered dangerous. We had the mumps, measles, chickenpox, red eye and scarlatina. I don't think any of these were serious enough to have to go see our family physician, Dr. Wedemeyer. But Mr. McGuiness, the druggist in the 55 residents-town of Walburg, regularly filled our prescriptions.

There were, however, three specific health issues that stick with me to this day.

The first is a tooth filling. My cousins who drank "Walburg water" never had decayed teeth. There was something in that water that discolored their enamel but preserved their teeth. I was not so fortunate. I had to have a tooth filled (probably hastened by the reality that as a child I never brushed my teeth).

My memory is that in the mid-1930's the dentist used no anesthesia and the drilling was painful. But that's not what was the most painful. What hurt most was that the after-school dentist appointment came on the exact date that Zion school played softball against another school – a rare event. I simply could not believe that my parents thought it more important for me to go to the dentist than it was to play this softball game. I knew my team would miss me. I knew my substitute at the shortstop position, Wimpy K, could not play up to my standard.

So, it was with mixed feelings that I learned the results of the team having to play without me. We won and all the students said that Wimpy was a great shortstop, made two great plays and hit a double. (As stated above, this was nearly 70 years ago and I remember it still. And, Wimpy grew up to be called "W.A.," was a successful banker and married my cousin Genelle.)

Second health memory. We went barefoot all the time, except that we needed to wear shoes when we went to church on Sunday. There are consequences of always going barefoot. The soles of the feet become hard as leather, but not hard enough to avoid being pierced. We stepped on glass that lacerated our feet. We stepped on nails protruding from boards and they pierced our soles. We would come home from the cotton fields with thistles embedded in our feet. We dug them out with needles or tweezers. Mercurochrome treated the wounds and if there was a slight infection, we had a famous "black salve" that cured everything.

But some 15 years later a surprise reminder of those barefoot adventures suddenly was revealed. I played college football and broke my ankle. The doctor who examined the x-rays noted the break but had a more interesting question. "When did you step on that needle now firmly embedded in your heel?"

My mother always worried that the needle would move, get to my heart and kill me. I ignored it. In 1958 I played basketball in Hong Kong, had an x-ray and heard the doctor ask in Cantonese, "Where did that needle in your heel come from?"

The last time I had to have that ankle x-rayed was when I was in my 60's. The needle continues to rest comfortably in my heel.

∞☙

EARLY YEARS: CHORES AND WORK

During my primary school years, I almost never had to do any school homework. Since I attended a two-room school there was always time during school hours to complete our assignments (We did that while the "other grades" were "up front" for their specific subjects). The only homework I recall was my mother listening to me recite my "Religion Recitation," memorized Bible verses, Catechism lessons and hymns.

Household chores were shared (after all, eventually there were nine of us kids). I often helped "do the dishes" and got an earful from one or more of my sisters when I tried to be excused from this as I suggested this was "girls' work."

We lived in the church's teacherage, which was located on several acres of the congregation-owned land. So, there was room for our home, barn, stables, hen house, large pasture, small field for crops, a large garden and a big cemetery. Our lawn was immense and the grass was always mowed by me using a hand-driven mower.

The cattle, chickens and pigs needed twice daily feeding. We shucked corn and shelled it for the chickens with the hand-driven corn sheller. We sometimes had fun shucking corn, seeing who could shuck 100 ears the fastest. Or we would get a thrill out of shucking an extra amount of corn and hiding it. Then when we were told to "go shuck corn" we gleefully exposed our already completed work.

From very early on, I milked the cows. The cow was let into the stall and her calf was allowed to come suckle. Then we roped off the calf, sat down next to the cow and milked her. The milk was immediately taken to our home and run through our hand-cranked separator that separated the cream, which was then made into butter. I always liked to drink my milk when it was still warm, having just come from the cow's udder. When the calves reached a weight of a couple hundred pounds or so they were sold to the local butcher.

We slaughtered our hogs ourselves on cold days with the assistance of neighbors. I recall how they were killed (usually by slitting their throats). They were bled and then dropped in hot water so that the hairy skin could be scraped off. We had wonderful fresh pork and also preserved smoked sausages and hams (and occasionally also the stomach). One of my jobs was to keep the bark of logs smoking in the smoke house where the pork was cured.

We ate lots of eggs and chickens. My mouth still waters as I recall my mom catching a young rooster, chopping its head off, getting the feathers off and then frying that wonderful chicken in home-made lard. The price I paid for getting those always fresh and tasty meals was two-fold. 1) Feed those chickens plenty of corn and 2) Keep scraping the chicken "droppings" to keep the hen houses clean.

Summertime meant it was time for us to earn some cash for the family. We kids never kept a penny of those earnings for ourselves and we never had an "allowance." Those meager resources all went into the family coffers. While others "chopped cotton," I never had that chore. It entailed hoeing very close to the young cotton plant, removing weeds and surrounding the cotton plant with fresh soil. I think the fear was that if I were given this task, I would too often chop out the whole plant. But I could "pick cotton." An eight to ten-foot-long bag was strung over our shoulders and dragged behind. We "crawled" between two rows of cotton plants and extracted the soft cotton bolls. The load was weighed, placed in a wagon and when some 1,300 pounds had accumulated was taken to the gin. There the lint was separated from the cottonseed and debris, then packaged into 500-pound bales and sold. On a really good sun-up to sundown day of picking I might make between 50-75 cents. But I was such an inept cotton picker (my sister out-picked me every time) that rumor has it that the verdict was, "Melvin will never make it on the farm. He'd better go to work for the church as a teacher!"

And that is what I did.

෨ଓ

ELEMENTARY SCHOOLDAYS: HELPING GRANDPA

In my elementary school age, it was always a very special treat to go visit Grandma and Grandpa Kieschnick. They lived in a farm outside Lincoln, Texas, about 60 miles from my home. The trip to and from was itself an adventure. We loaded our 1929 Model A Ford with kids and excitement. The roads, of course, were unpaved and the 60-mile trip took in excess of two hours, especially since it was not at all unusual to have to stop and fix a flat.

Once at Grandma's place we were sent to the garden to hoe weeds, prop up plants and often harvest some vegetables and/or fruit. If I (or my sister Leona and I) stayed over for a week or more our jobs got more interesting. I remember picking beans, then placing them on a tarp to get good and dry. After a few days we beat the beans to separate the kernels from their pods. After another day or so of dry heat we would find a windy spot. Then we threw the beans into the air and let the wind separate the kernels from the chaff. The chaff was fed to the animals; the kernels we consumed.

A special treat while at Grandpa's was to make hay. The hay was in a field some distance from the farmhouse. That was good because we got there by riding on the back of my Dad's faithful horse, Dan. I remember my job when the dried hay was made into bales. I sat on one side of the baling machine and reinserted baling wire so it could go from one side of the bale to the other.

We had an hour off for lunch to eat and rest. One time I think my sister and I sat on some kind of a tick nest. That evening our bodies were covered with blisters and we both believed that some of those ticks had embedded themselves permanently into our flesh. We struggled to extract them from our own and our sib's body.

At the end of the day there was a special treat. Grandpa would say in German, "Melvin, go take the horses down to the tank to water them." This meant unhitching them from their wagons and then leading them to a tank (pond) where they drank the water. I loved being in charge of those horses, then unbridling them, feeding them and getting them into their own stalls for the night.

A job that I did poorly and hated was "cutting maize." Milo maize grew to be several feet tall and the stalks contained seeds. The job was to use a knife, cut off the head, put it into a bag and then load it onto a wagon. That was tough work. Worse yet was that something about that milo maize created a terrible itch over my whole body – and of course the rule was "bathe only once a week, on Saturday." One of God's great gifts to kids like me was the invention of the combine, which eliminated the job of "cutting maize."

Many years later when as a school principal I was confronted with an upset parent or an angry teacher I always comforted myself by saying, "This surely beats cutting maize!"

ഇരു

EARLY EXPERIENCE WITH DEATH

Death and dying were certainly not far removed or never spoken about in my early life. After all, my home abutted the church cemetery, a couple of hundred steps from our front yard. From very early in my life I watched the volunteer grave diggers; I went with Dad who tolled the funeral bells; I

175

watched the earth being dropped upon the in-grave coffins as the pastor intoned, "dust to dust, ashes to ashes."

The death of animals in front of my eyes was a regular event. Mother killed fryers for dinner; hogs were slaughtered for ham and sausages. Our heifers were always sent away for butchering. I was still in elementary school when I assisted my cousin Ben Jacob in his weekly ritual of butchering cattle. Fresh beef was always available in their Andic General Merchandise Store.

Two animal deaths did disturb me. I was so sad when my father needed to shoot to death my beloved pet dog, Rover. Rover had been bitten by a poisonous snake. The bite around Rover's mouth became terribly infected. Rover could not eat. Seeing a vet was never considered. The bite looked fatal and besides we had no money for vet costs. So, Dad shot, killed and buried Rover, the closest pet I ever owned.

The second instance was a pet lamb whose name I cannot remember. We played with it from its infancy. Then came time for it to be butchered, but I could not get myself to eat the meat.

The third recollection relates to a near-death (but no death) experience. Some of my relatives were visiting and showing off their newly acquired 22 long-range rifles. They spotted a near-by bird and gave me instructions on how to aim, fire and kill that beautiful meadowlark, head held high and singing. I missed and I was glad! In that moment I resolved to never again fire a gun at a bird and I have kept that promise.

I am amazed that I claim to have a memory of when I was only 3½ years old, but I think it is a real memory. My cousin Milton Kurio who lived only a mile away died at the age of only 10 months. My memory is of overwhelming sadness seeing that miniature coffin being lowered into the ground.

The other strong memory is when I was 5 years old and being told of the untimely death of my cousin Ben Siek who was also 5 years of age. Uncle Ben (young Ben's father) and Aunt Elizabeth had just had electricity installed in their Austin home. They joyfully replaced the old icebox with a new electric refrigerator. The icebox was awaiting pick-up for disposal. Cousins Helen and Ben were curious. They climbed into the old icebox, Helen in the ice storage side and Ben in the food storage side. We never learned how both doors became slammed shut. By the time frantic Aunt Elizabeth and Uncle Ben found their trapped children both were unconscious. Helen survived, apparently because some life-saving oxygen worked its way up the ice drainage pipe but Bennie was beyond recovery. I had played with Bennie just days before his tragic death. Sadly, 15 months later Uncle Ben died and I remember the faith, courage and strength with which Aunt Elizabeth and Cousin Helen carried on after those shattering experiences.

Of course, in the years since these early encounters with death I have been at the bedside of many deaths, have presided over burials ranging from Forest Lawn in Glendale, California, to hillsides in Hong Kong, to burial at sea in the Pacific. My childhood images of heaven and the after-life have changed in many ways. I continue to marvel at the mysteries of eternal life and I am confident in my trust in a benevolent God and confident that peace is what yet awaits us all.

ഇൻ

EARLY CHILDHOOD: POVERTY AND POLITICS

I grew up poor. I was born in 1927. The market crash was in 1929. The national unemployment rate rose above 25%. Income from farm products plunged. Dad's salary was about $50 a month. Often the congregation was unable to pay even that. At one point the congregation owed him (I think) $300. They had a special fundraising effort, raised $150, gave that to him and called it even.

We never went hungry. We raised lots and Mom canned tons of vegetables. When all else failed we had boiled potatoes covered with beet juice. I loved it. I can still smell and taste the homemade bread. We raised and ate our chickens and pigs. The heifers were sold and we bought the beef. Even after our family grew to seven members Mom would send me to buy $1.00 worth of round steak and it would feed the whole family. When we "butchered hogs" the meat was cut off the bones and made into sausage. But the bones were kept (some of them canned). When things got tough, Mother cooked these bones, we applied mustard and ground off the remaining bits of meat.

I had my first-ever food in a restaurant when I was 14, a hamburger.

For me the Great Depression is associated with the anti-poverty efforts of President Franklin D. Roosevelt. We listened on the radio to his fireside chats and made fun of his references to his dog, Fala. In those days we were all Democrats. (I don't think I ever met a self-proclaimed Republican before I went to college!)

Two of the New Deal programs, which provided some government sponsored employment, were the Civilian Conservation Corps (CCC) and the

Works Progress Administration (WPA). As one part of its assignment WPA built better "out-houses" and one was built for us. Of course, we had no indoor toilet facilities and that outhouse was a welcome luxury. (And yes, it was always supplied with a Sears Roebuck Catalog. Real toilet paper was only for "the rich people.")

Even though we benefitted from the WPA it was ridiculed and looked down upon by the adults whom I heard speaking about it. Those WPA workers were considered poor citizens for "relying on government handouts." The belief was that if you were in trouble you just got by, trusted your family and if you got hungry then subsisted on "jelly bread." I do not believe that a single member of Zion Lutheran Congregation ever "stooped so low as to go on public welfare" and take one of those government hand-out jobs!

In the midst of it all, we kids always took along our Sunday church offering, a nickel every Sunday! In reflection, I feel sadness at how hard my parents struggled to meet our needs; yet I am also grateful. Those years taught me "to be content with what I had," to always try to find some kind of a job, and to be a very conservative spender. It also taught me to have a very deep appreciation for those rare and special days at our church picnic. I was given a nickel and for that got a big double scoop of ice cream!

୫୦୯୫

END OF ELEMENTARY SCHOOL

The 8th grade, my 14th year of life, marked a significant transition point. There were several clear indications that I had moved from being a young child to being a young man.

One of those rituals was Confirmation at my church. This was a ritual in which we expressed a re-confirmation of our status as beloved children of God. This first happened at our infant baptism but was then "confirmed" when we were 14 or in the eighth grade.

Significant rituals marked the Confirmation occasion. In my time it was always on Palm Sunday, the Sunday before Easter. First was the matter of dress. My parents took me to Walburg Mercantile General Store. There we picked out my first-ever store-bought suit. It was smart and cost a total of $7.00, a major investment for clothes. I got a nice tie and a new pair of black patent leather shoes. I wore my new attire with pride for years and still have that now 73-year-old Kodak photo to prove how proudly I wore that suit.

178

The second phase of the ritual was a "public examination" in front of the entire congregation. The pastor asked the questions, called upon a "confirmand" to answer loud enough so the whole church could hear. The anxiety around this ritual was somewhat reduced by at least two factors. We pretty well knew what the questions would be and even the preferred exact words in the answer. Also, the pastor wanted to prove that he had taught us well; so, he knew on whom he should call for the easy or the more difficult responses.

The ritual was also important because each of us was given a "confirmation verse." This was a short text from the Bible. Mine was Romans 1:16: "I am not ashamed of the gospel of Christ for it is the power of God unto salvation to everyone that believeth."

In those days, Confirmation also meant we were allowed for the first time to partake of the Sacrament of Holy Communion, a very important ritual for me to this day. "First Communion" was always on Maundy Thursday, the Thursday after Palm Sunday. We used a strange procedure as a part of this ritual. We knelt at an altar rail on the left and received the host (bread). Then we got up, walked behind the altar and knelt on the other side and received the wine.

Of course, those were always several social dimensions to the religious ceremony of Confirmation. One was that our sponsors (godparents) joined us for the service and at the big meal in our home afterwards. My sponsors all made it (except for one who had tragically drowned while he was still a young man). Of course, the sponsors gave us gifts. I remember the incredible gift of a full $5.00 and leather-bound King James version of the Bible. That Bible (though twice rebound since) is still a treasure to me.

There was still another coming of age privilege attached to Confirmation. We were now allowed to become members of The Walther League. The Walther League was the official young people's society of the church. The very first ritual after our Palm Sunday Confirmation which we, as new Walther Leaguers, could participate in was an Easter Egg Hunt on Easter, the first Sunday after Palm Sunday. It was a thrill for me to look for those eggs hidden in the pasture around our home.

৪০০৪

HIGH SCHOOL: DORM LIFE

As mentioned previously my four high school years were at a residential prep school (preparing for ordained ministry in the church). It was small; less than 100, all boys.

The facilities were sparse. I remember especially the long concrete corridor of our second-floor dormitory. A favorite midnight prowl was for a student to take a big 16-pound steel shot put and roll it down the entire length of the corridor. The whole floor reverberated, especially in the bedroom of Dean George Beto who slept in his room one floor below ours. I recall one night he came up to investigate. Of course, every student was fast asleep. Nevertheless, he went to the end room, opened the door and screamed at the two occupants, "Steyer and Krueger, you are both 'campused' for next weekend." Which meant they were not allowed to step their feet off campus.

Another very daring adventure (remember this was way back in 1941) was to sleep on the flat deck serving as the roof over the dining rom. I guess what made this exciting was that it was forbidden – and we had to pick a lock to gain access. But when we lay there on our blankets on a starry Texas night, we felt daring – and maybe even romantic.

Naturally, there were no computers or cell phones then. There was one pay phone in the main hall. To make a long-distance call home was out of the question, way too expensive. My memory is that I made a total of two calls in my four years there, both times calling "girls" and asking for a date. Once I succeeded. It provided me with the only real date in those four years at Austin Concordia.

I am embarrassed to remember that I never did my own laundry. As was the custom, I placed my dirty clothes and bed linens in a cardboard laundry box and mailed it home! My mother washed, ironed and then sent me back my newly laundered clothes.

Only upper classmen were allowed to smoke. If a freshman or sophomore was ever seen with a cigarette, that cigarette was confiscated along with any others the smoker had unsuccessfully hidden.

Showers were, of course, communal. I recall no doors on the shower stalls. As adolescent boys it was a time for much "comparison," pride or embarrassment.

There was supervised "study period" every night from 7:00 – 9:00 p.m. I still recall how I shuddered when, one evening, Dean Beto opened the door to my room and bellowed, "Kieschnick, what are you doing? You're supposed to be studying!" My memory is that I was writing a message on the penny

180

post card I was mailing to Mother the next day.

I still have some feelings of guilt about an "extra expense" I caused my parents. In my sophomore year I got a new roommate, Mike, who now lives five minutes away from me in Encinitas, California. He wanted to place venetian blinds on our room windows. I agreed and my share of the cost was, I think, $8.00! This was an extravagance my parents paid with great reluctance. I can assure you the home in which they lived had no fancy window coverings like blinds.

As I reflect now on those experiences some 70 years ago my memories are warm. I learned to live in community, to budget time and money, to develop my own set of values, to appreciate friendship, to resolve conflicts without resorting to violence and to survive the teen years in an all-male environment.

ഈൻ

CONCORDIA COLLEGE (ACADEMY) AUSTIN

Even before I was in Grade 1 of my elementary school, I knew what I wanted to be/do when I grew up. I was going to be a teacher in a Lutheran parochial school. That's what my Dad was and he was my ideal. So, it was an unquestioned given that Melvin was going to be a Teaching Minister. Only once (maybe when I was in the fourth grade) was this plan ever discussed. Mother was very sad and I recall her looking at me with loving eyes and saying, "Melvin, are you sure you want to be a Lutheran school teacher? There must be something better than that!" I was shocked. My guess is that Dad had not been paid even his meager $60 a month salary and that it was hard for Mom to feed and clothe her children and she really did not want her oldest son to go through that. Of course, I protested, "I want to be a teacher, just like my Papa!"

So, there was no question about it. The first step was Austin College, now Concordia University, Texas. It was also called Concordia Academy. It was never called Concordia High School, although the only grades it included were Grades 9-12 that were always called freshman, sophomore, junior and senior. It was a prep-school for recognized ministers in the Lutheran Church-Missouri Synod. There were two classifications: "Ordained Minister" and "Commissioned Teacher."

It was small. I don't think that in my days the total school enrollment

181

ever exceeded 100. It was for "boys" only. And it was 100% residential. So, at the age of 13 I left home for Concordia.

My memories are almost all positive. I loved sports and the school was so small that I could, of course, play all varsity sports. The professors all knew and respected my father who was chair of the All Texas Lutheran Teachers Conference, my Uncle Reinhold was on the Board of Control and the Director of the school (Studtman) was often a dinner guest in my home.

We lived in dorm rooms on the second floor; had our meals, classes, and chapel on the ground floor. There were two students in each room. We each had our "Murphy beds" which folded up and rolled into the closet each day. There was a central shower and toilet. To this day my high school friends all know that "Room 210" means shower and rest room.

As was typical of the day, there was some hazing of lower classmen. Any senior could scream, "Freshman! Sophomore!" and we were expected to run to the person who screamed and follow his orders. I escaped physical attacks and really had very few assignments beyond shining the shoes of the upperclassmen.

The day was highly routinized. Breakfast at 7:00, bed inspection at 8:00, classes till 4:00. Chapel services every morning and every night at 9:00. Lights out at 10:00 with the Dean making inspection every night to be sure we were in bed.

ℰℚ

BIRTHDAY TIME

I was born December 10, 1927. So, it's time for my 87th birthday.

Birthdays are, of course, personal. After all it is my time on this earth that I am observing. But birthdays are also always communal. Without Mom and Dad there would be no "me." So, I want to spend a bit of time this birthday reflecting upon my 87 years of life, both personal and communal.

It has been and continues to be a good life made so by a host of human connections, Divine Guidance and my own response. Here are just a few examples of how this has all transpired.

Faith
My parents were people of faith. They saw me as a gift from God. They brought me to baptism just days after my birth. They taught me to pray, to trust, and to believe in a good and forgiving God. During my years my faith

182

has changed. It has been deepened, been threatened, been modified, exists among doubts, keeps me going, gives me hope for the future.

Family

My family is my greatest earthly gift. My parents sacrificed much for me, sending me off to "study for the ministry" beginning at the age of 13. My two older sisters had to turn down college scholarships (and never went to college) so they could work "outside the home" to help pay for my schooling. My six sisters and one living brother continue to care about me and tell me they respect me. (In fact, as I write this, I have paused to answer phone calls from them wishing me "Happy Birthday.")

I am profoundly blessed through my five kids. All are persons with wonderful values, professional success, caring hearts, liberal supporters of good causes and people in need. They have, I think, forgiven me for some of my unwise decisions and actions I may have made as a part of my less-than-perfect parenting. They know how greatly I love them and how deeply I respect them.

Jane, my wife of 63 years, is my anchor. I do not want to live without her. Someone recently made the slightly enigmatic comment, "You know that the longer the two of you both live, the less time either of you will be living alone." Celebrating a birthday without Jane is something I don't want to think about and celebrating with her is a high delight.

Friends and Colleagues

I have had more than my share of co-workers, people reporting to me, neighbors, bosses, and colleagues. Most were wonderful supporters, a few hard to take, a very few impossible. At first it was just Rosa Bush and me in a two-room school. Then it included hundreds and even thousands who were part of a throng of Lutheran teachers with whom I shared responsibilities. I have been challenged and affirmed, knocked down and pulled up, cursed at and prayed over. In almost every setting we had some great and wonderful birthday parties and cakes, including one massive sheet cake with a beautiful birthday greeting in Chinese characters delivered to Concordia Kowloon, enough for 65 servings! --- My number of close friends is now, regretfully very small. I can probably count them on one hand, but in my mind, I can go back to a multitude of times together in quiet conversations, at conventions, sharing good Scotch and honest talk, great dreaming and exchanging quarters won/lost on the golf course.

Experiences

I am blown away in gratitude for the incredible set of experiences I have had in my life. I've taught in Grades 1-8 and in graduate school. I've been the CEO of a staff of two and over 60, had responsibility for budgets totaling $20,000 and over $26 million. I've picked cotton, set bowling pins in a bowling alley, supervised, managed multi-million-dollar building projects, peeled potatoes, waited on tables, had meetings in squatter huts, in State Senate chambers and the White House. I have conducted workshops, preached, presided at baptisms, weddings, anniversaries, and funerals – around the world. I honestly, greatly and humbly can feel that I have made a difference.

I was born in the country, a mile from the town of Walburg, Texas with a population of "44 friendly citizens and one old grouch." In my early years, a trip of 60 miles was a major experience. Last week I saw an ad for the10 top cities of the world and the top hotel in each of them. I did not stay in all those top hotels but I certainly visited those top cities. As I looked at the list of cities, I reflected upon cities which I have visited, usually as part of a speaking tour or similar. I decided to list some of these cities, not in a spirit of braggadocio, but in the hope that as readers see names of cities, they have visited they may stir pleasant memories as it did for me. Take a look: Tokyo, Seoul, Taipei, Hong Kong, Macau, Shanghai, Beijing, Xian, Urumchi, Lhasa, Bangkok, Singapore, Calcutta, New Delhi, Karachi, Islamabad, Jerusalem, Cairo, Beirut, Istanbul, Athens, Rome, Zurich, Vienna, Paris, Prague, Berlin, Amsterdam, Copenhagen, Stockholm, Oslo, London, Edinburgh, Madrid, Barcelona, Bermuda, The Bahamas, Rio de Janeiro, Cancun, San Juan, Tahiti, Sydney, Auckland… I have been blessed to have been in all 50 states of our country and made some kind of group presentation in all but five of them. Blessings upon blessings.

Health

Health is another great gift for which I am thankful. My body still works reasonably well – most days. I even shot my age again twice this year. But I am getting older, weaker, hear less well, forget much more, tire more quickly, have low sexual impulses, less stamina, think more slowly.

Decision

I have decided to stop making any more speeches, delivering any more sermons, conducting any workshops, being responsible for any more events. I want to do only one-on-one stuff like visits to the sick or lonely. I want to be available to my wife and family, especially to our eldest son David who has serious cancer. I want to get more involved in the retirement community in which Jane and I live. I want to continue to support organizations making a positive difference in the lives of people. I want to continue my autobiography via this blog.

So, I celebrate my birthday with gratitude and in faith, hope and love.

ℰℭ

KIESCHNICK REUNION: "I"

Some years ago, I had an important personal insight. I learned that wherever I go I take my self along. And I have learned that this "I" is ever changing midst other constants.

The "I" that I took to the Kieschnick Family reunion this year had some of the ever constant: I am one of nine children, deeply influenced by my parents. I am a person of faith and continuing commitment to integrity, justice, and inclusivity. That "I" once again went to Walburg, Texas, the place of my birth more than 87 years ago that has in some ways stayed pretty much the same.

Yet the "I" of this Reunion was also very different. This "I" was feeling its age. I moved more slowly. My reaction time was slower. My energy level is lower. My driving now depends more on my GPS than just recalling, "Take Highway 29, then 72, then 190 and get off at Friendship Ave." My hair is more white than gray. Then it got really serious. I once had to ask, "Tell me again what's trump?" in the annual Texas 42 (dominos) competition. Now that is a serious new dimension of my "I."

It just happened that during the Reunion weekend Concordia University, Texas awarded me the George J. Beto Award for Leadership. It was presented at Zion Lutheran Church just 200 yards from the room in which I was born and one hundred yards from where I attended Grades 1-8 in Zion Lutheran School. So, I took the opportunity to reflect upon how my "I" was formed by my extended family, my Lutheran school and my church. I gave thanks to God and the community for those formative impressions.

What I did not share with those present was the great surprises since I left Walburg. Included in those forces and experiences are my world travels and work in tens of cities from Helsinki to Karachi. That I have lived in the

185

urban areas of Chicago, Hong Kong, New York City greatly changed me. My wife of 64 years and our five children have had a tremendous impact upon me. Books continue to challenge and expand my world. Spending one-on-one time with people of many ethnicities, varying socio-economic levels, all sexual orientations, atheists and fundamentalists, greatly influenced the "I" that is still being formed.

So, as I reflect on my "I," I give thanks, seek forgiveness and look forward to who the "I" will be should I be around to go to our 25th Kieschnick Family reunion next year.

ℰℭℛ

PERSONAL HEALTH CARE PART 1: THE GOOD NEWS

I have been blessed with good health and good health care whenever I needed it. Mother birthed me under the care of Dr. W. C. Wedemeyer, the old-fashioned country doctor of the rural area of Walburg, Texas. He literally came with the traditional black bag. I seldom needed him. Mom knew how to deal with it when I (and my siblings) had measles, mumps, chickenpox, red-eye, infections in bare feet that had stepped on broken glass, sharp nails or really tough-to-get-out cactus needles.

When I was about seven, I had a ruptured appendix with puss all over my intestines. This was before antibiotics had been discovered and I was on the "critical" list. My cousin-by-marriage, Dr. Harlan, took very good care of me at King's Daughters Hospital in Temple, Texas and got me out of intensive care and home safely.

When I started teaching in Tracy, California my very seldom if ever seen doctor was Dr. Longley, the well-respected father of Louise, one of my fourth-grade students.

When we moved to Hong Kong, we had Dr. Rankin, an all-around expert who was there as a Southern Baptist Missionary who treated me as a colleague.

When my wife Jane developed an exceedingly difficult to diagnose illness, she was visited by one of China's very best doctors, the personal physician for Madam Chiang Kai Shek. Without an angiogram or other modern device, he diagnosed a cerebral aneurism. We flew her (in a coma) to the USA where the attention of Dr. Livesey and excellent care at Baptist Hospital in San Antonio and my Texas family brought her healing.

186

Now I have the person who must be the best primary care doctor in the world, Dr. Joel Diamant. And I must tell the story of how he happens to be available to me. I needed a new personal physician. I was told by reliable sources that Dr. Diamant was tops. By wonderful coincidence, his wife is also an M.D. and she and I were members of the same church. By further good circumstance Dr. Diamant's mother-in-law Ruth attended my Bible Class whenever she visited here from her home in Illinois. She was a conservative, very Biblically literate, of strong convictions who monitored my every word. One day after church I said, "Ruth, I want to talk to your daughter." "Why do you need to talk to Carrie?" she asked. I explained that I wanted her son-in-law to take me on as a patient. "He'll take you," she pronounced.

The next day I called Dr. D's office. I explained my need. "Oh, sir," his secretary explained, "Dr. Diamant has not taken on a new patient in three years as he is now head of the entire hospital's Fellows Program." I explained to her, "His mother-in-law said he would take me." Twenty-four hours later I became Dr. Diamant's first new patient in three years.

The list goes on. Dr. Dennis Gile is my caring and competent dentist. Dr. Jan Ryan treated my ears and loss of hearing as she would her own.

All of this brings me to the care our son David, who has been diagnosed with terminal neck and cheek cancer. The technology has been wonderful. They got his mask right for his extensive radiation. The hyperbaric treatment was there to increase blood flow. The acupuncturist is helping with his eyes and drug reactions. Dr. Murphy took lots of his expertise and time to diagnose and prescribe – and then to stop radiation when it no longer worked. He was kind, compassionate and professional in giving us the much-dreaded advice that there was no further healing help he could offer.

So that is all good and I am grateful - and in my next blog entry I'll talk about "Health Care: Part II. The Bad News."

෧෬

PERSONAL HEALTHCARE PART 2: THE BAD NEWS

For the last several years my biggest health care connections have related to our eldest son David, who just today went into hospice care because of continuing aggressive cancer in his mouth and cheek.

In my previous blog entry, I gratefully acknowledged some excellent care he received. Unfortunately, other aspects of his care have been horrendous.

Scheduling

It has been a nightmare getting appointments. More than once he arrived for his appointment (bringing with him a copy of the email with the details of the appointment) only to be told that he was not on the schedule.

Primary Care

His primary care physician chooses to ignore him, just hoping that the specialist will treat him.

His primary cancer doctor is a great clinician. He really knows the current field and the latest research. However, when we see him, we feel that he would be more comfortable if David sent in his cancerous cheek in a brown envelope. In fact, in three successive visits this doctor chose to not have David remove his bandage and expose the terrible large cancer tumor which had broken through his cheek. He actually asked David to go home, take an I-phone photo of his tumor and send it to him.

Two weeks ago, we were in the Emergency Room three times in four days. The reason: each time his bleeding face cancer needed a new bandage. Once we were there because a doctor in radiation had removed the bandage but had explained, "There is no nurse here who can replace a bandage." So, we waited in an emergency room for four hours before someone could put on a new bandage.

We called for Home Care to have them send a wound care specialist. He arrived (three hours after his appointment) but he brought no bandages, no tape, nothing!

When David was first diagnosed, he had good care from Kaiser Permanente. Then he changed jobs and his new company's insurance did not include Kaiser. So, he went with a team associated with another prominent local hospital. That doctor loved cutting. He removed cheek, jaw and gums from ear to chin on the right side of Dave's face. He then recommended doing the same on the other side of his face. Again, we switched providers, to one of the best-known reputable health organizations anywhere. Again, as indicated in my previous blog entry, Dave got some good care and he continues under this care (although just today he transferred to hospice care.) but once again all of our effort at a real team approach has proved frustrating. (And I won't even mention that the cost of all of the above is in the hundreds of thousands of dollars and involves hours of negotiation with his insurance company.)

But enough of this rambling. We are grateful for the care, expertise and concern of so many. And we want to be advocates for better service, especially also since we know that David's care by far exceeds that available to millions of others in America.

So, we commend ourselves and all who are ill, into the hands of the Great Physician.

ഇൻൽ

WAITING FOR DEATH

This is a tough blog entry to write. Reading it may be more than some would like. I get that.

I sit here beside my 62-year old eldest son, David, hoping and praying that each breath may be his last, finally bringing him eternal peace.

It all began about four years ago. His dentist suggested doing a biopsy of a nodule in his cheek. It was malignant. A major portion of his lower jaw was removed, followed by hyperbaric treatment, radiation and chemotherapy. After that he was well enough to go back to work, to cruise Europe with sister Peggy, and to provide a sanctuary in his granny flat for a refugee from Afghanistan.

After months of good and not so good experiences with several medical systems he attempted all options: vegan, non-protein and non-lactose diets, higher, healthier doses of supplements, more radiation, more chemo and acupuncture. The final verdict: "There is nothing more medically that can be done." He and we decided to manage the pain, no more liquids and no more nourishment. Stay at home under hospice care and await death.

So now for some two weeks that's what we do. He is home. His siblings, his friends from here, from Chicago and elsewhere sit with him briefly. We had our family farewell with David himself concluding the session by him saying, "It's time for us to say The Lord's Prayer together."

So, I sit by his side. His eyes stare blindly into space. The bandage hides the entire right side of his face which, when I looked at it last, brought back terrible memories of seeing those same features in people whom I saw in Hong Kong dying of leprosy.

As I sit, I hum hymns and folk songs. I tell him softly of his youthful

189

escapades with snails, of his wandering the streets of Hong Kong enjoying the wah muis he bought from street vendors. I recall him at age 12 caring for three younger siblings on a transpacific flight while I was attending his mother in a coma up in first class. I recall how his high school friends ridiculed his strict English school politeness – which his teacher admired. I recall for him briefly the challenge of his being a college student body president in the early 70's.

I come to tears as I recall my initial prejudice and ignorance when he first invited me for a just-the-two-of-us weekend retreat during which he disclosed that he was gay. I remember with gratitude how he bore evangelical witness to the Church, how he repeatedly visited those dying of AIDS for whom he was the only family and friend.

I smile as I recall good family times, especially at Christmas, or at his wonderful vacation home, our trips together or more recently just the two of us sharing a beer at a neighborhood bar. And I remember our shared anger at the prejudice, ignorance, and rejection shown him and gays around the country and world.

Then I force my mind to the father-son bonds that are inseparable. I contemplate all the mysteries of the life to come. And then I stroke his arms once more and whisper loud enough for him to hear in the depths of his soul, "Come sweet sleep. Come sweet peace."

⊱⊰

SON DAVID AT PEACE

Our eldest son David about whom I have been posting died peacefully, surrounded by family on Saturday morning, Feb. 14. He is at rest. See below for his bio.

⊱⊰

DAVE KIESCHNICK OBITUARY

Childhood

David Allan Kieschnick was born on Sept. 14, 1952 in Tracy, California, the first born of Mel and Jane Kieschnick. He was baptized at St. Paul's

Lutheran Church in Tracy. After living briefly in Glendale, California, he moved to Hong Kong with his parents at the age of four.

In Hong Kong he lived a happy ten years exploring neighborhoods where few foreign children ever roamed. Soon after settling in Kowloon, Hong Kong he was enrolled in a Chinese-only kindergarten. Following kindergarten, Dave attended Kowloon Junior and King George V schools where he learned the Queen's English, Latin, and a unique combination of British/American/Chinese culture ("Three cheers—and one for the tiger!"). On his 13th birthday his family (by then he had two sisters and two brothers) returned to the United States, where he graduated from Huron High School in Ann Arbor, Michigan with a National Merit Finalist honor and then from Concordia Teachers College, Chicago, where he served as student body president at the height of the turbulent 60's.

Career

In the early 70's Dave served as Director of Christian Education for Hyde Park Lutheran Church, a radical church community operating out of "The Mansion," (which is now the Chicago home of the Obama family). He also worked on the streets of Glen Ellyn, Illinois, helping troubled teens. Then Dave surprised us all when he made a dramatic career shift to become Director of Training for Evans Furs of Chicago, where he immersed himself in the finer points of high fashion. After Evans, Dave founded "Off-Site, Inc.," his own HR and computer consulting agency. Finally, in 2007 Dave moved to San Diego to be near his aging parents, continuing to support small businesses with his unique combination of technical expertise and a rare ability to translate between techies and regular people.

LGBTQ Advocacy & Support

Dave was a founder of Lutherans Concerned-Chicago, the leading advocacy and support group for the LGBTQ community in the Lutheran church. At a time when the only places for LGBTQ people to find each other were bars and bathhouses, Dave helped create safe places for people to meet, worship, socialize, and support each other. Dave was President of the founding Board of Directors of Gay Horizons (now the "Center on Halstead"), the Midwest's largest LGBTQ social service agency. Dave wrote and spoke extensively about grace and inclusion and was a leader of the Maywood House Church, that met for worship and fellowship for more than 30 years.

At the height of the AIDS crisis in the U.S., Dave traveled to many parts

191

of the country, providing comfort to many who would otherwise have died alone. He sponsored and supported persons seeking political asylum from Communist China, provided sanctuary for Afghan refugees, and challenged Americans to live up to the ideals on which our country was founded.

Lifestyle

A consummate host and gourmet cook, Dave relished good wine and fine cuisine, and celebrated life with finesse and style. He sure knew how to throw a party! Dave made many, many people feel welcome who didn't feel welcome anywhere else. He loved to travel internationally, was fascinated by history and culture, and seemingly remembered everything he ever read or learned.

Dave loved music, theater and film. He had an eye for beauty whether in fine art, a relic from some exotic place, the colors of an insect's wings, or a discarded treasure scavenged from a Chicago alley. He didn't just appreciate art; he made it. Dave was a storyteller extraordinaire and an eloquent writer. He was a gifted potter who combined his aesthetic sensibilities with great personal discipline to create many beautiful things.

Dave was a courageous voice for the oppressed, adamantly refusing to accept injustice. And most of all, Dave was a man with a huge, compassionate heart who gave shelter to wounded and weary hearts. Even now, he continues to give us all strength for the journey.

Family

While in Chicago Dave lived in a committed relationship with Doug Wilmore for more than 30 years. He was at the center of a large and extended LGBTQ family, many of whom had no other family. He was a loving and devoted son, a great brother and uncle, and a steadfast friend.

David died February 14, 2015 at his home in San Diego at the age of 62. He is survived by his parents, Mel and Jane Kieschnick, and by his siblings: Peggy Kieschnick (Phil Hatcher), Tim Kieschnick (Wendy Fiering), Elizabeth Kieschnick (Jim Flanders), John Kieschnick (Regina Llamas) and his nephews and nieces: Christina Hatcher (Ariel Osharenko), John Hatcher, Anza Fiering, Jon Flanders, Ryan Flanders, Maria Flanders, Antonio Kieschnick, Clara Kieschnick and a community of friends both here and around the world.

A REMEMBRANCE OF MY SON, DAVID KIESCHNICK

David Kieschnick, Sept. 14, 1952 to Feb. 14, 2015

The writer of Ecclesiastes had it right: "For everything there is a season and a time for every matter under heaven."

A time to be born. It was a great time for David, our first, to be born. His was a much longed for arrival. While he was being delivered around 3:00 a.m. I was sound asleep in the waiting room. People chided me for my seeming lack of concern. But I reply that his Mother Jane and even David never were dependent on me. From his birth Dave was strong, self-reliant, capable, showing up on time. "Dad, I can handle it."

A time to die. It's hard to admit that 62 years of age is a time to die. For David it was. In a long personal conversation with me right after his oncologist told him, "Six months." Dave said, "Dad, I'm ready. I trust my God. I have no spouse or children dependent on me. I've accomplished my significant goals. I've made a difference. I've had a good life. "It's a time to die."

As that horrific cancer ate up first his jaw, then his cheeks and then descended into his throat and ascended into his brain sending excruciating pain along every cell along the way, the time came for hospice at home, massive pain killing drugs, always unbelievable support from his sibs and then final prayers and tearful goodbyes. It was a time to die.

A time to mourn and a time to dance. Of course, we mourn (with hope). Already I have moments of "Oh, I must talk to David about this." Or "I've got to call Dave to see if he has time for us to have a beer together." So, I mourn.

And I recall the time to dance. David knew how to dance and have fun. His parties (especially hat parties – he kept 39 of those hats right inside his door), his love of food, his travels to the rivers of Europe with his sister, his singing, attending the theater for music and drama, his pottery and those who joined him there. Yes, David knew there was a time to dance.

A time to keep silent and a time to speak. Sometimes it was tough for David to keep silent, when honest disclosure would have brought more pain to him that he could bear.

But he also knew there was a time to speak. So, he spoke for those outside the "norm," the poor, the disenfranchised, the refugee, the alienated.

A time for war – and a time for peace. Yes, David fought his wars, for the cause of persons of all sexual orientations, for those who had trouble finding God in the "organized church," against incompetence at work. And he fought his cancer with vegan and non-lactose diets, with chemo and radiation, with acupuncture and hyperbaric, with enhanced food supplements, with cancer support groups and writing seminars – and above all a desire to live and to make a difference.

And in the end, a time for peace. A time to rest from his wars, his pain, his weakened body and a time for peace with himself, with his family, with his God, with eternity.

"For everything there is a season and a time for every matter under heaven."

৪৩০৫

FUNERALS, BURIALS, CELEBRATIONS OF LIFE

Rituals to remember the deceased have been a part of my life as long as I can remember. I grew up in a Lutheran "teacherage" where our home bordered the church cemetery. In elementary school we attended all the congregation funerals in the church next door to our parochial school. I accompanied my father as he tolled the church bells as the coffin was taken from church to cemetery. I watched gravediggers prepare the gravesite, and then fill it with dirt. Often, I have been in the country home parlor with the corpse as it stayed there for the night prior to being taken to the church for funeral services.

I bargained in Chinese with street-side coffin makers over the size and price of a coffin in Kowloon. I renegotiated the price coolies were charging to carry a coffin up a hill. I stood with the weeping mother as only three of us were there when the son had been killed in a bicycle-truck crash. I have spoken at tens of funerals delivering the meditation or the eulogy. I have sung a solo at a funeral in Forest Lawn in Glendale, California. I accompanied a father to the beach when he took his son's ashes out to the waves, and presided on a boat three miles off shore as ashes were reverently lowered into the ocean. I have written instructions for my own funeral.

All of that was a part of me as a month ago I was there for my son David's rituals after his way too early death. A couple months ago when I asked him his wishes, he said little other than "The rituals are for you the survivors - do whatever you want."

And so, it was that on Friday night just the immediate family gathered as we together recalled his life. I presided as we all participated. It was a simple ceremony filled with memories around the topics: prayers, songs, Bible verses, rituals, memories and promises. It was good.

On Saturday we had the Celebration of Life ritual. It was in the patio of David's home. The atmosphere was intimate as we crowded under a canopied space. The tone was intimate, reflective, sad and celebratory. In four segments of about 15 minutes each we had beautiful music (both religious and popular) performed and sung by Dave's incredibly gifted family members, remembrances by people from many parts of the country, with varied experiences of David. A common theme: Dave's concern for those on the edge, his commitment to people who were hurting, his unfailing faithfulness, his deep spiritual roots, his incredible generosity and his multitude of talents. When we closed with the traditional Biblical benediction with its seven-fold "Amen" sung beautifully by some of Dave's family members I knew we had done it right.

But that was not the end. Emails, telephone calls, letters and cards have been coming in commenting not only upon the ceremony but upon the legacy of David to which it all pointed. Two examples: One couple spoke with me and then wrote. They recalled that after the ceremony they sat and talked for over an hour about David and his example. "We have decided to be better people," they reported. "We want to be more generous with our time and gifts. We want to make more of a difference like David did and they sent a generous memorial gift.

A second person read about these events. She lives in Colorado. She wrote, "I want to be more like David. I have lately not used my experience as an immigration lawyer. Tell me how I can better reach out to those who have suffered from government sanctioned torture overseas and are seeking sanctuary in America."

So, in this Easter season I rejoice in the Resurrection and in all resurrections to which end of life ritual can so vividly point.

෨෮෬

I AM NUMBER ONE

I really have never thought much about it. Yet I suppose that it would be nice to be recognized in some way as "being number one in the world!" I recently realized that I do deserve that honor. If there were a designation

"Most Sloppy Person in the World," I think I would deserve to be at the top of the list.

Let me present my credentials: On Easter Sunday we had our usual wonderful dinner with the Paulovich's. We had not yet finished eating when I looked down and saw the mess I'd made around my plate. There was evidence of every course. As I looked around the table, I saw that every other of the 12 places was spotless. I don't think Barbara would have had to wash the tablecloth – but Mel was there and that tablecloth needed laundering.

This morning I looked at the big stain on our bed sheet! No, you would never guess. It was chocolate ice cream. Honestly, I took only a couple little teaspoons, which I thought I had finished before reaching the bedroom. Wrong: I had left my mark.

It doesn't matter if my dress shirt is white or colored. It is sure to have evidence of the fact that I had coffee during our church's coffee hour and some of that coffee somehow gets embedded in my shirt.

Our living room is really quite neat and the carpet is in pretty good shape, with one exception: the area around my lounger. It is not just crumbs, peanut shells or salsa that show up but significant areas that can only be red wine spots and I don't even fill my glass to the brim.

I need to make my amends to my mother. She tried so hard to have me be neat, to use my napkin, to lean over my table settings when I eat, to not over-fill my fork or spoon. In spite of her best efforts I continue to be worthy of the very title she wanted me to avoid: "Melvin you are a Slop Hans."

So, I have decided to not fight it, but to accept it and be grateful that there is at least one thing in the world to which I can claim to be NUMBER ONE!

ഇന്ദ

CLOSURE AND MOVING ON

It is now more than three months since our son David died. The literature says, "It's time for closure and moving on." That might be good advice. Yet something about those words does not ring true to me. I want to remember and I also want to move on, but I will move on aware that my life has a new reality. I have changed. I want to "move on" but as a changed person. That is what I am trying to do.

But first there are some elements to the closure that I want to always remember. I want to be grateful for the many letters, notes, cards, emails and memorial gifts that help me recall the best of David. So many stories of him reaching out to those looked down upon or ignored by others. The story from a Community Center he started when AIDS was a bad word not to be mentioned in polite company. This Center now serves some thousand clients a day. The letter from Finland informing me that more than 3,000 copies of his "Home for Christmas" article had been distributed. The old newspaper clipping we discovered in which teen-agers and their parents wrote letters to the editor in affirmation of his work on the streets of Glen Ellyn, IL on behalf of young people who were losing their way. A couple pastors even sent copies of sermons they preached built around recollections of David's faith, positive attitude and advocacy for the persecuted (and I try to forget that in the midst of this there were and are others claiming the name Christian who call for the death and eternal damnation for people like David).

So, I think of all this as I seek closure.

And then comes another flood of memories: Family. Dave's sibs have been incredible, both in supporting him in his last months and in dealing with all that comes after a death. They have divided the tasks. Peggy is CEO responsible for selling the house, car, etc. Tim is dealing with all those medical bills that will be coming in for another year. John deals with the finances associated with credit cards, insurance proceeds et sim, Liz worked on all the Celebration of Life issues around caterer, tarps for the patio etc. etc. And they are doing this all without any sibling (or parental) acrimony.

Family extends also to my birth family, with special appreciation for the support also demonstrated by the attendance here for the last rituals. They came from Texas. They made their own arrangements for accommodations. They spoke lovingly and emotionally at the ceremonies. They took care of "the elderly" among the group.

All of this marvelous family harmony and support stands in strong contrast to what I have unfortunately seen in others who deal with these matters with great disagreements, arguments and even bitterness,

Anyone who has dealt with taking care of post-death arrangements knows there is pain involved in things like conducting an estate sale, taking care of the cremains, disposing of personal items like clothes and favorite art objects.

In the midst of this has been the care of seven members of one Afghan family who just arrived in the USA, escaping the Taliban who had already killed their father and elder brother. David had been providing housing and other assistance and now other sources of support need to be identified.

I realize that I am certainly not alone in all this. Thousands around the world do this every hour. I have the special advantage of a spouse who is with me all the way sharing not only the tasks but also the emotions.

And now I move on, determined to live each day as fully as possible, to put people first, to have my house in order and to confidently trust the One who walks beside me every day, now and forever.

ಹೃದಯ

HIGH SCHOOL DAYS: SPORTS

Sports was probably number one in my life as a high school student. As mentioned in previous blog entries, I attended Concordia Academy in Austin Texas for my four high school years. This was a boarding school, boys only, which during my days there reached an enrollment of 100.

With such few students it was pretty well assured that if one wanted play varsity sports one would make the team. The biggest team sport was basketball and I lettered all four years. I was short, but reasonably fast. It was during these days in the mid-forties that the one-hand jump shot came to be popular. I practiced it endlessly.

We had no gym and had only an outdoor dirt-covered court. All games were "away games." The only indoor practice facility was a basement room we called "the boiler room." Apparently at some point there was a plan to have central heating for the campus, but they could never afford a big boiler. So, the 20x20x12 foot room became our gym. I spent hours there - often with my roommate Mike Mitschke who beat me about nine times out of ten in our one-on-one games. We played other small schools, some church youth teams, but the biggest rivalry was with the Texas School for the Deaf.

George J. Beto, who later became head of the Texas prison system, was our coach. However, the term "coach" was not really applicable. He was more monitor, driver, and disciplinarian. I doubt that he had ever played basketball He had no real knowledge of how to put together either an offensive or a defensive plan. But he ran the show. My memory is that we lost more games than we won and I enjoyed every minute of them. One big thing about the basketball team: we actually had uniforms - the only team at the school with this distinction.

Dr. Beto was not only coach but also the dormitory supervisor and was in charge of our recreation time. So, he umpired our every-day softball games that were played after dinner and before our mandatory 7:00 to 9:00 p.m. study period, which he also monitored. I played shortstop mainly. Sometimes I also played the outfield. I was a pretty good hitter and I thought I had a strong arm. It was only after college when I was playing for a local amateur team that I finally had a coach. I remember especially the coaching I then received that, on a throw to the plate from the outfield, it was very important to keep the arc of the throw low as that extra second saved would mean the difference between an out or a score.

We also played six-man flag football. For a few weeks one year we interrupted that. Somehow or other we heard of a group of guys (all of whom were black) who also had a pick-up football team. Neither of us had uniforms or even helmets and yet we played "tackle football." We discovered that the University of Texas did not lock the near-by Memorial Stadium after Saturday home games. So, on Sunday afternoon we battled it out right there on that hallowed turf. I also remember my nose getting terribly battered but I was not allowed to disclose this, as "tackle football" was prohibited. To this day I still have a severely separated septum in the middle of my nose.

Every spring we had a big Field Day in which we ran track events. Again, I did them all, winning very little, if any. However, I did do fairly well in throwing the discus. My discus throwing was always influenced by an event that took place in my freshman year. The senior who was throwing the discus let it slip. It struck a by-stander right in the face and he had to be taken to the hospital for treatment. I made sure I didn't let loose the discus and I can assure you I never set any record for how far I threw it.

The camaraderie was great, the exercise helpful, the discipline enduring, the enjoyment wonderful and I think it helped me keep an interest and even a certain ability in sports that endures to this day

෨෬

HOPE SHATTERED - DREAMS DESTROYED

ON THE 20TH ANNIVERSARY OF TIANANMEN SQUARE MASSACRE

Weeping students in the quad of Beijing University surround me. It's the evening of June 5th, 1989. Mournful funeral music sweeps from speakers across the campus. The banner in front of the campus gates, in black characters on white cloth, laments, "Tiananmen bathed in blood. The whole world weeps."

By now the world knew what those milling about us had experienced in the hours before. The People's Army did fire on students. Tanks rumbled through the streets and the square. Bodies were bullet-ridden and crushed. Soldiers were captured, strung up from light posts and burned while the crowd cheered. Buses were parked together to form barricades. One side or the other torched them. Sporadic skirmishes and resulting deaths would continue for another day. But the outcome was immutable. The student-led foray for freedom had failed. The Party won.

Now cadres of students come into the weeping cauldron, returning from the morgue with news of whose bodies they found and who was still unaccounted for.

My two sons and I are the only Americans in the crowd and so the target for unrealistic pleas. "Can't you contact President Bush? Can't the US military intervene? Will the free world just stand by and let hope be crushed?" It was a cry not only for themselves, but also for their fallen colleagues and their now-under-suspicion parents. It was the unrealistic plea for some kind of rekindling of the flame of hope that had been definitively quenched.

We weep with our new student friends. We wince as we they show us wounds in their bodies. We remember with mixed feelings the female student friend of John who was safe in the countryside. The day before, her mother had come and physically carried her out of the square where she had been on a hunger strike. We know we cannot reach our family back home but are confident we will get there. Other student friends will not make it home. Without a doubt many others will make their homes in prisons. It seemed almost secondary to think of two years of John's work reflected in Chinese to English translations now stored "somewhere" on campus. Yet in the magnitude of the suffering, death, and shattered hopes those concerns seem minor. Many have died. More will. It's a long, long road to freedom for too many.

ളാ

THREE SATISFYING DAYS: RETIREMENT

I've been retired now for more than 22 years and it has been good. I am blessed to live with Jane, my wife of 64 years. The retirement community in which we live is wonderful. Our health is good. Our congregation, Calvary

Lutheran in Solana Beach, is supportive.

Probably the best thing about retirement, in contrast to my previous working environment, is that I do not feel responsible for an organization and I actually go through a whole week without any meetings.

Into this environment there come some special days that are extraordinarily satisfying. I recently had three of such days.

Day One

I had a terrible cough; my body was weak. I did a most unusual thing. I stayed in bed late. At 10:00 a.m. the phone rang. A volunteer at church called. She knew I had volunteered to fill in if there was any emergency situation as our pastor was out of town. She told me that a phone message from the previous day (Sunday) said someone was dying and there was a need for a pastoral call. My initial response was negative. "I'm not feeling well. Pr. 'N' is also on call; he could do this - and why is yesterday's message being responded to only today?"

But I acted. My phone follow-up gave me the message, "Ellen is not just very sick. She is at the point of death."

I hurried over. I was greeted by Mary whom I soon discovered was the best, kindest, most able and compassionate hospice care provider I have ever met. Ellen was indeed dying but conscious. I stroked her arm. I spoke into her ears and looked in her eyes. I recalled happy days. I read to her from John's Gospel, "In my Father's House are many mansions. I go to prepare a place for you." Together with her caregiver we recited the 23rd psalm. I prayed a prayer and we did a ritual for those dying.

I asked if it would be possible to have Holy Communion. The aide assured me it was. I was concerned about Ellen swallowing even a little bread and wine. But the caregiver provided a small syringe. We consecrated the sacramental elements, merged them, put them into the syringe and we three partook of the blessed elements, I spoke the Biblical blessing and left.

Twenty minutes later I arrived home. Jane said we'd had a phone call from Ellen's caregiver. Ellen had died a few minutes after I left. She had let go. She died in peace.

I was grateful to have been a part of a day very well spent.

Day Two: Memorial Day

The retirement community in which we live includes a great many retired US military personnel. Since we are near San Diego and Camp

Pendleton there are especially many former Navy and Marine veterans. Memorial Day rituals are a big thing here.

But this year I decided to observe Memorial Day "off campus." I volunteered to feed the homeless at TACO (Third Avenue Charitable Organization) at First Lutheran in downtown San Diego.

So, I gathered with the 20 or so volunteers to meet them and get acquainted, to get our arrangements and to have a community prayer. I was honored to be asked to lead that prayer.

Soon the 2,000+ guests arrived and gathered in the church courtyard. We had a special birthday cake for those who had a birthday in May. I was again asked to lead the prayer. But first I asked all veterans to raise their hands. Tragically there were more than a dozen now living on the street, homeless and hungry. I thanked God for their (and all veterans') contribution to preserving American's best values.

As they all marched through the food line I tried to look into each face, the mentally ill, those on drugs, women, men, children, all colors and ethnicities, each one a hungry brother or sister.

They all responded in gratitude, humbly and sincerely. As long as the food lasted, they could come back for seconds or thirds – or even for take-out.

I wished them all God's blessings and drove back home to my well-supplied and secure home. And I felt good about my small role on the different kind of Memorial Day – a day well spent.

Day Three: Committee Meeting

I mentioned above that one of the blessings of retirement is the greatly reduced number of meetings one is required to attend.

Yet I recently chaired a very small committee meeting. On the face of it, it sounds like the dullest of all possible committee meetings.

I chair the Governance Committee of a local organization called Survivors of Torture International. We provide a safe haven, psychosocial support and immigration support to persons who have fled to the USA to escape government-sanctioned torture now so very common in too many parts of the world.

I've spent my life working for "not-for-profit" organizations so it is no big deal for me to help our organization with training board members, putting in place staff succession processes, ensuring proper accounting. So, my committee does that. The three other committee members all know their stuff, bringing competence, compassion and commitment. So, we did our thing for a couple of hours.

Really all very simple and straightforward. Yet as I drove home that evening, I felt satisfied. I was using my time, talents and experience so that others might find a life much better than what they had experienced in their home country. It was a satisfying day for me.

ളഗ

FAMILY REUNION IN TEXAS

I love going to the annual Kieschnick Family Reunions and I love going to Texas to celebrate that. But I must also admit to what many Texans (including some of my relatives) may consider a set of mortal sins. There is stuff going on in Texas that I hate. I hate the idea of arming the Texas National Guard to protect it from an invasion by the USA. I hate the reality of everyone insisting that it's important to carry guns to school, church and family picnics. I hate it that too many Texans think sexual orientation is a choice that must be stopped. I hate it when I experience (at best) paternalism for Blacks and downright denigration of Hispanics. And if any of my Texas relatives or friends have gotten past this paragraph and have not deleted this blog entry and inserted a two-word expletive in its place then I am ready to proceed and tell you why I love Texas.

On my recent flight to Austin we had not proceeded very far east of El Paso before I began to enjoy the beauty of that vast and varied state. Texas had wonderful spring rains and the fields were unusually green for late July. The hills were alive with lush green trees. Herefords and Holsteins roamed the fields. Massive rolls of hay were strewn in the vast fields. The few visible clouds added just the right touch to a beautiful landscape. The feeling that I have when looking across or driving in the rolling green hills of Texas brings me to bliss.

When my sister Mimi welcomes me into her house with her beautiful slight Texas drawl and the temperature of the house is just right and the refrigerator is filled with cold beer and there is a bottle of Scotch nearby, what could be better!

In the morning I join a couple of my California and Connecticut kids and some of their family for breakfast. I get upset when my wait for the table runs to 30 minutes. And then the waitress comes, and it's true joy. Her Texas accent flows from her sweet and accepting face. She offers us all the options we might want with unusual graciousness. Then she brings the just baked biscuits, the cream gravy and the strong black coffee. I could stay here all day.

In the evening we go to the first of a series of feasts. The backyard is as immense as it is inviting. The beer is on tap for everyone. The pork butt bar-b-que is so wonderful I think it can't get any better until I add just a bit more of that bar-b-que sauce and I check whether or not I am already in heaven.

The style of the Pitching Washers game has changed a bit but there is room for all from ages 8 to 88 - and from then on. The Super Bowl could not be more competitive but it is all in good fun.

My granddaughter has come from California to experience Texas and she gets the full treatment. The first gentleman with whom we converse at the first party is a former rodeo competitor and tells about bucking broncos and calf roping. The next day she goes to buy her western straw hat and the salesman discovers she is from California and within minutes figures out that she is here for the Kieschnick reunion and tells her he is a housemate of a person from the Kieschnick clan. He gets just the right hat for her!

The next few days I continue to be immersed in some of that good stuff that is essentially Texan: marvelous chicken-fried steak, freshly picked ripe peaches, crisp pecan pie, fried okra, five or even seven layered dip. And I visit an ancient smoke house where a generation ago at least seven deer a year were smoked, dried and preserved to provide meat for an entire year.

I drive by the old cotton gins. Brother-in law Raymond's longhorn cattle come to the edge of the fence to greet us, and the country western tune on the radio blares "Beautiful, beautiful Texas the land where the bluebonnets grow. We are proud of our forefathers who fought at the Alamo."

As I walk down the airport corridor for my return flight to California I take one more look at all those U. of Texas Longhorn caps, shirts, etc., hear one more "Howdy" from a Stetson-wearing exec and I head into the plane thinking, "Sure hope we come back to Texas next year for another Kieschnick Reunion."

෫෬

HIGH SCHOOL MUSIC

While in high school I may have had only one date, seen only six movies and never went to a dance. But at least I was a normal enough teen-ager to enjoy music. In 1951 Frank Sinatra and the Hit Parade were still big. So, every Saturday night I listened to The Hit Parade, eagerly waiting to see which popular song would be number one for the week. There were other singers and my favorite was Bing Crosby. Three female singers were always welcome: Dinah Shore, Ella Fitzgerald and Peggy Lee. Glen Miller was always good and Duke Ellington had his own style. Of course, there was no TV and I owned no record, disc or LP player so I heard these on our small radio. These were the days of WWII, so patriotic songs were featured. Songs to which I sang along, included "Praise the Lord and Pass the Ammunition," "I'll Be Seeing You," "I'll Be Home for Christmas" and "Accentuate the Positive."

I am surprised that I do not have more memories of country and western songs as I was certainly surrounded by them. I did memorize old favorites like "I'm An Old Cowhand," "The Yellow Rose of Texas" and "Deep in The Heart of Texas." I knew nothing about, or ever even listened to, classical music.

I am forever grateful that my musical tastes did not stay fixated at that terrible teen-age stage. Many wonderful people have since instructed me and led me to one of the many blessed aspects of my life: the enjoyment of all kinds of good music ranging from "Let Me Call You Sweetheart," to "A Mighty Fortress is Our God," to "The Barber of Seville."

ℰℭ

WORLD WAR II PART 1

Preface: I want to be very clear. World War II was *not* about me. I did no heroics, performed no great acts, and endured no great personal sacrifice. Compared to so many others, my life was easy. Millions suffered and died. Many Americans (and other) families suffered terrible deprivation, pain and loss. Many of my fellow Americans were incredibly brave. They represented me. They saved the USA from enemies. I am the beneficiary of all of this valor, patriotism and sacrifice. So, while I reflect upon my life during those days I do so in great humility and clarity of understanding that I had it easy.

My years in high school very nearly match the years of the USA being officially at war in WWII. I entered high school September 5,1941 and Japan bombed Pearl Harbor on December 7,1941. Germany surrendered to the allies on May 7, 1945; I graduated from high school on May 10, 1945 and Japan surrendered on August 14, 1945.

205

I had gone home for the weekend and was "playing catch" out in our back yard with my siblings on that December 7th afternoon. My father came out and in a very serious voice ordered us all into his "study." There he informed us that the Japanese had bombed Pearl Harbor. He knew it meant war and that would have incredible consequences for the world. He had us all sit and join him in prayer.

It immediately came close to home. The son of a neighbor was in the Navy and at Pearl Harbor. He was serving on the US Arizona and we knew Japanese bombs hit it and by New Year's Day the family had received word that he was officially "missing in action." We feared the worst. He was eventually declared, "killed in action."

In a spirit of patriotism many of the young people enlisted. Soon, my father received confidential letters from the military. We lived in a German community and many of the servicemen from that community volunteered or were chosen to do confidential interpretation, code breaking and similar work. My dad had been their grade school principal and knew that many of them never went to high school. He very carefully documented their expertise in their native German language and vouched for their patriotism.

It became a time for us to follow the news with great interest. We listened to the radio. At Concordia Academy we had only one newspaper available to us in the library and we perused it eagerly.

Soon the streets were filled with men (and a few women) in uniform. Then we all experienced rationing. My parents carefully used their sugar-rationing card to get sugar to can fruits and vegetables. Dad had an A classification for his gasoline allotment and he was always determined to use as little gasoline as possible. No new tires. Old ones were recapped.

The military training activity around us became intensified. When we lived in Walburg we saw tanks rumble by our house on maneuvers from Fort Hood to Camp Swift. When we moved to San Antonio, we were completely amid airmen from all the airbases there. My trips to and from home were all by "hitchhiker's thumb." The courtesy rule for us non-military was that we would stand at the end of the line so that military hitchhikers would get preference.

Even as there was good news about the Allies advance there was always great anxiety, as we personally knew so many friends and relatives on the front lines. We kept the newspaper maps and articles handy. New names became familiar: Iwo Jima, Anzio, The Desert Fox, Doolittle, MacArthur, and Eisenhower, etc. etc. It was a time of great anxiety always mixed with the hope for an early victory.

206

WORLD WAR II PART 2

I experienced WWII as an average American teen-ager, but also with a bit of a difference from many. I was a child in a "German Lutheran Church" (The Missouri Synod). Within that context I spoke German before I learned English. When I was with my grandparents, I was expected to speak German. Almost all our Lutheran Church worship services were in the German language. I memorized Luther's Small Catechism in German.

Thus, there was an especially great interest in things German and what was happening in Germany. This intensified with the rise of Hitler. I vividly recall my father getting Adolph Hitler's speeches over short-wave radio. He listened intently as Hitler raged and raved. Dad understood the words better than I. He heard enough to be very disturbed. He saw Hitler as a dangerous and evil man. Dad told me that Germany was in the wrong in its aggressive policies and unprovoked war. So, when war against Germany was officially declared there was no doubt that our allegiance was 100% pro-America.

As I have written earlier, many of the young people from my congregation enlisted. Others were drafted. For each one a star was duly embroidered on a large white cloth poster prominently displayed in the front of the church. Sadly, the white star was replaced with a gold star when one of the members had been killed in action.

Lutherans (including the very narrow Missouri Synod) supported the concept of military chaplains and many of the pastors served with distinction. At the same time the church supported its clergy as being exempt from military service and received approval for those of us "studying for the ministry" to receive a 4D deferred status in the military draft.

Prayers for peace and protection were in abundance at every worship service. Members were encouraged to do their part in conservation of products and in supporting the war effort via agricultural production, work in plants producing planes etc., and in buying war bonds and donating blood.

In the midst of these, two very negative images still stick in my mind. The first has to do with Zion Lutheran Church in Walburg, Texas. Someone had written a hymn asking for God's protection and an early end of the war. Most Missouri Synod churches chose to sing this hymn as the final song each Sunday. However, at Zion there was a protest against singing an English song even though it was a prayer for peace, as part of the German worship service. I still recall how each Sunday a small group of men and women would walk out because of this.

The second image forever seared into my soul happened at St. Paul's Lutheran in Austin. A young 1st Lieutenant in full uniform entered, walked about two-thirds of the way to the front of the sanctuary and took his seat in the pew. After a few minutes, two ushers came and asked him to leave that seat and to come to the back of the church. That lieutenant was black and was not supposed to sit among the white worshippers.

Neither the Germans nor us Americans can claim pure holiness of motive or action.

ഇ൯ന

HIGH SCHOOL ACADEMICS

Concordia Academy was clear on its mission: train young men for the rostered ministries of The Lutheran Church-Missouri Synod - both those ordained for pastoral ministry and those commissioned for the teaching ministry. I was in the second category following in the footsteps of my father.

Our training was in the old tradition of classical education. We took at least one course in religion every term. Next in priority came the languages. I took English, German (all using German script) and Spanish. Those studying for the pastoral ministry added Latin and even some Greek.

I do not think any of our professors ever took a course in educational methodology. They were clergy and were probably chosen because they scored high academically. Dr. Studtmann who was also the school's Director taught religion and German. The eccentric and brilliant Dr. Viehweg taught Latin and Greek. Dr. Martin J. Neeb taught us public speaking and he assured us that even though we were in high school he used exactly the same curriculum he used while concurrently teaching that course at the University of Texas. The theologian George J. Beto taught physics. For two years Dr. Robert Schroeder taught whatever no one else taught. He was an excellent teacher and should also have been the basketball coach!

True to the values of the day, there were no women on the faculty. One woman was allowed to teach individual students the piano. I was among her notable disastrous failures (not due to any deficiencies on her part, I can assure you). The other woman who was allowed on campus (and she wasn't even a Missouri Synod Lutheran was a Mrs. Lillian Bedicheck. She taught Spanish. She was wonderful. She loved us. She gave it her best. We were disrespectful, came to class barefoot, not studious and failed to do our homework. But she hung in there with us, was extremely gracious and kind and I have wonderful and fond memories of her.

Caveat on Mrs. Bedicheck: One of the reasons we loved her is that her husband was a big wheel in University of Texas athletics and he got us free passes to Texas Longhorn games etc. Twenty years after leaving Austin I was in a tailor shop in Hong Kong. I met a tourist from Austin Texas. I disclosed that I went to Concordia. The surprised comment from the tourist, "Oh, that is where my best friend, Mrs. Bedicheck, taught Spanish. She loved those boys and still talks about them!"

When I compare the quality of my high school education with that of my grandchildren, I see again how inadequate my high school years were. There was way too much indoctrination, too much rote, and too little project work. No cooperative work assignments, little creativity, no problem solving, no understanding of different learning styles and very little appreciation for the arts. On the other hand, our teaching gave us strong faith and moral grounding, dedication to hard work, and a desire for more learning.

Another caveat: Prof Viehweg tried to teach us music appreciation. One evening he had a select group of us meet with him to listen to some classical music played for us from a wind-up Victrola. When I got back to my room, I told my roommate how bad it was. I said to him, "We listened to that one song and all they sang was 'Hosanna' over and over!" Of course, it was from Handel's Messiah and just too far removed from country and western for me to think it could come anywhere close to expressing what one truly feels!

I guess something was done right. I still remember most of the Lutheran doctrine taught me. I can still diagram sentences. I have been able to have quite a bit of my writing published. I enjoy classical music; and still read old German script. Just don't expect me to play you a song on the piano or send you a greeting in Spanish!

ജയ

HIGH SCHOOL YEARS AND GIRLS

As with all (or at least the vast majority) of high school boys, members of the opposite sex were on the agenda of my classmates and me. Yet it was a far from normal situation. We were in an all-boys school. It was a dormitory school and we were not allowed off campus five days of the week. We were all in a town other than our hometown. So, we had very little interaction with girls.

The one weekly opportunity came each Sunday when we all went to church. We walked the two miles each way to St. Paul's Lutheran Church and were required to attend both the morning and the evening services. There, at least, we were in the company of someone not of the male gender. The good news is that that church had very unusual architecture, which placed the choir in front of the church behind the altar. Thus, our eyes always looked right to the soprano and alto sections. The choir was robed in traditional garb. We could try to make some eye contact and that was about as close as we could get. Even so, we discussed the various girls and tried to figure out who was of an age to attend the Walther League meetings on Sunday afternoon. Those meetings were hardly great social events. I remember us having some appropriate topic to discuss, some project to plan and then a game to be played. We did that and then walked back to our dorms.

Yet some of us some made some contacts. Rumors on campus floated about which girl had her eyes on which boy - and which boy might daringly ask a girl for a date. Actually "having a date" was rare.

My memory is that in my four years at Austin I had two dates. Each time I met the girl whom I had telephoned and fearfully asked for a date. I made my way to her house via city bus. I got checked out by her parents. We took the bus downtown to a movie. We took the bus back to her home. I walked her to the door. I turned around and took the bus back to the campus. (Except that on my second of those memorable dates, my bus got to downtown too late to get the last bus to the college and I had, as I remember, 30 minutes to run the three miles back to campus and be in bed for the 10:00 o'clock bed check by Dean Beto).

In my senior year I did a very daring thing. I made a telephone call and asked a non-Lutheran girl to join me at a party. She was one of the twin daughters of the boarding house mother at which my sister Erna lived. I had met her. Moreover, she was really beautiful and well known as she was a cheer leader for the Austin High School, I finally got the courage to call her, remind her that we had met and asked her to join me for a birthday party of a classmate. She told me she had another activity already scheduled. I believed her. But I never called her again!

I did exchange some letters with "D." I had had my eyes on her already in the 7th and 8th grade at Zion Elementary School and we did exchange a few letters. Also, we went Christmas caroling together and at the end of the caroling she became the first and only girl I ever kissed before college.

One other girl was one from the near-by town of Thorndale. We met at a Walther League event. She was very nice and I liked her a lot. We exchanged a few letters. I remember she came to my high school graduation (presumably driven there by her parents). There we spoke briefly. But after the ceremony I went out with some of the guys to an amusement park. She was really nice and I always thought fondly of her but neither of us pursued the relationship. Later she did marry a Lutheran schoolteacher who had been with me at Concordia College, River Forest and I am sure they had a good marriage.

As I reflect on all this, I do have some regrets. High school years should be a time for good fun with both young guys and girls. It is a good time to explore one's values and social skills and to have some good clean fun. I regret missing that. And I am most grateful that I did not meet my future wife at that time, as that would have prevented me from marrying Jane; and nothing coming out of high school, or any other relationship, could ever be as good and blessed as that.

ॐ

SEX

Sex in the public arena in the 1940's was very different from what is it today. This was 20 years before the pill, 20 years before the work of Masters and Johnson, and 10 years before the first issue of "Playboy" magazine. Condoms were hidden behind counters or in machines in men's rest rooms. Couples known to have sex before marriage were subject to church excommunication processes. Yet none of this really explains my early teen years' ignorance and naiveté about sex.

I still marvel at what a slow learner I was. We raised and bred cattle and hogs. I remember telling my best friend that I found it interesting that roosters played tag with hens. (He laughed a little titter which I did not catch on to for another few years!) I am number three of nine children so my mother had several children after me, yet the word "pregnant" was never mentioned in mixed company. My instruction came in very uninformed conversations with my sister Leona and finally from the book which mom and dad left prominently displayed in the bookshelves, entitled "What Every Young Man Should Know."

211

But when I started living in an all-male dormitory filled with teen-agers, sex and sex talk was not a secret. Some at least played the game of knowing all about it. Others remained quiet. Maturing boys did a lot of comparisons in our public showers. It was my guess that only one of the boys in our entire school was having sex with his girlfriend and this was especially scandalous because he was the son of one of our professors. The rule was absolute: "No sex before marriage." In spite of all this I know that at least three of my small class "had to get married" within two years of them being my high school classmates. And it was a time in which high school girls loved to wear very tight sweaters (even to church) and we boys were sure to notice and comment.

It is with considerable regret that I recall being completely in the dark about homosexuality and all I knew about homosexual activity came from dirty jokes all using the usually pejorative terms of the day.

Nor was there any "sex education" under any pseudonym in the high school curriculum and if it was ever spoken about in class, I have no memory of it.

But somehow, I guess I learned. My wife and I are the parents of five. And now some 70 years after graduation from high school I have had a very satisfying and blessed sex life and I am not so sure I would change my experience with that of my grandkids now in their teen years.

80CR

HIGH SCHOOL: WORK FOR PAY

Working for pay was always a high priority for us kids growing up in the Depression years of the 1930's. Of course, we never got paid for any work around our own home. A weekly allowance was something we only heard about. So early on I mowed lawns for my relatives and then picked cotton for neighboring farmers during the summer. I was good at the first and very, very poor at the second.

Therefore, when I went away to dorm living at Concordia Academy in Austin in 1941 it was assumed that I would find some paying jobs. This was complicated by the fact that we were not supposed to go off campus from Tuesday a.m. through Saturday noon. So, I found work on campus. The first job was to help take care of the grounds. I was assigned a partner, Mike Mitschke. We worked especially on the rose bushes. Our work was carefully monitored by the school's head, Director Dr. Henry P. Studtmann. The pay was 20 cents an hour.

In my junior and senior years, I got another assignment. I managed the "school stationery." This was a small operation originally set up to sell stationery supplies to students. Gradually it was expanded to a much more productive service namely that of selling candy, soft drinks and such. We were open for a few minutes after chapel each morning and then again after evening chapel services. Everything was supposed to be on a strictly cash-only basis, but there were always some students who asked for credit. So, I kept a log of that. However, every accumulated bill had to be settled by Friday evening or no more goods would be sold to that person.

Since these were the years of World War II, it was extremely difficult to procure candy, etc. to sell. Every week I would go in the "college truck" with the school custodian to a wholesale provider. There I put on my most friendly and beseeching face in an attempt to get a supply of Milky Ways, Mars Bars, Butterfingers, et sim. Sometimes I succeeded, other times I came up empty. I am somewhat ashamed to admit that once I procured these favorites, I was not always completely fair in making them all available for general purchase to all students. I must admit that at times I did hold some back for favored roommates or other friends.

In retrospect I find it amazing that there was virtually no supervision nor accountability. Each week I simply told Director Studtmann how much gross income there was, turned that amount over to him and then moved on. It was a good job.

In my junior year (11th grade) I got a good break. The Wukasch Brothers Café operated on the main drag just across the street from the big central library tower of the University of Texas. They were looking for workers. Again, Mike Mitschke and I quickly jumped at the opportunity. On Saturday afternoons (except for when the Texas Longhorns had home football games) we walked the few miles to the café and got to work in the kitchen. I remember especially peeling pound after pound of potatoes. But we also helped with doing dishes, cleaning the floor, etc. A free ice cream cone occasionally supplemented the 20 cents an hour at the end of the day.

This job turned out to also be available over the summer, so I grabbed it. I actually rented a small room at the home of Teacher and Mrs. Wilkening and got in as many hours as possible. I was promoted to waiter, which meant that my 20 cents an hour was supplemented by tips. I don't recall ever getting a tip larger than 25 cents but those nickels and dimes did count up. And I got my meals provided, as long as the cost did not exceed the 40 cents that was the price of our standard plate lunch. Now that I think of it, the café

213

also got a good deal. They wanted me there early in the morning through about 2:00 p.m. then wanted me "off" without pay from 2:00-5:00, returning again to work from 5:00-7:00. It all worked out.

One other benefit of that job was it expanded my horizons. I became very close to Joe the dishwasher. He was an African American and for me to work with a non-Anglo was a good and positive experience. To this day I recall our banter, our 5 cents a day wager on how many lunches would be sold that day, my covering for him when he took off for June "tenth" (the Remembrance Day of when slaves were first freed in Texas). One other "handyman" there was a mentally challenged gentleman and he, too, was my teacher. Furthermore, my sheltered life had in no other circumstances put me in contact with any non-Lutherans. Here I worked with people of many or no religious beliefs. Some of my co-workers were females (both single and married) whose life experiences, language, and other escapades help expand my world. I also learned that of all meals, breakfast is probably the most difficult to serve. I never knew there were so many different interpretations of what it means to have eggs "over-easy" or to have bacon that is "slightly crisped" or toast that is "toasty but not too brown." The size of the waffle or the appropriate thickness of a pancake was always open to argument, all in all this was a very good experience and later some of that family were generous in helping me find funds to go on to college.

I believe that today, after 60 years, there is still a café on that site, but I bet one cannot get a steak sandwich for 30 cents!

ℰℭ

65th ANNIVERSARY PART 1: PEOPLE

September 10, 2015 marked the 65 anniversaries of my commissioning as a "Teaching Minister" in The Lutheran Church-Missouri Synod. So, these have been days of reflection and remembering. I realize that recording some of these will be of absolutely no interest to many who may on occasion look at my blog. I write them because it feels good to me to do so and there may be a few others of you who may even find them of a bit interesting.

I recall first of all some of the people through whom I was blessed during these 65 years. I begin with Lydia Zielske. She was the woman who opened her house for me as I spent the first year as a single male in Tracy, California. She cleaned my room, prepared my meals and did my laundry. In a quiet, unassuming way she was always there to support and assist. Two other families which offered special support to this single guy: the Paulsons who farmed sections of tomatoes and other crops and made their house always open for a good meal and secondly, James and Mary Elhard who taught me how to drink black coffee.

Hong Kong, then and now, means masses of people and unbridled energy. Even on the day we arrived the place was being overrun by the tens of thousands fleeing Mao Zedong and his takeover of China. They came on boats, on foot, by rail, bus, walking, swimming, in the bottoms of sampans, below deck of steamers. They were everywhere, sleeping on the streets, on the hillsides, the roofs, the stairways.

I will never forget one of the persons whom I saw in my first week. I had immediately started teaching an education course for Lutheran teachers and was on my way home at 10:00 at night. I saw a young man lying in the arms of his father. He was starving to death. It was the first time I realized that stomachs might bloat under extreme malnutrition. I gave him some money and to this day recall the look of gratitude from his father.

The Chinese people were incredibly wonderful to me. They were patient with my arrogance, forgiving of my mistakes, open to learning, eager to move forward. Students and staff alike were motivated and deeply appreciative of any opportunity to move ahead. They changed my life forever. Mr. Hung Chiu Sing taught me Cantonese and even more importantly taught me Chinese customs and traditions, warned me of social faux pas, gave me the right words to say, the proper place to sit at meals, the appropriate way to address an elder, the place to put my chop sticks, the way to present a diploma.

A most unexpected Godsend in Hong Kong was a Mr. David Kowalke. He was head of Kodak Far East, a massive enterprise in those days. He and his family traveled over an hour each Sunday, taking a car ferry to attend English/Cantonese worship services held in a storefront. I am tempted to say that even more important was that he had some very close connections to top decision makers at the Royal Hong Kong Golf Club. He got me moved up that long waiting list, helped me pass my inspection by the membership committee and for about $250 I became a member. Weekly golf for 10 years kept me sane and gave me some British contacts which helped shape the entire building programs of Lutheran church and schools in Hong Kong.

Back in the States I was blessed to have the best possible team ministry trio, with Don Kell and Roland Boehnke in Michigan and a very diverse and competent staff in St. Louis. The principals of the Lutheran Schools in New

York were an incredible group of people who simply did what needed to be done, who accepted and affirmed me and held my feet to the fire. In between I moved in an entirely different world of Parent Effectiveness Training where I met and worked with people from all over the world. They were both my students and my teachers and helped continually to blow open my mind to new adventures, insights, problems and opportunities.

People. They have shaped me, angered me, empowered me, given me joy, despair and hope. And in each of them I saw a glimmer of what was impressed upon me as my lifelong duty when 65 years ago the pastor speaking at my commissioning said simply that my job was to respond to One who called "Feed my sheep. Feed my lambs."

ഇൻ

65TH ANNIVERSARY PART 2 PLACES

In these days I am recalling my 65 years since I was first commissioned as a teaching minister in the church. The focus of this reflection is the places we have lived. I have actually lived in 14 different apartments or houses during these years. The casual reader would conclude, "Mel was unable to hold a job!" It is really a bit more complicated. One reason for the different places is because I often lived in "church supplied housing." So, my quarters were determined by church budgets and sometimes even by a committee, which chose an apartment without ever having listened to any of our considerations.

The locations of those houses included California, Texas, Illinois, Michigan, Missouri, New York and Hong Kong. Each had much to love and enjoy. Tracy, California in the 1950's had a population of some 10,000. So, I got to know many of the residents and when one walked down Main Street one was likely to be called by name. Hong Kong is my favorite place in the entire world. I love the Chinese people. The energy of the place carries one along. The food options are unlimited. The streets are safe. If one has air conditioning (which we did not have) and good solid windows (which we mostly had) then one can ignore the heat, the 96 inches of rain per year or the terrible typhoons. New York comes close to Hong Kong as a favorite and if I had lots of money (and a different wife) I could enjoy living in Hong Kong or New York as my place of choice even for today in retirement. Chicago was great. It has excellent public transportation, great art and entertainment and every imaginable type of food. Ann Arbor, Michigan (even in the tumultuous 60's) is a place of intellectual stimulation, roads cleared of the worst snow imaginable, and not too far from Frankenmuth chicken dinners. And we now live in San Diego county California by choice. The weather, the multi-ethnic communities, the golf courses, the range of political opinions, the beaches and nearby mountains… It is great!

Of course, there are "places" other than just our residences or the cities that contain them. My life has been spent in classrooms. I love teaching. 65 years ago, that meant 45 kids in one classroom of 4th - 8th graders. Later on, those classrooms were found in colleges and seminaries in Hong Kong and several USA campuses. I have given the keynote address or led a workshop in each of the Districts of the Lutheran Church-Missouri Synod and all the Regions of the ELCA.

Work with Effectiveness Training gave me the opportunities to teach or do business or just stop in on places like, Germany, Switzerland, France, Norway, Sweden and best of all Finland. There were plenty of challenges (and good people) awaiting me in Australia, New Zealand, Tahiti, and Pakistan.

In retirement I was blessed to lead some tours with incredibly wonderful cadres of friends. These tours took us to China, Tibet, Greece, Turkey, Germany, the Czech Republic, Austria, Slovakia, Hungary, Brazil, Argentina, Israel and Palestine.

Places I visited (usually with Jane) just for fun and to be with family and friends hold special niches in my heart. Before we were frightened off by drug wars, we had wonderful times in Mexico. Visiting son John and his family in Barcelona, Madrid, Taiwan and England were special. Len and Ruth Galster were wonderful hosts in Bangkok. And since we were careful not to break the law by chewing gum in public, we had a great time in Singapore

Just naming these places stirs up masses of differing feelings. There is admiration for those poor kids who attended our rooftop schools in Hong Kong. All they got was rudimentary stuff of the basic three "Rs," but they took that and became wonderful citizens of the world. I think of the children sitting in out-door schools without textbooks in Pakistan and how they are now being challenged by the Taliban, et sim. I admire the great work we witnessed at Christmas Lutheran Church and School in Bethlehem and the God-blessed incredible work of Pr. Raheb. I pray that the improvement in wealth distribution is bringing hope to the many, many poor people I saw in those long lines awaiting treatment in small Wheat Ridge-supported clinics in south India and I hope that all of them will someday get the opportunity to just visit and admire the Taj Mahal in the heart of their own country.

None of the above places would be so favorably remembered were it not for Jane, family and friends. Jane has made each of our homes, places of refuge from stress, centers of beauty, locales of peace and the abode of love. No matter where else I may have been in the world the thing that kept drawing me forward was the anticipation of being safely home. Even today when she is there and also if by chance some or all of the kids come join us, I have no desire to be any place else. For as my family always reminds me "Home is where the heart is."

৪৩৫৪

65TH ANNIVERSARY PART 3: OPPORTUNITIES FOR MINISTRY AND SERVICE

In these days I am recalling and reflecting upon the occasion just 65 years ago when I was commissioned as a teaching minister of Lutheran Church. I want to recall some of the many unexpected opportunities for ministry and service that I have faced during these 65 years.

Lutheran Church Leadership

It had been my life-long ambition to be a Lutheran elementary school teacher. To me that usually meant a small two or three classroom school that was one aspect of one local congregation's educational ministry. That was a wonderful dream for I know that such a setting can shape the lives of students, provide a close-knit support system and allow one to observe the effects of one's ministry over many generations. I got to experience that for about six years and I am grateful for that. What I still can't quite get used to is that those opportunities became so vastly different. I never dreamed that I would play a role in establishing a Lutheran School system in Hong Kong, a system that today has kindergartens, elementary and high schools in Chinese and English with an enrollment of some 25,900 students. Nor did I ever imagine that I might play some role in a wider jurisdiction of the Lutheran Church. I not only had some responsibility for 51 Lutheran schools in the Metropolitan New York area and 117 Lutheran schools in Michigan, but then also some general leadership support/assistance for all the Christian education of some 6,000 congregations of the LCMS. And what a special blessing to later be a minor player for Lutheran education in the ELCA with its vast number of preschools and nearly 30 universities. For many and complicated reasons those systems in the USA are facing extreme challenges these days and all who serve and support them deserve our continued admiration and encouragement.

Parent Effectiveness Training

I certainly never dreamed 65 years ago that I would spend eight years of my career in a position outside the church. But I did that with eternal gratitude for eight years as I headed up Parent Effectiveness Training. As a colleague of its founder, Dr. Tom Gordon, this organization reached over one million parents and countless parents and children learned the value and joy of strengthened parent-child relationship. Parent-child relationships share many values regardless of the nationality of the family involved and I played a role in getting that program started in tens of countries around the world

From Classroom to Unexpected Situations

Teachers learn to expect the unexpected. I know that saying well and experienced it often. Just three of the unexpected places my teaching career took me include Tiananmen Square, The New York World Center and hospital intensive care units. I have written a previous blog entry about the terrible experience of being in Tiananmen Square on June 4,1989, of having bullets fly over my head as we were escaping, and of being with students mourning their slain classmates. The World Trade Center begins with much more pleasant memories as I recall the absolute joy of having lunch with principals of the Lutheran Schools Association of New York in a beautiful private dining area on top of Tower Two and then later watching in horror from my Hong Kong hotel room as that building collapsed on 9/11. And that reminds me that just by being a teacher I have often found myself at the bedside of people dying. The saddest include being there as a student expired after being hit by a truck. But it also includes the much more peaceful deaths of older persons, usually the parent or grandparent of a student.

After being commissioned 65 years ago, I served "full-time" as an educator until I turned 65 at which point, I retired. And what a glorious retirement it has been. I have been surrounded by a faithful, loving spouse and wonderful people and opportunities: work with Wheat Ridge Ministries, which brings health and hope around the world, the Center for Urban Education Ministry, which works so hard and effectively to bring hope to children living in our large urban centers, and serving on the Board of Survivors of Torture International, which provides a safe haven, healing and integration into American society for those who have suffered government sanctioned torture in countries around the world. During the years I have been encouraged, challenged, confronted, saddened, and supported though membership and leadership at Calvary Lutheran Church, Solana Beach, California. This congregation, which probably has the greatest unrealized potential of any Lutheran congregation in America, has been an arena for service, disappointment and everlasting hope.

And so, I bring to an end this little three-part set of memories with a determination to be grateful for the past, content in the present and hopeful of the future.

ଛଠଣ

ROSARIO: LISTEN

Once a month we gathered to tell our stories, share our pain and look for signs of hope. The group, which I helped facilitate, was made up of first-year teachers in New York Lutheran elementary schools.

The new teacher's question surprised me. "How do I deal with a group of students who make fun of their classmate?" "What's the issue?" I asked, knowing she was in a multi-racial ethnic school. "Well, the kids tease Rosario. They tell her she smells. The problem is: She does! Her clothes are clean enough, but I doubt if she ever takes a bath."

I suggested that the teacher get some very private one-on-one time with her student. I suggested she gently ask her about her bathing habits and then just listen, not judge, not condemn, not teach, and just listen to the response.

When we next met the new teacher could hardly wait to share her experience. She had followed my suggestions. Her student had said it was true that she didn't bathe. "It is too scary!" she said. The teacher listened. "Scary?" "Yes, I'm afraid I might die." "You're frightened that taking a bath might cost you your life. That is scary."

Slowly the whole story came out. This little second grader had seen her mother get into the bathtub. While she was rinsing her hair, she had a stroke and died right there in the tub in front of her child's terrified eyes.

The teacher held the trembling tearful child as she related the story. More conversation ensued. A consultation with the very silent surviving

220

father was productive.

After a while, Rosario came to school all fresh and bright. "I am not afraid to take my bath," she said. The one thing that opened the door was listening. The power of empathic, nonjudgmental active listening is a power beyond words. All of us who have access to listening ears or to the Listening Ear know this.

ဆလ

65th WEDDING ANNIVERSARY

Yesterday Jane and I celebrated our 65th wedding anniversary. It was a good time to give thanks, reflect and look forward. Jane and I had a long and wonderful conversation on the context of the traditional Christian wedding vows plus a list of what it takes to have a good marriage. A few of the thoughts that struck us are listed below.

We promised to live together in the holy estate of matrimony. Our time together has been made holy by a gracious, generous, forgiving God. We are aware that our spiritual insights, beliefs and values have both remained firm and have significantly changed. We are much more open and less dogmatic. We are more comfortable with mystery and not in need of certainty about non-essentials. We are less provincial and feel a stronger shared unity with all of God's people and the whole creation.

We have experienced poverty and riches. We recalled how in our early years of marriage Jane took our meager check, cashed it, and carefully placed the appropriate amount in individual envelopes, even $1.00 for postage. We have always tithed and more and as the years went by included more and more "non-church" causes in our designations. We realized that after 10 years of marriage we were still making less than $300 a month (plus housing) and now we live in a wonderful retirement community where our monthly fee is well in excess of our annual salary in the first 10 years.

Like others, we experienced together sickness and health, both to an extreme extent. Our daughter Liz was once not expected to live through Christmas Eve to the next day. We flew Jane home from Hong Kong while she was in a virtual coma. We watched our son Dave's face be destroyed by cancer and held his hand as he breathed his last. And at age 88 both of us still travel the country without cane, wheel chair or oxygen tanks.

We have learned to love and cherish each other with a love that grows

221

deeper with each passing year even as the sexual expression of that love that we so much anticipated and enjoyed for so many years is now sometimes more a memory than a current reality.

Our personal intercommunication has been strengthened by our ever-deeper commitment and practice of active listening, non-blameful confrontation, win-win problem solving and honest sharing of values and beliefs.

Family members including our children's spouses and grandchildren are sources of joy, pride, new insights, challenges and satisfactions.

Colleagues and work experiences enriched us. 65 years ago, both of us anticipated spending our professional careers in the elementary classrooms of Lutheran parochial schools. That would, of course, also have been a very satisfying calling, but we have been blessed by all kinds of other opportunities for service from California to New York to tens of cities and countries around the world, ranging from Hong Kong to Helsinki to Pakistan and places in between.

The marriage vows conclude with "as long as you both shall live." How long that will be is, of course, unknown to us. Yet this we do know. It's has been and is great. We are blessed beyond what we ever imagined possible on that Saturday afternoon in Zion Lutheran Church, Ft. Wayne, Indiana, 65 years ago.

଼ଠ୶

AFGHANI FAMILY PART 1

Five years ago, a young woman whom I will call "Sarah" lived a reasonably contented life, as contented as possible for a middle-class Afghan family enduring the on-going conflicts in that ancient country. The father ran a business including a money-exchange component. The mother was an active supporter of women's rights. The children of school age were attending school. And that is where the trouble started.

One day as Sarah was coming home from school she was stopped by the Taliban. "Who is sending you to school?" they demanded. She told the truth: "My father." The response, "Tell him he must stop doing that immediately! In this country girls do not go to school!"

After about a week, Sarah was again stopped on the way home from school. This time it got even more serious. The Taliban discovered that she was not only going to school, she was learning English. The next day her father disappeared. It was soon obvious that he had suffered the same fate as his eldest son who had previously disappeared. Both father and son were murdered by the Taliban. When the mother heard this distressing news, she suffered a heart attack and died.

The remaining seven family members, all under 20 years of age tried to manage. Then a government agent arrived at their home with information provided by the USA forces. The threat was clear, "You, Sarah, are next on the list for extermination by the Taliban. Escape at once." The entire family scrambled out of their home in the middle of the night making their way to a neighbor some distance away. The escape in the dark, was hurried and in the process a younger sister fell and broke her leg.

Someone related to the USA again arrived, this time with one ticket for a flight to the USA. S-1 was given the strong advice to flee for her life, get on the next flight and find freedom in the USA. S-1 arrived in Washington DC.

Meanwhile back in Afghanistan the nearby family was helpful but only for so long. It was announced that their six siblings could stay, but there was one new condition. The youngest girl in the family was to become an added wife to one of the care providers. He was 65, the girl, 12! They refused. They decided to get what cash they could for all their goods, car, home, and other possessions. Every penny of the proceeds was given to an underground group that got the family safely out of Afghanistan into hiding in Pakistan. About this time our family and Sarah's were about to get connected.

෪ඏ

AFGHANI FAMILY PART 2

When "Sarah" (the Afghani woman I mentioned in my last blog entry) was sent to San Diego she was advised to contact Survivors of Torture, International. This is an organization that helps people who have fled to the USA because they have suffered government-sponsored torture. I had assisted this organization to secure a start-up grant from Wheat Ridge Ministries more than 10 years ago. I was a member of its Board of Directors. By coincidence our late son David had contacted this organization with an unusual offer.

David lived alone in his home here in San Diego. On his lot he had refurnished a beautiful small "granny flat." Originally, he intended to rent it out. Then he came to the conclusion that he did not really need rental income and that some needy person might find it a wonderful place to live. So, he contacted Kathi Anderson of Survivors of Torture, International. Within 24 hours she had identified S-1 who was overjoyed to find a place to live other than the small one-bedroom apartment she was sharing with three refugees from Africa.

When she moved in, she was in a very difficult situation. She spoke virtually no English. She had recurring headaches. She knew her parents were dead, her elder brother also murdered and her siblings in hiding.

David sprang into action. He provided cooking utensils, bedding, helped her get a bus pass and assisted her in enrolling in a local community college. She responded with deep appreciation, incredible hard work at her studies, and got a job cleaning rooms in a hotel. She regained hope.

After about a year her siblings found refuge in America under the sponsorship of several human-care agencies. Unfortunately, two of her sibs were assigned to San Diego and four younger ones placed in a foster home in Hemet, CA some 90 miles away. David assisted in cutting miles of red tape, got the family to at least have telephone connections, and all this while he was suffering from growing throat cancer. Then David's cancer worsened and he died. Like the rest of us I was devastated but determined. Against unbelievable odds and with massive assistance, especially from David's estate and generous members of Calvary Lutheran Church, Solana Beach, she got herself named "foster parent" for her siblings. The entire family was reunited in San Diego with six of them now living together in a rented home.

All seven of this family are now in school. Two have found part-time work. "Sarah," who is in school full-time, foster parents the younger ones and manages it all. They are all determined to make it. She has sworn that they will stop needing "outside assistance" as early as possible.

The challenges continue. Getting a used car and driver's license is a continuing major issue. Women do not drive cars in Afghanistan and roads do not have lanes or stop lights. The house got bed bugs. The kids who had not seen a dentist for five years have terrible teeth and no money for dental care. Her eyes are a mess and her insurance does not cover eye care. Their Muslim headscarves bring them occasional taunts.

But they persevere and with the help of friends they will make it and be a valuable addition to this country that they now very thankfully and proudly call home.

AFGHANI FAMILY PART 3

The saga of the seven children who fled torture by the Taliban by coming to our country continues unabated.

First, the good news. The eldest, a young woman whom I call "Sarah" continues to amaze us. She is in her last couple weeks of junior college. She has amassed a grade point near perfect A's, all with knowing barely a word of English when she arrived here some three years ago. She is the designated foster care provider for her six siblings. She managed to get dental care for her family, who had not seen a dentist in five years. She has applied for admission for university-level work and just yesterday was informed that she was accepted at the prestigious University of San Diego, as she awaits word on her other applications. She passes weekly very meticulous in-home inspections conducted by a very legalistic representative from the foster care agency.

The second oldest son whom I will call "Rafeek" is also doing very well. He works (for $10 an hour) at McDonald's, keeps a to-the-penny budget, incredibly saved $5,000 and last week purchased (on credit) a nice used car. His plan is to go to school full-time, work full-time and also drive Uber and Lyft, save enough money and then open an Indian bakery. The youngest, aged 12, is doing great in school and speaks "American" without even the hint of an accent.

Yet the challenges continue. The first is the changing attitude about them that they perceive in society. They are increasingly hearing terrible slurs about their Muslim faith. They fear that threats about deportation will be carried out even though they are here 100% legally and have green cards. They face some outright discrimination when they go in public wearing their headscarves.

The second oldest sister, "Shakira," is having the hardest time. She is really struggling with her G.E.D. classes and her English. Her mental health is still not well. After all, when her family was informed, they were next on the Taliban death list, they fled in the middle of the night and she fell and broke her leg as she ran. Then some "friends" took them in but after a while demanded payment: in the form of her (a 12-year-old at the time) becoming the third wife of her protector who was aged 62. That is when they fled to Pakistan where they lived in exile for some two years.

Now money has become a significant issue. "Sarah" cannot at the moment come up with the $300 university registration fees, much less the university tuition. They have exceeded their medical expense limits on health and dental care and so are going without, including not getting eyeglasses badly needed. "Sarah" really thinks she will pass her driver's license test this Christmas season but does not know where she can find the money for the car insurance for a car that friends have found and paid for. And then comes the message from their landlord: "I intend to sell the house so you'd better start looking at an alternative."

Yet - their determination is undeterred. All of them daily "show up." All of them still see America as the land of dreams and opportunities. Their gratitude for all who have, and are now, helping continues to be expressed most profoundly. Together, under God, they will be blessed and will be a blessing to our country and to the world.

ຂໍແ

AFGHANI FAMILY PART 4: THREE STRIKES, BUT NOT OUT

The amazing family, of seven young persons who fled the Taliban and are now our friends here, continues to face challenges and to persevere.

We rejoiced with them 18 months ago when they found a wonderful four-bedroom home to rent at the very good price of $2,100 a month. Now the owner has officially announced "I am selling the house. You have three months to vacate." So, the search is on. A computer site listed a deal: "For rent: three-bedroom stand-alone home with two-car garage in a desirable neighborhood." The eldest, "Sarah," replied via email and then phone. It got better. The rent is only $900 a month. Then it got even better: Utilities included. Then it got suspicious: the house interior could be viewed only after a $2,900 deposit was paid. Keys would be handed over after the by mail deposit was received. More phone calls, more emails, all to the Afghan woman. When I sent an email, made numerous phone calls there was no response. I explained to her, "This is a scam! Do not send any money to the suggested Texas mailing address." The owner had not responded to me but was very persistent in calling the Afghan woman saying, "Just send the money. Keep the house clean. Trust me. I am a very religious and righteous person." I finally convinced my friend to forget it. She cannot afford sending a check for $2,900 to a Texas address to rent a house from a guy she has

226

never met, who won't let her see the house and can't explain why he is renting his place at well less than half of the going rate. I am convinced we dodged a scam.

I missed seeing the eldest son "Adil." I was told, "Oh, we forgot to tell you. He is back in Pakistan. He is there for two reasons: 1. He wants to get married to an Afghan woman whom he met at the immigration center in Islamabad which helped the family get asylum status in the USA." The second reason: "He has found a way to contact the smuggler who got our family out of Afghanistan. However, in the process our five-year old sister disappeared." Now "Adil" wants to make contact with that smuggler and see if we can find our missing family member. "Adil" has now been somewhere in Pakistan but he does not have the money to pay for a phone call back to the States so we don't really know what's happening.

With wonderful assistance from a friend of mine who runs several McDonald's we got work for three of the family members. They are very eager to work, are willing to go to school, work and do anything to "get ahead." However, time schedules are very complicated. English language skills vary. Work ethics for them range from extreme dedication and hard work to something less than that. But then the reality is that in San Diego (at least at these McDonald's) 95% of the employees are Hispanic, speak only Spanish at work and look out after their friends and relatives with whom they share work at the same store. When one of the Afghan young men decided that he was being discriminated against, was never allowed to "work up front," spent week after week doing only the lowest and least satisfying work like sweeping the floors and cleaning stoves, he rebelled. He refused to obey an order. He was appropriately fired on the spot. Now all three are out of work.

Meantime the climate in our country has become more challenging. Racial and religious slurs are coming more frequently. Job applications from Muslims are placed at the bottom of the pile. Yet they, and we, carry on. There is an unsinkable conviction, "America is the land of opportunity. We are blessed to be here. We are most grateful to all the people who are making great efforts and sacrifices to help us. We are determined to get our citizenship status and make a contribution to this country and to those who are supporting us. With God's help we will not only survive but we will prosper."

୫୦୬

AFGHANI FAMILY PART 5: SUCCESS AND CHALLENGES

It is now eight years that my family has been involved with a specific Afghan family who came as refugees to the USA. The long, complicated story includes our late son, David, learning of the eldest female, named "Sarah," through Survivors of Torture, International. David provided this young woman a place to live, helped her register for school, helped her extended set of siblings all make their way to San Diego, etc. etc., etc.

It is a remarkable story of achievement. "Sarah" learned enough English to attend and then graduate from junior college and get admitted to UCSD. She has one more year to get her degree. Her eldest brother works at Subway, drives Uber and Lyft and is a full-time student in junior college. The next, a female, works at McDonald's, is a student in Continuing Ed. and just got her certification to be a childcare provider (all of this while suffering post-traumatic stress syndrome from abuse while a refugee). The next young man helps "Sarah" with the family etc. and also works at a bakery and drives for Amazon. The next one just went on his own, works at a bakery and is also in pre-college classes. The younger sister will graduate from high school next month and the youngest was recently told to just skip the 7th grade and move to 8th grade and is a sought-after young soccer star. "Sarah" has just received her USA citizenship and hopes next month to get her much-prized USA Passport. On top of that, she was named the top achiever in a major competition with Soroptimists and even went to Tokyo to receive her $25,000 award as the top winner of their "Live Your Dream" award.

And I cannot tell all this wonderful news without acknowledging all my family and friends at Calvary Lutheran Church and other places who have been generous beyond words with all kinds of support including funds, furniture, automobiles, etc.

Given all of the above, it would seem there would be nothing but celebration and a big "let's keep on doing it." True – and, there continue to be challenges.

America and Afghanistan have lots of different ways of dealing with everyday life issues. For example: paying attention to time. We are still working on the American concept that days of the month often have strict time limits. Thus, "Sarah" has missed classes at school because she did not register on time. She has failed to get rentals because she applied too late. She has missed scholarship awards because she filed late. Just this morning I received a request to write a recommendation for a scholarship. Deadline for this is "later today!" After arriving late for doctor appointments or at the

DMV et sim she is now also working hard to "get" that in America, 10:30 does not mean "any time after 11:00."

We also have not solved the question, "What is your name? The name she uses for rent contracts is different from the one she uses as a student. I have no idea what name she will put on her American passport. I say her family name is "Abad." Then I get a request for a reference and her name is "Sarah Safar."

She was almost denied the opportunity to go to Japan because the date of her birth as shown on her passport did not match her date of birth on her American green card. Of course, this is partly explained by the fact that she left Afghanistan in an emergency situation and brought no "official papers" with her. Also, when her sibs arrived here (also without papers as they were in a "leave tonight and flee situation") the American official here gave them all an estimated year of birth and assigned them all January 1 of that year as their official birth date.

Just yesterday I was frustrated with myself and others. I asked whether the younger sister who is a senior in high school had been granted admission to any university for next year. I knew that she had applied at many of them. I was told, "Oh we just got the news that ALL of her college applications were denied because she had never taken and therefore never listed any SAT scores!" How can that happen after four years in American high schools! And how could I not have asked her "Mahala", how did you do on your PSAT or SAT?"

The demands on "Sarah's" life are overwhelming: caring for six siblings, going to school, getting citizenship - and now, another "cousin" family arrived from Afghanistan with no means of support and lots of health issues and they all turn to "Sarah" to assist with all this. So, I stress to "Sarah" that for her own sense of control and priorities she really needs some regular things like a "To Do List" or a budget or some kind of filing system. To date I have gone 0 for 3 on these!

Yet do not let these take away the big lesson: America is still a land of opportunity. Migrants who come to us from places like Afghanistan work incredibly hard, faithfully, and honestly to make it on their own. Every single member of this family is determined to be a good citizen of the USA and of the world and to pay back ten-fold and more all that has been invested in them.

৪০৫৬

TEACHERS COLLEGE PART 1

There was never any doubt as to which college I would attend. I think I was only FIVE years old when I announced to my Mother that I was going to follow in my father's footsteps and become a teacher in the parochial school system of The Lutheran Church-Missouri Synod (LCMS) and that is where I landed.

In 1945, Concordia Teacher College (CTC) was a very closed institution. It enrolled only LCMS Lutherans aspiring to be parochial school teachers. While it was co-ed it was far different from today's co-ed colleges. Males were not allowed to visit the women's dorms except on a few rare occasions and the women were ordered to keep their room doors open at any of the rare times when males were allowed on the floor. Once a year a wife of one of the profs gathered the "girls" and gave them a lecture on sex. The women had to be signed into their rooms by 11:00 p.m. except for once a term when they received a special permit to stay out until 1:30 a.m.

Academically the school was very traditional. The profs were committed to their students and all of them had to be rostered ministers of the LCMS. Of course, there were no computers and I had no typewriter. Teaching by assigning group projects was unheard of.

I did not do well in my freshman year and in one term made three grades of "C." Then I caught on and did well, always being on the Dean's List and eventually graduating with highest academic honors.

Our education courses turned out to be not very helpful. However, we had an English professor, Diesing, who taught me how to read, to organize, to write, to appreciate theater. It was also obvious that the teachers really cared about us students. Their office doors were always open. They always knew my name, and gave me much positive affirmation. My piano and organ teachers were unbelievable. All students were required to play an instrument. Teaching me to do that was hopeless, yet my teachers were kind, kept my weekly sessions with them short and encouraged me to fully use my other talents.

The school helped shape my spiritual values and beliefs. I am grateful to Doc Koehler who indoctrinated me in the Lutheran tradition. Daily chapel attendance was required and not very creative. I now realize that all of this helped my spiritual formation but I also realize that I no longer believe much of what I was taught, especially as it relates to the role of women, the insights on all world religions, the wide arms of grace, the definition of church, the inclusiveness of the sacraments, etc. etc. I am grateful for what I was taught

230

and that I have continued to learn and develop.

In retrospect CTC helped shape me, gave me a commitment to learning, prepared me for graduate work, gave me my first teaching placement and maybe most important of all: gave me the opportunity to meet a young woman named Jane Scheimann about whom I will write in another blog ENTRY.

৪০০৪

TEACHERS COLLEGE PART 2

By far the most important outcome of my college education had nothing to do with academics or career options. It had everything to do with my meeting, courting, loving and becoming engaged to Jane Ann Scheimann.

I was hardly a big "ladies' man" in either high school or college years. In high school I think I had a total of two formal dates and they led to no special relationships. In my freshman year at college I dated some but nothing special clicked. In my sophomore year at college I did fall for a young woman, but she jilted me. Then a colleague suggested I ask for a date with Jane Scheimann, a woman I had not previously noticed. Not noticing her was my bad judgment. Our first dates were very simple. We'd attend a basketball game together, then maybe go to Petersons' Ice Cream Parlor for a Sundae.

Dating during my college years presented some challenges: I had no money. Cars were forbidden. "Girls" had to be back in their dorms early, 10:00 p.m. most nights. The Dean of Women quickly admonished public displays of affection.

But we managed very well. Some of our best dates involved taking the Chicago "L" to go the Loop in downtown Chicago. Of course, we walked the two miles each way to and from the "L" station. If we could save a few bucks we would buy discounted tickets to the Goodman Theater, which staged very good plays. Or we would just walk around the Loop, find our way to Lake Michigan and then hold hands, madly in love, staring at the Buckingham Fountain. "Eating out" would be very simple until we had been together for over a year when Jane's father came to town and took us to Berghoff's in the Loop for a fancy dinner that included not only great food but also wonderful, romantic violin music.

Intimacy options were limited. But love finds a way. Our first kiss was behind the college gym. The Catholic Monastery, not far away, had massive

231

grounds with secluded trees perfect for smooching. Old-fashioned vows of chastity were self-imposed until our wedding night.

In our senior year we had a date that could have turned out to be very embarrassing. Cousin Blondie Doering's mother from Texas was visiting. She arrived in her Buick. After we all went out for ice cream, we stopped the car in front of the dorm, and Blondie who had been driving said, "Here, you two take the car for the rest of the evening." I slid behind the wheel of the car with the engine running. By 11:00 we were in the secluded parking lot of a nearby forest preserve. A policeman arrived and informed us that the park was closing and we had to leave. I attempted to start the car, but simply could not find the starter. Sweating profusely, I looked everywhere and was still fruitlessly searching when the officer returned. "I warned you two. Now get going or I will arrest you!" I was in a car in Illinois with Texas license plates. I had no ownership papers and I was unaware of where the starter was. In my panic I stomped my feet in every direction. Somewhere I hit a starter button (under the clutch?). The car started! The officer gave us one more incredulous look and sent us on our way back to the college dorm.

And we have been hitting starter buttons and heading on our way together ever since.

୫୦୧୪

TEACHERS COLLEGE PART 3: STUDENT GOVERNMENT

One of the most enjoyable and long-term beneficial aspects of college life was my involvement with student government. I think it started already in my freshman year when I was a "floor rep." It got amped up on my junior year when I became head of the Men's Council. It ended in my senior year when I served as Student Body President. The last was fun even before it started, as there was a long and interesting campaign season.

Two cousins, Blondie and Blackie Doering, were schoolmates one year behind me. When I decided to run for office, they chose to be my campaign managers. That was fun as we made signs, had slogans and made some campaign speeches, etc. They were great and we succeeded. If my memory is correct, I received some 90% of the popular vote. Which probably totaled some 600 in this small school.

The task of Student Body President involved quite a bit. I chaired all Student Council meetings, oversaw a whole host of student committees and met weekly with the college dean to discuss campus life. One of the perks of the office was that it carried with it a school grant in the fabulous amount of $100 for the year. (This sounds infinitesimal now, but since my total college costs for the year were around $500 this was a nice little help.)

One minor aspect and very strange "duty" of the student body president was to lead the entire campus in table prayers each day for the evening meal. In those days we had a very limited and set time for dinner. It was served "family style" and there were no food options. We ate what was set before us or went hungry. The members of the Student Council sat at an elevated head table. I led the table prayer or designated someone else to do it. In retrospect this all seems very strange.

One of the heavier assignments was that the Dean consulted me when serious discipline actions needed to be taken against students. I still have some regret over one particular case. One of the young men had been caught stealing some money from another student. He confessed and seemed truly repentant. I also knew he came from a rural family and his parents were extremely proud that their son was entering the teaching ministry of the church. But the dean was adamant, "This may be his first offense, but it's serious. He's out of here." Despite my not-strong-enough protests and pleas he was sent home to his devastated parents and to this day I wonder what he did with the rest of his life. I still regret my failure in giving him another chance.

One of the things I did of which I was most proud is that I suggested, then organized and finally chaired the very first nationwide conference of all student body presidents from each of the Lutheran Church-Missouri Synod colleges across the country. This was unheard of at that time and our college president was very afraid of this. He feared it might lead to some kind of inappropriate demands from these radical students. It was, of course, nothing of the kind. It was just a good time for us to get together, learn from and support each other. One of the wonderful results of this was that for many years after that I would run into those student leaders and see what a positive difference they were making in the life of the church and society.

There is one other aspect of all this about which I have very good feelings. It turns out that in 1920 my father, Oscar Kieschnick, had served as "Sem Buck' for this Concordia. In 1950 I had that title and some 25 years after me our son, David, was elected Student Body President at this same school. Just a quiet satisfaction. And the lessons I learned in that position served me well in a variety of positions I held later in my professional life

TEACHERS COLLEGE PART 4: SPORTS

I have a friend who often reminds me that when I speak of my high school and college sports activities, I should always begin by explaining that I played in a very small pool. His point is that when one is in a small pool one can be a tiny fish and still seem to have volume. He has made his point ever since he discovered that my high school had about 100 students and my college some 600.

When I arrived at Concordia, I had never played legal tackle football. (I say "legal" because, as referenced in a previous blog entry, we had an unauthorized little team that played without uniforms and which snuck onto the wonderful turf of Memorial Stadium of the University of Texas and played against a similar unauthorized team made up of local black young men from the neighborhood.) I was eager to play college football. I was assigned the position of right end and played both offense and defense. I had a couple of things going for me: 1. I had spent the summer in San Antonio heat digging foundation trenches at construction sites using only pick and shovel. So, my body was rock hard and 2. I had played lots of "take away" where we competed to grab fly balls snatching them away from other pursuers. Thus, I did pretty well at catching passes, grabbing five of them in the first quarter of an early game. The bad news is that I was a very slow runner and the coach reminded me on the sidelines "Kieschnick, if you could run, we would have a bunch of touchdowns!" Then I broke my ankle - but I did play all four years.

Probably the biggest surprise of my days as a footballer is that I was elected team captain. It was in my junior year. I had returned after a year of being a teaching intern. The coach assembled the team and asked then to use a secret ballot to elect their captain. I won, getting almost all the votes. It had been entirely kept from me by my teammates that they were planning this.

I was on the varsity basketball team for a year, but the other players, especially those from basketball-crazy Fort Wayne, Indiana were all better that I was. So, after my freshman year I settled for intramural basketball, did a few things on the track team like throwing the discus and shotput, but you will certainly not find my name in any record books.

I did play four years of varsity baseball. In high school I always played shortstop, but that position was sewed up by an upper classman and I took to the outfield. My arm was not bad, but after college I played some under a very experienced coach. He always (correctly) insisted that my throws from the outfield had too high an arc and therefore took too long to reach their destination. He was right. My baseball colleague Rudy Block (who died way too young) really monitored batting averages and he assured me that my batting average was number two on the team, second only to his.

One other memory: Once I was removed for a pinch hitter even though the coach knew that I had the second highest batting average. And Coach Waldschmidt had seen my two previous plate appearances against this very small but canny left-hander who struck me out in both my previous two trips to the plate. I simply could not connect with his curve, which broke toward my body. I guess some moralist will tell me that it was a good learning experience for me to have to sit on the bench.

An interesting and fun intramural game was badminton. By some coincidence my roommate and fellow Texan Roland Trinklein and I battled it out for the school championship.

All in all, I am very grateful for my college sports activities. It kept me in good physical shape. Being part of a team is a very rewarding and learning experience. Learning to lose (which we did often) taught me that life often has bitter losses and I have experienced and survived my share of them in the many years since I last played college sports - and being on losing teams prepared me well to be a fan of the San Diego Padres and Chargers.

ഇരുജ

TEACHERS COLLEGE PART 5: PAYING FOR COLLEGE

Paying for college in 1945 (the year I entered) was a whole different story from what our children are paying for our grandchildren's college in 2016. My recollection is that I figured my total cost for college, including transportation between Texas and Illinois, all tuition and room and board, came to about $600 a year. That was because the church charged us no tuition as we were all studying to become commissioned teaching ministers on the official roster of the church. My recollection is that my father (who provided most of the money) was making about $3,000 a year. Yet he sent in all the money for room and board. My two sisters, Erna and Leona, who "went to work" rather than go to college themselves and helped pay my fees for four years at Concordia Academy, had both married and were no longer providing

235

funds for me. Costs for daily activities, laundry, books, etc. were up to me

So, of course, I worked over the summer. The first couple years I worked as a waiter at Wukash Brothers Café in Austin. The last two years, I worked at constructions jobs. And work I did! I was at the lowest level of skills and pay. I think I was paid 40 cents an hour and spent most of my time digging foundation trenches and then fabricating the steel foundations. It was often over 100 degrees of Texas heat. I wore shorts and no shirt. I was turned a very dark tan and my muscles were as hard as the steel I fabricated. I also learned about the language and conversation of people who were far removed from "church work" and the curses and oaths that surrounded very graphic descriptions of sexual activity were, at first, very foreign to my ears.

I remember one of the first little jobs I took on a Saturday in River Forest. It was to install storm windows in a private home. I didn't even know what a "storm window" was, but the two female residents of the home who hired me were very kind and forgiving and we did eventually get all those storm windows installed on both levels of that big two-story house.

By far the best job I had during the school year was "setting pins" in the bowling alleys of the private Oak Park Club. I was responsible for two adjoining lanes from 7:00 - 11:00 p.m. Obviously that was before there were pin-setting machines and so it was all hand labor. While I was responsible for the lanes up to 11:00 p.m., it was also agreed that if no one was there after 10:00 p.m. I could take off and head back to the dorm. I was paid $4 a night and often worked two nights a week and in those days $8 was enough to take care of my incidental expenses. Obviously "incidental" could not allow for any restaurant meals, cigarettes, alcohol, et sim. but just enough to take the "L" to the Chicago Loop and enjoy the sights.

The good news: I graduated from college without debts (other than the $100.00 I borrowed to start grad school) and it was good financial discipline! It blows my mind that last night when Jane and I went out (as guests of family and friends) our dinner bill for the two of us came exactly to the same dollar amount as what my salary was for my first month of teaching in a Lutheran school.

೮೦೧೩

TEACHERS COLLEGE PART 6: THEOLOGY AND SPIRITUALITY

The Good News

Religion, church and doctrine were all-important at Concordia Teachers College (CTC) in the late 1940's. We were never to forget that we were being trained to serve as "ministers of religion" serving as Commissioned Teachers of the Church. The big thing was Lutheran doctrine (specifically The Lutheran Church-Missouri Synod version). We knew that in our oath of office we had to swear faithfulness to Lutheran doctrine as explained in the creeds found in The Book of Concord.

We took an overview course on the Bible and studied selective books of the Bible in courses devoted exclusively to the various individual books. We had a course in church history and another on the Lutheran Church in America. All courses (not just those in religion) were taught by duly authorized ministers of the church.

Worship was deemed important. Even at the college level daily attendance at morning chapel services was compulsory and attendance checks were taken. Attendance at worship every Sunday was assumed to be the practice of us all.

I am grateful that I really knew the official teachings of the church. I am glad that worship attendance was stressed. I appreciated the efforts of those in the church who came before me.

The Bad News

In retrospect, I think my religious training at CTC was very inadequate in many respects. The teaching methods were most unfortunate. Especially our courses in Christian doctrine were all taught in very rote fashion. We learned "A Summary of Christian Doctrine" from a book taught by the book's author, Doc Koehler. He was kind and paternalistic. He called male students "sonny" and women students "honey." He told us when to pick up our pencils and exactly which phrases in the text to underline, some of them twice and he came to our desks to make sure we had exactly followed directions. Of course, there was no discussion. He told us exactly what "the word of God" was regarding each matter and our duty was to know it, believe it and correctly state it at exam time.

In retrospect, I find it amazing that while the religious world of the day was facing the rise of "the historical-critical" approach to Biblical interpretation I never once heard that term in any of my courses. The possibility of ecumenism was never broached. Our brothers and sisters in the

Roman Catholic Church were seen primarily as purveyors of "false doctrine." Discussion in class was, in my memory, never substantive and the big argument was whether "engagement between a man and a woman" was "tantamount to marriage."

Especially disturbing to me now (though I admit it did not bother me at the time) was our introduction to the creeds other than The Apostles Creed and The Nicene Creed. We were instructed to read the creeds according to a schedule and to then write a summary of the key teachings expressed in that creed and "hand that in." It was soon obvious that no one ever read our summaries. To prove this some of my colleagues wrote the appropriate doctrine name in the title and then copied sports reports from the newspaper into the body of their "essay." This was done more than once and no student was ever "caught."

Daily chapel worship fell far short of its potential. It was always led by staff (never by students). The "order of worship" and liturgy never varied. I remember absolutely not one single service in which silence was called for; no service in which prayers or prayer requests from those assembled were asked for; no special music, only the wonderful organ music. The tragedy is so that so many opportunities were missed.

In Summary

I am grateful that I really learned the teachings of the Church. I am grateful that worship was just a normal, yet essential part of life. I learned well to appreciate the great choral music and hymns of the Lutheran tradition. Even though he taught by rote I knew that Doc Koehler really cared about his students and he had a special interest in me as he had taught my father 20 years earlier. And he knew that the method he used for my father was also the absolutely best for me.

ଚ୍ଚର

TEACHERS COLLEGE PART 7: MUSIC

It is a great pleasure to recall music from earlier days of one's life - and I have lots of wonderful memories of the music of 1945-50, the years I was in college. Being a Texan I carried with me the classic country western melodies of "I'm An Old Cowhand," "The Yellow Rose of Texas," "Pistol Packin' Mama," "Cotton-eyed Joe" and all the rest.

238

Being in love left me wide open to be stirred by "I'll See You in My Dreams," "You'll Never Know Just How Much I Love You," "Sentimental Journey," etc, etc. I never had a portable radio or record player but managed to hear all those great popular songs by Frank Sinatra, Bing Crosby, Nat King Cole, Peggy Lee, Glen Miller, Perry Como, etc., etc.

Religious and classical music were new to me in those days and I am forever grateful for those who introduced me to them. I sang in the college choir under Director "Tante" Beck (who let me join the choir because he remembered singing with my father in college 25 years earlier). He even asked me to become the manager of the choir tour and in my sophomore year I arranged for an on-road choir tour of some ten days that took us to many parts of the Midwest. Of special blessing was what we simply called our Mass Choir because it had well over 100 voices and was directed by Dr. "Kelly" Waldschmidt. We did Handel's "Messiah" and Bach's "St. Matthew's Passion." This was accompanied by a full orchestra and professional soloist. Again, wonderful memories.

The student body at the time included an incredible number of musicians who helped shape Lutheran liturgy and music for the last 60 years. They included Richard Hillert whose liturgies are sung every Sunday now in hundreds of Lutheran churches, Carl Schalk whose choir compositions continue to be top-sellers, "Pinger" Pelz who for many years was chief organ instructor at Bethany College, Ralph Schultz who continues to compose and direct orchestra and church masterpieces, etc., etc. And I will include my wife Jane in that list. She was a top organist among that elite group. (Later she made the switch from multiple rank massive pipe organs to playing the portable knee-pumped little instruments we carried from chapel to chapel in Hong Kong.)

Surrounded by all this great stuff, I was an abysmal failure. After four unsuccessful years of piano instruction during my high school years I kept up the poor piano performance for two more years at college. At that point the piano teachers were so frustrated by this non-practicing pianist that they turned me over to Dr. Carl Halter for instruction in playing the organ. To no-one's surprise my inability to find time for practice resulted in my reaching my peak performance skill as being able to play "Glory Be to Jesus" and forgetting about the foot pedals!

So, I gratefully carry all of that musical heritage with me and am still stirred by great music and its incomparable power to enrich my life and to help me experience the deepest emotions of faith and life.

TEACHERS COLLEGE PART 8: CALL/JOB ASSIGNMENT

Like every other student at my college, I was there to prepare to serve as a teaching minister of the Lutheran Church-Missouri Synod. We knew that if we were certified for service, we would receive our "assignment" from the church through the school's placement office. This assignment was to a teaching position in a specific Lutheran school. Our Director of Placement was Dr. Albert Maurer. As part of the process each of us graduates did have a one-on-one interview with him regarding our "placement." He was very clear that while he might listen to our ideas and wishes, the responsibility for our first position rested with "the Church," not with us.

I explained that I was eager to serve. It did not make much difference what grade-level I was assigned. I explained that I could not serve as a church musician but all other options were open. My assumption was that I would be assigned to a congregation in the state of Texas. Texas is where I was proudly from. Most Texans were assigned back to congregations in Texas.

The day of assignments arrived. About 150 of us gathered in Room 105 of the Administration Building. I do not even remember that the occasion opened with a word of prayer. The Placement Director had a big pile of envelopes that contained the info. for where each of was to go.

Our assignment came after a meeting with the Placements Directors of the two LCMS Teachers Colleges with the appropriate Director of Schools from the various Districts of the church. Each of those District Directors made their case for their respective vacancies and then an "assignment of candidates" was negotiated.

I dutifully awaited the calling of my name, then went up and took an envelope. I hastily opened it. The assignment stared me in the face - "St. Paul Lutheran School, Tracy, California, teacher of Grades 4-8 and principal of the school. Additional assignments: Director of Youth Ministry, assistance with Sunday School, remuneration: $200 per month. The school was only four years old. Total enrollment about 70 in Grades 1-8. The other teacher was Mrs. Rosa Bush, wife of the congregation pastor.

This assignment was fine with me. I was surprised it was not in Texas, and that I was to serve as principal but was quite naive as to what the duties of the principal were and so was not overwhelmed by that.

More important: where would my girlfriend (soon to be my fiancée) Jane be assigned? As I recall we were seated in alphabetical order and I had to wait until all had received their documents. Then Jane and I hurriedly met and disclosed to each other where we were headed. Jane was assigned Grades 1 and 2 at Peace Lutheran School in Saginaw Michigan. (She had been requested by name by the principal of that school and by the Superintendent of Schools for the Michigan District, Sam Roth, who was very influential and almost always got the persons any school in his District sought.

So that was it and that is where we served, I in California and Jane in Michigan. She served there for only one year. Then we married and the two of us shared our ministry, first in Tracy, then around the world for more than 65 years.

As I reflect on this process, I feel okay about it. We trusted the Holy Spirit and the responsible church people of the day. And I think everything worked out just the way it was supposed to!

∞∞

TEACHERS COLLEGE PART 9: GRADUATION/ENGAGEMENT

I know that I graduated from college even though when I just now searched for it, I could not find my diploma. But I found the diploma for my wife Jane and she and I graduated together. And her diploma clearly lists our graduation date as June 9, 1950. Frankly I remember very little about the ceremony or the words of the speaker.

I suspect that the reasons my diploma and graduation ceremony are not clear is because that date was more important to me for a different reason. That is the day I gave, and Jane accepted, her engagement ring. The ring itself has its own little history. My parents had met, admired Jane and were very pleased about our relationship. They knew we hoped to be married. They also knew that I was a flat-broke student who could not afford to buy an engagement or wedding ring. So, my dad had a proposal. The Lutheran "teacherage" in which they lived outside Walburg Texas had about ten acres of pasture around it. Dad offered and I bought for $10 a newborn heifer calf. It pastured on the grass and after about 10 months it was sold at auction for the wonderful price of $110! So, I had $100 with which to buy an engagement ring.

Fortunately, Jane's mom and dad also approved of our relationship and when I visited with them the Easter before our graduation her mother wisely

241

suggested that I spend a little time with some very good friends of theirs who happened to own a jewelry shop. And there I found it: a one-quarter karat gold solitaire engagement ring! Cost: $100. To me it was as amazing and beautiful as any million-dollar giant sparkler.

The time and moment of me giving the ring to Jane does not reflect well on my romancing skills. It was a couple hours before graduation. I was saying, "see you" to Jane as she went to her dorm room to put on her graduation gown. I handed her the ring and said "Here is a little something for you." Of course, when she got to her room and opened the package she screamed and all on the floor came to gush and admire.

I now have some regret that I did not handle this in a manner more worthy of her. I wish I had formally asked her to become my wife. That formality never occurred. We just grew into it. I had, however, very formally asked Jane's dad for permission to marry his daughter. In fact, I did that just an hour before I handed her the engagement ring.

As mentioned above, we then went to the graduation ceremonies. After that we did an unusual thing: we all went out for a late dinner at Nieman's Restaurant on North Avenue with her parents, grandmother and my folks. This was unusual because we were both so broke, we simply could never go out for a nice dinner and it was unusual, because my mother actually joined in the celebration by drinking a cocktail, another first. And, of course it was the formal announcement of our engagement It was all great.

It is now more than 66 years since that graduation/engagement event. The ministries made possible because I have that college degree and because Jane accepted that ring have been wonderfully blessed, amazingly interesting, and still going on at a fairly respectable pace!

ဆာ

WHATEVER HAPPENED TO......?

Soul Accounting

Soul Accounting is a term coined long ago. It was used especially in congregations of The Lutheran Church-Missouri Synod. It described a very good practice. It was a process to track and follow-up on the status of their members. The Senior Pastor had primary responsibility. Often, he was assisted by a team of lay persons (in those days always men) who shared responsibility with the pastor. The goal was to monitor as best as possible the

242

spiritual well-being of the congregation members. It focused on frequency of communion attendance, regularity of attendance at worship, consistency of financial offerings, ensuring that children were enrolled in the Lutheran school, et sim. It really had a noble purpose and when properly carried out greatly assisted the congregation in its responsibility for the spiritual welfare of all of its members.

If I were to use that term today in my ELCA congregation I would get a blank stare and the honest question, "What in the world do you mean by 'soul accounting'? Is that some new computer tracking system?" My congregation keeps no formal record of communion or church attendance. It has no lay committee charged with monitoring how things are going in the families of the church. I know of no system in place for laity to visit the ill, no functional utilization of our apparently dead Stephen Ministry. I know of no effort to have private conversations with members who have stopped making financial contributions. All of this leads to my lament "Whatever happened to soul accounting?"

Lutheran Congregation Singing

Again, I have wonderful memories of robust total congregational singing in the Lutheran churches of my youth. There were old hymns (especially chorales) accompanied by a full pipe organ. Men, women and children joined in, often in the four-part harmony of soprano, alto, tenor, bass. Now many new songs are filled with, what to me, is simply a repetition of quickly succeeding 16th notes. Maybe one-in-ten congregants sing along. In my congregation the singing of hymns is a lost art.

Home Visitations Among Congregation Members

It is, I am sure, not just nostalgia that recalls all those Sunday dinners we used to share with other members of our congregation. They were augmented by big at-home beer- and barbeque-filled wedding receptions, birthday celebrations, and remembrances of years of marriage. The pastor was certain to have been an invited visitor in every single congregation home. Now it usually takes death or a near death experience to have an in-home pastoral visit.

But it is not only church related stuff that I am nostalgic about this morning. Rather, I ask more WHATEVER HAPPENED TO...

Eating Out At An Affordable Price

This week my wife Jane and I celebrated her birthday at a wonderful top-level steak house. It was generously paid for by friends and family. Here is what we had: one serving of French onion soup, asparagus, dessert, one glass of good house wine, the smallest filet on the menu and the lowest cost full-sized steak. The bill (without tip) was $175. Now, I want to be clear: it was great, the gift from friends and family deeply appreciated. But $175! What retired Lutheran schoolteacher in the world could ever do that without assistance from family and friends!

A Decently Long Golf Drive

I just watched the golf tournament at the magnificent Bethpage-Black Golf Course in New York. I saw and relived the hole where 30 years ago I won the long drive contest with a drive of about 275 yards. Today it takes me a good drive and another wood to reach that distance

That Mel Who Always Had A Positive Spirit

The truth is he is still very much alive. He knows that the whole scene of congregational life has changed in the last 75 years and the good ole' days have been replaced with lots of good multimedia worship. He knows that Lutheran congregations are still places of care, good pastoral ministry and music that lifts the souls of many. Good dinners can be found and paid for without taking out a loan, and it does feel good to hit golf drives that are straight even if they're not very long. But I just decided to let it all hang out for a few minutes, post it on a blog and then go have a good glass of wine and be grateful for the past, the present and the future.

ഇരു

GRADUATE SCHOOL PART 1

Graduation was great. Having Mother and Dad there from Texas was greater. Having Jane accept my engagement ring was the greatest. And four days later I began the next chapter: graduate school. Graduate school had always been on my long-range plan but I had no idea as to when I would start that. Dean of Students Huegli had other ideas. In my college senior year, I was Student Body President and Dean Huegli and I met for a full hour every day, Monday through Friday. Shortly before graduation he told me, "You are going to grad school and you will start this summer." He received his Ph.D. from Northwestern U. and that is where he wanted me to go. So, I followed his orders and applied. It seemed like I had a somewhat reserved response from Northwestern. Then suddenly I received new communications not only welcoming me, but also urging me to come. Apparently, Dean Huegli had made some contact.

When I told him, I had no financial resources he again stepped up. He arranged for me to live on campus at Concordia (at no cost) and work on campus facilities upkeep during the summer. When I needed course fees, I approached my cousin Ben Jacob. He came through (all be it reluctantly) and loaned me $100 with me paying him back $10 a month for 12 months. I figured that was a pretty high interest rate but I paid that and Ben accepted the full $120. In fact, I paid it off ahead of time out of my $180 month salary.

I studied psychology and had excellent courses. Two were outstanding. One was called Human Personality and I remember getting certified to administer and interpret the Minnesota Multiphasic Personality Inventory. Another course was Diagnosing and Treating Mental Disorders. Tough and very good. One important lesson I learned: Work very carefully and long on the symptoms and only then make a diagnosis.

A couple of minor aspect of life during those summer months: the first was that I had a very enjoyable time playing summer softball. The quality of pitching in the games was very low and at the end of the summer I was informed that I had won the batting title with an average of well over 400. (As I said, the level of pitching was very low.) The other incidental has to do with one of the two gentlemen with whom I shared rides to and from the university. That friend's name was Don Dinkmeyer who was working on his doctorate in psychology. Twenty-five years later we "met" again under some stressful circumstances. He had developed and was aggressively marketing a parent-training program and called it Systematic Training for Effective Parenting (STEP). It was based very heavily on the PET skills. In fact, it had so many almost exact concepts, words and steps as PET (I was then working with PET) that we seriously considered legally charging him for plagiarism and copyright infringement. Eventually we decided against that and I am glad we never had to jointly appear in court.

Summer was soon over and I needed to get to Tracy, California to begin my teaching ministry, the next phase of my long and blessed life.

ഇൻ

GRADUATE SCHOOL PART 2

As mentioned above, it was always my intention to get a graduate degree and I started my master's program at Northwestern University the week after I graduated from college. But then I hastened to Tracy, California and my first teaching assignment at St. Paul's Lutheran Church and School in Tracy, California. The nearest university offering graduate work was the College of the Pacific (now University of the Pacific) in Stockton. At that time, in my eyes, it was most famous for its wonderful 5'8" quarterback, Eddie LaBaron, who was a top football quarterback on offense, great safety on defense and punter on special teams. And the school offered a master's program at an affordable price.

The entry process surprised me. I took standardized tests in General Knowledge and in Education. I scored in the ninetieth percentiles in both and that taught me a lesson. In a day when so much emphasis is placed on getting into just the right undergraduate school - I learned that sometimes it does not matter that much how highly the school is ranked. Concordia Teachers College certainly was never in a "top schools" list. I went there. Did my best. Got the most I could from the school and when it was time for grad school, I had nothing to worry about. I think that is as true in 2017 as it was in 1951.

Since I was working full time, I went to school in the summer and in the evening. My degree was in Psychology. The mid-fifties were a time when there was much emphasis on non-directive teaching and learning. One of my most disappointing classes was a class where the prof did no formal teaching. All learning was to be self-directed by the members of the class. My class did not do much "directing." It spent most of the time arguing how the prof could assign a letter grade to students who only talked and gave each other feedback.

I had a good Philosophy course and an outstanding course in Statistics. And I was fortunate that the Statistics prof was on my thesis committee. I did my research across the LCMS elementary school system on what standardized tests were used, how they were used and what was done with the results. The most challenging aspect of that whole process may simply have been in getting the findings into published form. It was all made possible by the incredible efforts of my wife, Jane. When we were writing this, she was the mother of a new baby. She did all the typing which was, of

246

course, on an old manual typewriter. We needed two copies without any corrections on any page, all on paper of a particular nature and very strict unyielding rules on proper footnotes and citations. Because of everything else that was going on in our lives, that entire thesis was written and typed by the two of us, typically beginning at 10:00 or11:00 p.m. working until around 1:00 a.m. and then going to bed so that we could be up and at work by 7:30 in the morning. Together we made it.

Interesting footnote:

The week before my orals, the US Supreme Court issued its famous Brown vs. Board of Education ruling against school racial segregation. That became a significant area for the committee to address in asking me how that would influence Lutheran schools in the USA. Little did I know then that, some years later, I would be visiting all the black Lutheran schools of the USA south and later working for the Center for Urban Education Ministries that served many schools that were the first in the LCMS (Lutheran Church-Missouri Synod) to be truly racially integrated.

ഇൻൽ

TRIPS

Graduate work at summer school passed very quickly. Then it was time to head out to St. Paul Lutheran Church and School in Tracy, California for my church-assigned duties. My memory is that the congregation offered to pay my bus fare from my home in Texas to Tracy. I chose to go by a route other than bus. As I did quite often, I checked the newspapers and found a car that needed to be delivered to California: a beautiful two-toned brand-new Pontiac. A friend from Texas joined me. We went from Chicago to Central Texas to San Francisco all without incident other than one stop by the Highway Patrol in Arizona. I think they had seen me speed down a long hill but were too far behind me to track the exact speed. So, I was stopped, the officer examined my papers, I told him about my "sacred call "and he wished me well and sent me on with his blessings (and no ticket).

This was my first of quite a few trips between Texas and the Midwest, always by some means other than public transportation or my own car. I had been at St. Paul's school only a few months when the PTA very graciously raised money as a gift to allow me to visit my fiancée, Jane, who was teaching in Michigan. I always remember Mr. B telling the parents "I know Mr. K. Let's not buy him a ticket; instead let's just give him the cash. I bet he will come up with an alternative plan." He was right. I joined a group of men (found through a newspaper ad) and again we drove straight through. I did have one stress-filled hour. We arrived in Salt Lake City around 1:00 a.m. Of course, there were no freeways in those days and we needed to drive through the heart of the city. The driver said, "Watch me. I am going to drive through this whole city without stopping once," And he did, though it meant just running through the many red lights we encountered. The Mormon gods were with us and we made it safely.

After a wonderful Christmas with Jane, a friend who was the coach at Concordia College in Oakland found a car in Detroit that needed delivering to San Francisco. Again, we drove without spending a night in any hotel. However, we did have a New Year's Eve incident. Just after midnight a car was suddenly stopped in front of us in the middle of the road and another car was coming up the mountain to meet us. We had a minor collision. The highway patrol arrived but they said they were too busy on this New Year's Eve to write up an accident report. They ordered us to go the county court house in the next city and write the report. We went to the courthouse arriving around 2:00 a.m. We had to wait for the lone official there to first perform a wedding ceremony for a couple which had decided at midnight that they wanted to get married at once. The other party involved in our accident never arrived (we think the driver of that vehicle actually did not possess a valid driver's license). We went on our way and got stopped in California (maybe we were speeding) but then it got interesting. We told the officer about our deal on delivering the car. He asked for the name of the company to which we were headed etc. etc. etc. Then I showed him the papers. "WOW!" he said. You are lucky. This guy is famous for bringing cars into California illegally and changing registrations in an improper way. You are one lucky gentleman. I will not confiscate this vehicle." And he sent us on our way rejoicing.

There are other stories of this kind of travel. Jane and I drove a vehicle from Fort Wayne to Muskogee, OK because our new car had been nearly totaled on the way to the wedding and had to be repaired in Muskogee. Once we drove an almost new Cadillac from Detroit to Orange County. The air conditioner went out in the middle of that summer heat, but again we made it.

They say that the journey is as important as the destination. But my destination was the more important because it was time for me assume my exciting new role as teacher of grades 4-8 and principal of St. Paul's Lutheran School and I was rarin' to go.

ഔൗര

BEGINNING MY CAREER AS AN EDUCATOR

When the day after Labor Day arrived in 1950, I was ready for my first day of teaching. I had decorated the classroom. I made sure the desks, which were bolted down to 2 x 4 runners, were all perfectly aligned. I had carefully prepared a set of watercolors and brushes for each student. I had tried to memorize the names of the 32 students in my room in Grades 4-8. I had bought extra gel for the clumsy purple ditto copy trays. Of course, I was somewhat nervous but also quite confident. After all I myself had gone to Grades 1-8 in a two room Lutheran school. I'd had a full year of internship teaching Grades 1-4. I was excited and ready to roll.

I loved teaching and I loved my kids and I think I did a fair job. Now some 65 years later I remember especially one teaching activity that went very well. Tracy was a town of about 10,000. We did a total classroom project across grade levels. Students got themselves into self-selected groups with each group choosing one aspect of the city to study and report on. The groups included making a map of the city, meeting with the city's Director of Recreation, meeting with the Chief of Police, going to the big tomato processing plant, interviewing the editor of the town weekly newspaper, etc. Each group did its homework and then reported to the entire classroom. As various city leaders heard how "those kids" from St. Paul's Lutheran school had interviewed their colleagues, there was a very positive reaction.

I used an organization design for teaching that I had learned from my father. Religion, social studies, music, and art were taught to all five grades at once. However, reading and arithmetic were taught grade by grade. I had the kids from each grade come to the front of the room, gather around a table and we studied and learned together. Meanwhile the other classes were busy with workbook assignments. We focused on the basics and our kids really excelled way above state and local norms on standardized tests. I think I was reasonably effective but I never did consider classroom discipline to be one of my strengths. We faced the reality of widely different student abilities with not too much trouble. Since we were multi-grade the brighter kids could join the grade above them for specific work and the weaker students could get

249

reviews by listening to the lessons taught in the grades below them.

The 1950's were days when the whole paradigm of Lutheran Church-Missouri Synod schools was changing and my school represented the new realities. We made the switch from when all children in the school were Lutheran to an enrollment predominantly non-Lutheran. We moved from children paying no tuition and all costs being covered by funds from the congregation budget to charging tuition and receiving very little (if any) congregational financial support. My memory is that our tuition was $10 a month.

Fund-raising was a pretty new thing for Lutheran schools then but it was central to our financial viability. Thus at least once a month I was joined by boy students as we used a borrowed truck and went throughout the city collecting newspapers that, of course, we sold. My other fund-raising methods were not at all creative and not very effective. I now often wish I could go back to those days and do a better job.

When I compare my experience with my colleagues of today, I see great differences. All my students were white and native speakers of English. Pick-up permission slips from feuding divorced parents were unheard of. Peanut butter allergies were not yet on the agenda. Cell phones and computers were distant dreams. It was usually assumed that if a student and a teacher had a conflict the teacher was in the right. Mandatory state tests were nowhere on the horizon for non-public schools. "Titles" were names of books and unrelated to government programs or requirements. LGBTQ were random letters of the alphabet.

I was accountable to a School Board made up of congregation members (all male). They were very supportive (though I had to agree to disagree with the chairman of the Board who refused to have his three children in our school vaccinated against any disease).

Naturally, I have some regrets: I had a few kids with some relatively serious behavior/adjustment problems and I wish I had been more helpful. I did not teach enough creative writing. I wish I had challenged the brightest kids more. As a principal I was seriously lacking in providing support to my teaching colleagues. During my years at Tracy I had two first-year teachers. I do not think I visited their classrooms for even one day. I did not seek classroom aides for them. The best I can say for myself (and that is not much) is that I was available to them and stood behind them when they had any issue with an unhappy parent.

The boys in the school would probably be in agreement that the best thing that Teacher Kieschnick brought to their school was that (for the first time) the school basketball team had uniforms and was actually allowed to play a game or two against another school team. They and their female classmates would also applaud that sometimes when we got into really close soccer games, recess time just kept getting extended until one team or the other scored the winning goal. And I do hope and pray that every one of my former students went away convinced (and still believing today) that God loves them.

As it turned out, I ended up spending only six years of my over 50 years as an educator being a classroom teacher. I enjoyed it and to this day have nothing but the greatest respect for the "ordinary" classroom teachers who just happen to be among the most important change agents on this planet.

ഇൗ

REMEMBERING STUDENTS

Obviously, teaching is all about students. My hope and prayer were, and are, that somehow or other my teaching has some effect (however minor) on each of the students I teach. Every teacher has the vision that students will be shaped, however slightly, by their teaching. In my days of retirement, I now once in a while just try to recall the names, faces and traits of students who at some time or other sat in my classroom. My list runs from those fourth through eighth graders in Tracy, California through that very small band of Grades 1-3 in Glendale, through the grad students I taught at the Concordias, through the students I taught through an interpreter in Hong Kong, to many others all around the world. But today I want to again go back to that very first classroom of some 32 kids at St. Paul's, Tracy, California.

I will just select four boys for this blog entry and let them be both individuals and also examples of tens of others who figuratively sat at my feet as students. For some unknown reason one of the first to pop into my mind is "Denny." I recall his unrivaled enthusiasm for life. He was small for his age. He had a rough life as the son of a single mom who dearly loved him and struggled with a couple of jobs to have the tuition to send him to my school. Denny was always full of optimism and energy. He was convinced we would win any basketball or softball game we ever played. He was sure he would do well on tests. He energized me and I will always remember that when I went back to Tracy 50 years after I had taught there, he was the middle-aged person who showed up all decked out in a smart jacket, shirt and tie, still with a zest for life.

At the other end of the energy spectrum was "Larry." He had been abandoned by his birth mother and cared for by a wonderfully loving aunt and uncle. Studies were a bore to him and he did poorly. He was not interested in any sport and seemed unaware of his classmates. I wondered what would ever become of him. Yet, some years later we were living in Hong Kong and received a telephone call from him! He was in the US Navy, had a short leave in Hong Kong, heard about us being there and somehow or other not only located our telephone number but ventured north of Boundary Street (the limit for US servicemen) to come see us. He was full of life and looking positively toward the future. He had much praise for his years at St. Paul's.

"Tim" was an only child. Both his parents loved him and wanted only the best for him. They even persuaded me to use some of my summer time to take him and a couple of other students on day-long trips to the California gold country and there learn about the early days of our state. Some years later a former high school roommate of mine who had become a pastor told me that he'd had a call to conduct a funeral in Tracy, 500 miles from his parish in San Diego. He got to talking to the Funeral Director in charge of the memorial. It was Tim, who upon learning that the pastor was Lutheran, told him about his Lutheran school experience and a teacher named "Kieschnick." He sent warm greetings to the person he claimed had had a life-long influence on him.

Richard Hamlow was in the sixth grade. My relationship with him was influenced by another factor. I was a very close personal friend of his parents. Thus, he often saw me in his home in a very relaxed atmosphere where his parents often shared a few beers with me. They always called me "Mel." His parents, however, made it very clear to him that it was not appropriate for him to do the same. They made sure that Richard always referred to me either as Mr. Kieschnick or as Teacher Kieschnick. While I was his teacher, I never heard him express any interest in becoming a pastor. But after I left, he made that decision, graduated from the seminary and then served faithfully for many years until his retirement as a parish pastor. Richard was the first of many of my students who chose to enter the rostered ministries of various churches. While I, of course, honor every occupation in which people find their vocation, I am also pleased that many chose their vocations as professional ministers of the church. And Richard was the first.

HOSPITALITY: A WONDERFUL VIRTUE

At one level it was just another dinner invitation. At another level it was a profound reminder of the great virtue of hospitality. We chatted on the phone, working to agree on when we would meet for a simple meal and deeper conversation. I offered pizza at our home. She said, "How about coming over to my place? I can grill some steak. I have a really nice bottle of wine just waiting for you." It took me less than five seconds to respond. "When should we arrive?" When I hung up the phone, I reflected upon hospitality. This is a custom expressed at all levels of society from the most primitive tribe in Africa through the Oval Office in the White House to China's imperial palace. Every society has its own centuries-old (and ever-newly-emerging) ways to answer the question: "How do you show hospitality?"

I reflected upon the graciousness of my host. She is a single woman, living alone. Her business takes her to assignments all over the world. Her schedule is full. Yet, she didn't hesitate to say, "Come on over." I think I know where some of that hospitality comes from and I want to honor it. I know that she attended a Lutheran elementary school and that her father was a Lutheran parochial school teacher. So, she and I share that mutual background. And I believe that hospitality was a key virtue I learned in Lutheran elementary school. I experienced it as people invited my large family over for many events. My mother demonstrated it when I suddenly brought a softball team of high school guys into our home unexpectedly and within minutes, she was setting the table and frying up scrambled eggs. So, my memory is that the Lutheran school of my day and those who taught in it really believed that hospitality was an essential aspect of Christian living. And, of course they had ample Biblical support for teaching it.

Am I correct in judging that hospitality expressed by inviting people over to one's home for a meal is now a less frequent experience? The number of times that Jane and I are invited into someone's home for dinner is far less than it was for my parents. When we are invited out, it is often (not always) an invitation following one we had initiated. At the same time, it is true, of course, that having a meal together with another couple at a restaurant is far more prevalent than when I was child. In fact, to the best of my memory, that never happened for me until I was 21 years of age.

So, customs around hospitality vary greatly from culture to culture and are ever-changing. In the midst of that, the command of Jesus to extend hospitality not only to our friends but also to those often excluded does not have an expiration date. In a recent class that I taught at my church I challenged all of us to this particular act of hospitality: "Invite to your house for a sit-down dinner an individual or a family who is of a different color, ethnic group, or speaker of a primary language other than yours."

So, this evening Jane and I will have a special treat. We will have a grilled steak (and grilling steaks is not permitted at the retirement community in which we live) a glass or two of good wine, lively conversation, and even keeping a tab on the Cubs vs. the Indians.... all instilled in the heart of a young girl attending a good Lutheran elementary school.

ഇൗരു

CHRISTMAS MEMORIES PART 1: CHURCH

Being baptized as an infant and raised in a very devout Christian family made it very natural for me to learn very early that Christ is the reason for the Christmas season. Thus, church attendance and church activities were (and are) at the core of my Christmas celebration.

I do not remember any special emphasis on the church season of Advent, though we thought a lot about getting ready for Christmas.

At the heart of the Christmas activities was the Christmas program at church on Christmas Eve. It was led by the children of Zion Lutheran School. By today's standards it was really simple and would be considered terribly boring. We had no manger scene or reenactment of the visit to the manger. No one played the role of Mary. It was very old-fashioned Martin Luther catechism inspired stuff. The children's program had three important components.

The first, was to tell the Christmas narrative through the format of questions and answers. The teacher asked the carefully prepared questions. He called upon students (one by one). Each gave the carefully prepared answer. I still remember the German question (though I do not remember the correct spelling of the German words) that always began the program "Welches hochest fest feiren wie in diesen tage?" (What high feast do we celebrate in these days?) Thus, the Old Testament prophecies and the infant birth story up to the visit of the Wise Men were recalled.

The second element, was that the children had to memorize their "Christmas piece." These were rhymes of poetry. In groups of about four students each we would march to the front of the church and recite our piece. There were no mikes and it was a big church so the instructions were drilled into us, "Speak slowly and very loudly."

Thirdly, of course, we sang the carols. It amazes me to recall that when we were in the upper grades, we always sang in two and even three-part harmony.

The Christmas Eve service was usually early in the evening. A huge 30-feet tall cedar Christmas tree was decorated and in my early years adorned with hundreds of lighted candles. Two special ushers were seated right next to the tree with buckets of water handy should a fire erupt. After the close of the service came another highlight. The ushers distributed a Christmas bag to each of us children. These were plain brown grocery bags, but they were filled with incredibly wonderful gifts. Even during the deepest part of the Great Depression, we each got at least one stick of Wrigley's Juicy Fruit chewing gum, an orange, an apple, some nuts and some ribbon candy. Wonderful, wonderful, wonderful!

The thoughts of those bag contents, and trying the figure out what to eat first, and what to save, occupied our minds not only during the worship on Christmas Day but even on the mandatory attendance at service on Second Christmas Day, December 26th.

ଛଔ

CHRISTMAS MEMORIES PART 2: GOOD FOOD

My memories of Christmas food and drink are all positive and wonderful. I was born in 1927 so my early years were during the Great Depression and we were poor - but I never felt poor at Christmas, and especially not when it came to the matter of food.

My first memories are of Mother making homemade candy. At the top of the list is wonderful divinity candy, then chocolate candy and finally date bars. All were filled with pecans which we had gathered earlier in the year at Grandma Doering's farm and then cracked and made available in abundance for Christmas baking.

And there was always stollen and fruit cake and lots of cookies. Homemade bread was just a common daily part of the diet

The primary meat was, of course, fresh pork. We raised our own hogs and slaughtering hogs was a big deal in early December. We had to pick a colder day to ensure the meat would not get bad. The neighbors (Schwausch, was their name, I think) came and helped. I was always just a bit taken aback when the hogs' throats were slit but that was overcome by my love of fresh pork. We had wonderful sausage, fresh pork cutlets, incredible hams and all the rest.

The term "all the rest' included what we called "bone meat." When sausage was made, the flesh was all taken off the bones, but always a little remained. These bones were preserved and, especially when money got tight, these bones were cooked and served usually with boiled potatoes and red beet juice.

We had a smoke house, a simple shack of about 20 feet by 30 feet with a tall roof. We always used the bark of the trees as the source for the smoke, because it burned slowly and produced a lot of smoke.

The sausage was always stuffed into thoroughly cleaned intestines. We even used the stomach of the hog and filled it with stuffing. And I especially loved the fresh or smoked bacon that was always sliced very thick and then fried - but not too crisp!

Christmas was time for Dad to buy the once a year bottle of whiskey. Parts of our county were dry - so he had to drive to a liquor store near Jarrell to get the annual bottle of Jack Daniels. I recall my mother's disapproval of this practice - as she was convinced that we could not afford it, and my mother, in spite of all the evidence to the contrary, seemed to often fear that we would "drink too much." The only way the Jack Daniels was drunk, was in eggnog. Of course, the eggs and the milk were fresh and the milk was supplemented by a generous amount of additional fresh cream. There was often an argument as to whether or not the eggnog should be cooked or drunk raw. Eggnog was front and center at the Christmas Eve party at Grandma's house after the children's service. Two large bowls were always in evidence, one with the whiskey already in one bowl and the other bowl alcohol free. It was a daring adventure for me as a kid to "accidently" take my eggnog from the wrong bowl.

Frankly, I do not remember Christmas dinner. What was important were all those homemade cookies, cakes and candy. Glorious memories!

ଽଔଓଷ

THE ZIELSKES

As written earlier, when I graduated from college I was "assigned" to St. Paul's Lutheran Church and School in Tracy, California. My job assignment was to teach grades 4-8, serve as principal, and be the congregation's Director of Youth and Christian Education. I was single. Upon arrival I was informed about the plan for my living arrangements. I was to live with the family of Lydia and Arnold Zielske and their three children. I was assigned a bedroom and a shared bath. It was just a block off Main Street and four blocks from the school. Lydia provided all my meals including packed sandwiches for lunch. I think the cost was $85 a month. It was a good deal in every way.

The Zielskes treated me with respect and then affection. Lydia introduced me to foods like lasagna that I had never eaten in Texas. And she had a brother in Lodi CA, 70 miles away, whom we visited together. He was the master wine maker at a well-known winery and introduced me to the wonderful variety of wines. Prior to that I only drank what I now remember as terrible: Manischewitz, a very sweet red wine!

Arnold was a devoted father and husband. He knew that his intelligence was not a match for Lydia's and he accepted that. He had a job as a radio repairperson and he did that well. The situation got a little complicated because I had the eldest daughter as a student in my classroom. She was a sweet but underperforming student who tragically died of cancer at a young age.

The Zielslkes had a most interesting and unique travel habit. As mentioned above, we often visited some of the Zielski family in Lodi. We would arrive home well after midnight. Arnie would drive the car into the garage and close the door behind him. Then, at his suggestion, we all stayed in the car and just slept there for about 30 minutes, then picked up ourselves and the sleeping kids and went into our beds in the house and slept there till morning.

The family stayed in touch with me through the years. Some 20 years later they came to visit me in St. Louis. One little interesting detail of that visit is that Arnie asked me to assist him in purchasing the full multi-volume set of all the writings of Martin Luther. I doubt that he ever got through that virtual library! But I am eternally grateful to the Zielskes for helping me get off well in my professional career.

ഇ)ൟ

257

THE PAULSONS

My life and work in my first post-graduation life was greatly enriched through the friendship of John and Margaret Paulson. They were the parents of two boys and two girls and were major Central California growers. At one point they had over a section (640 acres) of land under irrigation and production. They raised tons of tomatoes, loads of melons, bushels of almonds. All irrigated by Central California water lines. All of it picked by hand by migrant Mexican laborers and hauled to the tomato and other plants in massive trucks.

But more important than the crops they cultivated, were the people they raised: people, including me. They lived too far out in the country to send their children to my Lutheran school but they were amazingly open to this single guy and later to Jane, then to our son David and eventually to our whole family of seven.

I had barely arrived when they had me out to their beautiful home sitting among their vast acreage. Since I had no car of my own, they picked me up for meals and then returned me. They served wonderful food and introduced me to the whole concept of farming with irrigated water (something I had not seen in the Texas farms of my youth). They were by far the most generous contributors of the congregation and when money was short (as it seemed to always be) they would come through and eventually I would get my salary.

When our first son, David, was born naturally Margaret was a sponsor (godparent). Later when our first daughter was born, we named her Margareth.

Their children were models of good behavior and commitment. Their eldest became a Lutheran pastor, the next eldest a Commissioned Lutheran teacher who later married a pastor. The next daughter is my goddaughter and still is a successful California famer. The youngest son is a community leader.

But there is also sadness. One year, John borrowed a lot of money (as he did every year) to plant and irrigate his crops that in this particular year focused upon acres and acres of melons of various kinds. Just when the harvest season arrived, rains came - and they kept coming and kept coming. They prevented the fields from being harvested. Not a single melon was ever picked and delivered. So, there was not only no profit, there was no money to repay the short-term loan. The lending bank was merciless. It moved in, took John and Margaret's land leaving them only their home. This was devastating. But they remained steadfast, continued to work as tenant farmers and eventually retired. After John's death his son told me, "You know Dad scrimped and worked and saved and he eventually paid back every penny of that debt that they owed, but never got their farm back."

Meanwhile their friendship with us endured. They wonderfully took Jane and me to San Francisco on the night before we left for our first term of service in Hong Kong. They took us to the famous Mark Hopkins Hotel. There they treated us to a dinner in an environment the likes of which we had never experienced before. They sent us gifts while we were in Hong Kong. When my wife Jane was flown home due to a medical emergency and we had to spend a night in San Francisco between airplane flights, they heard about our situation. They came to the airport, picked up our five kids, took them for the night and returned them the next morning with every single one of them decked out in a completely new suit of clothes.

Later they suffered deep disappointment at St. Paul's church. The new pastor decided that "contemporary worship" was the only way to go. The Paulsons' (and others') preference for the traditional liturgies was ignored. (They were finally offered a Saturday morning worship opportunity.) The Paulsons left St. Paul's and when we, a few years ago, went to their burials and memorials, these were not held at St. Paul's. Nevertheless, the memory of them is forever etched into my brain and into my heart. They were critical in helping me (and Jane) get off to a wonderful start in our careers and ministry.

ഇൻൻ

PARADIGM SHIFT

1950 is so long ago that I think no one was even using the now over-used term "paradigm shift." But for Lutheran schools, the early 50's was indeed a time for great shifts in the Lutheran Church-Missouri Synod school model. The traditional model was as old as the Synod itself. LCMS congregations were expected to operate elementary schools. This was such an essential element for parish life that it was even written into the Synod's constitution that every congregation was expected to operate its own school.

Elements of that model included the following. The congregation would operate the school. It would employ exclusively teachers (almost always males) who had been trained in the LCMS teacher training system and the Synod had established two teachers' colleges (one in River Forest, IL and one in Seward, Nebraska) to ensure a steady supply of teachers. Teachers were to be "called," not contracted. They were considered "ministers of religion" by both church and state. They had life tenure and could be dismissed for only three reasons: teaching false doctrine, gross neglect of duties or public display of immoral behavior. They were to be provided housing by the calling congregation, usually in a congregation-owned home called a "teacherage." These teachers had special responsibilities in the congregation for which they received no special income. Most of them were church organists and choir directors and/or youth directors for the official youth group called The Walther League.

All congregation members were expected to send their children to the Lutheran school. I remember discussion when I was growing up as to whether or not a couple could be excommunicated from the church for sending their children to the public school rather than to the parochial one. Enrolling children who were not baptized members of the congregation was rare.

Financing was completely through the congregation budget - by the regular offerings of congregation members. Tuition was not considered an option. Receiving state or federal funds was not on any Lutheran school's agenda.

In 1950 the role of the principal was, to the best of my knowledge, not a full-time position in any Lutheran elementary school. All of this was changing in the 1940's and early 50's especially on the East Coast in New York and on the West Coast in California. And that was also happening at St. Paul Lutheran School in Tracy to which I was assigned. I did have the traditional "call." I was teacher of grades 4-8 and was the principal. I was the Youth Director responsible for meetings with the youth every single Sunday night. (Note: Today in retirement I often say to my wife, Jane, as we drive home from church on Sunday morning, "Thank God, I do not have Walther League tonight!") I was responsible for the Sunday School's teacher training meetings twice a month. I was not the organist (for which everyone was thankful) but I did play the organ while the organist went to communion. Later the organist was my wife Jane. More about that in a later blog entry. Of course, it was my responsibility to organize and run an annual Vacation Bible School.

But changes were coming fast. At least half of the children in my school were non-members of the congregation. They paid tuition, though I think it was only $10 a month. My first year we had a non-synodically-trained woman teacher in grades 1-3. It was important to know who the "non-member" children were. It was important to not have the reputation that the

Lutheran school was somehow there for kids who could not make it in the public school. In Tracy it was significant that both the small city's top medical doctor and the top dentist sent their children to "the Lutheran school." I am grateful to say that I embraced the "new paradigm" fully. I recruited from the entire neighborhood and was pleased that after three years we were over capacity in enrollment. I was also grateful that more women teachers were available and I utilized interns and graduates from both River Forest and Seward. The role of the principal was expanding and I was very pleased to attend a semi-annual principals conference with my area colleagues. Fundraising was a new and critical responsibility. It took a great deal of my time and I did not do an excellent job.

I was at Tracy for four years. It was a very different Lutheran school from the one I attended in Walburg, Texas but it was Lutheran, had member and non-member children, was supported by congregation and tuition, and was well respected by the neighborhood. It was challenging and rewarding and it prepared me for challenges and opportunities in my future career.

෧ාඥ

THE WALTHER LEAGUE

The Walther League played a significant role in my life. Begun in 1893, and named after C.F.W. Walther the first president of The Lutheran Church-Missouri Synod, the League was the official youth organization of that denomination. One became eligible for membership after the ritual of confirmation, usually at the 7th or 8th grade level. It was an important rite of passage to be accepted as a member. I vividly remember that I was confirmed on Palm Sunday in 1940 and it was a big deal that the following Sunday I was allowed for the first time to participate in the League-sponsored Easter egg hunt.

My father was the counselor for the Zion Lutheran Walther League of which I was a member. We met almost every Sunday evening. Every meeting was required to have three components: Christian Growth, which meant we had an hour or so of Bible study, which we always called "Topic Discussion." Then there was time to plan a Christian Service project, such as cleaning church property, raising money for national projects, et sim. And the third important function was Christian Fellowship which meant games, hay rides, scavenger hunts, wink-um, et sim. It was at Walther League that many of my contemporaries courted, fell in love with and pursued their first spouse. I can still sing the Walther League song, "Walther Leaguers, Walther Leaguers, one and all are we: Serving Jesus Christ, our Savior who has made us free; Walther Leaguers, Walther Leaguers, where-so-ere we roam; Working and praying for our church and home."

Part of my first official work assignment was to be Youth Director. I worked hard at it with our little Walther League group in Tracy. We faithfully focused on the three aspects mentioned above. We stayed involved at the "zone level" which took us to neighboring churches in Stockton, Modesto, and Turlock. And we got involved with our District Summer Camps at beautiful Asilomar. A little remembrance of Walther League Summer Camp: Our pastor's son joined us. He "enjoyed" his freedom from his parents so much that after the second year he was banned from attending.

The Walther League no longer exists. The denomination leaders got unhappy with some of the way-too-liberal activities of the League with the breaking point coming when the League invited Pete Seeger to attend and sing at one of their national conventions.

The League continued to impact me in a variety of ways through much of my career. When I was in Hong Kong it was the Walther League (and Wheat Ridge) that sponsored Haven of Hope T.B. Sanitarium that was a place of healing and hope for many. Years later I was a counselor for a tour group that took me to clinics all over southern India, the result of work begun by the Walther League and continued by Wheat Ridge Ministries. In my retirement I served as a part-time field rep for that same organization. These on-going connections were helpful in getting start-up grants for two recent organizations, which are still important to me: RESOUNDING JOY and Survivors of Torture, International.

Yet, in a strange way what I seem to remember most is that Sunday after Sunday my assignment was "go to the Walther League meeting tonight." Jane will tell you that now on more Sundays than not, as we drive home from Sunday morning worship, I announce, "Thank God I do not have Walther League tonight!

૭୦୧ଓ

PASTOR-PRINCIPAL RELATIONSHIP

Anyone who has been active in Lutheran elementary schools, knows that the relationship between the principal of the school and the pastor of the sponsoring congregation is vital for the school's success. And this was even more important in the 1950's when the relationship between the school and the congregation was more mutually dependent than it is now.

My first pastor was someone I will simply designate as Pr. RB. He entered the pastoral ministry later in life, leaving a successful business as a mechanic. There was a crisis in his life and he promised God that if God got him out of the crisis, he would become a pastor. I am glad the crisis was resolved and… I wish he had remained a mechanic. He was better qualified for that than for serving as a parish pastor.

He was a good man. He had a special heart for the poor, especially also the homeless. He never turned down a beggar who showed up at his door. He often found some small task or assignment for the needy, but then he helped.

He was very supportive of the school and was, in fact, the founding pastor of the school. His wife taught in the school. He was kind to me. But there was a major issue. He was (I am firmly convinced) an alcoholic. He denied this. His wife was an enabler. He kept liquor right next to him in his office desk.

The situation became very public more than once, but especially at a Lenten worship service. As he began to lead the service it was obvious to all that he "was under the influence." After the initial reading I hurried to the closed area behind the altar and met him there while the next hymn was being sung. I told him, "Pastor, it looks like you are not well. I do not think you can continue with the sermon. Just let me go out and explain that you are not well. I will give a brief message." He resisted me. When I insisted it almost became physical so I let him continue. By the next morning the word was buzzing throughout the town of Tracy. "Last night the pastor of The Lutheran Church showed up to preach - and he was drunk."

We attempted interventions with the District (Synod). Unfortunately, they just transferred the problem. He served one parish after another with the same "issue" making him ineffective. Seven years later we had a dinner appointment with him. When we got to his home his wife said, "I am sorry. R. cannot be with us. He is not well. He cannot speak to or be with you."

As I reflect on this whole experience, I recall that I may have been a threat to him. I was young and eager and creative. I had the full support of the school and congregation. People were coming to me with their "pastoral problems." I wish I had been more supportive and more confrontive. May he rest in peace.

ഇൽയൂ

COLLEGE TEACHING

I was surprised that immediately upon receiving my Master's Degree I was asked to teach a summer course at Concordia Teachers College, River Forest, IL (now Concordia University: Chicago). I accepted the request and thoroughly enjoyed teaching the course entitled "The Use of Tests and Measurements in Lutheran Elementary Schools." The students were all principals. They brought good questions and a variety of good insights. One much-unanticipated result of this class was that I met the remarkable and capable principal of St. Lorenz Lutheran School in Frankenmuth Michigan: Mr. Walter Bleke. Twelve years after my teaching him in this class it was Mr. Bleke who played a big role in me becoming Superintendent of Lutheran Schools for the Michigan District and then four years later (again with his influence) the head of Parish Education for The Lutheran Church-Missouri Synod. The next summer I taught again, this time at Concordia University, Seward, Nebraska.

My college teaching then continued at Hong Kong College in that British Crown Colony. And at Concordia Seminary and The Lutheran Theological Seminary there. I taught Christian Education, General Psychology and Pastoral Theology. While not of essence to the content of the courses, my strongest memories relate to the language used in teaching. At first, I taught in English with sentence-by-sentence interpretation into Cantonese by Mr. Isaac Ma and Dr. Andrew Chiu. Both of them were outstanding interpreters and of incredible help in my teaching. The saddest and most embarrassing feature of my teaching is the General Psychology course I taught at Lutheran Theological Seminary in the Cantonese language. I spent hours in preparation and made it only with the wonderful assistance of Pr. Daniel Lee Wing Ching. Yet even with his assistance my Cantonese was terrible. I messed up many of the tones of that language and must have said many incomprehensible things. The only textbooks available were translations from Russian and were all pure behaviorism in point of view. Yet those students did not mock me (at least not to my face). They stuck in there with me and I hope even learned one little insight that later on helped them in their ministry.

Strangely enough my memory of teaching at Hong Kong College has an unusual twist. I had one student who resisted everything I said, often in a rather belligerent manner. I was told that he was a strong Communist supporter who was there to expose the failure of the Christian witness. He endured me and I hung in there with him. Sometime later I learned that he had not only become a Christian but also had decided to become a Lutheran pastor.

Upon reflection I am deeply aware of the critical role that college/university professors play in the lives of students and in society. I am now blessed to have had a brother-in-law and a daughter who have been college teachers and currently have a son-in-law and son who are full-time college profs. These are honorable and worthy professions indeed. They are influencers and shapers of minds and of our world. I am grateful that for short periods of my career I was briefly numbered among them.

ക്കQ

MOANING AND COMPLAINING: LUTHERAN CLERGY

I have known, worked with, or heard of, several situations in which pastors have flat-out failed to be effective ministers. So, I am taking advantage of this blog entry to let all my frustrations shout out.

1. Some pastors just don't listen. A lay member of a pastoral call committee spoke with me recently. The congregation wisely decided to hold "cottage meetings" at which the members were to provide their input to the congregation committee in answer to the question "What are you looking for in the next pastor we are calling to serve us?" Unfortunately, an interim pastor decided to attend those cottage meetings. She took over. For the full 90 minutes she lectured, she gave instructions, she shared her personal experience. Not once did she allow the members to give their input to the question for which the group had been assembled. She just didn't listen.

This need to talk rather than to listen is also often demonstrated by pastors who teach adult classes. Way too often these are lectures only. Opportunity to gather the shared wisdom and insight of the group is simply not considered. The message seems to be "You folks listen up! I know. You don't."

2. Failure to Conduct Pastoral Visits to the Sick and Shut-ins. Some pastors are fantastic at this and give it a very high priority, but it seems to me

the current trend is in the opposite direction. I have a friend who is a member of a Lutheran congregation (not mine). She has kidney cancer. She carefully informed her pastor of the date she was to have it removed. There was no hospital or home visit made. After my friend returned home there were new complications. This time her husband sent an email to the pastor. No response. No home visit. No mention on congregation prayer lists. I became so disturbed by this that I wrote a very careful non-blameful email to the pastor. No response to me or to the ill member! And certainly, no home visit

In the old German Lutheran congregation of my youth I learned the term "siel sorger" which means, "concern for the soul." The pastor kept a careful record of those who were ill, those who had not taken communion for some time, those who had not been to worship for over a month. This was his (and it was always a male) priority list for home visits. Any suggestion that a process similar to this be instituted into today's church life would be met with derision and the strong declaration that I was out of contact with today's realities. Yes, I know the lay people can do a lot of this and I also know where the pastors have made zero effort to train, engage and encourage their members in home visits via e.g. Steven Ministries

3. Interim Clergy. These are clergy assigned to parishes which have a vacancy in the pastoral office and are in the process of calling a replacement. Again, there are some interims who do a great job, but by far the majority of cases about which I hear tell of great frustration, especially by congregation leaders. Too many interim pastors make the situation worse.

So that's my moaning for today. And I thank God for all those pastors who faithfully listen, really make those pastoral visits and really help hurting congregations eagerly awaiting a new pastor.

ಬಿಂಬ

"GOOD WIFE": PUT-DOWN OR COMPLIMENT?

It started very early in our married life. When Jane accompanied me to an event and especially if I was a featured speaker, Jane would usually be introduced to the group or to individuals. More often than not she would be introduced as "Mel's good wife." This happened especially at Lutheran Church-Missouri Synod gatherings and most especially if the person doing the introducing was a pastor.

It did not take me long to realize that whenever Jane heard herself introduced as "Mel's good wife" she inwardly flinched. We talked about it and I understood. When she was simply "Mel's good wife' it identified her not so much as her own being but as of one who got her identity because of her marriage status and her husband.

Of course, in those years (especially in the 1950's) being "a good wife" carried with it a pretty well-defined set of characteristics. It meant that the husband was the featured one. It meant that her role was that of obedient spouse. This was especially true since the roles that women could play in the church were defined and limited. She could not be a pastor, could not serve as congregation president, could not be asked to lead a prayer when men were in the group, etc. etc.

While this role assignment was informal in the churches I served in the USA, it became formalized in official church documents when I became a missionary in Hong Kong. The official rules of the then Mission Board stated that wives of missionaries were also to be considered missionaries. However, they were not to be employed in any church related work nor were they allowed to receive any compensation for any services they might render on behalf of the church or any of its agencies.

Now in the year 2017 it can still happen occasionally that Jane is introduced as "Mel's good wife." But that is rare. Whether it is stated or not, what I want to affirm is that Jane is indeed "a good wife." She loves me and forgives me. She shares with me in our roles as parents and grandparents. We are partners in ministry. Yet we also have our separate identities. We disagree about things. We have differing opinions in matter of food, drink, art, and church dogma.

Jane is much more than someone's "good wife." In Hong Kong she produced Sunday School materials for 10,000 children each week. She taught art and music and piano lessons, she served as an officer in the American Women's Association of Hong Kong. Later she gained her own role as a significant contributor to Women's Effectiveness Training programs around the world. She was a featured speaker on gay rights at the Lutheran Church of Finland. When we moved to New York with the Lutheran Schools Association, the schools' staff were wonderful in their affirmation of her strengths, her professionalism, her computer and editorial skills. On top of this, she is excellent in oil painting, weaving and playing the piano. And when the need arose, she has personally replaced the garbage disposal in our kitchen and the water pump in our car.

When I now, more rarely, hear Jane spoken of as "Mel's good wife" I still cringe but I also affirm the designation. I consider her one of God's greatest gifts to me and to many, many others. She is, indeed, a very good wife and more.

ഇ൞ര

HOLY PLACES, SAN DIEGO PADRES AND THE HOLY SPIRIT

Next Sunday at my church I am leading an Adult Class which will discuss "The Holy Spirit." Last night I spoke with my son John who is head of the Department of Religious Studies at Stanford University. There he teaches a course on Holy Places, places like churches, temples, cathedrals and others usually associated with the various religions of the world.

This semester he has a student who has signed a contract to play baseball for the San Diego Padres organization. At the beginning of the term he had explained to John that he wanted to be excused from attending some of the classes because he wanted to attend spring training. John agreed and assigned him the task of writing an extra paper on a topic related to the topic of "Holy Places."

This week John received the paper. In it the student explained that he was indeed at spring training. He described a particular place. He wrote that it was just an ordinary large room. It was virtually empty. It had only a large group of chairs. There were no pictures on the walls, no symbols or decorations on any of the walls. It was the place where the players gathered, sometimes the whole big squad of regulars and new recruits, at other times just the rookies. As he thought of sitting in that room, he recalled his own story, his hopes, his fears. Then he became aware of the reality that each person there had their own story: a story of excitement, fear, stardom, boredom, fantasy, anonymity, last chance and fresh hopes. In that moment he thought of what made each of them unique and what connected them all as one. He said he came to a profound realization: "This is indeed a holy place." And I agree. The more I reflect upon it, the more I realize the truth of the statement that the Holy Spirit moves among us as it wills, dwells in our midst, stirs up our memories and our visions and our faith. It is indeed true that spirit, the Holy Spirit, the San Diego Padres and all the rest of us are all connected.

ഇ൞ര

268

FIRST BORN

From the moment we were married (and before) my wife Jane and I knew that we wanted to have children. Moreover, birth control was not really a part of my life experience. My mother and father had nine children. We were married in July; by the end of December Jane was pregnant; and very early on the Sunday morning of September 14, I was at the hospital awaiting the birth of our first-born. Jane had the excellent care of the best doctor in Tracy California, Dr. Longely. When we arrived at the hospital, however, he was out of town and an unknown substitute was called in. In those days, fathers were not allowed anywhere near the delivery room so I was sent to the waiting area. There I immediately fell sound asleep to be awakened with the news "It's a boy!" When some criticized me for sleeping during Jane's labor, I explain that there was really nothing I could do to assist Jane and besides I had to get to church by ten o'clock, to teach my Sunday morning Bible class. We rejoiced and gave thanks for our first-born: David Allan.

We had no family living in California but members of the St. Paul congregation were very supportive and helpful to us in our care for our new baby. Elder members of the congregation joined us in celebration and care. Baptism followed quickly and was celebrated with a big dinner in our tiny apartment.

David was a wonderful son and brought us many learnings, blessings and unfailing support. My mind overflows with memories. Regretfully, he very early developed asthma and I still shudder as I recall fearing that he would suffocate because he could not get his breath. Both Jane and I hated to, but reluctantly gave him adrenalin shots. By the time he was ready for kindergarten we were living in Hong Kong and we sent him to an all-Chinese kindergarten. At that time, he spoke no Chinese - but loved it. When the kindergarten put on its big program for parents, he (naturally, as it seemed to his teachers) was assigned the role of an American Indian. He was a bright student in school, which included Kowloon Junior School, King George V High School and later Huron High School in the States. He graduated as a National Merit Scholar. He followed in the footsteps of both of his parents and enrolled at Concordia Teachers College, River Forest, (now Chicago). He became certified as a Director of Christian Education for the LCMS. He was in college during the very hectic 1960's. To my great delight he was elected president of the student body, just 20 years after I had held that position which had been 20 years after my father had held that position, all at the same college.

His career as a DCE, however, was short-lived as he became open as a gay man and thus was barred by the LCMS from holding office or (by many of that church) as even being deemed a Christian! My understanding of and acceptance of his sexual orientation could well be the basis of an entire book. Let me just say that Dave took the initiative and we spent a weekend of just the two of us at a retreat center to discuss this vital matter. To my everlasting regret I told him my opinion that at the time assumed that sexual orientation was a choice (and a very bad one!) I urged him to pray about it, to see a counselor and to not disclose this to his mother! His response: "Dad, I have seen a counselor tens of times and prayed about this, thousands of times. I am gay - that is how God chose to make me!"

Of course, I changed my mind and Jane never had to change her mind as she was much more knowledgeable and accepting all along. Dave had a successful career in serving youth street kids, retail business, hospital administration and computer services.

His faith remained strong in spite of incredible prejudice, judgments and rejection. He forgave me for my lack of understanding and misjudgments. As I have written elsewhere in my blog entriess, he became a leader in helping the Evangelical Lutheran Church in America adopt its current position of affirming the status, gifts, and ministries of gay people. He was the one person, many who were dying of AIDS, wanted at their bedside in their final moments.

Again, as I have written in my blog entries of early 2015, he died of cancer way too young. He lives in my memory every day. I consider him one of the very great and many gifts that God bestowed upon me.

෫෬

BAD HABIT

Very early in my professional career I developed a bad habit. It started while I was at St. Paul, Tracy CA and got worse through the years. I did not overcome it until after I retired. The bad habit: workaholism. I was a workaholic. At first it was something that had little effect on anyone else. I was single. I was living alone in a single rented bedroom. There were so many tasks to do. I was asked to do them. I felt I could do them well, so I did them.

In those early days I taught Grades 4-8. I was the school principal. I

270

taught Sunday School teachers every other week. I taught a Bible Class every Sunday. Weekly I went to choir practice. On a regular basis I went to school board meetings, church council meetings, men's club, P.T.A. Executive Committee and then regular PTA meetings. I served on the denomination's District Youth Committee, the area Principals Conference Committee. I attended graduate school and gathered used newspapers to sell to raise money for school supplies. On Sunday evenings I led the youth group (The Walther League). I played on city sports teams throughout the year moving from basketball to softball to baseball.

When I got married and had first one and eventually five children, I never slowed down. I took calls (new positions) with different specific responsibilities, all of which just spurred me on.

Of course, these actions had undesirable consequences. I was unfair to Jane and my children. The task of raising them fell very much to her. It was only rarely that I took time to read to them, bathe them or dress them or do fun things with them. In later years it got so bad that I did not even want to take vacations. I remember that after I had been in Hong Kong for four years without taking a vacation the Board for Missions sent me a formal warning, "If you do not take a vacation, we will no longer guarantee paying for your health plan."

Why all this hyper-activity? Several factors: 1. I really enjoyed what I was doing. I loved my work and the challenges it presented and the difference it made. 2. These positive results "felt good" and spurred me on to do more. 3. People affirmed me. 4. I was doing "God's work." Somehow or other it failed to register in my brain that spending time with wife and family, taking care of my body, getting a good night's sleep would also be doing "God's work." And so it was, that year after year, I just took for granted that I would work 70+ hour work weeks, never go to bed before 11:00, and on Sunday night (when I did not have another duty) I was sure to be at my desk from 8:00-11:00 pm.

Now, in retrospect, I see that I was stubborn and unresponsive to the good advice and incredible forbearance of my wife and family. I am eternally grateful that they (and God) have forgiven me. I have finally learned, at least most of the time, to say "No" when that is the appropriate answer.

I have learned to not work "after dinner," to enjoy reading good books, even before 11:00 pm. I have learned to admire my children, all of whom have done a much better job than I did at balancing work, family, self-care etc.

And I am grateful to know that having been forgiven by both God and family I need not lament my past failures. Rather, I have come to live the more balanced life to which God had called me now for almost 90 years and who knows for how many more.

ഇൻരു

GLENDALE, CA: CHALLENGES AND JOY

After serving as principal and teacher at St. Paul's Lutheran School in Tracy, California for four years I accepted a call to Zion Lutheran Church and School in Glendale, California. We were there only two years and the two years were years full of challenge and joy.

Challenges

My basic assignment in Glendale was to open a new school. In contrast to what was happening to Lutheran schools in many other Los Angeles areas, it was tough getting enrollment at Zion. The congregation's median age was well beyond child bearing. The school was located downtown on a small lot. Public transportation was unavailable. The public schools were good. I gave it my best shot, even personally picking up and delivering back home at my own expense several students who lived a distance away. The school grew very slowly. We had only13 students in Grades 1-4, all in one room. Yet, the school did grow, eventually enrolling well over 100 until many years later the elementary grades were dropped and a strong early childhood program still flourishes.

Our financial situation and living arrangements left much to be desired. When we arrived, the congregation had rented for us a small upstairs apartment with the landlady living on the same floor with us. She took it upon herself to teach our young son David "how to behave properly" and as part of that process spanked him when she thought that was what he needed. My salary was $200 a month (plus that apartment). One of the members suggested that it was time for me to get a credit card. I applied for a card for gasoline only with Texaco. My application was denied because of "insufficient income."

Jane was asked to serve as the congregation's organist and choir director. However, among other demands there were these two: when the Sunday School children left the church to go to their individual classrooms they must always, without exception, march out to the tune of "Onward Christian

Soldiers." Every single worship service must end with singing exactly the same hymn. Our pastor was very conservative. Once we had dinner at his home with some guests. He offered the table grace. But after the guests had left, he spoke with me. He explained that he hoped he had not done wrong by inappropriately joining in prayer with people who were not Lutheran Church-Missouri Synod members. He explained that the guests were actually Wisconsin Synod Lutherans.

Joy

We had left Tracy which was a wonderful small city of 10,000 residents heavily related to the agricultural community which surrounded it. Glendale is an integral part of the greater Los Angeles area. We took in many of the wonderful offerings that were right there. We listened to music at the Hollywood Bowl. We loved taking guests to the Grauman Chinese Theater, to Hollywood and Vine, to the homes of the stars in Beverly Hills. It was great to go to the Rose Bowl Parade and watch football there and at the L.A. Coliseum. I remember the extravagance of eating at a famous restaurant in the La Cienega area. Two friends took us there for a farewell dinner. It was the most expensive meal I had ever eaten: the wonderful steak cost an extravagant total of $4. (Remember this was 1956!) I must also admit that already in those years the city was often clouded over by a terrible layer of dark and heavy smog.

As is true wherever one lives, we were with some wonderful people. The DeVillers treated us with affection and affirmation. Mr. Roth saw to it that he always brought a good supply of beer when he came. Parents of my pupils invited us to their homes for dinner. The principals of the surrounding Lutheran schools were a marvelous source of learning, support and encouragement. I sang in an all-male chorus that practiced at Faith, Inglewood which introduced me to another urban environment. We took day trips to the California gold country and enjoyed an extended stay at Yosemite National Park.

We were in Glendale for only two years. I am grateful for those two years and they served as the transition point to our next adventure: Ten years in Hong Kong.

80C3

SURPRISE! SURPRISE!

It was a beautiful late Spring weekend in 1956. On Friday night a small group of members of Zion Lutheran Church, Glendale, CA invited Jane and me to a member home for wonderful steak dinner. As the evening drew to a close, they wheeled out a beautiful new television set. It was a gift to us, our very first TV. Surprise!

On Saturday I was on the roof of our house with a ladder next to the chimney and was installing the TV antenna, which was needed to get reception in those days. When the mailman came, I noticed he had a big fat brown envelope. I glanced at it, and saw it was from the national office of the Lutheran Church. I assumed it was just another mass mailing of church literature, completed the installation of the TV antenna and then joyfully sat down and enjoyed our very own TV. After dinner I decided to open the mail. Turned out the mailing was to me personally. More surprisingly it actually contained a call to service (a job opportunity in everyday lay language). And it was not an ordinary call. It was a call to serve as an educational missionary in Hong Kong. Surprise!

Hong Kong. I didn't even know where it was. I had never expressed any interest in overseas work. I had not been interviewed. I knew no Chinese. Yet here it was and the accompanying material made a big point. This is urgent. Please come and come quickly. We have already opened a few schools; another big one has been approved and most of the construction money promised. We need you to coordinate this whole program.

We dug out a National Geographic magazine, which had a feature on Hong Kong. It located Hong Kong for us and identified it as a British Crown Colony. It was being inundated as a refugee haven for the hundreds of thousands who were fleeing Mao Zedong who was making China a terrible Communist state. And we discovered that we actually knew three missionaries already in Hong Kong.

The details for the call were pretty straightforward. The call was to me (Mel) but Jane was expected to also carry on "missionary duties" but was not to be compensated for them. The salary was $3,000 per year plus adequate housing. The deal was that the Mission Board paid for our passage there and we were expected to serve a full five years before we were to be granted our first furlough back to the States. We were expected to learn the local language which was Cantonese. Ordinarily newcomers were allowed to spend most of the early time in language study - but in our case the demands of the job were such that I was to both study language and carry on the usual

274

duties of my assignment.

This was, of course, a major life-changing decision for us to make. It had appeared that my future lay in teaching at the college level as I had done that the previous two summers. I was in the early stages of exploring getting my PhD at UCLA. Of course, it meant leaving behind our family and Jane was the only daughter of her parents. David was a much-loved grandson. Also, David was suffering from severe asthma. Jane had been experiencing some undiagnosed ailments and the level of medical service in Hong Kong at that time was just developing. We had been in Glendale serving Zion for only two years.

In retrospect, Jane claims that she knew within 48 hours that I was going to accept that call. She may have been right because in any event I soon announced to the congregation that I was leaving my position as principal and teacher at Zion. We had decided. We felt this was where God wanted us. There were challenges ahead. We were going. And so, we started getting rid of most of our earthly possessions. We got our medical shots. We planned a trans-Pacific voyage on a passenger ship and were headed for a new life. It was scary. It was exciting. And it was all (we believed) a God imposed surprise!

ഇരു

GOOD-BYE CALIFORNIA, HELLO THE ORIENT

Of course, million have left America and gone to live overseas: the military, business people, the diplomatic corps, missionaries. Yet for each person or family doing this ,it is a unique experience. Since most missionaries from the Lutheran Church sent abroad were fresh out of the seminary, we had a very meager weight allowance for shipment of personal goods: 600 pounds if I remember correctly. So, we had to get rid of lots of stuff including, of course, our car, almost all furniture, boxes of memories, etc. But it was important to us that four-year-old David's toys make the trip.

The Mission Board travel department was very slow and inefficient in arranging for our travel and the folks in Hong Kong were ever more anxious for our arrival. After all, I was an educator and school terms were opening and teacher-training classes needed to be taught.

So, we got it done. Sold or gave away lots of stuff. Made a visit to our folks in Texas knowing that we would not see any of them for at least five years and aware that some would not be seen again on this earth. But it got done. We were to go by plane rather than ship. The farewell parties were held, the commissioning service was well done, the good-bye hugs were exchanged and we were on the Pan Am prop plane with first stop, Hawaii and change of plane. Then it got interesting. A plane engine failed. Emergency landing at Wake Island turned out to be a long stopover. The airline was helpful, even putting us on a bus and giving is a tour of the island while the repairs were made. Then off to the next stop, Tokyo. Again: engine failure. One engine was completely stopped. We made it to Tokyo, slept a few hours in a hotel and then were quickly loaded on a flight to Hong Kong.

Landing at Hong Kong in those days (as many pilots still attest to this day) was always a challenge. Had to avoid getting into the prohibited air space of China, stay above the high-rises along the landing path and come to a quick stop before the end of the taxiway which ended right at the Hong Kong ocean front. Another interesting aspect of the landing: the single taxiway actually crossed a public highway. When a plane came in for landing, a gate game across the car highway and the planes zoomed down the runway right in front of the line of stopped cars.

When we landed, we had quite a reception. We got off the plane and walked across the tarmac to the reception area. We still have the picture of little David all excitedly carrying his suitcase, me in coat and tie and Jane all decked out in formal dress, hose and hat. A reception committee of both missionaries and Chinese brothers and sisters were there plus a special greeter as well. By great coincidence for the first time in its history the President (Chief Bishop) of The Lutheran Church-Missouri Synod was making his first trip abroad. It was The Rev. Dr. John W. Behnken standing in line to greet us.

We went from that flight of many, many hours directly to a dinner for President Behnken and a welcome for us. This was an entirely new dining experience for us all - traditional Chinese food and service with no knives or forks, only chop sticks. It was great. And the after-meal activity was very disturbing. As we exited the not-so-formal restaurant on Nathan Road we were inundated with people: emaciated old people, young mothers with babies, crippled persons, all begging for food, money, anything. We had to push through them to get to our parked car jamming our way not only through the crowd of people on the sidewalk but also the never-before seen rickshaws, push carts, bicycles, taxis and busses.

Two of the women missionaries took us to their home where we stayed until we found our own apartment. Their apartment was on Tung Choi Street, just 20 feet south of Boundary Street in Kowloon. Boundary Street marked the official boundary between Kowloon and the New Territories. It marked which land was to automatically revert to China in 1997. We were the only non-Chinese residents in the area.

There was no time to waste. Within seven days of our arrival we were enrolled in Cantonese language classes at Hong Kong University and had a private language teacher assigned to us. I was teaching a course (through an interpreter) on Christian Education. Jane played the organ for a worship service which was all in Chinese and she had to rely on head shakes to know when to play the hymns or the liturgy. David had to follow the rule: Never leave the apartment and stay off the furniture inside! We were in a new land!

ഇൗരു

HONG KONG BY IMMERSION

When we received the "call" to Hong Kong we had no idea where it was. The atlas soon identified it for us: a speck of land on the southern coast of China. We learned that is was, in fact, a Royal Colony of Great Britain. It had gained that status as a result of the Opium War in 1841 and a few subsequent treaties. On Christmas Day 1941 it had fallen to the invading Japanese. By 1956 when we went it had reverted to its British Colony status. It's a small area of only 427 square miles including a main island (Hong Kong), a built-up peninsula called Kowloon and a rural area called The New Territories.

At the end of WWII Hong Kong had a population of 600,000. Then in the late 1940's as Mao Zedong forced China into Communism, people fled to Hong Kong at a rate of some 100,000 a month! By the time we arrived, its population was 2.5 million. Some of those who fled brought with them considerable financial resources. The vast majority came with nothing but the clothes on their backs. There was no place for hundreds of thousands to live. So, they just lived in whatever situation they could create. Multitudes slept on the street. Others thronged the hillsides, building their tiny shack homes out of whatever scrap they could find. Flat roofs and stairwells of buildings were filled with sleeping mats.

While our consciousness was overwhelmed by these realities, we moved into a two-bedroom apartment to live with two female missionaries We were urged to begin studying Cantonese and to teach classes through an interpreter. So, within ten days Jane and I made several trips a week to Hong Kong

University traveling by bus, then ferry, then bus again for the 90 minute each way trip, and I was teaching a Wednesday night class on Christian Education to teachers in the already existing Lutheran schools.

Two experiences of those first weeks are forever embedded in my memory. As I returned to my apartment around 10:00 p.m. after teaching my course, I walked past many street sleepers and beggars. However, one situation hit me in the face. A father's searching eyes found mine. He held in his arms a boy of about 12. He was starving. It was the first time I had actually seen with my own eyes the extended, bloated stomach of a person dying of starvation. I reached into my pocket and gave the man a one Hong Kong dollar bill. He looked into my eyes with such overwhelming gratitude that I still feel its piercing impact. All I had done was give him one HK dollar (worth about 15 US pennies!).

Two weeks later things got even closer to home. As I left my Wednesday night class, I thought there was more turmoil and anxiety than usual on the street but I thought it was just part of my getting used to a new situation. Within a block (by now I was in the middle of the street because the sidewalks were all blocked) a man came running up to me and waved a bag with a bottle in it right in my face. I was surprised to see a drunk on the street because I understood that that was one thing one did not find on the streets of Hong Kong. It was just a minute or more later that I caught on. That was not liquor in that bottle but an inflammable substance and maybe some type of firebomb. Kowloon was in the midst of a full-blown riot. I made it home through the next few blocks. The people in my class were less fortunate as they were unable to leave the building. The classroom in which I had just been teaching had bullets come through the windows. Those who had been in my class did not dare to try to walk home. Especially tragic was the news that the car of the Swiss Consulate General had been attacked in front of where I had been teaching and tragically his wife had been killed.

The riot was a battle between forces loyal to Chiang Kai-shek and those opposed to him. We listened to the news as the fighting continued, not daring to go to bed. The next morning, we heard more commotion below our apartment and we sneaked to the window for a look. The police had rounded up hundreds of rioters and were marching them down the street below us. They were taking this mass of people to the jail that was right at the end of our block. In this last block they suddenly forced the people to run. This was an intentional and successful effort to have the arrested persons lose their wooden clogs so they could not be used as weapons. Ironically within minutes those clogs were all gone as residents hastily slipped out of their apartments and secured those shoes for themselves.

Businesses, schools and public transportation were all closed down for a couple days and then calm was restored. We did not see such turmoil again at any time during the next ten years. For that I am grateful. Immersion does not be need to be repeated.

৪৩

STUDYING THE CHINESE LANGUAGE

One of the biggest challenges I faced after feeling called to serve among the Chinese in Hong Kong, was the challenge of learning the Chinese language and specifically the Cantonese dialect of that language. Chinese is spoken by some 1.2 billion people around the world. In its written form it does not have an alphabet but uses "characters"- each character being only one syllable. In its spoken form, it is tonal which means that the single character has a different meaning depending upon which tone is used. Cantonese has nine tones ranging from high to middle to low. Thus, the word "sic" can mean know or eat or color or thorn, etc. depending upon which tone is used in its pronunciation.

There is good news and bad news about my efforts to learn the language. The good news is that I had wonderful teachers. The second good news is that the Chinese were very forgiving of my very poor Chinese language skills. For example, it was only many years after I did it that a teacher told me that in one of my early attempts to use Cantonese at a faculty meeting I had opened the meeting by calling the attendees "old rats" when I had meant to call them "honorable scholars." I had used the wrong tones. The bad news is simply that, in spite of my good efforts, I spoke Cantonese very poorly. My wife Jane did much better. She has a good ear for music and so her tomes were right on.

My problem was especially bad when I tried to speak Cantonese over the phone. The person on the other end of the line heard my mixed-up tones, assumed I was a native Mandarin speaker trying to speak Cantonese so would switch to Mandarin which left me more in the dark than ever.

Because the never-ceasing efforts of my teachers and the forbearance of my colleagues, I finally was able to read the basic information on report cards, carry on a simple conversation, and memorize the Lord's Prayer, the Apostles Creed, and the Ten Commandments.

279

Jane and I studied Chinese at Hong Kong University, but much more important was the tutoring from Mr. Hung Chiu Sing. He was a wonderful scholar, a devout Christian and a very patient teacher. The name "Hung" is the Chinese version of what in English was translated "Con" as in Confucius. He was a direct descendant of Master Confucius. Thus, he taught us not only the language but also the customs, the special analects and, most importantly, proper Chinese manners. He was wonderful. And unbelievably patient.

Of equal importance were the marvelous interpreters who empowered and assisted me. Without them I would have been a complete failure. My first interpreter was Isaac Ma. He interpreted for me at the classes I taught both for Lutheran teachers and at Hong Kong College. I learned later that if I said something that didn't make sense to him, he just made up his own message. And it worked. Dr. Andrew Chui was invaluable in interpreting for me when I taught at the Bible Institute and Concordia Seminary. He had memorized almost the entire Bible and could always quote scripture absolutely accurately. Rev. Daniel Lee was unbelievable. He was especially helpful in assisting me when I taught (in Chinese) a course in General Psychology at the Lutheran Seminary in Dou Fung Shan. Daniel worked with me hour after hour helping me out because all the Chinese texts in psychology were translations from the Russian, pure behaviorism and thus not suitable for what I wanted to teach. Those seminary students bore with me, never laughed at me, and while they had, I am sure, plenty of comments out of class, they survived (thanks especially to Daniel). Slowly my own high school students became my interpreters, especially John and James Chu and then also Margaret Wong who was especially helpful in my office.

Now years later I dare to try my Cantonese very, very rarely. I can still recite in Cantonese the Lord's Prayer and the Apostles Creed and sing the common doxology. And an interesting sidelight: Our youngest son John was only a year old when we left Hong Kong but he is the one who developed a keen interest in all things Chinese. He now reads and writes in Chinese as easily as in English. His wife, a native of Spain who graduated from Beijing University, and their two children regularly speak Mandarin with each other. And I continue to feel a bit ashamed that 1.2 billion people speak some form of Chinese every day but I am not numbered among them.

ॐ

HONG KONG WATER CRISIS

"Water, water everywhere and not a drop to drink." When in high school I memorized those words from "The Rime of the Ancient Mariner," I never imagined that one day they would apply to me. Yet they did, in Hong Kong, especially in 1963-64. Hong Kong is surrounded by the South China Sea. But its very small land mass has no river and deeper wells are extremely difficult to dig because of a tough, very thick layer of bedrock. So, when the British Colony was overrun by refugees from China and its population suddenly soared into the millions there simply was not enough water, even for drinking purposes.

So, Hong Kong had to negotiate with the Chinese central government to get access to water from across the border. To the credit of that government they went out of their way to make water available to the people of Hong Kong. But still there was not nearly enough to meet the demand.

Severe water restrictions were put into place. The authorities simply cut off all water supplies to homes, schools, restaurants, etc. At its worst we would get water only every fourth day and then for only four hours. This placed an incredible burden on many, especially the hundreds of thousands who had no running water in their small tenement rooms or next to their hillside huts. So, they would line up for hours at the few available public water faucets. Already early in the morning on days when there would be some water one could see long lines of people of all ages. Each one had two five-gallon buckets. They would be attached to poles, which stretched across the back of persons, often even a young teenager or child.

The Chinese were incredible in making do. For example: we, of course, had strict school rules about the students needing to wear clean school uniforms. And some of the poor had only one set. So, they needed to wash their uniform in the evening, let it dry overnight and wear it again the next day. Yet, even though my schools had thousands of students and our rules were pretty strict, not one single time did I as principal have to send a student home because his/her school uniform was too dirty or stained.

Our family was very privileged. We lived in a situation where we had a small concrete water reservoir on our roof. On water days we could collect a little extra water there. And we used it very sparingly. For example, we would let some water come into our bathtub during that available 4-hour period every fourth day. We would dip it into small basins to wash the seven of us and then carefully take it from the tub to flush our toilets, which, of course had not been flushed for way too long. On "water days" Jane would fill the washing machine with a hose connected to the roof reservoirs, catching the used water in buckets and pouring it back into the washing machine for the next load.

Even though the authorities claimed the water was safe to drink no one believed that and everybody boiled all their drinking water. We would never consider brushing our teeth with water from the faucet. It had to be boiled. For years after we left Hong Kong, I still had difficulty allowing myself to use water directly from the faucet to brush my teeth.

One of the persons who was most amazing in managing water was our "tea woman" at Concordia Lutheran School. We were a large school with a staff of some 50 persons -and she always had hot tea available for us, delivered to the teachers' and my desks twice a day! I still don't know how she managed that.

There were some things one never saw during this time of water shortage. I never once saw a green lawn. Water at a restaurant table was more expensive than beer. There were no public drinking water fountains, not even at our schools. I cannot recall that water in a small plastic bottle was ever available for purchase. Yet we survived. More water and channels to move it were made available from the mainland. Hong Kong itself did dig some wells and even tried to dam up some water during the heavy rainy season. Now when I go to Hong Kong, I feel free to take a shower, I can putt on green grass at the Hong Kong Golf Club. I can flush the toilet after every use! But I just stick to my old ways and have a San Miguel beer in place of water when I have dinner.

ଽଠଓ

FOOD IN HONG KONG

I love to eat. So, enjoying good food is among the many good memories I have of living in Hong Kong. However, before I can speak of that I must face the reality that when we first arrived in Hong Kong in 1956 there were many, many people there who were going hungry. They had fled for their lives bringing with them nothing or only the barest of necessities. They lived on the street, in stairwells, in hillside shacks. When they had a little rice thy cooked it right there in the open. They often went hungry or underfed. I will never forget my early experience of seeing people on the verge of death due to starvation.

Fortunately, we were a small part of the many efforts to feed the hungry. Lutheran World Service provided food for thousands. When their food trucks arrived, people lined up, orderly but eagerly, for milk or rice packets. At our schools we regularly served milk to our pupils. This was a challenge because except for mother's milk it is not common for Chinese to drink a lot of milk. When we strongly urged our students to drink milk, they often had diarrhea as the initial response and that, of course, made it even more challenging. We added a bit of sugar to the milk and that helped. But what really helped is that it soon became obvious that those who drank milk every day were the ones who were gaining weight.

We faced a bit of a moral challenge in Macau. We had lots of flour and milk, but this was not what the people could easily use. They certainly had no money or space for baking ovens. We negotiated with a baker to use the flour and milk to bake fresh buns, which were enjoyed. We did not have funds to pay the baker in cash so we paid him "in kind" which technically we were not to do. But the arrangement did really save some lives and gave daily nourishment to others.

Inviting guests to share a meal is one of the basic forms of Chinese hospitality. This is almost always done in restaurants. In my ten years in Hong Kong I do not recall ever being invited to a Chinese home for a meal. Of course, most of the people with whom I worked lived in tiny, tiny apartments and hardly had room to accommodate guests. For people living in the resettlement estates it was not unusual that they had their small eating tables attached to pulleys and when it was not mealtime those tables were pulled up close to the ceiling to make room for movement or a place to sleep.

One of the eating customs is to have the number of courses served be the same number as the number of guests at a table, usually 10 or 12. This can make for a wonderful varied meal but, if funds are short, it can present a challenge. I remember a very early one. We had a big dinner for the teachers who had corrected the entrance exams at Concordia. We had little money but we needed 12 dishes so we ordered the most economical and that is why, for example, at one meal we served blood soup, fish stomach and similar very low-cost ingredients.

At our home we always had plenty of good food. We learned to go without any fresh leafy vegetables because they were all raised using human excrement as fertilizer. The local chickens were scrawny but good, especially in soup. Fish from near-by waters were fresh and wonderful. Lamb came from Australia. Pork from the New Territories and China was excellent. I survived five years without ever having a steak.

ഔന

FOOD IN HONG KONG RESTAURANTS

Already in the 1950's and continuing until today, Hong Kong has had wonderful restaurants for every taste and pocketbook. My mouth begins to water as soon as I think of some wonderful Chinese feasts. We were indeed blessed to enjoy meals at common neighborhood restaurants and at the most elaborate and expensive ones.

But before enjoying the meal we always had to go through the appropriate seating ritual. Each place at the table had its ranking in the hierarchy - both as to where the table was located and the specific seat at which one was placed. It was dictated by both Chinese and biblical mandates to seat oneself at the lower tables and at a seat facing away from the entrance. This would always result in the polite urging to sit up higher - which one would, of course, decline. Eventually we all got seated and course after course was served. Among my very favorites is shark's fin soup which is no longer available because it was the very sad practice to catch the sharks, just take the fins and discard the rest of the fish. It is impossible to beat traditional Peking Duck. This specialty came in courses: first the very fatty meat wrapped in a wonderful crepe and dipped in a pungent, delicious sauce. Later the meat was served in small pieces and still later in the meal, came the soup made from that same duck. Roast suckling pig was exactly that - with the whole piglet presented in the middle of the table. Elaborate meals had at least two soups plus fish, pork, duck, and several vegetables.

In contrast to the practice in mainland China, my Chinese meals in Hong Kong did not feature heavy drinking of liquor. Beer was really not considered liquor. In fact, children of any age could buy beer in neighborhood stores. Wine was never on the menu at any of the Chinese dinners I ate in those days. In Hong Kong whiskey meant Scotch.

The best and most exquisite place to eat on the Kowloon side was at the Peninsula Hotel and was (and still is) called Gaddi's. The service was impeccable. The place was quiet and always featured a wonderful small musical ensemble from the Philippines. It was considered very expensive and we ate there very rarely. Of course, "expensive" is/was a relative term. One could eat a complete dinner including a cocktail, soup, entree and fancy dessert for less than $15 (US). Our family often had our Sunday noon meal at a place called Garden Bakery. We could get soup, entrée and dessert for $1

(US) each! Another favorite was the Russian Restaurant. It had wonderful baked bread and it was there that I first learned of and got to appreciate borscht (Russian soup).

There were, of course, no McDonalds's or other fast food places in HK in our day. However, there was plenty of "fast food" available. There were hundreds (maybe thousands) of little noodle and rice stands. There were street vendors who wheeled their offerings into the residential neighborhoods.

As I write this blog in mid-June 2017, I am anticipating going to Hong Kong this fall. Top reason, of course, is to reconnect with former students who are now the wonderful and successful persons who have invited me back as their guest. It will be great to see them again and that experience will be greatly enhanced by fabulous meals at Chinese restaurants, at the Deep Water Bay Golf Club, and maybe even the extravagance of another meal at The Peninsula where a simple cocktail will cost more than the entire meal did in 1956!

SOCR

HONG KONG VISIONS

My years in Hong Kong were certainly among the most enjoyable and rewarding years of my life. One reason for that is that I was a partner in a visioning process. Chinese fellow-workers and missionary cohorts and I had the job and the joy of envisioning what a Lutheran School System could be in Hong Kong.

When in 1950 Missionaries Behling, Holt, Simon and Boss and others were evacuated out of Communist China and landed in Hong Kong they immediately began teaching. Very early they were not only teaching religion but were starting schools and a Bible Institute. By the time I arrived in 1956 they had already secured the land for a large K-12 school to replace the middle school they had started in a store front (Concordia Lutheran School). But we had bigger dreams.

We wanted a Lutheran School System. It had to cover kindergarten, Grades 1 through 12. It would include a target audience of very poor children and the children of wealthier families. It would in some case utilize the Chinese language and in other situations English. It would of course be taught primarily by certified Chinese teachers but also by non-Chinese foreigners. There would be schools for the deaf. And for those with other special needs.

In the midst of the diversity there were to be some common essentials. The schools were to be Christian and specifically Lutheran. By that we meant they would teach that there is one God and that God is good. That God's goodness was most evident in the reconciling work of Jesus Christ. The goal of Christian education is to set people free in Jesus Christ, enabling each student to more nearly become all that God intended each student to be.

We knew, of course, that all of this would cost a lot of money and that that money would not primarily flow from the USA, but would be raised locally through tuition, government assistance, special education grants, etc. etc. We knew that we would need a system of teacher-training focused on in-service learning.

The visioning was stimulated and greatly enhanced because of the values and experiences of my Chinese colleagues. They shared with almost all Chinese a great respect for education and for teachers. The refugee population included many persons who had been well trained in a variety of disciplines in China before they were forced out of China by Mao Zedong

In those days Hong Kong was a British Crown Colony and the British, too, had a deep commitment to schools. All Hong Kong land was owned by the government and was leased out long-term to businesses, not-for-profit organizations, churches, etc. The British had the tradition of allowing religion to be taught in schools and that practice was continued in Hong Kong.

My job title was Coordinator of Education and so I had the joy of trying to put all this together into a feasible plan and then find and utilize the resources to turn dreams into reality. Many, many days were spent in government offices studying the Colony's plans for redevelopment. For example, we selected one school site that, when we selected it, was all still under sea water awaiting future development (Kwun Tong). Another interesting incident was when I found a site for the Hong Kong International School on a lot which had somehow or other escaped zoning by the government.

All of this had to be done with a view to the time when Hong Kong would lose its status as a Crown Colony and most of the land (and accompanying conditions of lease) would revert to the Communist Party and its Beijing control. Fortunately, the Brits negotiated a very good treaty with one provision being that the Communists would honor all leases including those made to Christian Churches - and would allow the teaching of religion in all church-related schools during the next 50-year period.

In a couple months I plan to be in Hong Kong and celebrate how so much of that vision has become reality. What a thrill it will be to meet with colleagues who are daily turning those visions into reality as they operate the following: six secondary schools, two international schools, four night schools, six primary schools, one private school, two special- ed schools and 12 kindergartens. These schools enroll more than 23,000 students and are staffed by more than 1,000 teachers. Visions have become reality!

ഇൻൽ

TEACHING IN HONG KONG

I have always said that my profession was "teaching." I realize that I often spent much more time in administration, planning, supervising, consulting, grant writing, etc. But if you ask me what I really am I would say, "I am a teacher." When I spent some ten years in Hong Kong, I spent a great deal of that time teaching.

I had barely gotten off the plane when I first arrived in Hong Kong when Miss Behling informed me that I was scheduled to teach the next week. The Lutheran Church was requiring in-service training for its entire staff. Every Wednesday night the teachers from our various schools gathered for in-service classes. My first was "Basics of Christian Education." Naturally I taught through an interpreter and I had an excellent one: Mr. Isaac Ma. He translated my lectures sentence by sentence. Regretfully my teaching method was almost exclusively by the lecture method. To this day I admire those members of my class who sat through that – especially since they came there after themselves having taught all day and then returning to their classrooms again by 8:00 the next morning.

Concurrently, I taught a similar class at Hong Kong College. I taught there partially because in return for my teaching in the college, the college provided free space for us to conduct church services on Sunday or special church holidays. The students were all refugees of all ages and probably came to class as much to learn English as to learn about Christian education. Mr. Ma was my interpreter there. One of my strongest memories there relates to a student who objected or questioned almost everything I said (very rare in those days.) He eventually came around. In fact, he became a Christian and later a professional church worker in our Lutheran Church.

On Thursday nights I taught a class for Sunday School teachers. I really enjoyed doing this as the class members were very excited to be learning and then teaching the Bible stories. Teaching this class also assisted me in being supportive of my wife Jane who was playing a major role in producing the Sunday School curriculum. Our Sunday Schools became very popular and before long we were printing 1,000 Sunday School leaflets each week.

Friday night teaching was also wonderful. This was the Bible Study class for missionaries and spouses. We really kept our Friday night reserved specifically for getting together and study. We spent the first hour in Bible study and then the second hour discussing another book, magazine article or special topic of interest. We did this while also enjoying some refreshments. We moved from member home to member home to do. We took turns leading the class – and I learned a very great deal from all the men and women who shared the teaching roles.

In my second year I added a class on Teaching Religion. This, too, was very satisfying. I taught it to all the elementary school teachers and I gave them lesson plans to use in their classes the following week. This class was very interactive with the students (teachers) doing demonstrations, critiquing each other's teaching, etc. I was determined to do this job right - for a very special reason. When I announced that the Chinese teachers in kindergarten through Grade 6 would all be teaching religion, a veteran missionary spouse confronted me very sternly with the words, "Mr. Kieschnick, you are sowing the seeds of the destruction of the Lutheran Church by your actions!" She was convinced that no new Chinese Christian should be permitted to teach and that only missionaries had this right and skill.

Soon, I was also teaching in the Bible Institute and later, Concordia Seminary as well as the American Lutheran Church's Sha Tin Lutheran Seminary. I have made previous reference to my disaster in that last-named teaching assignment as I was teaching General Psychology, was teaching it in my very poor Cantonese, and the only texts available were very behavioristic translations from the Russian.

Now, as I near my 90th birthday, I do very little teaching. I have sternly requested my wife to let me know when my Sunday Adult teaching in my local parish is not up to standard. So far, she tells me I am still getting a passing grade, so I will carry on for a bit longer. Teaching is enjoyable and personally rewarding. And hopefully the class members find that this is true for them as well.

৪৩৫

90TH BIRTHDAY CELEBRATION IN HONG KONG: PART 1

I am not sure how my friends in Hong Kong heard that I was due to celebrate my 90th birthday on December 10. But when they heard, they immediately determined that part of that celebration needed to be in Hong Kong with them as hosts. So, they made all the arrangements and I gladly accepted being there November 1 to November 7. Jane felt the trip would be too much for her (and she was right) so son Tim accompanied me and that was also a good decision as his youth and internet skills made for very smooth international and local travel.

When I accepted my friends' kind invitation I had only one instruction: "Keep it simple." I suggested eleven names of people with whom I thought it would be extra nice to have a good Chinese birthday. We would eat in a room at the hotel and they would come get me for my dinner. I was told to be ready for dinner on the day after my arrival.

They came to my room at the appointed time. When I was escorted to the dining room I was greeted by a roomful of celebrants, 112 person-strong, in a brightly decorated room. They were all waiting for me. A very large birthday candle on a very, very large birthday cake was ignited and the group broke into a joyous version of Happy Birthday, first in English and then in Chinese and the celebration was on.

In the midst of an incredible ten-course meal accompanied by free-flowing wine, the program flowed - very ably emceed by Paul Chan Sing Kong - almost all in English! There was a "Biography of Mel Kieschnick Contest" at each table. Then each table selected one word to describe me. A spokesperson from each table came forward and explained why that word was chosen. Key words included trust, leader, farmer, inspiration, mentor, visionary, etc. etc. Each speaker at the podium brought with him/her a gift (more about that later) and made a three-minute speech which the master of ceremonies had a very difficult, yet humorous time controlling. After each little speech the entire table of 12 persons came forward and a group picture was taken and I had the opportunity to greet for a second or two each of the 112 wonderful guests. Of course, I was expected to make a speech, which I joyfully did.

The evening ended when I was presented with a very large artistically designed "Happy 90th Birthday!" card with many hand-drawn birthday candles and a very large folded poster that contained a picture of each table with each of the guests having signed their name.

After a rousing "Auld Lang Syne" sung twice and an even more joyous

"Praise God from Whom All Blessings Flow," the glorious party came to an end.

The second party, too, was a surprise. One of my hosts, John Chu, had told me that he was accompanying Tim and me to Concordia Church on Sunday morning for Sunday morning worship with that congregation. I was especially pleased with that, as so many years ago, I had worshipped with that congregation and helped write its first constitution.

We got stuck in traffic crossing the harbor between Hong Kong Island and Kowloon and arrived at church late. The service was already under way. Of course, we were escorted to the front row. The entire service was in Chinese but they had prepared an English Order of Worship and an outline of the sermon to help Tim (and me follow). After the service there were speeches and then opportunity for my former students -including also, four who (some with tears in their eyes) told me they learned to read and write in a simple little evening school I had organized some 50 years ago, then a big congregation dinner followed. The catered food (Chinese)' was wonderful. Naturally there had to be another gift-giving ceremony - and hundreds of photos as everyone had a cell phone camera and was anxious to record one more memory!

ఠఇ

90TH BIRTHDAY CELEBRATION IN HONG KONG PART 2

It was to establish and support Lutheran Schools that took me to Hong Kong back in 1956, so it was high on my agenda to visit a few of them now 52 years later. Therefore, the morning after we arrived, we were off to Concordia Lutheran School in Kowloon. The school had started with just a couple middle school grades housed in a storefront. Then we received a grant of land from the government and a $100,000 grant from the Lutheran Women Missionary League to build a stand-alone structure. That was my first assignment upon arrival those many years ago. We built a K-12 school, later added classrooms, added an evening school and enrolled some 1,500 students by the time I left. I was principal of that very large operation, completely staffed by Chinese personnel. It was a premier school with the highest rate of successful takers of school government-sponsored high school leaving exams in the history of Hong Kong.

Things have changed dramatically. It is now only a Grade 6-12 school.

The evening school is no longer necessary. It is completely funded with government grants. It continues to have high standards and a tough academic program. Its enrollment is 750. It has a new US $7M campus complete with all kinds of science and language labs, etc. etc.

The faculty and staff were eagerly awaiting my visit. Together they had arranged for a group of top students to meet with me and tell me about their school. Their presentation was all in English, fully illustrated with computer-generated projections. The students told me of current things that were never on the table in my day: optional sequences for high school students, courses in tourism and hospitality, courses taught in Cantonese, Mandarin and English. The students proudly told me of academic teams, sports programs, religious clubs and musicals, inter-school visits with schools on the mainland of China and on and on. Very impressive.

They had a carefully prepared session in which I was interviewed. I was pleased to respond to their questions regarding original visions and dreams and about differences between then and now. Finally, the interviewing student said "Just one more question, What is your opinion of President Trump?" That was the question they really wanted to ask!

The next school we visited was Saviour Lutheran School for Special Ed. What a treat. It had always been a dream of mine to reach out to this neglected portion of the population. I was there to help find the site, raise the construction money and get the building started but had to leave before completing the construction and I had never seen the final product. Now there has even been an addition to the building. Kids with special needs ages 6-16 are enrolled. The program is excellent and professionally conducted. A group presented a short musical program for me, including the singing in English of "Jesus Loves Me This I Know for the Bible Tells Me So." I left emotionally overwhelmed.

Then, primarily for son Tim, we went to the site of the home where he lived from birth to age 5. Of course, that building had long ago been torn down and replaced with higher density housing. The squatter hut village just a block away has been replaced with high-rise apartment buildings. But Tim tried to look over the fence to find where he had played on the slide and climbing bars.

A quick trip to where Tim had been born: St. Teresa's Hospital. All replaced. Good thing, as when Jane went there for his delivery, the labor room was on the third floor, there was no elevator and we woke a night watchman to let us in. Jane's water broke on the way up the stairs and Tim arrived before the doctor did. But he survived very well and the new building is helping many others do the same today, but I bet there are none named Tim.

The next day I was off to Hong Kong International School. This is another school which I planned, got approved, designed, and was building when a family medical emergency forced our family to leave. Now, it is one of the top schools in the world. The recently dedicated lower school is THE BEST I have ever seen anywhere. It even has a full-size swimming pool with a bottom that can be raised or lowered automatically so children can be in water ranging in depth from 1 inch to 8 feet. There is a full-sized kitchen for children to learn, and all play equipment is specifically designed for this school. The entrance features an incredible tiled mosaic with tiles made in Italy and laid in place by the kids. It meets all the demands of parents who pay up to $25,000 in tuition for their children to attend! It blows my mind, and while everything else that I designed has been replaced, the startling cross in the center still sends a message of love and respect for all.

When I spoke to some of the staff on the theme of excellence and learning they announced that the bursary to allow teachers from all over to come and learn here had been named in my honor.

ॐ

90TH BIRTHDAY CELEBRATION IN HONG KONG PART 3: FOOD

Chinese and Food: These two are inseparable. So, at my five-day 90th birthday celebration among Chinese friends this held true to tradition every day. I ate very, very well in Hong Kong, which might just be the best place in the world to eat.

It began with breakfast every day. My host knew that the manager at the Regal Hotel at which we stayed had been her former pupil. So, of course, she arranged for an up-graded room on the premier level with full access to the special afternoon tea, evening open bar, late night complimentary cocktails and full breakfast. Since Hong Kong is so international it was obvious that the breakfast counters featured not only traditional bacon and a form of hash-brown potatoes, but also all kinds of hot and cold cereals, porridges, congee, steamed buns, fish, Japanese dishes hot and cold beyond count, bagels and lox, fresh fruit of great variety, trays of pastries, etc. etc.

One of the features of dining in Hong Kong is that it is often done in private clubs. So, I was elegantly hosted for food at the Chinese Club, the Hong Kong Golf Club and the Bankers Club. I will here go so far as to actually list the specially-prepared (and carefully printed out, personally dedicated menu) provided by Tam Kim Chu and her husband at the Bankers Club. Here it is: Barbecued Whole Suckling Pig, Sautéed Scallops and Prawns with Vegetables, Deep-fried Crab Claws with Minced Cuttlefish, Braised Birds' Nest Soup with Fish Maw and Seafood, Steamed Sabah Giant Garoupa, Roasted Crispy Chicken, Fried Rice with Shredded Chicken in Cream and Tomato Sauce, Braised E-fu Noodles with Mushroom and Abalone Sauce, Sweetened Red Bean Cream with Lotus Seeds and Lily Bulbs, and Chinese Longevity Buns. Yes, that was one meal, all accompanied by outstanding, appropriate wine for each course!

Lunch at the Chinese Club and at the Hong Kong Golf Club was on a somewhat lesser scale but dinner at Hu Tong in Kowloon overlooking the harbor, and at Guincho a Galero in Macau, were also at the very top of any list of fine dining. In Macau it was wonderful to enjoy Portuguese sausage as it can only be made in that former colony of Portugal.

There were two large birthday party meals each attended by over 100 and each featured wonderful, more traditional Chinese food. At the alumni dinner the meal actually started with a huge birthday cake which was served before the rest of the meal. The meal was not served in traditional Chinese style with dishes in the center of the table and then on individual plates. Rather each entrée was a separate serving brought to each guest on a small plate with just that one item. This went on for 12 courses, most of which I did not have time to eat as I busy posing for photos with guests from the respective tables.

I was greatly surprised by the sumptuous, catered noon meal served at Concordia Lutheran Church after services on Sunday. It again featured a vast multitude of traditional Chinese dishes served cafeteria style. Two menu items were especially interesting. The first was proudly brought to me. It was a large bowl of charred mashed potatoes. This would never be seen at a traditional Chinese feast but the hosts figured I was an American and so they asked for this dish to be specially provided for me and it was brought to me with great flourish and humor!

The other feature of this meal was the birthday cake, actually three of them. At a ceremony in the church after the regular worship service, the ushers brought up two rather small and beautiful cakes that they asked Tim and me to ceremoniously cut. It was then served later at the dinner. However, at the dinner they brought me another piece of cake in a somewhat "messed up" condition. They explained to me: "This piece comes from the big beautifully decorated cake we had ordered for you to be presented after the church service. However, on the way to church there was an accident. The whole top of the cake with all its decorations was totally ruined." They did salvage some of the cake and wanted me to at least have a little piece of that, too.

In between all this Tim and I were ready for a simple dish of noodles from a street-side stand. So, we asked David Tzang to help us locate one. Well, that did not work out as planned. He and his wife knew of an old-fashioned noodle shop that had become so famous that it was listed in the Michelin Guide. It was so popular that the waiting line stretched half a block and the wait could be an hour or more. So, Margaret had gone early, stood in line and in we marched immediately, sat in the crude wooden booths, and with waiters whizzing by, enjoyed our noodles -accompanied by wonderful pig knuckles that Tim enjoyed so much that it was later announced that he had eaten three portions of them.

ಬಂಡ

90TH BIRTHDAY CELEBRATION IN HONG KONG PART 4: GIFTS

It all began when a former student and teacher on my staff, Margaret, heard that I was turning 90 this year. Her immediate response, "You must celebrate in Hong Kong and I will pay the airfare for you and Jane to come." This was followed by a message from her husband, David (also a former student), "And I will pick up the hotel bill!" Who can turn down an offer like that? Well, actually Jane could and did. She knew what the pace of activities would be in Hong Kong and she knew what it feels like to take that 14-hour non-stop flight from San Francisco to Hong Kong and return. So, she wisely chose to celebrate only vicariously and that turned out to be just the right decision. Our son, Tim, decided to go and the hosts said, "No problem. We will pick up all his expenses." and they did. Just to make the air flight a little easier, a couple from my home church, Calvary in Solana Beach, upgraded our flight to Economy Plus!

Public transportation in Hong Kong is excellent but we were going all over the place with a very tight schedule. So immediately another female graduate, Tam, spoke up. "I am making available my Mercedes and my full-time driver. She will take you wherever you need to go at whatever time you need her." We grabbed that opportunity.

When we got off the plane, the driver, together with Tam and friend John, were waiting at the airport in the chauffeured car. We had barely sat down when each of them handed me envelopes. Inside was cash both US and HK dollars to cover expenses, and a so-called "Octopus Card" that provides access to all forms of public transportation. And when we got out of the car at our hotel, we were loaded down with four bottles of outstanding French wine!

As indicated in an earlier blog, all our meals were more than covered, some by the persons already mentioned above, another by Heman, the Oxford graduate attorney son of Margaret and David, and by Paul who hosted a major dinner in Macau with Tam, of course having purchased the first-class ticket on the hover-craft that provided passage between Hong Kong and Macau.

At the first birthday party each table gave a gift, which ranged from a pen, through a lovely little statue of the goddess of longevity, to more little red envelopes, each of which contained cash. At the end of our visit, the Concordia School principal presented me with a wonderful photo album plus a remarkable flash drive wrist band which, when plugged in my computer, carried complete photo coverage of my entire visit plus photos of the history of the school, including shots of me with the graduates for each of the years I was there. The church at which I spoke gave tee-shirts with the Luther words, "Here I Stand." and appropriately logoed umbrellas, photo albums and a new Chinese Bible. During the previous day another pastor had given me a book stand in which the Chinese characters of the 23rd Psalm had been beautifully etched.

Naturally, gifts of jewelry, purses and wads of cash were sent along for Jane.

The evening before we left, I totaled up the content of all those envelopes. The combined total Hong Kong and US dollars was astounding. The total was not in the hundreds of dollars but was in the thousands! I sat there alone for a few minutes but then sang out loudly in both English and Chinese the immortal words of "Praise God from Whom All Blessings Flow!"

ନ୍ଦ

Places

I did not go to Hong Kong to go sightseeing or to explore places. I went there to be with people and to celebrate schools and churches. But the place of Hong Kong continues to be amazing. Now considered a part of China, it is classified as being part of one country two systems. Hong Kong is no longer a manufacturing center. All of that is in either the mainland or Vietnam and other southeastern Asian countries. Nevertheless, it is a bustling never-go-to-sleep business metropolis of some seven million energetic, ambitious, success-driven people. Its business is business. All the major finance companies of the world have offices there. It is a favorite place for shoppers from the mainland to come and secure both ordinary and luxury goods. Wherever we went over the weekend we were engulfed by people from the mainland carrying suitcases full of stuff to take home. And they all spoke Mandarin, not the local Cantonese. When we visited both the Chinese schools and Hong Kong International School it was stressed that while English is an important language there is now an emphasis that everyone also needs to learn to speak Mandarin.

When I lived there 50 years ago, it had no bridges or tunnels to connect the Kowloon peninsula with Hong Kong island - now there are three massive tunnels flowing with tens of thousands of cars. The underground metro system is inconceivably efficient, clean and economical. Where rice patties or steep hills formerly lay, we now find high-rise after high-rise.

Hong Kong is expensive. It is on par with Manhattan. Housing is unbelievably costly and people cram into very small spaces and often struggle to afford that. Even families with more than one wage earner may live in less than 800 square feet of home space.

The Hong Kong Peak, which Tim visited, has not changed much, but the scenery is very different. The harbor area keeps getting filled in with massive high-rise structures now standing where we used to catch the ferry. But the faithful Star Ferry is still there and Tim and I rode it, even being lucky enough to be there on a free-ferry-ride day!

Nathan Road in Kowloon is not much changed. We went to the old section of Hung Hom with its bustling, clogged streets, looking very much like it did 50 years ago. The Peninsula Hotel with the Bentley and Rolls Royce cars sitting in front remains unchanged. The Hong Kong Golf Club where I got in 18 holes of poor golf now allows pull-carts though my host insisted I use a caddy.

Macau is an entirely different world from what I knew. It is the Las Vegas of the Orient with all the Vegas gambling casinos and hotels reproduced and even done up more ostentatiously than in Nevada. When we stopped for cocktails in the Wynn Casino it felt like Vegas.

People

It's the people of Hong Kong generally, and those whom I got to know personally, that most inspire me. This time more than ever, many of them grew nostalgic. Over and over and over they recalled the early days, the days, they were newly arrived refugees and my students. They lived in squatter huts. They lived in stairwells. They slept on the corridors of huge resettlement estates. They got burned out. They went hungry. They had no shoes. When they got sick, they could not afford medical care. They had T.B. They had skin diseases. Even teenagers lost hair due to malnutrition. I heard those stories over and over. And now they are well-fed, they may be crowded in small apartments, but they own them. They are teachers, principals, money managers, medical doctors, nurses, attorneys, fashion designers, newspaper writers, pastors, and professors. It was all incredible. And one after another after another came and told me their story and expressed heartfelt thanks for the opportunity to go to school and get an education.

One of the most moving moments of my whole trip came on Sunday after worship. Four different older women came up to me. Each one of them told me that that their only opportunity to learn to read (they were very poor) was to come to a special evening school we had started that charged only 50 cents a month tuition. One of them came to me just before I left. She pressed into my hand a tiny very, very low-cost piece of plastic/glass beads. "These are for you, with my thanks!" she said, and quickly stepped away. That is the most wonderful way for me to celebrate my 90th that I could ever imagine.

෧෨

90TH BIRTHDAY CELEBRATION IN HONG KONG PART 6

When I lived in Hong Kong in the 1950's and 60's my Chinese friends were often reluctant to speak about their difficult pasts and why they had to flee China. Students, too, were quite hesitant to get very autobiographical. But when I was in Hong Kong recently this had changed. I was surprised by how candid my former students were as they spoke of their youth. More than once they recalled the extreme poverty they experienced growing up. Especially when a group of us had finished dinner one night in Macau, the group shared stories of their challenging backgrounds. I want to relate just a few of those stories here. I have changed all names and may have altered a few details to protect some identities.

Matthew started the conversation. "We were all very poor," he stated, "and I think I was among the poorest." He recalled that his father had been killed on Christmas Day 1941 when he served in the British forces protecting Hong Kong and the Japanese invaded and just demolished them. So, at about five years of age, he and his three-year-old brother were raised by his widowed mother. She found a few dollars to enroll him in Concordia Middle School, but soon she came to the Dean and announced, "I have to take Matthew out of school. I cannot pay both his tuition and still have money for his food." The Dean said," We will help with tuition and he can just eat with me. At lunchtime let him come to me and I will share my rice with him." Incidentally the monthly salary of that dean was US $30 a month. Matthew studied and did very well. A few years later the Dean informed me that Matthew's mother could now not even pay the reduced school fees. So, he and another colleague had asked her to iron their shirts and they would help with his tuition (and I found money to make up the balance of his school fees). He graduated with highest honors - one of the top five in the entire colony of Hong Kong. Soon the Lutheran Church chose him to study at a Lutheran College in the USA. There he was supported by faithful Lutherans from a congregation in the small town of Walburg, Texas. Matthew served the Lutheran Church in Hong Kong, then went into business as a major exec for an international conglomerate and ended up as a most senior officer in what is now the largest international insurance company in China. He never forgot God or the people who helped him, is a stalwart in the Lutheran Church and the community, and was a primary host and benefactor for my visit.

Mary was an excellent student in Concordia Middle School - excelling especially in English. I even used her as an interpreter when my Cantonese was inadequate. She was also a person with a very disturbing past. She was a very young girl when Mao's officials came to the farm where she lived with her extended family in South China. These officials came to take away her grandfather's land and keep it for the Communists. It got worse. The officials tied up her grandfather with his arms tied behind his back. They took him outside and brought the entire family including little Mary and made her watch as they shot and killed him. That vision stayed in her head. Eventually

298

she escaped to Hong Kong but carried with her the fear of what might happen to her when Hong Kong was to "return" to China in 1997. She badly wanted a USA passport as a safety net. Our son, David, sponsored her as an immigrant to the USA. She worked in the dress fur business and then in banking. She returned to Hong Kong as a successful businesswoman and teacher and supported her son through his graduation from Oxford University. She is forever grateful to those who assisted her and was the person most active in making all the arrangements and paying for my 90th birthday in Hong Kong.

Mark was the best athlete at Concordia, excelling especially in basketball and swimming. He studied very hard to excel in his academics. Unfortunately, he was also very poor and lived in a tiny study and sleeping area - which also had poor ventilation. As a result, he had barely finished his high school when he was struck down with tuberculosis - an all too common experience in Hong Kong in the late 1950's. Fortunately, space for recuperation was found for him at the Haven of Hope Sanitarium, partially funded by The Wheat Ridge Foundation.

While there the gentleman in the bed next to him told the sad story of his young son. "He is very bright and talented," said the father "but he is on the streets as I cannot afford to pay any school tuition because I lie here helpless in this bed." Mark suggested Concordia and said he would speak to his church friends to see if financial aid could be found. That worked. The student was especially interested in making slide projections of Bible stories for use in Sunday School. Today that student is in Beijing after producing Mission Impossible II in the USA and is known worldwide as Andy Woo. And Mark, the person who got him started, was a successful teacher and stock manager and the person who paid for my son Tim's airfare and for all our hotel bills (plus) while we were in Hong Kong.

Martha was living in a squatter hut when the terrible Shek Kip Mei fires of the early 1950's suddenly made tens of thousands of refugees homeless once again. Her parents found another very minimal place to live and she found her way to Concordia, getting up at 5:00 each morning to grab the public busses which got her there. After graduation she was blessed to get married into an old-time Hong Kong family that had the resources to have one of her children get a PhD and become a cancer research specialist. Another is a medical doctor with major responsibility. A third is an attorney in England. She hosted us wonderfully, provided all our Hong Kong and Macau transportation and made generous contributions for all the events.

John's family was also made homeless by the fires mentioned above. His mother was relentless in getting a teaching position and pushed and advocated for her children. John was an outstanding student, studied at Concordia Chicago, ended up returning to Hong Kong and headed up the multi-multi million dollars a year Lutheran Social Services of Hong Kong and was able to secure funding from multiple sources including Hong Kong's Jockey Club. His sister is a widely admired surgeon in Hong Kong and his brother owns a business in England. He was co-chair of the committee that planned all the events and was most generous.

When I knew these kids, they had to launder their school uniforms as soon as they got home from school so they could wear them again the next day because they could afford only one set of clothes.

The list goes on: Paul was the head Chinese for introducing MacDonald's into China. Timothy, a top professor at Hong Kong Chinese University, got his PhD at Yale and headed a major worldwide evangelistic education agency. Ron heads a Cancer Research Institute. And the list goes on and on.

They are all blessed products of the conviction that under God, hard work, solid education, multiple sources of encouragement and endurance can lead to untold opportunities and blessings – and then they thank their old friends and pay it forward for the next generation.

ℰꞬ

GRADUATIONS 2017 IN THE USA

There is no way on earth I could count the number of graduations that I have attended. In my career I have been principal of elementary and high schools and so presented hundreds (thousands?) of diplomas. I was a superintendent of schools, which took me to many more. I have spoken at several college graduation ceremonies. At all of those I sat on the stage. But this year I was there just to celebrate the grads, sit back and enjoy the ceremony and to have my own thoughts and responses.

The last few weeks have taken me to the graduation ceremonies of a public Junior college (Miramar), two high schools (both Catholic) and a public university (UCLA). Each of these was wonderfully inclusive. The grads' surnames reflected more ethnicities than I could count. Even just thinking of the actual grads who had invited me I was struck by the variety in their or their family's background. One was from Afghanistan whose parents were both killed by the Taliban precisely because they sent their daughter to school (girls are not supposed to go to school). Another was adopted because her birth mother was a drug addict and abusive. A third has a mother from Jamaica. Another had a father born in Hong Kong. They were Christian, Muslim and "other or none." By gender they were not all straight. But they were all Americans and determined to make a positive difference in this country and in the world.

I could not help but contrast these classes from my own graduations. All my graduation classmates from elementary school through college were white, all American born, all Lutheran. But beyond the differences in our backgrounds I was struck by common themes articulated by both speakers and grads. I rejoiced at the challenge to dream big, to pursue the common good, to live lives of service to humanity, to be a part of one world which needs the best from every one of us.

As together we recited the pledge of allegiance, I was proud to be an American. I am grateful for the heritage that welcomes immigrants, that supports both public and private education, that encourages upward mobility and that affirms our connection to the whole of humanity and all creation. And I said a silent prayer of thanks for all schoolteachers and administrators who nurture the hopes, dreams and abilities of all these grads.

One final shout-out. As stated above, I salute the students, teachers and parents of all grads and I extend a special plea to my colleagues in the Lutheran school business around the world. Keep the vision alive. Pursue the goal to always have each and every one of your students be set free and empowered to become all that God intends them to be.

৪০০৪

KIESCHNICK FAMILY REUNION 2017

Something Old – Something New

The 25th annual Oscar and Lina Kieschnick Family Reunion was held recently and it was another resounding success. Held in Austin, Texas, hosted by the Milton and Sylvia Kokel family, it had all the traditional trimmings. There was the wonderful opening Mexican dinner party in Julie's backyard. The hospitality suite was overflowing with all kinds of food and beverages. The golf tournament was especially great as my team won. Of course, the Texas 42 domino tournament was officiated well, the Texas bar-b-que very delicious, the Sisters' Luncheon fun. As always, we left after the Sunday morning family worship service, grateful and content.

Two unexpected wrinkles: Our golf foursomes were not the usual Saturday groups of four guys each. Our foursomes had both male and female players of all ages and a very wide range of golfing skills. The golf starter noticed that the group was a bit different and got the details from nephew Tim. Tim explained the 25-year history of the K Reunions, the respect for the values exemplified by grandparents Oscar and Lina and the inclusiveness of this event. It resulted in the starter's surprising reflection as he said, "You know my dad is in a nursing home in Dallas. He always asks me to come visit but I admit I have not gone in some three years." After a bit of reflection and urging from Tim, the gentleman said, "I will visit him." He pulled out his cellphone called his dad and said, "Dad, Saturday after next I will be at your place to see you."

The second memory is the result of a personal reflection. As we gathered for worship on Sunday, I let my mind recall my parents' history. Mom and Dad's families have all been Lutheran going back, I suppose, to the Reformation. The tradition of marrying German-Lutheran spouses and then having multiple children was the absolute norm up to the 1950's. In the year 2017, however I observed the following: We have family members who are Roman Catholic, Evangelical, Jewish, none, and probably "other." We have family members who were born in Taiwan, Hong Kong, China, Jamaica, S. Korea, Thailand, Spain, Brazil and Israel. Within the four seas all people are brothers and sisters and this was beautifully experienced at the 2017 Oscar and Lina Kieschnick Family Reunion.

ಇಂಟ

FEEDING THE HOMELESS

A couple nights ago I went to downtown San Diego to feed some of the thousands who live on the streets in that area. I stood at the end of the serving line offering a cup of lentil soup for each of the more than 200 persons who marched in front of me. I looked into the eyes of each one and asked if they would like a cup of soup. It was all a very moving experience and as I reflect upon it, several thoughts and questions flood over me.

1. Each of those persons has a life story. I suppose that a mother rejoiced at the birth of each one of them. Did they go to school? Serve in the

military? Do they have any current family contacts? How did they end up on the street homeless and hungry? Where will they be 30 days from now?

2. I was struck by the large number of women in line. I have been serving at this location occasionally now for some 15 years and I noticed how each year the number of women increases. I noticed especially how the women still tried to dress as best they could. While many of the dresses were obviously well worn, they were clean and some effort seemed to still be made to have colors match. Some of the women even wore a bit of lipstick. Most looked me in the eyes but a few diverted their look. Life on the streets must be especially difficult for women.

3. There were people of all ages. I was especially struck by a young man of about 18. He seemed quite self-conscious and appeared to be new to street dwelling. I did not see evidence of drug abuse and I could not help but wonder, "How did he get into this position?" Similarly, a person of about 25 who also seemed new to the situation appeared. He was neatly and nicely dressed. I had the feeling this was all a new and very uncomfortable experience for him. Of course, I also saw some faces of people who have been on the street for a very long time. I was reminded that study after study shows that there are several different groups that make up that population. There are those who have just recently lost their jobs and or their homes. Others are veterans with PTSD syndrome. Some are perpetual drug abusers, some choose street life, and others are trying desperately to get off the street. Some have to choose between eating and paying rent.

4. I was very saddened by the fact that many had no, few, or terrible teeth. I learned that tooth disease is the most prevalent illness of the homeless. And I was saddened to be told that the American Dental Association formally declined to have any part in any of our country's affordable health plans so all these people are ineligible for any kind of Medicaid or other aid for dental care

5. It was obvious that homelessness knows no gender, racial or ethnic boundaries. There were men and women of all ages and skin color. But I did notice that there was only one person (an elderly female) who proved false my assumption, based on my many years working with the Chinese, that the Asians' heavy stress on education, family and their work ethic result in no Asians among the homeless.

6. I also noticed the extreme friendliness and gratitude of our homeless guests. All but maybe four out of more than 200 said "Thank you." One gentleman with near tears simply said "Thank you. This is my first meal in four days!"

One final word: the sponsoring group was the Third Ave Charitable Organization affiliated with First Lutheran Church. They really know how to do this right. They prepare a healthy, good tasting and attractive dinner. They respect each of the homeless guests. They organize the process so that it flows seamlessly. They carry the trays of those unable to do that for themselves. They carefully control serving size and then allow people to return as long as there is food. They welcome, respect and join in prayer with those doing the serving.

As I go home from the event, I say a prayer of thanks that all of us, the hungry and the well fed are brothers and sisters. And the words of Jesus ring in my ears, "I was hungry and you fed me."

ഇൻൻ

KIESCHNICK FAMILY REUNION – 2018 No .27

The Oscar and Lina Kieschnick 27th consecutive annual reunion was, as always, a great success. This one, however, was a bit different for me. For the first time in its long history, I was the oldest person there, even though I am only 90 years of age and number three in birth order of "The Original Nine." Sister Erna who is 94 had fallen and broken a wrist and so stayed home in Florida. Sister number two, Leona, has severe Alzheimer's and stayed behind in her memory care unit. Thus, I was the proclaimed elder statesman.

On this trip I had some undeniable evidence that I am indeed aging. I had typed in the incorrect pick-up date for my car rental at the San Antonio airport. Procedures for checking in for flights have changed and I was slow to catch on and relied upon my patient, always more proficiently computer-skilled wife, Jane. When nephew, George put together the rules for the golf tournament, he allowed for persons older than 80 to play from the forward tees (and he knew that I was the only one who met that criteria). By the time the last of the Texas 42 players went to bed around 2:0c0 a.m., I had long before been fast asleep. Age cannot be denied - and it can also be celebrated. I drank my full share of the beer that flowed from the three full barrels of Shiner Bock and Bud Lite. I stayed within the one-minute time limit when giving the update on my life. I still sang from memory all the verses of the hymns at the wonderful closing worship.

Niece Kari, who did an unbelievably fantastic job of pulling together this entire event of well over 100 of our Kieschnick clan, did a super job of having an update on every one of the extended family. As I listened to all the jobs now held by all (and especially also by all the women) it hit me. My mother never had these options. She could be a teacher, a nurse or a secretary. Yet her contribution to her family, to the church and to the world cannot be surpassed even by the wonderful things the current generation is achieving. I remembered and thanked God for Mom. She raised nine children, lived through the great depression, and supported Dad. She sewed, washed, hung on the line to dry and ironed our clothes, canned 800 quarts of fruit and vegetables in one summer. She butchered and fried young chickens, week after week and year after year. She took care of all nine of us when we had mumps, chicken pox, red eye, measles, whooping cough, annual birthday parties, broken bones and broken romances. And I recall Dad and his ministry to the church and the world. I recalled how his mom and dad had put him on that solitary and slow train ride from Lincoln, Texas to Chicago in 1913, when he was only 13 years of age, as he left to prepare for his lifetime ministry in the Lutheran Church. He taught multi-grade classrooms, was principal, organist, choir director, janitor, church secretary, state-wide chair of Lutheran teachers, counselor to hundreds, toast master extraordinaire, etc. etc.

Our closing worship featured the singing of favorite hymns of Mom and Dad and of the Original 9, an essay on Martin Luther by a fifth-generation eleven-year old, William, and a powerful trumpeting of Taps by great nephew Brandon.

After arriving back home safely to our retirement community in California I reflected upon the fact that the annual cost to Jane and me for the reunion (covering airfare, car rentals, hotels, meals, golf, etc. etc.) comes to about $2,000 a year. So, I guess we have spent in excess of $50,000 to make all these 27 annual reunions. I came to a wonderful conclusion. Thank God we can afford this. It is worth every penny.

ഇൽ

TAXES: HAPPY TO PAY THEM

It was, of all places, a golf course that got me thinking about taxes, as a part of our annual Kieschnick Reunion

As part of the reunion ritual we played golf Saturday morning at a public course in New Braunfels, Texas. The service was outstanding. The staff had the carts ready with our names on them. There were signs announcing the event. The staff had even called earlier to tell us they would have the kitchen staff arrive extra early on that Saturday morning to prepare breakfast, if we wished that. I have never received better service, even at the finest private clubs around the world.

I reflected upon the fact that this was a public golf course undoubtedly supported by taxes. Maybe I even paid some tax support for it as part of the add-on taxes when I paid my motel bill in that city. I was happy to pay those taxes and get those nice benefits. The more I thought about this, the more I became aware of other things I get for my taxes.

I am happy to travel on our tax-supported highways. The police help keep me safe. Some of my fellow citizens, who are less blessed with resources than I, get housing or food or health support. The monthly social security checks deposited into my bank are certainly more than I ever paid into that account. My Medicare drugs tend to run to $8 per prescription due to tax support. While I think we spend too much on the military, I must admit that I am grateful for the men and women who serve to protect me. I get frustrated and angry when I see what my taxes are paying for at the DMV, yet the list of appreciated benefits goes on: free public schools, fire protection, clean beaches, airport security, assistance for poor and hungry people around the world. I am grateful that my California gasoline taxes help protect the environment and combat global warming. I get a lot for my taxes and I am grateful for the benefits.

I realize, of course, that I pay fewer taxes than many. I am aware that because of my income level I pay extremely little in income taxes. Whatever the amount: I do not regret paying it. I do not want to move out of my state or country to "save taxes." I follow Jesus' teaching to "render unto Caesar what is Caesar's." So, yes, I claim every deduction I can. I do not send extra "voluntary cash" to the government but I am indeed satisfied to pay my fair share of taxes and am grateful and pleased with the benefits.

ℰᘛᘎℬ

JANE'S 90th

Jane is about to have her 90th birthday and the celebrations are going on with a wonderful non-stop series of glorious events. Our four kids and most of their spouses and almost all our grandchildren have arrived from New

Hampshire, Connecticut and Northern California. Thanks to Airbnb and other options, they have places all up and down our nearby coast with fabulous views of the ocean and wonderful spaces for parties.

It started on Friday with a big shindig at one of the beautiful rented places. There was champagne, wine, special margaritas and homemade ice cream. There were balloons, and signs and streamers and tables of great food. Saturday dinner was here at La Costa Glen in a special room decorated with unique place cards featuring photos of Jane. A large bouquet of roses (sent by friends of daughter, Liz) added fragrance. The local kitchen staff outdid themselves with shrimp cocktails, sole, chicken, gluten-free pasta, etc. etc. But the highlight was not the food but the program. Toasts were raised by young and old, children, grandchildren and in-laws. They were loaded with stories of praise for Jane's incredible persistence, love, care and acceptance.

The memories of our children recalled times when they were young or when they gave birth or when they had appendixes removed or when they just needed a caring, listening ear. Special note was made of Jane's health issues including bad hay fever, asthma, both hips and both knees replaced, fibromyalgia, rheumatoid arthritis, cerebral aneurysm (flying from Hong Kong to San Antonio in a virtual coma), all lower teeth removed while she was still in her thirties and significant hearing loss.

Days in Hong Kong were recalled, times of learning a new language, of keeping kids in clean clothes when there was running water for only three hours every fourth day. While there she had a couple miscarriages and brought forth four children even if she had to wake up the night watchman to let her into the hospital and walk up four flights of stairs to get to the birthing area, where the doctor arrived after the baby did. In the midst of all that, she taught piano, sang in choirs, helped produce thousands of Sunday School leaflets (in Chinese) every week, and was an officer in the American Women's Society of Hong Kong.

There were stories of trans-Pacific plane rides with failing engines, of ferry rides to Macau, of giving missionary talks in 17 states. Also, good times in Hawaii, hay fever filled days in the Alps, secret support of gays and lesbians in Finland, visiting with an "adopted" daughter in Sweden, and grandkids in Taiwan. Spain, and England, finding family roots in Germany, falling three times on wet slick floors in Cancun and enjoying ocean views in Baja California.

In the midst of all this, Jane made time for artistic expression. Now her piano playing is no longer suitable for concerts solos. Her arm strength limits her woodcarving. Her favorite art teacher has died, but she continues to weave, crochet, sew, tat, bake wonderful cookies, learn new computer programs and tend to the plants on our balcony,

All of this was reflected in two most unusual documents. Liz had asked nine family members to each interview Jane and then write a summary of her life during one of her nine decades. Then she put all this (and more) together in a wonderful document. To top off all of this, these events were recalled in a marvelous ten stanza ballad complete with a repeated chorus composed by Tim, Wendy and Haven. Still it didn't stop. We filled a long pew at a Sunday morning eight o'clock service at Calvary Lutheran, joined the pastor in prayers of thanks, and then shared a marvelous big Happy 90th Birthday cake with the congregation.

As I write this it is still going on. The four kids (regretfully, yet thankfully, remembering David, now at eternal peace) decided to have a sib-fest with just the four of them. So, they are enjoying their seaside villa, going scuba diving, visiting San Diego and coming to our place for end of the day cake, ice cream and cognac.

Soon this will be over. Yet it will never be over. The memories will last. The gratitude for Jane will forever be remembered before our Heavenly Parent whom we acknowledge to be the giver of this and every wonderful gift, especially this marvelous human being: Jane.

ഇരു

HAWAII: UNFORGETTABLE MAUI EXPERIENCE

Big Plans - With a Major Modification

Dick Binford has been a warm, wonderful and generous friend for years. Then recently he came with an unbelievably wonderful offer. He was inviting Jane and me together with Pr. Fred Lubs and his wife Ruth to join him (Dick) for a week at Maui as his guests. Wow! That was an invitation to savor and readily accept. Then came a change, which even he did not anticipate when he first made the offer. He laid it out "I am getting married to Cheryl. We want you to perform the wedding ceremony and now there will be six of us on that Maui trip!" Well, being part of his and Cheryl's honeymoon was a new angle. So, we quickly offered to modify the plans so that the two of them would not have two retired ministers (plus spouses) along for this great experience. Both he and Cheryl, however, remained cool and said "Come along. It will be great. We will figure out enough one-on-one time and space for it all to work." And they did!

A Simple Yet Perfect Wedding

The wedding was held on Sunday evening at the Rancho Bernardo Inn. All was beautifully and carefully arranged and came off as planned. The site was a secluded outdoor space with green grass and lovely flowers with white chairs neatly arranged. Guests arrived on time, excited to support this new relationship. The simple procession down the grassy aisle went as planned with one wonderful little exception. At first the two flower girls were a bit reluctant, then they enthusiastically spread the blossoms. And when they realized that their supply of blossoms would run out before they got to the front, they simply went back, picked up some the strewn ones, and again delicately dropped them down the aisle. And then, spying some more blossoms on nearby plants, they picked some from there to replenish their supply.

The ceremony was direct and simple. The readings were attended to, the prayers spoken, the vows made, the rings exchanged, all accompanied by beautiful harp music. The newly married couple had their first public kiss and those assembled cheered.

The spirit at the reception with many drink and appetizer choices continued the warm spirit as family and friends wished the new couple an overflowing abundance of joy. There was a generous flow of hugs, tears, well-wishes and affirmations, not a single one of which was missed by the very professional photographer who got it all recorded.

The wedding dinner was just right for the group of 42, gathered around tables with assigned seats, and carefully served steak and fish with all the great accompaniments, with beverages of choice flowing freely, toasts earnestly made and concluded with special marriage cupcakes!

At 10:30 the next morning family and friends from out of town were treated to a great breakfast on the patio overlooking the tenth green of the golf course below. Once more the sentiments of joy and anticipation stirred through the guests.

First Class to Maui

On Tuesday, Jane and I joined Dick and Cheryl in their beautiful downtown San Diego condo where some of us watched the World Series game in which the Dodgers hung on to defeat the Red Sox in 13 innings. But

Dick was knocking on our door by 5:30 a.m. the next morning because it was time to head to the airport for the flight to Maui.

And what a ride it was. Outstanding first class on Hawaiian Airlines. The two flight attendants in the First-Class cabin were unusually solicitous. They made us feel like each one of us was the exclusive object of their attention. Even when I thought I really did not need another Mai Tai; it was furnished and I succumbed to the polite pressure of having to endure it. It might be a five-hour flight but it went so smoothly that I wasn't even sure I wanted to get off.

Room with a View - And then Some

Dick had made reservations for all of us at the Wailea Beach Resort Condo, D110 to be specific. It had three bedrooms, beautiful living room, full kitchen, stocked with every conceivable utensil including popcorn popper, waffle iron, three coffee makers, and a bar loaded with name brand drinks, outdoor grills etc. etc. Outside the door we were greeted by a wonderful sitting and viewing area with a flowing waterfall off to the right and the beautiful beach ahead. There was the pool, the beach, the ocean and the walkways with piles of large fresh white fluffy towels at every corner.

Luau

Among the many wonderful events, what stands out most is the private Luau that Dick arranged for us at the Wailea Golf Club Restaurant. It was strictly for the six of us. When we arrived the table on the outdoor deck was waiting - but we were invited in for pre-luau Mai Tais and appetizers.

There was a wonderful two-male music ensemble, playing a uke and a guitar. They sang and played for the full two hours we were there without repeating any number, and they were good - singing at just the right volume, choosing sentimental and appropriate music and ending with a beautiful rendition of "Can't Help Falling in Love with You."

They were easy to dance to. Even I (who cannot possibly dance even the simplest step), stood up and hugged Jane and once in a while moved my feet a bit. It didn't matter; it was love.

Then came the hula-dancing pair. When they came to chat with us after their perfect performance, we learned they were husband and wife and their words and body motions were just right for couples, whether newly married or married for 67 years!

It kept coming. This time an incredibly agile and gifted fire dancer who swirled the flaming torches about him in an amazing array of motions and angles. He, too, came to chat with us afterwards and that, too, was interesting.

All of this was accompanied by drinks and a mouth-watering eight-course dinner described below.

Not Quite to the Mountain Top

As was the case on several occasions, the two guest couples went out on their own while the newly married twosome had the opportunity to follow their own wishes. Fred, Ruth, Jane and I decided to go to the top of Haleakala to see the volcano site. Unfortunately, as we neared the top, we realized that the peak was completely enveloped by clouds. We went to the National Park Store and enjoyed reading about it and picking up a few souvenirs. With some effort we again found a great place to eat while admiring a still different view of appealing scenery

Tour of Lanai and Kihei

Traveling on well-traveled and very narrow one-lane roads made for excitement and enjoyment.

Always there was time for long walks on the beach, lounging on the shore, enjoying the pools or just reading on our Kindles, interrupted only by our choice of watching the World Series, with the ups and downs of the Dodger efforts cheered on by Cheryl in her newly gifted Dodger cap

And Don't Forget the Golf

The Wailea Golf Club offers three great courses and we played two of them. The first day on the Gold turned into disaster for me. That course must have over 100 sand traps and I found at least 20 of them. Fred hit the longest drives (some of which landed in the fairway) and Dick just hung in there to get the low score. When we played the Emerald Course, my partners felt compassion for this old man and let him play the forward tees. That worked great for me, and I actually ended up with five 3's on the scorecard, accurately recorded by Cheryl, and shot my age! On the once a year occasion when I shoot my age, I always buy the pitchers of beers, but when I wanted to do that at the Club House, we were told that on Maui the county does not allow serving beer by the pitcher. We adjusted quickly and well within that restriction managed to celebrate the day.

311

Looking and Feeling Beautiful

While we were playing our first round of golf, the women were having a very special good time. Dick had arranged an appointment for them to get the full treatment at a fancy spa. So, they got it all, steam and cream and tender care!

Food! Food! Food!

What's a vacation without special food - and we had plenty. Dick had asked me to grill steak the first evening. I was worried about it, but carefully packed my special steak marinade in my checked bag and it went safely through all the checks points. We picked up steaks and they actually turned out great. One night, Dick made a great spaghetti dish. The Lubs found some delicious pizzas to bring in. Brunch at the Marriott courtesy of Ruth and Fred was special and I had my first ever Maui Bloody Mary with a crispy slice of fried bacon as a swizzle stick. We ended our stay by going to the Far East for a simple Thai meal as our final selection. Previous to that we enjoyed the meal of a lifetime hosted by Cheryl at Momma's Fish House. The ambiance there is a very special conglomerate of half a dozen styles. The menu list is pages and pages, and the food are absolutely unique. We all had wonderful multi-course meals. My fabulous entree was mahi mahi and other fish in a perfect curry sauce all mingled with fresh and tasteful vegetables. To say "it was marvelous" is an understatement.

And there were all those homemade cookies. Jane brought a big batch of peanut butter cookies. Ruth brought blueberry muffin cookies. They disappeared so quickly that a trip was made to the grocery for the mix for lots more cookies. They smelled great when they were in the oven and tasted even better when they were in our mouths.

I will close the section on food by just listing the dishes served at the Luau. Here it is: Appetizer: Ahi Cake with Kula Greens and Wasabi Remoulade. Entrees: Macadamia Nut Crusted Fresh Catch with Pineapple Salsa accompanied by Kalua Pork Steamed Buns, followed by Hoisin Marinated Short Ribs of Beef with Mushrooms, and Wok Seared Vegetables in Curry Sauce with Lop Cheung Fried Rice and Purple Sweet Potato Mash on the side. All ended up with Selected Sweets! And the servings were so generous we took food home for the next four days!

Bumps Along the Road

Every ride needs a bump or two to help appreciate the smooth parts. We were disappointed not to see the volcano. More importantly, Jane caught a really bad cold and her cough made her draw upon deep resources within her resilient self to take in as much as possible. Dick and Cheryl did a little joy riding off the main drag and were greeted by a newly arrived boulder on the road, which extended a very firm welcome to them on the front right bumper of their car. The Dodgers disappointed. But what is that among the many joys, comfort, pleasures and just good times we had on Maui.

Yes indeed, **AN UNFORGETTABLE MAUI EXPERIENCE.**

ఐౚ

CHRISTMAS NOW (2018) AND THEN (1933)

Christmas continues to be The Most Wonderful Time of the Year. A great time to celebrate and to remember. This year I decided to remember Christmas 85 years ago (1933 when I was 6 years of age) and this year when I am 91.

Jane and I flew non-stop from San Diego to the JFK Airport in New York. This, of course, was undreamed of when I was six. To fly across the country in six hours (or even to board an airplane) was way beyond my greatest imagination. I had to think about the preparations needed for the 60-mile trip to Grandma and Grandpa Kieschnick in Lincoln, Texas. That meant packing our Model A Ford for a long trip. We had to be especially sure that we had enough patches for the inner tubes of our car. We had to anticipate the likelihood of a flat tire as we rode along those country roads, I recall how Mom and Dad and the kids (at that time there were eight of us) crowded into that slow moving car of ours and how we had to leave room for some of the vegetables or fruit Grandma Kieschnick was sure to send back home with us.

When we reached Connecticut, daughter Elizabeth had her home beautifully and wonderfully decorated. The candles were always lit, the fireplace always burning, the Christmas tree majestic. She even remembered special foods from my childhood -special fried sausage on Christmas morning, eggnog every night, homemade cookies and candies all over the place. I remembered the deep poverty of 1933 as we were in the heart of the Great Depression. We were thrilled then to get an orange in our Christmas stocking. I received back my little tricycle that the birds had carried away a couple weeks before Christmas and then reappeared all repainted and shiny under my Christmas tree.

The Christmas Eve worship experiences were radically different. When I was a child, the service focused on the children with all of us parochial school kids sitting in the front of the church, reciting our "pieces," singing the carols in three-part harmony and giving memorized answers to pre-assigned questions from our teachers, always beginning with "Welches hoest fest feiern wir in diesen tagen?" (Which high festival do we celebrate in these days?). This year the children's pageant had been presented the previous Sunday. More radical differences: the pastor was a woman!! Those in attendance included black people, Hispanics and people from India. I honestly believe that if any black persons had come to our Christmas Eve service in 1933, they would have been asked to leave the church or go sit in a secluded corner apart from the white people there. Once again daughter Elizabeth did honor tradition. After the service she took me to the big tree in the front of the church and there was that old paper bag and in it were the traditional orange, a few nuts and of course: a whole package of Wrigley's Juicy Fruit gum. In 1933, I got one stick and that was the total amount for the year!

When I was six, my family and all of my relatives lived within a day's driving distance. Now my kids live on both coasts and one daughter-in-law lives in Spain. Christmas contact included not only Skype but also email, texts, Facebook and all the other connections that were well beyond our Walburg days when we did not even have a telephone.

So, the differences abound. Yet Elizabeth and family were centered on that first Christmas - as she had the Advent wreath lit, the Scriptural prophecies read and the timeless message celebrated. God is love and came to dwell among us and daily invites us to bring Joy to the World, a world ever changing and ever the same.

৪০৪

CREMATION

Yesterday I attended the last of five funerals (Celebrations of Life) within the last two months. In reflection I noted that in each case the family has chosen to have the deceased family member cremated. This is something that was unthinkable to me growing up. I suspect I even considered it wrong and probably sinful.

Of course, by now I have changed my mind and I have spelled out my

314

own desire for cremation in the appropriate papers and have even paid for it in advance.

While most Protestant Churches (and some Roman Catholics) now approve cremation, I try to recall my earlier views and one still held by some today. Some opposed cremation because they judged that the person desiring it somehow or other thought cremation would make resurrection impossible. Resurrection is, of course, a belief that cannot be proven. It is a matter of faith and hope and for many a surety. Others decried cremation because it seemed to dishonor the sanctity of the human body. Still others just never considered that option.

It was not considered an option in my youth. I was born in and lived in a house with the Zion Lutheran Cemetery just a hundred yards or so away. Every single member of Zion was buried in that cemetery at a very low cost, maybe even at no cemetery charge. I know all the graves were dug at no charge by members of the church. Now even that cemetery has built a columbarium and my late brother-in-law, Raymond, will be the second person to have his cremains there. I have been active in my current congregation, Calvary Lutheran in Solana Beach, CA to install a columbarium in our sanctuary. Of course, a columbarium holds only cremains. In a couple of days, I am assisting in placing the cremains of a former military officer in a three-person space at Ft. Rosecrans National Memorial. In the San Diego area, burial at sea is very common.

Because I lived in Hong Kong, worked with Chinese brothers and sisters and participated in many burials (no cremations), I checked to see about current practices there. I found that cremation is now becoming quite popular and that in mainland China the government has dictated that in all major cities all bodies must be cremated. However, the Chinese often still seek very earnestly to have a gravesite for those cremains as they feel it a family duty to return to their ancestors' burial sites and bring offerings and remembrances.

I close this blog entry with a somber reflection on the death and cremation of our eldest son, David, just four years ago. My wife, Jane, and I took his cremains and decided to strew them in the sea at a spot we loved to enjoy viewing together from our balcony. That episode is fodder for another later blog. I am glad he was cremated and his remains are now part of the Pacific Ocean.

And this I believe: that while the mysteries of the after-life are many, the hope of the resurrection of the body whether after cremation or dissolution remains firm.

GROWING UP RACIST

On Dr. Martin Luther King Memorial weekend this year, I led an Adult Class at my church on the topic of racism. It once again caused me to confront the racism with which I grew up. I think it was unconscious and reflected the attitudes of all my acquaintances around me. In some ways it was not vicious or overtly destructive but it was there and it was wrong.

Of course, I never went to school with a black person, never worshipped with one, never played with or against one or knew a black person by name until I was in high school.

An early memory is that we knew of one black family that lived about five miles away close to the small town of Weir. The word was out that if anyone from that family came to the local Walburg Mercantile Store they had to be carefully watched, as they were sure to shoplift if they weren't monitored every minute. The mother of that family must have had a reason for her own actions toward us. I recall that as we sat in the back of a truck and drove by their home the mother had her children pull their pants down, turn their backs to us and expose their rear ends directly at us.

I also interacted a bit with a few black people when we visited at my Grandpa Kieschnick's farm. He had several black families living on his property. Some of them had been slaves or the children of slaves. I remember Grandpa as demonstrating benign benevolence. They paid no rent. Grandpa helped them out with their medical costs and paid them cash for work done on the farm. I know that when it was dinnertime, Grandma K always fed them a meal, she herself prepared. It was good solid food; however, it was not as choice as what we had at our table and the black people had to eat it at a table out on the porch, not with us.

All of this was in the context of very prevalent state and federal laws intended to preserve the superiority and purity of the white race. In 1930, for example, Alabama still had a law prohibiting white and black people to even play checkers or dominoes together. Another state law forbade blacks and whites to ride in the same boat or go fishing together. All railroads had to provide separate cars for black and for white people. All public restrooms were designated either "White" or "Colored." White baseball or other sports teams were not allowed to compete against black teams and no team could have blacks and whites on the same team.

I had never known of a black person who went to college or held a professional position like an attorney or medical doctor.

I had my eyes dramatically opened, with an incident when I was a high school sophomore in 1943. I was at worship at St. Paul Lutheran Church in Austin. A black serviceman who was a U.S. Air Force 1st Lieutenant entered the church with his black wife. They took their seat in the middle of the church. Very quickly two ushers came to them and asked them to leave. When I saw this my inner voice screamed, "This is not right!"

Also, during this time, I worked at Wukash Brothers Café on the main drag next to the University of Texas. If any black person came to order a meal or even an ice cream cone, they were asked to receive it "in the back - next to the alley." This again offended me, especially since I was working with a black gentleman dishwasher who was always kind, faithful, hardworking and nice to me, a silly teen-ager.

I am grateful that slowly I saw the errors of my ways and hopefully no longer practice racism. But I must confess that, as much as I hate it, there are still occasions where some of those old prejudices and misconceptions creep into some level of my consciousness. I ask God and my black brothers and sisters to forgive me. And I earnestly seek to now always be open to all people regardless of creed, color, or nationality and firmly and gratefully acknowledge that we are all equally created in the image of God.

෨෬

LET YOUR EARS DO THE TALKING

I have been asked to share a brief reflection at my church's Lenten supper next Wednesday. The topic is the charge given to the newly baptized to "Proclaim God's love in Christ in word and deed." When I saw that first word "PROCLAIM" I immediately realized that "proclaim" is not a welcome word to most people. It is not at all unusual to have people say that they are quite uncomfortable with making any public speech. An order with the word "proclaim" is likely to result in an initial response, "Not me! I am not a proclaimer!"

I am grateful that I learned long ago that sometimes our most powerful way to show God's love is by initially not proclaiming anything. Rather it is to just listen. That is why I truly believe that often the best way to proclaim God's love is to "Let Your Ears Do the Talking."

The power (yes, the ministry) of attending, of hearing, of active listening is sometimes the very best way of showing both human and divine love.

I recently did a little private experiment here at the retirement community at which my wife, Jane, and I live. I decided to either begin, or insert into a conversation, something about myself. It could be some experience I have had, some sharing of a previous encounter, an opinion about some current event or recalling a feeling I have been having. Then I would see if the person I was with would in any way follow-up on what I said. In the last 10 times I have done that, not once has the person really followed up on my lead. Instead the person(s) talked about their experience, their insight or thought. In one recent case both Jane and I tried at least three times to move the conversation to a piece of our life. In every case the other just went right back to their own train of thought!

I am sure that there are times when I too, failed to be a good listener. I do, however, place a high value on the importance of listening. For some reason or other I recall an experience of some 40 years ago. I was on a plane to Omaha, Nebraska. I had a speech to give and was going over my notes, not paying much attention to the woman seated to my left. However, I could not fail but notice that she was upset. So, I began with just a brief comment or "door-opener "as to whether she was afraid of flying. With just this little opening she began to speak, at first reluctantly, and then as I just listened, she let it all come out. She was worried, fearful, guilty, ashamed and more. She told me she was returning to the small town from which she had moved. She was returning there to see her father. She had to tell her father of her failed marriage and impending divorce. He would be upset - in fact - very upset, because in addition to caring for his daughter, he was the pastor - of a Lutheran Church-Missouri Synod congregation! I gave no advice, shared no comparable experience, and did not speak of my position. I just listened. By the time we reached our destination she had become composed. She asked if we could just have a brief prayer together just before we disembarked. I was grateful that I (at least on this one occasion) Let My Ears Do the Talking.

ℰℭ

WALKING WET

The baptism of an infant at my church recently was especially meaningful to me. The baby had two siblings who had joined the baptismal group around the baptismal font. When it came time for the actual baptism, the pastor asked the two little ones (about three and five years of age) to join in and to also sprinkle a bit of water on the head of their little sister as the pastor pronounced the words, "I baptize you in the name of the Father and of the Son and of the Holy Spirit." Then he took the infant in his arms and marched down the center aisle of the sanctuary. The beaming baby, still wet from the water, seemed angelic. It deeply touched me as I reflected that she was my sister in Christ. I tried to imagine the life that lay before her and the many joys and blessings she could bring to others. Her "Walking Wet" touched me deeply.

In my reverie I recalled another baptism now more than 50 years ago. It was an Easter service at Concordia Lutheran Church in Hong Kong. We baptized 200 students from the school of which I was principal. This was very significant. We enrolled around 2,000 students in that Kindergarten - Grade 12 school. New enrollees numbered only about 5% Christian. So, to add 200 or more baptized students to our enrollment meant a great deal. I wondered how they would make a difference. How would their classmates know that these friends were now baptized? I urged them to "Walk Wet." Just be what you are, a beloved child of God. Be honest in your schoolwork. Treat teachers and others with respect and kindness. Don't cheat. Use no bad language. Tell no dirty jokes. Tell others you love them. Remember to pray. Attend worship. Be pleased to tell others that you are baptized. Just "Walk Wet."

Now, these many years after that event, I find myself in a very different environment, a retirement community of some 900 residents. And I ask myself, "How many of the people here know me? Of those who do know me, how many know that I am a baptized Christian? How do I 'Walk Wet?' What words have I spoken, what actions have I taken, what behaviors have I demonstrated? How empathetically have I listened?" Of course, I realize I could do more things or say more words to "proclaim the love of God in Christ," but I am also grateful that in some small and big ways I am faithful to the baptismal call as, day by day, I try simply to "Walk Wet."

ॐ

SAY IT, "I LOVE YOU, SO DOES GOD."

One thing I have been absolutely sure of all my life is that my mother loved me. She certainly demonstrated that day after day, year after year. I was number three out of the nine children that she bore. It is impossible to count the number of loads of laundry she did, all before the days of automatic washers or dryers. Each of us kids took our turn at having the measles, whooping cough, mumps, and red-eye. I grew up during the Great Depression and even Dad's salary of $60 a month was not always paid, so she scrimped as she made us our daily portion of potatoes and gravy. And I will never forget her sound advice given to me when I was frustrated with our meager diet as she always said, "If you are hungry - then jelly bread tastes good." But three words I did not hear from her were "Melvin, I love you."

Maybe there was something in our German heritage that frowned upon expressions of endearment. Maybe it had not been the custom in her childhood. I just know that it was not part of my growing-up memories to hear those words. So, it is not surprising that it wasn't until I was in my late thirties and our family was going through some stressful times that I first recall her saying to me, "Melvin, I love you." And it was wonderful to hear those words - even if I had never doubted that truth.

Then, 10 years later, we had concluded a difficult talk in which I revealed that I was resigning a significant position in the Lutheran Church-Missouri Synod and was transferring to another Lutheran body, she said to me "Mel, I love you - and so does God."

I guess the fact that I remember those incidents today, decades later, proves how important they were to me. And they have been helpful to me in passing on to others. I have learned the lesson that at the appropriate time, I can assure another that I love them by saying those simple words, "I love you."

To add the expression, "And so does God,' is sometimes a vitally important addition. I think one must guard against using that phrase too flippantly or too causally as if it were just an everyday casual expression. But at the right moment, and said with genuine conviction, those four added words carry very special significance to the hearer. I know I have been told by others, "No one has ever before told me that they loved me and so does God."

One of the pledges of Christian baptism is that the baptized say that they will "Proclaim God's love in Christ through word and deed." One of the simplest and yet most profound way to do that is to simply and honestly say to another, "I love you. And so, does God."

ഇൽ

ORGAN RECITAL

I live in a senior retirement community. Small groups form in the dining room, around the coffee table or just casually in the corridors. One thing is the same: wherever two or three are gathered, an "organ recital" will be sure to happen. It may begin simply with, "My hearing is bad, so be sure to speak up." Within minutes all body organs will get their attention. Soon there will be early excuses to leave from the group because of incontinence and kidney weakness. Then the stories of lumps in the breasts of women and removal of the prostate from the men. It takes about 20 minutes to cover all the organs and then the recital moves to allergies. The list will include allergies to foods, to clothes, to smells, to an endless list of things tangible and intangible. It is important to go into details about how the stomach or the skin or the nose reacts. Unless something suddenly intervenes, the concert can last up to an hour. Efforts to change the subject to something important like baseball scores, the food in the common dining area, or trips taken, are all sure to fail. Organ recitals must take precedent. So, sit back and listen and resist the impulse to add your own encore!

ΣΟΩ

6/4 THIRTY YEARS LATER

The Chinese Government does not want to acknowledge the Tiananmen Massacre and the only reference one can find on the Chinese internet is under the designation 6/4 that stands for June 4, 1989, just 30 years ago. As I read the articles and look again at the photos my heart sinks and my total being recalls the feelings, sights, and sounds of that event.

I recall the incredible FEELING of hope that was alive in the square those days. Every student we spoke to, had the hope of more democracy, more freedom and greater prosperity. Yet, in the midst of that hope which we shared, we also had feelings of TREPIDATION. We knew that China was authoritarian, afraid of its own people and determined not to lose absolute power. Those feelings were quickly justified. On our return to the Beijing University campus in the afternoon, our bus was stopped. Citizens had heard the army was moving in and shooting to kill any civilians trying to stop them, even shooting and killing people on balconies who were observing the tragedy. The citizens wanted all buses (including the one we were in) to

321

block the military entrance. We were forced to stop in an intersection. Sons, John and Tim, and I quickly got out and walked back to the campus. Not many hours later, we were surrounded by students showing us the nametags of their killed comrades. They confronted us with pleas to contact the US government to intervene and stop the killings. Our hearts overflowed with sadness at the lives of old and young wiped out.

So many SIGHTS come back (without even needing the aid of photos). I can still see the goddess of democracy statue erected in the square, confronting the huge image of Mao Zedong just across Chang An Ave. I see the elderly woman brought to the Square in a wheelbarrow by her grandson, because he wanted her to get a view of democracy coming to her country. Then, I see all the destruction of the day after, the burned buses, the destroyed buildings, and the not-seeing of things we knew were there, bodies hanging from light posts.

I hear the SOUNDS. I hear the sounds coming over the loud speakers that the students had put in place, being careful not to interfere with the official sound system under the control of the authorities. I hear the sounds of excited students talking to son John, in Mandarin, and to Tim and me, in broken English, assuring us that for the first time in history, China was going to have a peaceful revolution because under no circumstances imaginable would the students resort to violence. Hours later I hear the sounds of students speaking through their devastation and tears, recalling classmates lying dead on the street or in the morgue. And after more than 48 torturous hours of non-communication, I hear Jane's voice on a long-distance call when, with the help of a young Chinese gentleman, I finally managed to get through (a man, who then refused to take my financial tip as a reward).

Now 30 years later I REFLECT. Deng Xioping who ordered his military to shoot and kill innocent civilians did have some (partially) redeeming actions. He opened up the economy, developing, for example, Shenzhen just across the border from Hong Kong, which is now exceeding Hong Kong in the volume of its exports. He took some of the manufacturing from very inefficient government-run companies, and allowed some aspects of capitalism to flourish. Now Premier Xi is again being extremely authoritarian, is removing freedoms, persecuting and killing Christians and Muslims, and is engaged in fierce competition with the USA president.

Yet I end with HOPE and the positive belief that the eternal human drive for freedom will eventually be heard and recognized. I am convinced that China will replace the USA as the greatest world power of the 21st Century, and I have the belief, that it will be a force for good in the world, that the

322

USA and China will not enter into a war against each other and that for many, the dream of a more positive future for more people around the world will yet come true.

(See previous blog entries: "Hope" and "Hope Shattered.")

੪੦੪

EBENEZER THANKOFFERING PART 1

It was late 1965. Our family was living in San Antonio, TX where Jane was dealing with a cranial aneurysm that doctors still feared might rupture at any time. My job future was uncertain. The hopes were that we could go back to continue working in Hong Kong. But every indication was that we would not be given medical clearance to return. The Mission Board was patient, gave me a couple short-term assignments, and we waited.

Then one morning I received a phone call. It was from Dr. Martin Koehneke, president of Concordia University Chicago, who was on leave, working for a US senator in Washington D.C. "Mel," he said to me, "I want you to grab a plane and come see me. Get an early flight. We will talk for two hours, and then you can return on the same day." I tried to analyze that request. But very soon I had bought and used my ticket, and was with him in Washington.

He explained that the Lutheran Church-Missouri Synod was about to undertake a churchwide fund-raising effort, that he was the director of that effort and he wanted me to be a part of his four-person leadership team. I was to be the Director of Organizational Services, whatever that might mean. I accepted.

Dr. Koehneke had a radical idea for a fundraiser. He was not going to use the usual tactic of first getting the majority of the funds from major donors and then reaching out more generally. He was not going to stress the need for funds, but rather he was going to stress the need to give as an expression of gratitude for gifts received. The primary leadership for the whole effort was to come from lay persons rather than the clergy. And the name of the project was going to have the strange moniker of EBENEZER, remembering a stone by that name that the ancient prophet Saul had erected with words "Hitherto has the Lord helped me." The theme hymn was going to be "The Lord has helped me hitherto."

Another major new idea. The project would use the resources of the just-newly-developing technology called computers. The plan was to have each of the 6,000 congregations of the LCMS submit the names, addresses, home mailing addresses and birthdays of all of their members. Using computer technology, these would all be entered into a massive database. Then, on the date of each person's birthday, they would receive a card and an invitation to express gratitude for the gifts in their lives by sending in a gift. The size of the gift was to be calculated by taking one's age and multiplying that by any number one chose and to then send in that amount of dollars for a Thank Offering.

My job was to put together, train and mobilize the organization needed to support this effort. The entire denomination was divided into seven regions: each region had about five districts, each district having about 175 congregations and each congregation having about 330 members. So, we wanted to gather some 3 million names. My goal was to find, and train and support the Regional Directors, and then help them do the same for a director for each district, and each district director was to, hopefully identify a director in each congregation and each congregation would select a director for each month of the year.

The hope was that each congregation would list and honor all persons who shared a birthday month and stress that this year they would show their gratitude for another year of blessings by sending in a gift in response to the greetings they received in the mail from the national office.

଼ଓଋ

EBENEZER THANKOFFERING PART 2

As mentioned in Part I the use of a computer system for a church wide mailing was a new and unheard-of endeavor in 1965. When I was taken to the IBM center, which we contracted to do this task for us, I was shown a line of computers that stretched some 30 feet long and 6 feet high. The close to two million names, addresses and birthdates were all entered via punch cards. There were many errors and a near-full-time person worked for months just to make the corrections

In the year prior to the actual offerings, I worked to establish and support the effort's organizational structure. It was wonderful to identify and support a vast cadre of outstanding laymen (and they were all men) around the country. I spoke at District Conventions from Edmonton to New York to

324

Orlando to Los Angeles to Little Rock and many in between.

Co-workers Dave Stein, Robert Hopmann, Max Heinz and Donna Behnken were capable and marvelous colleagues. Marty Koehneke kept us strong and exemplified faith and courage.

As soon as the offering mailing began to roll in, we discovered a significant problem. The return envelopes had poor sealing wax and some envelopes returned open - so we did not know if we lost any contributions. We fixed that.

Many congregations did a great job of celebrating members' birthdays and we received wonderful stories of grateful expressions. However, we were deeply disappointed at both the rate of return and the size of the average gift. At the end of the effort we had raised some $15 million.

Sometime after the effort, the official magazine of the LCMS declared our work "a disastrous debacle" (or something like that) because it failed to reach our goal of $40 million. I have a different view. Those $15 million in 1965, have a 2019 equivalency of some $120 M. A significant moment came to me several years later. The Chinese Headmaster of Concordia Lutheran School in Taiwan came to embrace me with the words, "Sir, I cannot thank you enough for your fund-raising efforts. Because of EBENEZER we were able to build our entire school, complete with dormitories for live-in students. We are now one of the premier schools in all of Taiwan teaching students English and the Christian faith." And because of the money we raised many others throughout the world can still daily exclaim "EBENEZER. The Lord has helped us hitherto."

જીભ્ર

EBENEZER THANKOFFERING PART 3: IMPACT ON FAMILY

In my previous blog entries I have commented upon my work on the staff for the EBENEZER Thankoffering. This blog will reflect upon how assuming that position affected our family. As indicated in Part I of this series we suddenly found ourselves resettling in the Chicago area and specifically on Iowa Street in the suburb of Maywood.

We found a very supportive community of colleagues and friends. A woman named Mable Warnke, whom we had first met when she was a tourist visiting us in Hong Kong, was always there. She was aware of Jane's limitations because of her health. Mrs. Warnke brought us many household appliances. She frequently brought food. She helped identify sources for medical prescriptions, she came to the house and did most of the clothes ironing which was still required in those says. Whatever was needed she provided.

The wives of faculty members of Concordia Teachers College-River Forest (now Concordia University Chicago) took turns baby-sitting when Jane had medical appointments, introduced us to the best places for shopping, provided items for our house to replace those left behind in Hong Kong. The pastors and teachers of St. Paul's Lutheran Church and School in Melrose Park just did whatever was needed, especially also helping our kids move from a British to an American school system.

Of course, there were challenges, many of them similar to what other people faced and still face. My duties took me away from home a great deal, often by plane. This became painfully clear one day when Jane pointed out an airplane that was overhead. Son Tim, who was about five years of age at the time said, "I hate airplanes!" Jane replied, "You don't like airplanes?" Tim's response, "I don't like airplanes at all. They always take my father away from me."

We chose to add another challenge. Three of our kids went to Texas to spend Christmas with Grandma and Grandpa Kieschnick. Just before returning we got a long-distance phone call with an urgent plea, "We have just found the most wonderful, the cutest, the most loving little dog in the world. Can we bring him home? Please, Please!" We explained it would be hard to get the dog on the plane. There was no yard or fence where we lived, etc. etc. Two day later Tex was happily rampaging through our house. Unfortunately, he also liked to rampage in the neighborhood and slipped out any moment a door was left often. It became a ritual. The phone call to Jane, "Mrs. Kieschnick, your dog is here at school again." I had the car at the office so, ailing Jane walked that three-quarter of a mile to the school, rain or shine, with toddler John, in a stroller, to pick up "that cute little MONSTER."

Yet, all in all, our days in the Chicago area were good days. Later our first grandchild was born there to daughter Peggy. And son David lived happily in Chicago for some 20 years. Chicago is still my kind of town!

෩ශ

WORLD CONFERENCE

While winding down my assignments for EBENEZER, I was blessed to concurrently be doing something else which had been a decade-long dream of mine: organizing and chairing a World Conference on Lutheran Education with an emphasis on schools. With the support and generous funding from the Board for World Missions, the gathering took place in Hong Kong in 1968.

After most insightful end-route stops in Lebanon and India, I called the gathering to order at the Hong Kong International School (HKIS) in Hong Kong. Present were Lutheran school leaders from the USA, Japan, Hong Kong, the Philippines, India, Ghana, Nigeria, Argentina, Brazil and New Guinea. Top Lutheran education leaders of Lutheran constituents around the world, including Martin Koehneke, James Mayer, Walter Wangerin, Francis Schaeffer, Delbert Schultz and Bruno Reith, shared insights.

Walter Wangerin conducted powerful morning worship services at the beautiful new chapel of HKIS. A most inspiring aspect of each morning's worship was that the entire group gathered in a circle around the altar and shared the Eucharist, for which, the words of consecration had been spoken in a different language by each person using his own native tongue.

Each country's representative had the opportunity to speak of the successes and challenges of the Lutheran schools in their particular country. These varied greatly and ranged from very simple literacy efforts among the aborigines of New Guinea, through schools for low caste poor people of India, to the high American university admission st   of HKIS. Daily Bible studies were led by Koehneke. At the conclusion of the conference, the representatives adopted a "Manifesto on Christian Education."

Hong Kong was the ideal site for this event. V   procured. The beautiful Repulse Bay Hotel was perfect for   d was within walking distance at the HKIS meeting site. The entire group shared a most enlightening tour of the Lutheran Schools of Hong Kong, which included the prestigious Concordia Lutheran School and the very humble roof-top Boys and Girl Clubs, and ended with all doing their best at utilizing the chop sticks provided for a sumptuous 12-course closing Chinese feast.

Tragically, a few years later a new Mission Board disagreed with the Manifesto and broke off all official relations with many of the fellow Lutherans who had attended the conference. Yet for a few shining days, Lutherans from around the world gathered and supported one another in their shared goal of building schools designed to ensure that each student had the opportunity to encounter a loving God who had come to set them free and desired that each one more nearly become all that God intended them to be.

ℰᏮ

SUPERINTENDENT OF MICHIGAN DISTRICT LUTHERAN SCHOOLS

As I was nearing the end of my service on behalf of the EBENEZER Thankoffering, I was very unsure as to what my next calling would be. Then suddenly I had two very attractive offers. The first came from Concordia University: Chicago. It was a professor position in the education department with the quiet understanding that I would immediately complete my Ph.D. studies for which the University would provide funds. The indication was that a long-term administrative position was envisioned for me.

The second call, was to serve as Director of Christian Education and Superintendent of Lutheran Schools for the Michigan District of the LCMS.

It was a tough decision. I chose the latter because I wanted a closer, more direct connection with teachers and their schools. It was a good decision. My four years in Michigan were very satisfying and fulfilling.

I succeeded Dr. Sam Roth who had served the District for tens of years. He was great – and - it was time for fresh blood and new energy. It was also extremely fortunate that the two associate director positions were open and the District was very open to my input on who that would be.

I was blessed to work with three outstanding colleagues. Don Kell had been a very successful principal and his expertise was exactly in those areas where I felt weaker. Roland Boehnke had been a very successful parish pastor with special skills in relating to young adults. And Elinor Donohue continued in her role as Administrative Assistant and she was the best.

The District had 117 schools headed by 116 male and one female principal. They were always responsive and actually appreciated our visits to their schools - which they saw as support and not as threat.

I spent a great deal of time in government relations - always working with the Michigan Association of Non-Public Schools, which included Lutheran, Catholic, many Christian and some independent schools. These contacts got me on a special education committee of the State Senate and eventually also an appointment with then-President Nixon. Equally unusual was that I was probably the only Lutheran ever invited to attend a national meeting of all the Catholic bishops of the USA.

The Lutheran schools shared a great diversity, ranging from - the incredibly well-designed, fully-equipped, generously-congregation-funded school of St. Lorenz in Frankenmouth - to Gethsemane Lutheran School in inner city Detroit with and a student body fully dependent upon tuition. The rest of the schools were everything in between. I had a special love for the urban schools and so it hurts me deeply to report that of the 17 Lutheran schools in Detroit, that we served then - not a single one is still in operation today.

Another disappointment: We succeeded in getting the State legislature to approve A financial subsidy for non-public schools and actually received our first very-generous allocation. Then a constitutional amendment (Proposition C), to ban all aid to non-public schools, was then passed by a statewide referendum and we lost all further state funding.

A couple non-district positions, that I held during that time included serving as the national Vice-Chair for the Citizens for Education Freedom Foundation and Chair of the Conference of Education Executives of the LCMS. There I worked with experts who are still remembered for their competence and dedication including Ben Eggers, Dean Dammann, Wally Hartkopf, Dick Engebrecht, Art Wittmer, Don Rosenberg, Ed Keuer, Eldor Kaiser, Willie Tewes and others.

We served congregations and schools small and large from inner-city Detroit to the smallest towns - and what still amazes me: I usually was there exactly on time - as the state of Michigan Highway Department did an incredible job of keeping the roads open, even after a couple feet of snow fell unexpectedly.

ഇറര

FAMILY LIFE IN ANN ARBOR IN THE LATE '60s

As reflected upon in my previous blog entry, my four years as Superintendent of Lutheran Schools of Michigan was a great experience. One aspect of that which I did not mention was that this was from 1968-72, years of great turmoil, unrest, assassinations, urban riots, weed-smoking long-haired college students, etc. etc. Since Ann Arbor is, of course, the home of the University of Michigan, we were in the midst of it all.

I remember 17-year-old son David agreeing that I could join him as we headed toward the U of M campus to experience my one and only rock concert. We were still quite a way off when the aroma of smoking weed filled the atmosphere.

Peggy went to a public junior high. She said that she had to learn which girls' bathroom to avoid and when to say, "Hi" walking down a corridor and when to just look straight ahead. But she had found the one rest room, which was safe to use, and she always found that. On the other hand, I recall a different very good experience with Peggy. It was a Saturday night and she had attended a house party with friends and, when it was time to be over, I drove and picked her up. As I watched the partygoers leave, I noticed that the youth seemed to all be black - and a few Chinese. When Peggy got into the car, I asked her, "Where you the only white person at this party?" She reflected for a moment, surprised by my question, and then said, "Yes, Dad, I guess I was. I never noticed."

Ann Arbor provided the first opportunity for son, Tim, to play Little League baseball and I was always impressed by the energy and enthusiasm he brought to that and to the basketball court of St. Paul's Lutheran School. What he lacked in size he made up for with energy, zest and real commitment to the game. I also clearly recall two goals he had at the time, namely, to play on the U of M football team and to then also play in the U of M Marching Band for the half-time show.

Liz had to endure a very authoritarian teacher who forced her into silence that was not over until she finally got Mrs. Foelber as her teacher and that was great. Liz's flute playing was exceptional and she was often in concerts.

John had a ball as he joined his best friend Bruce as they explored and built fortresses in the big open-spaced field just across the street from our home. I also recall that once, when he got bored in kindergarten, he just left the campus and walked the short distance away to where he was sure that his brother David was doing some lawn maintenance.

Jane kept on healing and fighting weight gain later to be discovered caused by a drug she was taking. She was always taking the kids to one place or another. It was great for her and me to head to Frankenmuth for some Zehnder's chicken. She probably saved her neighbor's life. One day little 4-year-old Amy came over from next door crying, "My mommy needs you!" Jane hurried over to discover that her Mom had, in fact, attempted suicide brought on by post-partum depression. Her life was saved.

A few years ago, Jane and I revisited our home there on Nixon St. We were thrilled to see the two little evergreen trees that Tim had planted. They were now (50 years later) fully grown and adding a stately presence to the entire back yard.

ℰↃↄℛ

EDUCATION EXECUTIVE FOR LCMS

After only four years as Superintendent of Lutheran Schools for the state of Michigan, I took the position of Executive Secretary for the Board of Parish Education of The Lutheran Church-Missouri Synod. I took the position even though I had been in Michigan only four years. I took the position knowing that it was the "highest office" available to any "called teacher" of the LCMS. I took the call at the urging of even my colleagues in Michigan because they felt they wanted a voice at the highest levels of the church. I rook the call even though I knew the LCMS had just elected a new President who had vowed to radically change everything in the church. I took the call because I felt it came through the work of the Holy Spirit.

There were some great things about my years in St. Louis. I had an incredibly supportive and capable staff of some 45 persons. During my tenure there, we were able to carry on or introduce many effective new ministries: we added an Associate Director for Schools, a Director for Early Childhood Education, a Director of Effectiveness Training for Lutherans (which was the Lutheran version of Parent Effectiveness). We provided excellent week-long couples training for pastors and their spouses. We conducted nationwide Sunday School conventions. We gained an important voice in Washington DC through the Council for American Private Education. I was invited to speak at important Christian education events around the world. I carried on or introduced very exciting new joint ministries with the then American Lutheran Church and The Lutheran Church in America. Together we produced some exciting material and events to deal with urban America and with people of color or language other than English. I was named head of the entire Division for Parish Services and had important input on the annual expenditure of some $28 million of church-wide funding. I was able to secure several hundred thousand dollars' worth of grants from "outside sources." I was a part of group of church leaders who had a great inclusive vision of a church grounded in the Good News of God in Christ, working together with fellow Christians, across the USA and around the world, for people of all ages and ethnicity or color.

331

And those four years were by far the worst four years of my life and if I had not resigned when I did, I may well have died of a heart attack or similar at the age of 49. As mentioned above, a new president had been elected and he and his supporters were determined to get rid of any staff or point of view that was incoherent to their very fundamentalistic theology, centralized power, and narrow vision of the church. I need not go into detail, I will simply state that when I was asked to sign a statement which forbade me to continue my work with non-LCMS Lutheran leaders, to never consider any biblical interpretation of Bible other than literal, to publicly pray only with LCMS Lutherans, to not attend Holy Communion anywhere other than in LCMS churches, etc. I could not accept those conditions of my employment and so I resigned. Tragically, I had also to terminate the calls to ministry of many staff members who had been faithful servants of the church.

In retrospect, I am grateful for the experience even though I feel that I was unsuccessful in my attempt to bring reconciliation to a fractured church. I learned anew the powerful message that is central to my faith. God is love. God is good. God reaches out to all God's children with grace, acceptance and hope. That is the God I worship and the God who sustains and drives me and all that I undertake.

೮ාҨ

FAMILY LIFE IN ST LOUIS YEARS

I recall with regret that I was not a good husband and father while I served the church for four years in St. Louis. I was so preoccupied with the challenges of my calling and all the turmoil in the denomination that I was not either physically or emotionally as available to my family as I should have been. Instead of me being the primary support for my spouse, it was she who was ministering to me. I went for a couple years without once sleeping through the night. I worked way too many hours per week and was away from home too many days.

Meanwhile the lives of my wife and children continued. David, our eldest, was doing exceptionally well academically and was elected student body president of Concordia University Chicago (just as his father had been in 1950 and his grandfather in 1920). And he was faced with the reality that if he came out publicly as a gay person, he would immediately be barred from serving as a rostered minister of the church into which he had been baptized.

Tim and Peggy were a bit on the fringe of things at Lutheran High South as they advocated for persons who were continuously being fired from their calling at the church headquarters and seminary. Then they got wonderful financial aid at Valparaiso University and were outstanding students there (with Tim surviving being jailed for an ill-considered entry into an unoccupied campus building). And Peggy, must have been the youngest freshman there when she enrolled as a 16-year-old college freshman - having been in advanced placement classes when she first started school back in Hong Kong. Liz and John had mixed experiences at the Lutheran elementary school they attended - as John had a very controlling and fundamentalist teacher and Liz had encouraging, evangelical, caring and competent ones.

Jane had the new experience of living in the first house that we were actually purchasing, and even that got off to a bad start. The people from whom we bought the home could not get occupancy in the new home they were building, so they and we lived together for some six weeks! Jane also faced the difficult reality that she listened to the cries (especially of wives) of co-workers who were all being evacuated from their homes at the directive of the then church leaders. She was powerless to do anything about it. She had to resist the urge to just go to downtown St. Louis with a protest sign in her hand. The stress level reached a new high when she got a phone call with the voice on the other end anonymously announcing, "You are a terrible Mother. What your children are doing in supporting heretics, will lead them straight to hell. And you will be the one who put them there!" The good news is that she also had a marvelous support group of a few women who joined her not only in tears but also in great moments of shared conversation, Bible study, music, laughter and mutual support. In the midst of all this, she found time to host my staff of over 45 for annual Christmas party meals and to provide room and board for two students who had to leave their dorm rooms at the seminary.

It is now 40 years ago that my family and I experienced our years in St. Louis. We choose to remember the support of friends; the joy of visiting the Budweiser Clydesdale horses that were pastured just down the street from our home; the great love and care extended to us by many; and, new and deeper insights into the power of the Gospel and the ever-growing conviction that the church must be a place where all are welcomed and open to the incredible ways in which the Spirit gives life and hope.

PARENT EFFECTIVENESS TRAINING

When I resigned my position as Executive Director of Parish Education for The Lutheran Church, I had no other job offering. However, almost immediately I received a wonderful opportunity. I was asked to be the director of a program called Parent Effectiveness Training (PET). This program, developed by Dr. Thomas Gordon, was and is, by far, the most widely used program ever carried out to assist parents to be the best possible parents. I had met Dr. Gordon when we, at the Board for Parish Education, adopted his model for the parent training we offered throughout the Lutheran Church. His financial advisor Thomas Blakistone had taken a liking for me and my set of talents and strongly advised him to hire me for this position.

Our model consisted of us providing teaching instructions and materials to be used in classes that typically ran for three hours per session for eight periods. Classes were taught by persons we trained in intensive full weeklong instructor training workshops held - first in the USA and then, around the world. Parents paid a fee to take the course. The instructor used our model and our materials and sent us a fee for each participant. It was a multi-million-dollar operation and eventually was and is in practice around the world.

Key concepts that were taught included how to listen to and assist children experiencing personal problems. A key tool: active listening. We also stressed that unacceptable behavior needed to be confronted (without corporal punishment) with assertive I-messages. Conflicts were to be resolved in a no-lose (win-win) manner. Values are important and values collisions between parents and children must be satisfactorily resolved and communication skills for that were taught.

The model was adapted and taught for applications in other relationships and the courses were called Teacher Effectiveness Training, Youth Effectiveness Training, Leader Effectiveness Training, Clergy Effectiveness Training and Effectiveness Training for Women. I had partners for each of those programs, plus a full-time editor, and about half a dozen other staff.

I thoroughly enjoyed doing some of the training myself - and conducted training for both instructors and parents. To this day (some 40 years later) one of the really great satisfactions I get is, when people hear that I was associated with PET, they tell me: "It changed my life. I learned then how to have great relationships with my kids and now that extends to my grandchildren!"

Another great satisfaction came from teaching Clergy Effectiveness. I taught this to leaders in all the major denominations and US military chaplains. Also my role took me to many countries around the world and I negotiated contracts or taught in Germany, Sweden, Norway, France the Netherlands, Switzerland, Finland, Pakistan, and China. PET continues to be adapted and used around the world in many languages and its current directors are Dr. Gordon's widow, Linda Adams, and step-daughter Michelle Adams.

One of the many lessons I learned while holding this position, is that almost 100% of parents love their children and want to do a good job of raising them. They believe this is one of life's most important duties. Yet there is almost never any formal training for this vital task and many parents feel that they are failing to be as effective in their parenting role as they would like. For me to have spent eight years helping parents be the kinds of parents they really desired to be, is indeed a most rewarding experience and I have many good memories of that period in my life.

ഇരു

FAMILY LIFE DURING PARENT EFFECTIVENESS YEARS

Working for PET involved moving our family from St. Louis to the San Diego CA area and specifically to Encinitas. Our first arrival there as a family had a moment of anxiety and then a roar of laughter. I had gone to California and purchased a house without Jane or family seeing it. When we arrived there just ahead of the moving van, I was excited to proudly show off our new home. So, I was stunned with their initial reaction. We pulled into the driveway. The family got out of the car. Then in unison they groaned, "Oh, No, Dad. Not this!" I was devastated for just five seconds. Then they all burst out laughing. They had conspired (under Jane's direction) to play this trick on me. The house was great. We found schools for the kids, a church for all of us, new doctors and the beach.

After a while Jane began working at the Effectiveness Training offices (not reporting to me). She assisted with the operations of Instructor Training which took place all across the USA. Then she became assistant to Linda Adams for Effectiveness Training for Women. Of major impact in those years (the late 1970's early 80's) was the introduction of computers into the workplace. Our offices acquired computers and then with zero training handed them over to office staff (including Jane) to figure out how use them. (For security reasons the instruction manuals were stored off-site in a locked box!) Jane learned computer skills very well. She consistently improved upon and expanded her expertise, eventually setting up all kinds of systems and today in our retirement community is considered our floor computer guru.

Dave had a dramatic job shift in Chicago. For a few years, he left working with street kids to become an exec for a company that ran exclusive stores selling high-quality furs to women. Soon he was flying corporate jets to places from Las Vegas to New York. Peg and Tim continued at Valparaiso University with an interesting stopover on their way home for Christmas. They traveled by Greyhound bus. They had a stop in Salt Lake City. They discovered that close to the bus station the Mormon Tabernacle Choir was about to have a concert. They changed their tickets, went to the concert and came home to San Diego a bit late but had a great experience. Liz did very well in school, greatly enjoyed Moonlight Beach, was student body president and had lots of great social times in the vast bonus room on the second floor of our home. She went to college at Claremont McKenna College. John was pretty bored with school, but got into duplicating famous paintings on the walls of bedrooms both at home and for others, developed in interest in Mandarin Chinese, applied for university at only one place, U of California Berkeley and got accepted.

We "adopted" an exchange student from Venezuela, Eliana Odreman. That was a good experience for all of us. Tragically she is now in Venezuela struggling with all the unrest and chaos of that country and we feel powerless to assist her.

We enjoyed our years in Encinitas. The California climate and multiple activity options were very satisfying. When we left after eight years, we, even then, had the feeling that someday we would like to return there for a satisfying retirement. But first, to New York.

ಜೋಡ

NEW YORK SCHOOLS ASSOCIATION AND URBAN CENTER

Parent Effectiveness gained such a wide acceptance that a national writer even called it a "national movement." But it is hard to maintain such a phenomenon. My staff and I struggled to maintain and grow the movement and were not succeeding. In spite of our significant efforts and generous use of funds for consultants and specialized staff, slowly the number of participants and dollars began to decline. The growth in foreign participants was significant, but unfortunately that did not generate income at the same rate as in the USA. I felt a deep sense of responsibility to the staff and became increasingly frustrated at my failure to grow the program. Maybe it was time for someone else to try his or her hand.

At that time, I received an unexpected invitation from Dr. Les Bayer and Dr. Richard Engebrecht from New York. They both urged me to get back into a leadership position within the Lutheran school system of the world. They came up with an offer that was both scary and challenging. They urged me to come and be the part-time Director of the the Lutheran Schools Association of New York and the Director of Projects for the newly formed Center for Urban Education Ministries (CUEM). There was one major catch: neither of the two organizations really had any money. The LSA had some $15,000 in its bank account and the CUEM depended upon regularly writing grants and the continued financial support of a visionary couple: Charles and Mary Gundelach. So, they made me an offer. Come to New York. We can guarantee you $25,000 a year - but you will be free to use half of your time to do your own thing of consulting, speaking or whatever you need to do to get enough money to make it. With the incredible support of an ever-faithful Jane, I accepted.

Our eight years in New York were wonderful. The challenges of running some 50 Lutheran schools in the metropolitan New York community were formidable. Parents had high and varied expectations. The student bodies and staff were extremely multi-cultural (Queens Lutheran School had some 16 different native languages spoken by their students). The principals were challenged beyond what most people could imagine. So, my major focus was simply on supporting those principals. We organized and maintained mutual support groups. We arranged for events that built morale and acknowledged the significant contributions they were making to church and society. We chose to be available 24 hours a day to address needs. We kept busy traveling to Albany to keep strong and supportive relationships with the State Education Department and the State Superintendent of Public Schools. We made sure that Catholics, Lutheran, Christian and Jewish leaders supported one another.

The Center for Urban Education took the learnings from New York and shared them across the country. We addressed a new major change in local Lutheran school leadership with the emergence of female administrators,

337

where for decades the principal had always been a male. We helped Lutheran schools across the country change their funding model from dependence upon local congregation support to being self-supporting through tuition and ever on-going local development and even government support. We helped teachers learn to adjust to multi-cultural classrooms with students coming from all of the world religions or from non-religious families. It was all very challenging and exciting. We gathered the top principals of urban Lutheran schools nationwide in special convocations for mutual support, affirmation and inspiration

We raised money through grants from Thrivent, the Lutheran Women's Missionary League, individual donors, golf tourneys, fund-raising dinners, etc. etc. I was able to find alternative sources for my personal income. I became a staff associate for Wheat Ridge Ministries (now We Raise); I spoke at events across the country; did consulting and training events for a variety of agencies around the world; and served as a part-time staff assistant to Bishop Lazarus of the ELCA Metro New York Synod.

Housing in New York was even more expensive than in California. We were first assisted by Dr. Ralph Schulz, president of Concordia New York, who made faculty housing available for us. Then an incredible, if sad, coincidence enabled us to purchase a nice home. A young man who been in my youth group at Glendale Cal. in the 1950's had accepted a position at Concordia New York. Then tragically he and his wife were killed when their private plane crashed. Their home became available and the family sold it to us at a most generous price. My wife Jane and our kids refurbished the house basement and turned it into the office for LSA and provided it rent-free to LSA for all those eight years.

I loved New York and I was thrilled to be part of an education ministry which endeavored to make life better for those living in the major urban concentrations in the USA - especially those in underserved community where the challenges and the can-do attitude of the multi-ethnic families is a constant source of my admiration and respect.

ജേരു

NEW YORK YEARS

The eight years Jane and I spent in New York were full, full, full!! It all started when Jane became architect, electrician, carpenter and computer guru as we set up offices in the basement of our home. She put up wall paneling, rewired the whole basement, laid new carpeting - and then set up a new computer system. To this day we recall, how in those early days of 1984, she explored computer options and even installed a very special Bernoulli Box to store all of our data. Then she took over as LSA Office Manager and Editor of the LSA Newsletter. In between, she fielded telephone calls from upset parents of kids in Lutheran schools as we had an agreement with the NY State Education Dept. that any complaints they received, would automatically be referred to the LSA office. There, Jane responded with powerful active listening skills and empathic understanding.

Our five kids were going through their own transitions - gaining new partners, children and occupations. Liz got married in New York while John did the same in Taiwan. Grandchildren were welcomed in Chicago and Michigan.

We (I more than Jane) loved the city of New York and tried to take it all in. It was always great to see the Christmas lights in Times Square. Worship and prayer were very meaningful at St. Patrick Cathedral and the Cathedral of St. John the Divine. Half-price tickets lured us to the Broadway productions. Yankee Stadium, Shea Stadium and Madison Square Garden were all places for special sporting events. Museums and art galleries of all kinds, and restaurants with every conceivable food option were right there. This was prior to the 9-11 tragedy, so we always took our guests for cocktails at the top of the World Trade Center and we even hosted a very special luncheon for Lutheran principals there.

We left New York to explore the world. Either just I, or sometimes the two of us, went to Pakistan, Canada, Finland, Germany, Switzerland, Hong Kong, Taiwan, Maui and Kauai, Puerto Rico, Bermuda, and the Virgin Islands. Unfortunately, Jane had to endure three days of incredible anxiety when our sons and I got caught up in the Tiananmen Square Massacre in China and were unable to communicate. So, she had no idea where we were or even if we had survived. As I reflect upon our years together in New York, I do so with great satisfaction and gratitude. They were years of special bonding between Jane and me. It was a time to meet, work with, support and be supported by a great variety of good people and to celebrate exceptional experiences. It was also while I was in New York, that I turned 65 and decided it was time to retire.

ഇ൦ര

CHICKENS

Chickens. That may seem a strange topic for a blog entry, but I relish it. Chickens have been and continue to be an important part of my life. Yet what really brought this topic to my mind was a recent surprise. Jane and I were having dinner (steak) at a friend's home. At the backyard of her suburban home I spied a chicken, "Oh yes," she said, "that is Rosie my wonderful friend." Subsequent conversation revealed that Rosie was a friend, someone to be looked after, taken into the house at night, prepared for bed and made comfortable so it could have a good night's sleep. That was a new way of looking at a chicken.

I grew up with lots of chickens outside that rural teacherage in Walburg, Texas. We raised chickens to provide us with the eggs we ate some 365 days a year. It was the chickens that my mother fried for us accompanied by mashed potatoes and cream gravy, that delighted my soul and sustained my body through years of the Great Depression. Mother would go out, grab a chicken, cut its head off with a small hatchet, pluck its feathers, cut it up, cover it with flour and then deep-fry it in lard. My dream of heaven is that God uses that recipe for dinner in heaven.

Chickens also meant a lot of work, much of it messy. As winter came to an end, I was assigned the task of cleaning out the little shed where we had stored the wood for the fire that kept us warm when a "norther" blew in. Then dad would go somewhere and bring back 100 or so tiny, day-old newly hatched baby chickens. They needed to be kept secure from coyotes and hawks, fed daily and assured enough water. When they were old enough, they joined the rest of their family in the big chicken house next to the barn. There they laid their eggs, served as a source of entree for many meals, sometimes hatched their descendants and always made a mess. It was a part of my assignment from as early as I can remember to scoop up that mess and keep the place reasonably clean. This took on immense proportions when, as an eleven-year-old, I helped Aunt Elizabeth Sieck, who ran a commercial chicken business. I scraped more chicken dirt than I even want to recall.

In Hong Kong we ate lots of chicken. Sometimes our Chinese cook would go to market and buy a live one and prepare it. Raw, as well as cooked chickens, were always hung outside the shops in the market. Every 10 course Chinese feast had at least one chicken course. Our son David went to the market, bought a young live chicken and placed it up on the flat roof of our apartment with the dream that it would be the beginning of his booming business. Unfortunately, the heat of Hong Kong had killed that chicken before the week was out.

Now raising and selling chickens is a major worldwide immense business with fast-food chains finding new ways to serve parts of chicken in all kinds of variations. Chicken parts are distributed internationally, and chicken raising has become a focal point of disagreement, not only among gourmet cooks but also among environmentalists, vegetarians and animal-rights groups.

In the midst of all this, Rosie found a friend who secured her safely in bed, that is until tragically one night she slipped out and became a late-night dinner for a neighborhood coyote.

၈၀၉၃

SPANKING CHILDREN

I read two sentences last week that really impacted me. The first, "The more you whip your children, the better they will turn out." And, "Love is not only an emotion. It is also a skill." The first one just made me cringe. There is overwhelming evidence that that statement is not true. Yet it seems that many people do believe it and they argue (and even quote Bible verses to justify it) that spanking is a good option for parents. I regret to say that I did spank a couple of our children and even spanked a first-grader in my first year of teaching.

When I did it and when many parents do it today, they will say that it is an act of love and I do not argue against that. But I do want to point out that even though it may be motivated by love that does not justify it. Love is not enough. Love is also a skill. My experience is that most parents who spank do that because they have not learned other more suitable options. They believe that the only alternative to spanking is permissiveness. They are wrong.

In my many years of doing parent training around the world, one important lesson I learned, is that almost all parents do indeed love their children. I also learned that they have had no formal training in how to raise them. Thus, they rely on what they recall about their own childhood, either copying or else rejecting how they were raised. In that process parents tend to move into one of two opposite directions: They become quite authoritarian relying on rewards and punishment, including spanking, or they go the other way and become entirely too permissive. Both approaches are ineffective. Incidentally, I noticed that this was most obvious in recent child raising practices in China. Under the former one-child policy each couple was permitted only one child. In some cases, the parents said, "This is the only child we will ever have. We will give the child anything and everything he wants. We will never spank the child or deny him his way." Other parents said, "This is the only child we will ever have. He will be the bearer of our family name. He must be an upright good citizen and we will ensure that by being very strict and super-controlling. Any misstep will be physically punished."

There is, of course, a third way. It is the process I taught and still believe in called Parent Effectiveness Training. It teaches child-raising techniques based on mutual respect. It teaches parents how to listen when a child is experiencing a personal problem. It teaches effective non-punitive confrontation of unacceptable behavior. It provides skills for win-win solving of conflicts. It gives lessons in sharing values. With the incredible partnership with Jane, that is how we raised our five children and how I hope they raised or are raising our eight grandchildren and our great-grandson.

∞∞

REMEMBERING HOWIE CAPELL

I write this on 9-11-19 remembering that sad and infamous day 18 years ago. Sadness continues to overwhelm me as I recall all those innocent victims. I recall especially also those 60 children, who were all students in the Lutheran Schools of New York, who on that day lost either a parent or a grandparent. I recall those trapped, those who leapt to their death. And I recall the public servants who did all they could to assist. Painfully I remember those misguided men who perpetrated this unthinkable evil and did it in the name of God.

I remember with special admiration and gratitude the many who rendered all kinds of supportive services to those so terribly affected by this event. I recall with special gratitude and admiration the incredible work of Lutheran Disaster Relief New York under the extremely capable leadership of John Scibilia.

In the midst of the throng that passes by in my mental image I recall one who, was not at the Twin Towers that day but later assisted many of those affected by that disaster, HOWARD CAPELL. Howie was an incredibly gifted and big-hearted New York lawyer. Howie was my personal lawyer and he was the official lawyer for The Lutheran Schools Association and of many other Lutheran friends, churches and schools.

Of special interest is the fact that he was the persistent, patient, unrelenting and capable attorney for Dr. David Benke. Dr. Benke was the President (Bishop) of the Atlantic District of the LCMS. He joined thousands in a public outpouring of prayers at Yankee Stadium, praying for all those affected by 9-11. Some high church officials deemed his prayerful participation contrary to Lutheran doctrine and practice and sought to have President Benke defrocked. Howie was his legal representative and hung in there for years until Benke was finally cleared.

Howie did more. He pleaded the case of many public service employees or dependents who lost their lives or whose lives were severely negatively affected by all that went on in, under, and near to the those fallen towers. Of special note were the appropriate benefits that he secured for many police officers and their families. I have written in a previous blog entry how he became known throughout the city for his tenacious advocacy and how police officers quickly recognized his automobile, cleared traffic for him, found him immediate parking spaces, always free and within close walking distance of his destination, even in the midst of Times Square.

Previous to the 9-11 situation Howie was always there for The Lutheran Schools in New York and elsewhere. He fended off suits brought by upset parents or angry former teachers. He was especially helpful in more than one case through his unbelievable contacts and pleadings with the IRS and other government agencies. On at least three occasions he aided schools that had withheld FICA payments from employees but never sent them in to the IRS or Social Security. In each case Howie used his skills and contacts to have fines written off and the balances reduced.

He helped write all the documents to have the Lutheran Schools Association be properly registered with government agencies - and he did it all pro bono.

He wrote my will. When, by God's special grace to me, I made a significant profit on an investment, he insisted that I tithe the profits with a gift through a church-related charitable remainder trust. Now, 25 years later, I still get a generous annual interest payment and at my death a trio of my favorite causes will receive their remainder.

And he was fun to be with. He was not a drinker of alcohol but always invited his guests to enjoy a libation. He took me to New York steak houses that were way out of my price range. He brought guests to benefit golf events and purchased more lottery tickets than anyone else. Of special interest to me was when he and Sheila accompanied me on an incredible tour of China and Tibet. He met everybody, left the group when he wanted to do his own thing and made friends with all whom he encountered. And a couple of years after that China trip, he joined me and a few others for an unbelievable and unheard of "week-end expedition to Hong Kong for golf."

He was a strong family man and it was fun to watch and listen to his family interactions. His sons wisely chose not to be his business partners and loved him dearly. His marvelous wife, Sheila, and he were always at odds on foreign travel, eating choices, how much time to spend in their Florida home and lots of other stuff - but always loved each other, stood up for and by each other and were 100% mutually faithful.

Howie loved doing work not only for Lutheran churches and schools but also for many other churches, and he had the reputation as the right one to go to if any religious organization in New York ever needed legal advice or representation.

His heritage was 100% Jewish. He was not one to be overly committed to observing the Sabbath. But especially in his later days, as he (way too early) suffered and eventually died of cancer, it was important to him that appropriate religious rituals and expectations be observed.

And so today I remember my friend, my advocate, my model, my brother: HOWARD CAPELL.

ဆဝဿ

MILKING COWS

One of my childhood tasks, which I really enjoyed, was milking cows. From the time I was born until the time I went to college, my parents always had at least two cows. We had them to provide milk for our families - and to produce calves. We raised the calves until they weighed a couple hundred pounds and then sold them off to be butchered. But the main reason we had cows was so that they could provide us with daily milk.

My job was to milk them in the evening. During the day the cows roamed in our pasture while the calves were fenced into a small corral. Around sunset the cows were brought into a small fenced-in area between the barn and the chicken coops. The calves were brought to their mothers and were allowed to suckle milk for a while. Then they were roped off and tied away from their mothers. I would take my milk bucket, a very low small stool and get down (always on the right side of the cow) and did the milking. I remember that I always laid my head up against the side of the cow. That felt good and made the whole process a relaxing one. When the milk had been drained from the cow's udder the calves were released and they often tried to get a bit more milk from the cows.

Then the milk was taken into our home. We always had a mechanical milk separator. As its name indicates, this rotary hand-turned little machine separated the cream from the milk, with the cream coming out one spigot and the whey the other. The whey was fed to our pets. The cream was kept for baking, cooking, adding to coffee and for making butter. I always made sure that somewhere in this whole process I drank a goodly portion of the fresh milk. It was always best if the milk was still warm coming only minutes before from the cow's udder. No thought of any pasteurizing ever entered into consideration.

Something that happened only once or twice brings back very pleasant memories. It was in the middle of the day and Mom decided it would be a special treat to just stop everything else we were doing and make a gallon of homemade ice cream. I was given a bucket and told to go out into the pasture, go up to the cow and milk it of the required amount. My recollection is that Mother made the custard for the ice cream without boiling or heating it. The ice cream was perfect!

I find it interesting that in my adult years I never drink milk. I honestly now cannot recall the last time I drank a glass of milk. Our kids have other memories. Four of the five were born in Hong Kong, not a place at which I went out to milk cows. Getting fresh milk there was a challenge and we almost never had any. Instead all milk was from powder. The kids got used to that and liked it. When we went home on leave, we stopped in Japan. At breakfast they asked for and each was served milk. They took a taste, made a face and said, "This stuff tastes funny. We don't like it!" It was their first experience with fresh cow's milk.

I wonder if anybody around Walburg, Texas still milks cows by hand. If not, they are missing a good experience.

AFTERWORD: IT'S WRITTEN IN A BOOK

My son, John, gave me Susan Orelan's masterpiece, "The Library Book," as a Christmas gift. I devoured it. The main thread of the book is about the fire that destroyed the Los Angeles Central Library in 1986, the investigation of how the fire started and the subsequent rebuilding. But it is more than that. It is an affirmation of the role of books in the history of the world. And she makes the point that the days of the importance of books has not ceased. Even in the age of all kinds of electronic and other means of communications there is now and always will be a place for books. I agree.

So, I made the decision. I will put my name on a book. Not a book that will ever become famous or widely-read, not a book that will make a difference in the lives of many, not a book that is likely to ever be ordered by a library. It is just a compilation of the blogs I have written over the last number of years.

I arbitrarily decided to close the book with this blog entry and to put into print my postings up to my age of 92. I plan to continue to post blogs on line at melsmyths@blogspot.com And, if the Lord grants me the years and the mental awareness, I have made a pledge to do a printing of these in another book after I turn 95.

Contents

Made in the USA
Middletown, DE
14 October 2020

21964501R00213